S0-AWM-726

THE FATE OF FREEDOM ELSEWHERE

THE FATE
OF FREEDOM
ELSEWHERE

Human Rights and U.S. Cold War
Policy toward Argentina

William Michael Schmidli

CORNELL UNIVERSITY PRESS   ITHACA AND LONDON

Copyright © 2013 by Cornell University

All rights reserved. Except for brief quotations in a review, this book, or parts thereof, must not be reproduced in any form without permission in writing from the publisher. For information, address Cornell University Press, Sage House, 512 East State Street, Ithaca, New York 14850.

First published 2013 by Cornell University Press

Printed in the United States of America

Library of Congress Cataloging-in-Publication Data

Schmidli, William Michael, 1979– author.
   The fate of freedom elsewhere : human rights and U.S. Cold War policy toward Argentina / William Michael Schmidli.
      pages cm
   Includes bibliographical references and index.
   ISBN 978-0-8014-5196-6 (cloth : alk. paper)
   1. United States—Foreign relations—Argentina. 2. Argentina—Foreign relations—United States. 3. Human rights—Argentina. 4. Human rights—Government policy—United States. 5. United States—Foreign relations—1945–1989. I. Title.
   E183.8.A7S36   2013
   327.73082—dc23   2013004908

Cornell University Press strives to use environmentally responsible suppliers and materials to the fullest extent possible in the publishing of its books. Such materials include vegetable-based, low-VOC inks and acid-free papers that are recycled, totally chlorine-free, or partly composed of nonwood fibers. For further information, visit our website at www.cornellpress.cornell.edu.

Cloth printing   10 9 8 7 6 5 4 3 2 1

To Elisa Da Vià

He knew that the tale he had to tell could not be one of final victory. It could be only the record of what had had to be done, and what assuredly would have to be done again in the never ending fight against terror and its relentless onslaughts, despite their personal afflictions, by all who, while unable to be saints but refusing to bow down to pestilences, strive their utmost to be healers.

—Albert Camus, *The Plague*

Contents

Acknowledgments

First, I would like to thank my editor at Cornell University Press, Michael McGandy. Michael showed patience, professionalism, and enthusiasm throughout the publication process. I also thank Fredrik Logevall for his invaluable encouragement and engagement in my research; Raymond Craib for deepening my interest in Latin American history and for pushing me to seek a balance between "the view from the North" and local narratives south of the U.S. border; and Elizabeth Sanders, whose ability to move between the fields of U.S. foreign relations history and political science proved very useful throughout my research and writing.

I am grateful to the anonymous readers of the manuscript at Cornell University Press, as well as the readers of related articles in *Diplomatic History* and *Cold War History*. I also thank the participants in panels I have served on over the past seven years at the annual conferences of the Society for Historians of American Foreign Relations.

I particularly thank the individuals who agreed to participate in oral history interviews for this book, notably F. A. "Tex" Harris, who, in addition to discussing his own experiences in the U.S. Foreign Service, offered invaluable assistance by sharing his vast list of contacts connected to the issue of human rights in U.S.-Argentine relations. I also thank Patricia Derian and Roberta Cohen for generously allowing me to examine their personal papers. Additionally, I am grateful to the archivists at the John F. Kennedy Library, the Lyndon Baines Johnson Library, the Jimmy Carter Library, the Gerald R. Ford Library, and the Ronald Reagan Library, as well as the National Archives in Washington, DC, along with the archivists at numerous universities, particularly Boston College, Dartmouth University, and the University of Texas at Austin.

This research could not have been completed without generous financial support from Cornell University's American Studies Program, Latin American Studies Program, Peace Studies Program, and the Society for the Humanities. I am grateful to the John F. Kennedy Library for providing an Arthur M. Schlesinger, Jr. Research Fellowship, the Lyndon Baines Johnson Library for offering a Moody Grant, and the Society for Historians of American Foreign Relations for providing a William Appleman Williams Junior Faculty Research Grant. I also thank Bucknell University for generous research funding.

I wish to acknowledge the editors of *Diplomatic History* for granting me permission to adapt portions of my article "Institutionalizing Human Rights in U.S. Foreign Policy: U.S.-Argentine Relations, 1976–1980" 35, no. 2 (2011): 351–377; the editors of *Cold War History* for permission to adapt sections of my article "Human Rights and the Cold War: The Campaign to Halt the Argentine 'Dirty War'" 12, no. 2 (2012): 345–365; and the editors of *Diplomats at War: The American Experience* (Republic of Letters Publishing, 2013) for permission to adapt portions of my chapter "Robert C. Hill and the Cold War in Latin America."

Finally, I would like to thank the members of my family for their lifelong encouragement and inspiration: my mother and father, who first kindled my love of history and instilled in me the imagination to conceive of lofty goals and the work ethic to achieve them; and my sister, whose sound advice, intellectual insight, and abiding friendship I value immensely. For her steadfast support I owe special thanks to Elisa Da Vià, to whom this book is dedicated. Enduring almost daily conversations on U.S.-Argentine relations, human rights, and Jimmy Carter, Elisa not only exhibited remarkable patience but has made me a better scholar in the process.

Abbreviations

AAA	Alianza Anticomunista Argentina (Argentina Anticommunist Alliance)
ACLU	American Civil Liberties Union
AID	Agency for International Development
ARA	Bureau of Inter-American Affairs
BM	Burson-Marsteller
CADHU	Comisión Argentina por Derechos Humanos (Argentine Human Rights Commission)
COA	Council of the Americas
COHA	Council on Hemispheric Affairs
CONADEP	Comisión Nacional sobre la Desaparición de Personas (National Commission on the Disappeared)
DCM	Deputy Chief of Mission
EA	Bureau of East Asian and Pacific Affairs
ERP	Ejército Revolucionario del Pueblo (People's Revolutionary Army)
ESMA	Escuela Mecánica de la Armada (Naval Mechanics School)
Exim	Export-Import Bank
HA	Bureau of Human Rights and Humanitarian Affairs
IACHR	Inter-American Commission on Human Rights
IADB	Inter-American Defense Board
IBRD	International Bank for Reconstruction and Development
IDB	Inter-American Development Bank
IFI	international financial institution
ILHR	International League for Human Rights
IMET	International Military Education and Training
IMF	International Monetary Fund
INR	Bureau of Intelligence and Research
MAAG	Military Assistance Advisory Groups
MAP	Military Assistance Program
MDB	multilateral development bank
NACLA	North American Congress on Latin America
NSC	National Security Council

OAS	Organization of American States
OPIC	Overseas Private Investment Corporation
OTDC	Olga Talamante Defense Committee
PEN	Poder Ejecutivo Nacional (Argentine prisoners held under executive authority)
PM	Bureau of Political and Military Affairs
PRM	Policy Review Memorandum
SALT	Strategic Arms Limitation Treaty
SOA	School of the Americas
SOUTHCOM	United States Southern Command
WOLA	Washington Office on Latin America

THE FATE OF FREEDOM ELSEWHERE

HUMAN RIGHTS AND THE COLD WAR

Jimmy Carter's victory in the 1976 presidential election was a defining moment for U.S. foreign policy. Over the previous quarter century, Cold War national security concerns had dominated U.S. relations with the developing world. It was an approach particularly evident in U.S. policy toward Latin America; guided by visceral anticommunism combined with an abiding fear of Latin American leftist insurgencies in the aftermath of the 1959 Cuban Revolution, American policymakers cultivated close ties with politically ambitious Latin American military leaders.[1] By the mid-1960s, the imperial nature of U.S. Cold War policy was unmistakable in Latin America, where generous transfers of U.S. military equipment, extensive counterinsurgency training programs, and a shared anti-communist fervor had largely succeeded in creating an unprecedented hemispheric alliance system with the United States firmly at the helm.[2]

In the early 1970s, however, the emergence of a broad-based movement advocating the promotion of human rights in U.S. foreign policy stimulated a major reevaluation of U.S. actions in the Third World. Rooted in the struggle for civil rights and the anti–Vietnam War movement, and gaining strength thanks to widespread domestic disillusionment with U.S. support for repressive allies, the effort to institutionalize human rights in U.S. foreign policy and improve the protection of human rights overseas blossomed over the course of the decade. Focused on raising public awareness and utilizing congressional control over foreign aid funding, the human rights movement—a loose coalition of grassroots organizers, lobbyists in Washington, and sympathetic members of

1

Congress—was a counterforce to the politicians, diplomats, and military leaders who sought to maintain close U.S. ties to staunchly anticommunist, authoritarian governments, particularly in Latin America.

The direction of U.S. foreign policy in the 1970s was thus fiercely contested between advocates of moral imperatives and defenders of security goals rooted in self-interest and the maintenance of power. Put differently, over the course of the decade the idealist initiatives of human rights advocates vied for primacy with the realist Cold War policy prescriptions that had undergirded U.S. relations with the global South since the late 1940s. Roiling the political landscape during the fraught Nixon-Ford years, the battle between cold warriors and human rightists reached its climax following Jimmy Carter's successful 1976 presidential election bid.

For human rights advocates, Carter's victory over the incumbent Ford administration represented an extraordinary opportunity to integrate human rights into U.S. foreign policy. Carter's outspoken emphasis on human rights during the presidential campaign reflected his religious beliefs and moralism, but was also a savvy recognition of popular support for human rights in the post-Vietnam, post-Watergate era. Fueling the hopes of the human rights community, in his inauguration address Carter asserted that "our commitment to human rights must be absolute," and "because we are free we can never be indifferent to the fate of freedom elsewhere."[3]

Significantly, Carter also recognized that the issue could win the support of both Cold War hawks, who were eager to indict the Communist world for its treatment of subject peoples, and liberal idealists troubled by U.S. ties to right-wing dictatorships. "I was familiar with the widely accepted arguments that we had to choose between idealism and realism, or between morality and the exertion of power; but I rejected those claims," Carter wrote in his memoirs. "To me, the demonstration of American idealism was a practical and realistic approach to foreign affairs, and moral principles were the best foundation for the exertion of American power and influence."[4]

In this book I consider the Carter administration's effort to translate human rights rhetoric into clear-cut foreign policy initiatives, using U.S. relations with Argentina as the primary case study. As elsewhere in the Western Hemisphere, from the late 1940s until the late 1970s, Cold War considerations dominated U.S. policy toward Argentina, muting U.S. opposition to the military's overthrow of President Arturo Frondizi in 1962 and, over the course of the decade, adding legitimacy to the "praetorian behavior" of Argentine military leaders.[5] Indeed, U.S. military training and aid over the course of the 1960s played a significant role in creating the conditions for the 1966 military coup d'état and contributed to the formulation of the Argentine military's national security doctrine—the blueprint facilitating the systematic use of extralegal tactics against perceived subversives following the military's return to power in March 1976.

Referred to by Argentines simply as *el Proceso*, the National Reorganization Process implemented by the Argentine military junta after the 1976 coup d'état ushered in an era of state-sanctioned terror without precedent in Argentina's history. By the end of 1977, the Argentine Permanent Assembly for Human Rights reported that at least six thousand *desaparecidos*—"disappeared persons"—had been "sucked up" (*chupado*) by the ruling military junta's unbridled campaign to eradicate perceived subversives, and estimated that the actual number was between ten and twenty thousand.[6] Kidnapped by groups of heavily armed men, victims were transported to one of the more than three hundred clandestine detention facilities, where they endured torture and extreme privation.[7] Following interrogation, the vast majority were secretly murdered, their bodies burned or buried in unmarked graves, or thrown from military aircraft into the South Atlantic. "Only God gives and takes life," one interrogator told the detained journalist Jacobo Timerman. "But God is busy elsewhere, and we're the ones who must undertake this task in Argentina."[8]

In the United States, the Nixon-Ford era marked the zenith of realism as the lodestar for executive branch foreign policymaking. Accordingly, the White House consistently supported the political ambitions of the Argentine military. "U.S.-style democracy won't work here," Richard M. Nixon told journalists in Argentina during a tour of South America in mid-1967. "I wish it would."[9] Nearly a decade later, with the military again in power and the so-called dirty war fully under way, the secretary of state Henry Kissinger offered a similar assessment. "Look, our basic attitude is that we would like you to succeed," he bluntly informed the Argentine foreign minister César Guzzetti in a secret meeting in mid-1976.[10]

Yet by mid-1976 Argentina was emerging as a focal point for a transnational human rights movement. In the aftermath of the coup d'état, human rights sympathizers in the U.S. Congress such as the representatives Robert F. Drinan (D-MA) and Donald Fraser (D-MN) peppered the Department of State with information requests on Argentine human rights cases and used hearings and floor speeches to raise awareness of U.S. ties to the Argentine military government. These efforts were bolstered by a surge of activism from dozens of nongovernmental human rights organizations such as the Washington Office on Latin America (WOLA) and Amnesty International (AI), as well as Argentina solidarity groups such as the Washington office of the Comisión Argentina por Derechos Humanos (Argentine Human Rights Commission [CADHU]). Notwithstanding fierce opposition from the Ford administration, top-level U.S. policymakers were forced to confront the issue of human rights in U.S.-Argentine relations, as human rights advocates established broad grassroots support, organized an influential lobby in Washington, and demonstrated an ability to mobilize effectively.

The competition between cold warriors and human rights advocates culminated in a fierce struggle to define U.S. policy toward Argentina during the Jimmy Carter presidency. Entering the Oval Office at the height of state-sanctioned violence in Argentina, the administration aimed to shift U.S. policy from subtle support for the military's "dirty war" to public condemnation of human rights violations. In no small measure due to leadership provided by Patricia Derian, the newly appointed assistant secretary of state for human rights and humanitarian affairs, human rights became the defining feature in U.S.-Argentine relations, and the Human Rights Bureau (HA) oversaw a remarkably extensive U.S. effort to convince the military junta to end its campaign of extralegal violence. Indeed, by mid-1978, the Department of State had blocked an estimated $800 million in U.S. military and commercial transfers to Argentina on human rights grounds.[11]

By using the backlog of pending U.S. sales to Argentina as leverage, the Carter administration played an important role in convincing the military junta in mid-1978 to accept a formal visit by the Inter-American Commission on Human Rights (IACHR), an organ of the Organization of American States. Stimulating a significant decrease in state-sanctioned violence, the IACHR visit was an important success for the Carter administration's human rights policy. More broadly, the administration's use of the IACHR to advance its human rights agenda marked a notable transition from the previous quarter century of U.S. Cold War policy.

Yet such successes were few and far between during the Carter administration. Translating the president's human rights rhetoric into practical policy initiatives was an ongoing challenge, and the lack of a clear set of guidelines on the role human rights should play in U.S. foreign policy, coupled with intense bureaucratic opposition, dramatically limited the implementation of human rights initiatives. At the U.S. Embassy in Buenos Aires, for instance, supporters of the human rights policy faced fierce resistance from the majority of foreign service officers. Similarly, in Washington, Derian's effort to cast international opprobrium on the Argentine military junta confronted stiff opposition from policymakers in the Department of State, U.S. business leaders, and top-ranking members of the Carter administration. Indeed, private sector resistance to delayed or denied sales to Argentina on human rights grounds peaked in mid-1978, and effectively curbed the State Department's subsequent use of economic leverage to promote human rights overseas.

In addition to these institutional pressures against a robust human rights diplomacy, Jimmy Carter's increasingly hawkish stance in foreign affairs in response to a resurgence of Cold War tension with the Soviet Union edged human rights to the back burner as a U.S. policy priority. Most significantly for U.S.-Argentine relations, in the immediate aftermath of the Soviet invasion of Afghanistan in December 1979, Argentina's strategic significance for the United States increased dramatically. Specifically, in the opening months of 1980, the fear that the South American nation would offset the U.S. grain embargo on the Soviet Union rapidly accelerated a rapprochement between Washington and Buenos Aires that resulted in a profound muting of human rights diplomacy. By the time Ronald Reagan entered the White House in January 1981, the Carter administration's idealism had largely been supplanted by a more traditional brand of Cold War realism.

* * *

Although much has been written on the competition between realism and idealism in U.S. foreign policy, the history of human rights advocacy and transnational movements has only begun to receive sustained attention by historians in general, and U.S. foreign relations scholars in particular since the early part of the twenty-first century.[12] By conceptualizing the 1970s as a defining struggle between human rights advocates and cold warriors, in this book I offer an analysis that integrates more fully the U.S. domestic context into studies of international relations—the so-called intermestic.[13] In particular, my work provides a unique lens to examine the evolution of diverse strains of activism on both ends of the political spectrum as the human rights movement developed. My narrative moves far afield of traditional diplomatic history (often confined to Beltway politicians, the Department of State, and the diplomatic corps) and draws from social and cultural approaches to historical interpretation to grapple with the disparate actors engaged in the struggle to define the role of human rights in U.S. foreign policy.

In this book, then, I emphasize the importance of individuals operating on the political terrain below the top-level elites of the U.S. foreign policymaking process. By weaving an analysis of midlevel actors into the broader pattern of U.S. foreign policymaking, including civil rights activists, second-wave feminists, Chicano/a activists, religious progressives, members of the New Right, conservative cold warriors, and business leaders, I aim to illustrate the complex motivations that guided political activism in the 1970s from both sides of the political spectrum, and balance an analysis of the importance of individual agency with an assessment of the shaping power of the Washington bureaucratic structure. Correspondingly, I show how traditional boundaries between state policy and nonstate advocacy are blurred in actual contests over policy and power. Illuminating these relationships advances our understanding of the complex processes involved in the formulation and implementation of U.S. foreign policy.

My interest in tracking the many players who shaped the U.S. human rights movement during the 1970s is also part of a larger trend in recent historical scholarship that has sought to identify human rights as an evolving political construct rather than a universal moral sensibility. As the historian Kenneth Cmiel has written, "The language of human rights is fluid. The term has meant widely different things at different points in time. It may be too much to say that 'human rights' is an empty signifier, but given the range of uses over time—the phrase can mean diametrically opposed things—that seems to be a useful starting point."[14] Following Cmiel's lead, in this book I illustrate the disparate principles—including liberal internationalism, religious moralism, anticommunism, and anti-imperialism—that animated individuals and groups in the U.S. human rights movement. Indeed, for many U.S. human rights advocates, internationally recognized documents such as the 1948 United Nations Universal Declaration of Human Rights were far less significant than national, local, or even personal sources of activism.

This analysis should also shed new light on the foreign policy of the Carter administration. Situating Carter's policy toward Argentina within the broader struggle between cold warriors and human rights advocates allows one to assess the degree to which the Carter administration's initial emphasis on human rights constituted a watershed moment in the evolution of the movement as a whole. I contend that the Carter administration created an unprecedented, government-sanctioned arena for the human rights movement—a development particularly evident in the formulation of U.S. policy toward state-sanctioned violence in Argentina. Focusing on U.S.-Argentine relations is thus critical to any assessment of Carter's human rights policy, and to a considerable extent, my research complements existing "revisionist" foreign relations scholarship that underscores the significance and foresight of Carter's human rights policy.[15] Nonetheless, my work also indicates that multifaceted resistance to Carter's human rights policy—not only by the military government in Buenos Aires but also among Washington bureaucrats and the U.S. business community—significantly constrained the administration's ability to elicit improvements. Moreover, the erosion of Carter's support for human rights in the latter half of his presidency served as a catalyst for the administration's larger failures in the foreign policy arena after 1978. This conclusion lends considerable credence to prevailing critical scholarly analyses of the thirty-ninth president.[16]

This book, although it centers on U.S. state and nonstate actors, has much to offer scholars of modern Latin America. Heeding the historian Gilbert Joseph's call for a "more vital cross-fertilization" between U.S. foreign relations historians and Latin Americanists, in my research I underscore the importance of considering the Cold War in terms of Latin American political development.[17]

In particular, my analysis illuminates the important and largely overlooked regional role that Argentina played in the U.S. effort to bolster Latin American internal security against the perceived threat of Communist insurgency in the 1960s and early 1970s, while also demonstrating how Argentina utilized U.S. military aid and counterinsurgency training in ways United States policymakers did not anticipate or necessarily support. In addition, I shed new light on the Argentine dirty war era (1976–1983).[18] By integrating the conflict into a hemispheric context, I show the significance accorded to Argentina by U.S. human rights advocates and break new ground by situating Argentina at the center of Carter's human rights policy. Correspondingly, a recurring theme found in the diplomatic archives is that the Carter administration had limited ability to influence Argentina; as a State Department report pointed out in late 1978, the Argentine military was willing "to sacrifice temporarily close relations with the U.S. if that was the price for continuing the counterterrorist war and its attendant abuses."[19] By attending to the complex Argentine response to U.S. human rights initiatives, I highlight the diplomatic and political power of Argentina, redescribe U.S. power in the region during the Cold War, and show the multifaceted Latin American response to U.S. regional engagement.

FROM COUNTERINSURGENCY TO STATE-SANCTIONED TERROR

Waging the Cold War in Latin America

The 1976 Argentine coup d'état was a swift and bloodless affair. On the official television network, the Sunday afternoon soccer match was followed by an uninterrupted World War II documentary, and most Argentines were unaware that the military had arrested President Isabel Martinez de Perón until the ruling junta was firmly ensconced in power.[1] When the commanders of the three branches of the Argentine service appeared on television to gravely announce the inauguration of the "National Reorganization Process," however, few Argentines expressed genuine surprise; in the days preceding the coup, it was an open secret that military preparations for a political takeover had advanced to the final stage, with meticulous orders distributed to units across Argentina.[2] And after years of political instability, economic stagnation, and social upheaval, news that the military had incarcerated Perón, disbanded the Congress, and suspended the constitution was widely received with quiet relief and hopeful anticipation.

A similar sentiment pervaded the U.S. Embassy, where officials had been confident of an impending political sea change since the previous autumn. "At this point, whether she [Perón] remains as President is a question of almost academic interest," the U.S. ambassador Robert C. Hill cabled Washington in September 1975. "There is a power vacuum at the center and it is not she who will fill it; hence, whether she remains a figurehead President for yet some time or whether a new government . . . takes over from her, Mrs. Perón is no longer at the center of the equation."[3] Like much of the U.S. foreign policy establishment, Hill looked to the Argentine generals as the best hope for restoring political stability in Argentina.

When the military assumed power on March 24, 1976, Hill offered full and unequivocal support. "This was probably the best executed and most civilized coup in Argentine history," the ambassador cabled Washington three days after the takeover. "Argentina's best interests, like ours," he concluded, "lie in the success of the moderate government now led by Gen[eral] Videla."[4] U.S. policymakers in Washington concurred with Hill's assessment, greeting the coup with extraordinary enthusiasm. Immediately after the takeover, Secretary of State Kissinger forwarded a Bureau of Intelligence and Research (INR) analysis of U.S.-Argentine relations to all U.S. diplomatic posts in the hemisphere. "U.S. interests are not threatened by the present military government," the report bluntly stated. It continued: "The three service commanders are known for their pro-U.S., anti-communist attitudes. . . . Investment problems will be minimized by the junta's favorable attitude toward foreign capital, while the government's probable intention of seeking U.S. aid, tangible and/or moral, to overcome pressing economic problems will provide added insurance against openly anti-U.S. attitudes and policies."[5] Dismissing the customary examination period, within forty-eight hours Washington extended formal recognition to the military, while the International Monetary Fund delivered a previously approved $127 million loan.[6]

On one level, Hill's consistent support for a military coup in Argentina reflected a deep-seated skepticism regarding the possibility of a civilian solution to Argentina's political and economic challenges. The ambassador's encouragement of the Argentine military's political aspirations, however, went beyond a simple faith in the generals' short-term ability to reestablish stability. Indeed, Hill's response attested to the profound anticommunism that had guided U.S. foreign policy since the late 1940s, combined with the fear of Latin American leftist insurgencies that captivated policymakers in the fiery aftermath of the 1959 Cuban Revolution. U.S. support for the Argentine military takeover thus exemplified a defining feature of its policy toward Latin America during the Cold War: quiet cultivation of robust ties with politically ambitious Latin American militaries to protect U.S. national security.

* * *

Robert C. Hill's engagement in Latin American affairs began at the end of the 1940s when he was appointed assistant vice president of W.R. Grace & Co., a major shipping firm with strong commercial ties to Latin America. The position required Hill to travel extensively throughout the region, and the young executive immersed himself in hemispheric affairs. It was, he later recalled, "the most informative period of my life."[7] Hill's education could hardly have come at a more dynamic moment in U.S.-Latin American relations. While U.S. military interventions in the Circum-Caribbean area dated to the late nineteenth century, and U.S. military training programs had been established throughout the hemisphere in the initial decades of the twentieth century, the concerted effort by the United States to establish military predominance in Latin America had begun during the Second World War. Following the U.S. declaration of war on the Axis powers, Latin America's strategic importance surged as German U-boats prowled the Atlantic with near impunity and U.S. military planners considered the possibility of a Nazi invasion launched from North Africa. After securing a series of bilateral treaties, the United States dispatched one hundred thousand soldiers to military bases throughout the region. More significantly, the size and scope of U.S. military training missions in the region increased dramatically, and Latin American military leaders found themselves awash with $500 million in equipment and weapons supplied through the Lend-Lease Act.[8]

Significantly, the deepening of U.S.-Latin American military ties during the war corresponded with a surge of democracy that swept Latin America at the tail end of World War II. Propelled by the combined effects of the global struggle against fascism, the relative benevolence of Franklin Roosevelt's Good Neighbor policy, and, to varying degrees in each Latin American nation, the rise of an "emerging middle class and urban working class that joined with students, intellectuals, and in some cases a militant peasantry," the region witnessed unprecedented demands for democratic reforms.[9] Moreover, the United States actively assisted in the outpouring of Latin American democracy; flush with victory over authoritarian regimes in Europe and Asia, in the heady aftermath of V-J Day a phalanx of hardheaded U.S. diplomats fanned out across the hemisphere, pressuring Latin American authoritarians such as Paraguay's Higinio Moríngo and Guatemala's Jorge Ubico to hand over the reins of power via electoral transitions. As a result, in 1946, Latin America could boast fifteen democracies out of a total twenty nations—a startling figure considering there had been only four democracies two years earlier.

Dovetailing with the outpouring of Latin American electoral transitions, the Second World War sparked a broad-based effort to include human rights as a core component in the emerging postwar global order. Indeed, Latin American states played a significant role in the successful inclusion of human rights in the text of the United Nations Charter, drafted in San Francisco in the spring of 1945.[10] Human rights achieved far greater international recognition following the drafting and adoption of the Universal Declaration of Human Rights by the United Nations General Assembly in December 1948. Blending political, economic, and social rights, the declaration's thirty articles, writes historian Paul Gordon Lauren, "proclaimed that all people everywhere possessed certain basic and identifiable rights, that universal standards existed for the world as a whole, and that human rights were matters of legitimate international concern and no longer within the exclusive domestic jurisdiction of nation-states as in the past."[11]

Although lacking any legally binding enforcement mechanisms, the Universal Declaration arguably created the foundation for modern human rights advocacy.

Even as the Universal Declaration was being drafted, however, the onset of the Cold War ensured that it would remain largely an aspiration. Indeed, by the early 1950s the document had been appropriated as a propaganda weapon by both sides in the superpower competition. "The Soviet Union used the Declaration's antidiscrimination articles and its social and economic provisions to berate the United States and its friends, while the Western bloc badgered the Communist countries for failing to protect free expression and free elections," writes historian Mary Ann Glendon. "A wedge was driven through the heart of the Declaration, severing its firm link between freedom and solidarity."[12]

The deepening Cold War had a particularly significant impact on the role of human rights in U.S. foreign policy. On one level, despite having assumed a leadership role in the drafting of the Universal Declaration, the United States almost immediately made an abrupt shift away from supporting multilateral human rights initiatives. Fearing that human rights treaties could supersede existing domestic law, in September 1951 Senator John W. Bricker (R-OH) introduced legislation—subsequently referred to as the Bricker Amendment—that would amend the U.S. Constitution by preventing any treaty from altering U.S. domestic law without special congressional approval. The legislation, Bricker argued, would "bury the so-called covenant on human rights so deep that no one holding high public office will ever dare to attempt its resurrection."[13] Although it ultimately failed in the Senate, the Bricker Amendment debate, combined with the globalizing U.S. Cold War commitment, reversed the trend of rising U.S. participation in multinational human rights initiatives.[14]

On another level, the onset of the Cold War infused U.S. foreign policy with a realism focused on projecting American power overseas and protecting U.S. national security interests—a development particularly evident in U.S.-Latin American relations. Indeed, by the time Robert C. Hill began working for W.R. Grace, the onset of the Cold War had once again cast Latin America's geostrategic significance for the United States in sharp relief. As the United States moved from the Truman Doctrine's March 1947 promise to "free peoples who are resisting attempted subjugation by armed minorities or outside pressures," to the stark, ideologically charged superpower competition outlined three years later by National Security Council Report 68 (NSC-68), the centralization of power in the hands of Latin American military strongmen came to be increasingly perceived by U.S. policymakers as a more stable bulwark against Communism than democracy.[15] Recognizing the region's armed forces as a significant *political* force with which the United States could cultivate powerful allies in the effort to protect the hemisphere from Soviet territorial ambitions, in other words, the

Truman administration revived and deepened U.S.-Latin American military ties. "Contact with Latin American military men," as the Joint Chiefs of Staff asserted, "would in reality mean contact with very strong domestic political leaders."[16]

Accordingly, in 1947, the United States successfully lobbied for the signing of the Inter-American Treaty of Reciprocal Assistance in Rio de Janeiro, binding the twenty Latin American signatories to mutual defense in the event of an external attack on the region. The following year Washington made little protest when elected governments were overthrown by staunchly anticommunist military officers in Peru and Venezuela, and although Truman's initial efforts to authorize substantial transfers of military equipment to Latin American governments died in the Senate, the outbreak of hostilities in Korea galvanized recalcitrant lawmakers on Capitol Hill, and between 1951 and 1952, Congress appropriated nearly $90 million in direct military aid to Latin America.[17]

The close cultivation of U.S.-Latin American military ties was continued under the Eisenhower administration. By 1955, bilateral U.S. Military Assistance Programs (MAPs) were operating in eighteen Latin American nations, and by the end of the decade Washington had provided $400 million in military assistance to the region. Moreover, eight hundred U.S. military personnel were assigned to Latin America, and U.S. military missions crisscrossed the continent, establishing close personal and professional relationships with Latin American military officers. Nearly eight thousand additional Latin American military personnel underwent training at U.S. facilities in the Panama Canal Zone or in the continental United States between 1945 and 1959. The unprecedented degree of U.S.-Latin American military cooperation was underscored by the successful initiation of an annual Conference of American Armies. Organized in 1960 by the commander in chief of the U.S. Southern Command (SOUTHCOM) and hosted in the Panama Canal Zone's Fort Amador, the gathering was attended by top-ranking officers from seventeen of the hemisphere's armed services.[18]

Deepening U.S.-Latin American military ties underscored the degree to which the perceived exigencies of the Cold War pushed human rights promotion to the back burner as a U.S. policy priority. Indeed, although American leaders continued to champion the noncommunist West as a bastion of political rights, by 1955 more than half of the nations of Latin America had returned to dictatorial rule. To be sure, this reversal was primarily the result of local political developments, as coalitions of large landowners and conservative military, religious, and industrial leaders in Latin American states successfully launched counterrevolutionary political movements. Nonetheless, as Cold War national security concerns came to dominate U.S. foreign policy, the United States played a critical role in advancing the interests of Latin American conservatives—not least by cultivating the political aspirations of conservative Latin American political and military leaders.

"The United States certainly preferred and favoured constitutional democracy," the historians Leslie Bethell and Ian Roxborough write, "but this did not mean a commitment to wider participation and broad-ranging social reforms and certainly not to an enhanced role for labour and the Left (particularly the Communists): all this, it was feared, could only prove antagonistic to United States' strategic and economic interests."[19] Human rights rhetoric notwithstanding, by the early 1950s U.S. policy had moved sharply toward advancing national security concerns, a development that would define U.S.-Latin American relations over the first quarter century of the Cold War.

In its effort to protect the hemisphere against Communist incursions by deepening U.S.-Latin American military ties, the Eisenhower administration recognized a kindred spirit in Robert C. Hill. A native of Littleton, Vermont, Hill had spent his childhood skiing barrel staves and delivering the *Saturday Evening Post*.[20] After graduating from a private preparatory school in 1938, Hill was accepted at Dartmouth College, making a name for himself as an athlete and digging ditches during vacations.[21] Badly injured in a football game, Hill was deemed ineligible for military service in World War II. Having developed an interest in foreign affairs at Dartmouth, after graduating in 1942 Hill joined the U.S. Foreign Service and was first assigned to Calcutta before becoming a State Department representative with the rank of captain at the U.S. Army headquarters in New Delhi. Returning to the United States in 1946, Hill married a former Baltimore tennis champion, Cecilia Bowdoin, and briefly served as staff assistant to the U.S. Senate Committee on Banking and Commerce before accepting the assistant vice president position at W. R. Grace.

As Hill traveled across the hemisphere on behalf of W. R. Grace, the fear of Communist expansion that permeated the Truman administration's Latin America policy formed the core of his education in hemispheric affairs. In fact, by the early 1950s Hill had established himself in the vanguard of private sector leaders advocating the threat of Communist machinations toward Latin America.[22] The United States, Hill bluntly told Eisenhower's secretary of state, John Foster Dulles, in 1953, was "on the road to losing Latin America."[23]

Dulles demurred. Hill's staunch anticommunism and pro-business approach to hemispheric affairs fit nicely with the Eisenhower administration's approach to Latin America, however, and in 1953 the president appointed the young executive ambassador to Costa Rica. At thirty-three, Hill was the youngest ambassador the United States had ever sent abroad.[24] Notwithstanding his diplomatic inexperience, Hill quickly won praise for developing a close working relationship with President José Figueres, as well as constructively mediating between the Costa Rican government and U.S. private investors, particularly the United Fruit Company.[25] Reassigned to El Salvador in 1954, Hill was reportedly one of a small coterie of U.S. diplomats assisting in the top secret CIA mission to oust the Guatemalan president Jacobo Arbenz.[26]

Despite the successful overthrow of Arbenz, during Eisenhower's second term in office, top U.S. policymakers increasingly worried that Latin America was becoming *less* secure, and *more* vulnerable to the spread of Communism. In 1958, the vice president Richard M. Nixon was nearly killed at the hands of an angry mob during an official visit to Caracas. According to the vice president, the rioters were "communists led by Communists, and they had no devotion to freedom at all."[27] Greater setbacks were yet to come. In 1959, U.S. policymakers were stunned by Fidel Castro's revolutionary overthrow of the Cuban dictator Fulgencio Batista, whose credentials as a U.S. client dated to the late 1930s. By early 1960, Castro's reform agenda—largely targeting U.S. private investment on the island—had precipitated an increasingly acrimonious relationship with the United States government. Threatened with the closing of U.S. markets to Cuban exports, particularly sugar, in February Castro dramatically propelled the island nation into the Soviet sphere, signing a trade agreement with the Soviet premier Nikita Khrushchev and intensifying nationalization and expropriation initiatives. The response in Washington was electric; in March Eisenhower approved a multifaceted covert operation to overthrow Castro, and before the end of the year the United States had initiated an almost total embargo on U.S. exports to Cuba.

Few articulated the mix of fear and fury that captivated U.S. cold warriors in the aftermath of the Cuban Revolution with more intensity than Robert C. Hill. In fact, Hill proudly identified himself as the first U.S. diplomat to openly label Castro a Communist, and situated himself in the vanguard of Latin American hands who perceived the island nation as an immediate threat to U.S. national security.[28] Three months after the Cuban revolutionaries triumphantly proclaimed independence on January 1, 1959, in a three-day conference of U.S. ambassadors assigned to the Circum-Caribbean area, Hill—who had succeeded Francis White as the U.S. ambassador to Mexico in 1957—demanded a forceful statement regarding revolutionary activities in the region, raising the ire of career diplomats advocating a more conciliatory strategy. The meeting became so heated that according to one delegate, threats of "resignations were a dime a dozen."[29]

Hill's fierce anticommunism was especially evident in his diplomatic relations with the Mexican government. When the Mexican congressional leader Emilio Sanchez Piedras declared an "attitude of solidarity" with Cuba in July 1960, Hill spearheaded U.S. Department of State demands that the Mexican government retract the statement. As tension between the United States and Mexico increased, five thousand Mexican students marched past the U.S. Embassy hurling insults at Ambassador Hill and chanting, "Cuba yes—Yankees no."[30]

Disdained by Mexican progressives, Hill's strident advocacy of an unyielding U.S. position toward Cuba gained credence in Washington in the final months of the Eisenhower administration. "Loss of any part of the area to Communist control, or even its neutralization," he wrote Robert Kennedy—the president-elect's brother—in December 1960, "would strike a mortal blow to the defense of the Western Hemisphere." Hill continued: "Cuba under Castro is no longer a peaceful tropical island but an advance landing strip of the Soviet Union and Communist China at our very doorstep. It is the Communist take-off field for the penetration and subjugation of Mexico, Central America, Panama, and the nearby areas of South America." Accordingly, Hill advocated deepening ties between the United States and Latin American militaries. "In almost every Latin American country," the ambassador asserted, "the armed forces literally stand between the Communists and the Palace." The United States, Hill concluded, should thus provide extensive military assistance and training programs geared toward internal security.[31]

* * *

The Kennedy administration agreed with Hill's assessment. With Soviet support, John F. Kennedy believed that Castro was embarking on a major effort to foment Cuban-style revolutions throughout the hemisphere, a perception strengthened by Khrushchev's championing of "wars of national liberation" in his 1961 report to the Moscow Conference of Communist Parties. With the Soviets "in the front rank with the peoples waging such struggles," as the national security adviser Walt W. Rostow wrote, U.S. efforts to stem the spread of Communism in the developing world faced unprecedented challenges from the "scavengers of the modernization process."[32]

As the success of the Cuban Revolution dramatically illustrated, guerrilla warfare—or internal war, as U.S. policymakers often put it—was particularly threatening because it largely neutralized the effectiveness of traditional standing armies. "Conventional military forces are usually essential to deter overt invasion and to strengthen the political cohesion of new states," the State Department Bureau of Intelligence and Research reported. "For meeting guerilla [sic] aggres-sion, however, conventional organization, doctrine, equipment, and staff outlook are inappropriate."[33] The vast U.S. nuclear arsenal was also deemed insufficient to stem the spread of Communist insurgencies in the Third World. "The so-called nuclear stalemate has not served to inhibit violence," asserted the INR director Roger Hilsman in early 1962. "If anything, it has enabled the Communists to resort to a wider variety of force. Their new strength in nuclear weapons makes them all the more tempted to adventure with internal war."[34]

Moreover, U.S. policy analysts worried that the Soviets had developed a sophisticated internal warfare strategy that far surpassed U.S. counterinsurgency capability. "Soviet techniques in internal warfare have steadily developed, ranging today from political subversion to guerrilla aggression," the INR asserted. "Western techniques for meeting internal warfare, on the other hand, have lagged."[35] The threat of Communist subversion thus required the United States and its allies in the developing world to learn how to "adopt the tactics of the guerrillas themselves," according to the INR, "combining courtesy and firmness toward the population with hard-hitting military operations."[36]

The Kennedy administration was determined to meet the guerrilla threat head-on. As part of a sustained effort to make counterinsurgency top priority for the U.S. armed forces, Kennedy established a committee on counterinsurgency in January 1962, "to assure the use of U.S. resources with maximum effectiveness in preventing and resisting subversive insurgency in friendly nations," and two months later he mandated counterinsurgency education programs for all government agencies involved in internal security. Kennedy also worked to incorporate counterinsurgency into the U.S. military curriculum; by 1963, branch officer career courses dedicated nearly thirty hours to counterinsurgency instruction, while at West Point students participated in counterinsurgency training exercises in a summer camp and had sixty-six mandatory lessons in counterinsurgency in the classroom.[37]

Kennedy also oversaw the expansion of U.S. Special Forces, increasing U.S. guerrilla warfare units to roughly three thousand soldiers in the first year of his administration. By 1963, the expansion of training facilities at the Special Warfare Center at Fort Bragg had produced 5,600 elite counterinsurgency specialists. Underscoring his concern (and fascination) with guerrilla warfare, the president personally assisted in the selection of the elite Green Berets' state-of-the-art equipment, including canvas sneakers with armor-plated soles.[38]

In the global struggle to contain Communist-sponsored insurgencies, the Kennedy administration considered Latin America a central battleground. Significantly, Kennedy recognized the potential for unrest generated by the region's extreme socioeconomic inequality, and with Castro providing an unprecedented alternative to the hemispheric status quo, the United States could ill afford to be perceived as the bulwark of illiberal Latin American regimes. As Arthur M. Schlesinger Jr. wrote to the president with characteristic eloquence, "If the possessing classes of Latin America make middle-class revolution impossible, they will make a 'workers-and-peasants' revolution inevitable."[39]

Kennedy responded with a major policy initiative that claimed the mantle of Latin American revolution. Loftily designated the Alliance for Progress, it was an initiative, Kennedy promised, that would transform the region's political and socioeconomic landscape. Capturing the sense of possibility—and hubris—at the heart of the alliance, Kennedy eloquently declared at the program's inauguration:

"Let us once again transform the American continent into a vast crucible of revolutionary ideas and efforts—a tribute to the power of the creative energies of free men and women—an example to all the world that liberty and progress walk hand in hand. Let us once again awaken our American revolution until it guides the struggle of people everywhere—not with an imperialism of force or fear—but the rule of courage and freedom and hope for the future of man."[40] The United States, the Kennedy administration confidently asserted, was capable of giving Latin America a dynamic push along the path to development, and, more significantly, was willing to bear the brunt of the economic and administrative burden.

At its core, the Alliance for Progress consisted of three facets. First, in a dramatic shift from the close U.S. ties with dictators that marked the Eisenhower era, Kennedy pledged to support Latin American constitutional development. As a State Department strategy guidelines paper made clear, "We must disassociate ourselves from reactionary forces which decline to respond to the needs of the people, and learn to discriminate between legitimate expressions of dissatisfaction with the existing social order and communist inspired agitation."[41] Second, the United States pledged to underwrite Latin American economic growth. The alliance promised $100 billion in Latin American investment over a ten-year period, with the United States providing 20 percent. Moreover, in addition to industrialization, land redistribution, and tax reform, the Alliance for Progress ambitiously set out to improve Latin American health and education systems, leading U.S. policymakers to optimistically predict that within a decade, Latin America would experience a lower rate of infant mortality and major increases in life expectancy, literacy, and access to primary education.[42]

It was the third component of Kennedy's Alliance for Progress, however, that would have the most significant long-term impact on the region: increased U.S. military assistance and training programs to enhance Latin American internal security. Like his Cold War predecessors, John F. Kennedy believed U.S. national security depended on defending Latin America against Communist aggression. As the Cuban Revolution made evident, however, the nature of the security threat to the region had shifted. Rather than an externally based Soviet attack on the hemisphere, in the 1960s the primary threat, in the words of the secretary of state Dean Rusk, was "the appearance in Cuba of a Marxist-Communist regime committed to promote subversive, Castro-communist movements throughout Latin America."[43]

Internal security was thus the foundation on which U.S. policymakers aimed to build the Alliance for Progress. Although envisioning a region of stable, pro-U.S. democracies fueled by dynamic local economies, in the short run, U.S. policymakers feared the alliance would create unprecedented susceptibility to

Communist subversion, a "disease of the transition to modernization," in Rostow's clinical description.[44] As the under secretary of state Chester Bowles informed U.S. embassies in Latin America in mid-1961, the process of social and economic development "will take time. Castro-communism in [the] meantime can be expected to infiltrate and subvert established governments and to disrupt positive development program." Underscoring the relationship between the alliance's political and socioeconomic initiatives and internal security, Bowles concluded, "It is essential [to] build up defenses against this danger so Latin American countries can get on with development plans."[45]

More significantly, in addition to preventing Communist insurgencies, U.S. policymakers anticipated Latin American militaries would advance the goals of the Alliance for Progress by assuming a lead role in national socioeconomic development. Well aware of Castro's successful guerrilla campaign in Cuba's sparsely populated Sierra Maestra, U.S. counterinsurgency experts perceived Latin America's underdeveloped rural areas as easy targets for Communist infiltration. "The fields of battle are hunger, inflation, hardship, disease, ignorance, discrimination, and unrest," army Lt. Col. (ret.) Harry F. Walterhouse declared in the April 1962 edition of *Military Review.* "The enemy is communism which seizes every opportunity to identify itself with the fulfillment of the frustrations and yearnings of emerging populations. Communism fans embers of unrest, hinders the assistance and reform efforts of legally constituted governments, and incessantly propagandizes its own cure-all nostrums."[46] Determined to prevent Communist inroads while shepherding the region along the path to modernization, the Kennedy administration boldly set out to transform the core mission of Latin American militaries. Henceforth, the United States would assume responsibility for defending the hemisphere against external attack, while Latin American armed forces would concentrate on "contributing to the defense of the hemisphere by maintaining internal security against communist-Castroist guerrilla and subversive threats."[47]

To convince reluctant Latin American military leaders to establish internal security as the primary objective, Kennedy expanded U.S. military assistance, while focusing the program on providing equipment considered intrinsic to internal security. Beginning with the Foreign Assistance Act of 1961, this emphasis was evident in the administration's annual requests for congressional funding for U.S. military assistance to Latin America. Security forces were of "paramount importance," Brigadier General William Enemark testified in 1962. "If the Alliance for Progress is to have its chance, governments must have the effective force required to cope with subversion, prevent terrorism, and deal with outbreaks of violence before they reach unmanageable proportions," Enemark continued. "They must be able to sustain themselves against attacks by the international Communist organization and its indigenous members."[48]

Despite congressional opposition to repealing the prohibition on aid to Latin America for internal security purposes, Kennedy took advantage of a loophole in section 511(b) of the Foreign Assistance Act of 1961, allowing the administration to furnish internal security assistance to Latin America if the president "promptly reports such determination to the Senate Committee on Foreign Relations and to the Speaker of the House of Representatives." Accordingly, Kennedy authorized a grant of $34.9 million in military assistance for internal security in Latin America, in 1961, and two years later, half of all Latin American military assistance was geared toward internal security.[49] The administration had less difficulty obtaining congressional approval for civic action programs in Latin America—U.S.-led development projects aimed at winning Latin American hearts and minds. In addition to Agency for International Development (AID) funding, beginning in 1962, Kennedy utilized the Military Assistance Program to fund civic action programs, and by FY1963, MAP provided no less than $14.1 million for Latin American socioeconomic development programs, compared to a mere $5 million from AID.[50]

In addition to military assistance, the Kennedy administration sought to prioritize internal security in Latin America through U.S. training programs for Latin American soldiers. United States Military Assistance Advisory Groups (MAAGs) and military missions operating as part of the "country team" at U.S. embassies were instructed to integrate internal security into their daily operations.[51] Often responsible for working with the local Department of Defense to prepare a military budget and suitable tables of organization and equipment, MAAGs were in a unique position to encourage expenditures geared toward internal security. MAAGs also took a lead role in translating U.S. training manuals into Spanish or Portuguese, considered by the Department of Defense a fundamental element in establishing internal security as a priority for Latin American military officers.[52]

Law enforcement agencies were also recognized by U.S. policymakers as playing a key role in maintaining Latin American internal security. In August 1962, Kennedy issued NSAM no. 177, mandating that "the U.S. should give considerably greater emphasis to police assistance programs in appropriate less developed countries where there is an actual or potential threat of internal subversion or insurgency."[53] Building on training programs established during the Eisenhower administration, Kennedy directed the founding of Inter-American Police Academy in the Panama Canal Zone in 1962. Relocated the following year to Washington and designated the International Police Academy, the institution provided students with instruction in "surveillance techniques and intelligence gathering, interrogation procedures, methods of conducting raids, and riot and crowd control."[54]

More significantly, the Kennedy administration dramatically expanded training programs for Latin American officers at U.S. military facilities in the Panama Canal Zone and the continental United States. By mid-May 1961, plans were being formulated in the Department of Defense to "increase and strengthen the training of Latin American military personnel in anti-subversion, anti-guerrilla, and riot control techniques."[55] Four months later, Kennedy pressed for more rapid development of training programs for regional officers in NSAM no. 88, and asked to know what "steps we are taking to increase the intimacy between our Armed Forces and the military of Latin America."[56]

At the president's urging, U.S. training programs for Latin American soldiers expanded rapidly, particularly at the U.S. Caribbean School, renamed the School of the Americas (SOA) in 1963. Located at Fort Gulick in the Panama Canal Zone, over the course of the decade the institution continuously provided between 350 and 500 Latin American officers with Spanish-language military instruction in two- to forty-week courses. Counterinsurgency formed the core of the SOA's curriculum; as the authors of an early study on internal security in Latin America noted, instruction covered "every aspect of counterinsurgency: military, paramilitary, political, sociological, and psychological. Stimulation of economic growth by military civic action is [also] emphasized."[57]

Latin American officers were also invited to receive military training in the continental United States. A specialized program for Latin American officers was established in 1960 at the Army Special Warfare Center at Fort Bragg in North Carolina, with instruction focusing on unconventional warfare, counterinsurgency, and psychological-warfare operations. Additionally, in October 1962, the Inter-American Defense College was established at Fort Lesley McNair in Washington. With courses "comparable to that of most advanced military educational institutes," the college targeted students at the rank of colonel who had graduated from advanced command or staff schools in Latin America. By 1963, Inter-American Defense College boasted more than one hundred graduates from throughout Latin America.[58]

The expansion of U.S. military training programs aimed to instill in Latin American officers the will to reorient their armed forces' mission to internal security, as well as increase U.S. leverage in the region by cultivating close personal and professional bonds with future generations of politically powerful military leaders. "Our military schools afford a direct way of reaching this influential element of the governments in Latin America," Kennedy's military representative, General Maxwell Taylor, informed the president in October 1961.[59] Similarly, a State Department memo in early 1962 asserted that in order to solidify alliances with Latin American militaries and capitalize on their internal defense capacity through training and equipment-transfer programs, "the United States must be the paramount foreign military influence in Latin America." Accordingly, "a favorable political orientation on the part of the Latin American officer corps is vital to our interests. This calls for continuous effort in solidifying the bonds between our military forces and those of Latin America."[60] Indeed, as early as mid-1962, the expansion of U.S. training facilities had largely succeeded in drawing the hemisphere's armed services together under the mantle of U.S. hemispheric hegemony. As the veteran reporter Juan de Onís noted in July, "The top military leaders of Latin America nearly all know each other personally through the conferences for inter-American defense that United States regional service commands promote, primarily in Panama."[61]

U.S. military assistance and training for Latin America continued following Kennedy's assassination in November 1963. Reflecting an extraordinary reliance on the career diplomat Thomas C. Mann, from the outset of his presidency Lyndon B. Johnson sought to cut away the fat of Kennedy's idealistic rhetoric and get down to the meat of economic development. The new president emphasized the need for clear goals for the Alliance for Progress, and for streamlining the layers of U.S. bureaucracy involved in the project. Moreover, Washington cut back on the alliance's support for Latin American democracies and promises of rapid socioeconomic development.[62] Instead, the 1964 "Mann Doctrine" called for a halt to U.S. interventionism on behalf of democracy—with nations threatened by Communism as the major exception, and laid out three factors on which the United States would base its political recognition of Latin American governments: the fostering of economic growth, the protection of U.S. investments abroad, and anticommunism.

In particular, the perceived threat of Cuban-style insurgencies in the region would define the Johnson administration's approach to hemispheric affairs. Although Johnson curtailed the CIA's efforts to assassinate Fidel Castro, top U.S. policymakers saw the fiery Cuban leader's influence in nearly every instance of political upheaval and social unrest in the region. "Cuba continues to devote considerable effort to assisting subversive groups in the hemisphere," the Central Intelligence Agency warned in 1966. Citing the Tri-Continental Conference held in January 1966 as evidence, the agency continued, "Propaganda support for revolution in Latin America emanating from Fidel Castro and other high-level Cuban officials has again reached the crescendo of the early 1960s."[63]

Accordingly, the Johnson administration maintained the focus on counterinsurgency initiated under Kennedy, and expanded U.S. military assistance and training programs for Latin American soldiers. After resisting a major legislative reorientation of U.S. military assistance to Latin America since the final years of the Eisenhower administration, in 1965 Congress bowed to White House pressure and amended the Foreign Assistance Act to expressly include U.S. military assistance geared toward internal security.[64] In the same fiscal year, the Johnson administration budgeted 52 percent of MAP funds for "the maintenance of security against communist and other threats of violence and subversion, including guerrilla warfare, and the movement of armaments and men clandestinely across land, sea and air borders for subversive purposes."[65]

Increased MAP funding corresponded with hundreds of U.S. military missions operating throughout the hemisphere. By 1964, nearly nine hundred U.S. military, civilian, and local personnel were assigned to U.S. military missions charged with advising and training Latin American soldiers, as well as programming and monitoring MAP equipment deliveries.[66] An additional 252 individuals served as military attachés, and by 1967, the United States had military missions in all Latin American countries except Haiti and Mexico.[67] The Johnson era also witnessed an increase in U.S.-funded civic action programs in Latin America. Glowing reports flowed into Washington detailing road building in rural Brazil, the construction of clinics in Chile, potable water projects in Ecuador, and a hot lunch program in Guatemala feeding more than two hundred thousand children in three thousand schools.[68] "U.S. policy in this regard has been an almost unqualified success," a Department of Defense report claimed in early 1965. U.S. civic action initiatives, the report continued, "helped give local military forces a sense of mission, a greater interest in the welfare of their countries and a better relationship with the civil population."[69]

U.S. military training facilities also expanded under the Johnson administration. By 1968, more than 25,000 Latin American soldiers had trained in the United States since the end of World War II, and thirty thousand had taken military courses in the Panama Canal Zone.[70] In the latter half of the decade, the U.S. Army School of the Americas had expanded to include four instructional departments staffed by roughly sixty officers and 130 enlisted men—with guest instructors from Latin America constituting roughly 25 percent of the faculty—offering forty-two separate courses, some as many as three times a year. Hundreds of Latin American students also underwent training at nearby Fort Sherman's Jungle Operations Training Center. In such courses, one author wrote in the journal *Military Review,* "assaults, ambushes, and patrols are carried out both day and night in the thick, insect-infested, obstacle-ridden rain forests bordering the Panama Canal."[71]

Correspondingly, in the late 1960s Latin American students at the Inter-American Defense College attended lectures in a one-hundred-seat auditorium featuring simultaneous interpretation into Spanish, Portuguese, English, or French via a state-of-the-art headphone system. Moreover, in addition to a bachelor's quarters for nearly three dozen officers and a mess hall, the institution had accumulated a library with more than three thousand volumes, an equal number of pamphlets and documents, and held subscriptions to roughly three hundred periodicals. By the end of the decade, the college had nearly three hundred Latin American graduates.[72]

* * *

By the mid-1960s, extensive transfers of U.S. military equipment and training and a shared anticommunist fervor had thus largely succeeded in drawing politically ambitious Latin American militaries into an unprecedented hemispheric alliance system with the United States at the helm. "The fact that there are today no significant foreign military missions, other than those of the U.S., resident in Latin America is an index of the success of the U.S. in establishing itself as the predominant military influence in the area," a Department of Defense memorandum bluntly asserted in 1968. The memo continued: "The fact that the military as a whole are probably the least anti-American of any political group in Latin America is another indication of this influence. A third indication, not traceable wholly to U.S. policy, is the strong anti-Castro and anti-Communist attitude of the military. The adoption generally in Latin America of U.S. military doctrine, tactics, training methods, organization and weapons is both a result of and a contribution to continuing predominance of U.S. influence."[73] Moreover, U.S. policymakers championed Latin American militaries' adaptation of doctrines of national security linking economic and social development to internal security. At the annual five-day Conference of American Armies in 1964, Lyndon Johnson praised military representatives from seventeen Latin American nations for their "sincere desire to benefit—both economically and socially—the people we serve."[74]

U.S. policymakers were not oblivious to the risks inherent in the effort to reorient Latin American militaries' primary mission to internal security. Indeed, State Department memorandums reveal an awareness dating to the initial months of the Kennedy administration that U.S. military training and assistance could whet Latin American officers' appetites for political power. "Intensive aid and training can give the military leaders in these countries a sophistication, skill, influence, and material power beyond that of the civilian authorities," an INR analyst wrote in 1961. "This can create both the conditions and the rationale for a military coup." The zealous U.S. effort to contain the spread of Communism in the Third World through military counterinsurgency and civic action programs, the INR asserted, could be understood by Latin American military leaders as implicit U.S. support for anticommunist military regimes. The report continued: "Our present training programs may easily—and quite inadvertently—add to these difficulties. Trainees may come to believe that we desire the military to take over their governments and to implement social, economic, and military reforms. Emphasis on means of controlling the population, as in the antisubversion course at Fort Bragg, may lead officers to believe that we favor authoritarian regimes—provided, of course, they are anticommunist." Staunch support against

Communist insurgencies notwithstanding, military coups d'état, the INR concluded, "have not generally proved to be in our interest."[75]

By and large, however, the Kennedy administration dismissed fears of politicizing Latin America's military leaders. Instead, top U.S. policymakers repeatedly emphasized the positive effects of military training and assistance programs. As the Department of Defense secretary Robert McNamara told a congressional committee, "The exposure of the military officers of those nations to our schools acquaints them with democratic philosophies, democratic ways of thinking, which they, in turn, take back to their nations."[76] Similarly, Maxwell Taylor told Kennedy that Latin American officers "gain an appreciation and understanding of the U.S. more or less by absorption while attending these courses."[77]

The president himself expressed a similar view while discussing the Inter-American Defense College with the Venezuelan ambassador José Antonio Mayobre. The ambassador began by boldly informing Kennedy that "to bring senior officers to Washington for nontechnical, political training would, in the Latin American climate, inevitably stimulate their interest in taking political power." The program, Mayobre continued, "might establish a mutually supported network of Latin American military interested in taking power."[78]

Kennedy sharply disagreed. Military assistance and training programs, he asserted, strengthened U.S. ties with Latin American officers and thus increased coordination on hemispheric issues. Moreover, the U.S. military, Kennedy maintained, enhanced Latin American officers' respect for constitutional democracy. Dismissing the ambassador's fears, Kennedy "could not help but believe that close association with the American military, who understood so well the need to subordinate the military power to the civilian, would be helpful in dealing with the problem with which the ambassador was concerned."[79]

In fact, the Kennedy administration's belief that U.S. military training programs would instill increased respect for constitutional democracy in Latin American officers bore little relation to reality. Instead, U.S. counterinsurgency training and aid played a fundamental role in enhancing Latin American officers' belief in their ability to solve Latin American nations' complex socioeconomic challenges, thus serving as partial justification for the wave of military coups that swept the region over the course of the decade. More broadly, in the zero-sum atmosphere that permeated U.S. Cold War foreign policy, Kennedy's promise to spark a middle-class democratic revolution through the Alliance for Progress was quickly and irreparably undermined by the administration's overriding fear of "losing" Latin American nations to Communist subversion. As Kennedy admitted to his advisers after the assassination of the brutal Dominican dictator—and long-standing U.S. client—Rafael Trujillo, "There are three possibilities in descending order of preference: a decent democratic regime, a continuation of the Trujillo regime, or a 'Castro' regime. We ought to aim at the first, but we can't really renounce the second until we are sure that we can avoid the third."[80] Unwilling to risk backing a vulnerable democracy, Kennedy not only recognized a nondemocratic regime in the Dominican Republic in September 1963, but between 1962 and 1963 he extended diplomatic recognition to military governments that assumed power by force in Argentina (March 1962), Peru (July 1962), Guatemala (March 1963), Ecuador (July 1963), and Honduras (October 1963).[81]

The shift away from U.S. support for Latin American democracies accelerated in the aftermath of Kennedy's assassination in November 1963. Describing Latin American military leaders as, "on the whole, a pretty decent group of people," and dismissing congressional resistance to U.S. military assistance to the region as "a tempest in a teapot," Thomas Mann focused on economic growth and internal security and largely ceased to differentiate between democratic and military governments.[82] As a result, Washington made little protest as the region became increasingly ensnared in the dictatorial rule of repressive military regimes; during the 1960s, Latin America experienced no fewer than sixteen military takeovers, led by officers who had almost inevitably trained at U.S. facilities.[83]

Throughout the decade, however, U.S. policymakers and diplomats repeatedly denied that U.S. military predominance in the hemisphere had any deleterious effects on Latin American political development. Responding to a February 1964 State Department query, the country teams in Chile, Colombia, Ecuador, Guatemala, and Peru uniformly rejected the possibility that U.S. military assistance had played a role in facilitating Latin American coups d'état.[84] Even the U.S. Embassy in Honduras emphasized the positive contribution of U.S. military assistance and aid, despite an ongoing cutoff in response to the previous October's military coup, executed by soldiers in U.S. Army uniforms, brandishing U.S.-made machine guns, and patrolling in troop carriers sporting a sticker "showing the symbolic hands of the United States and Latin America clasped in friendship."[85] The coup, the embassy contended, "would have been entirely possible . . . with or without aid and training equipment furnished [to] forces under [the] Military Assistance Program." Although admitting that the "ease with which [the] military golpe [was] carried out testifies to improved discipline and ability to plan operations which [are] not unrelated to U.S. training," the embassy nonetheless maintained that it was "undeniable that expert planning and [the] rapid transport of troops had [the] effect of reducing bloodshed that might otherwise have accompanied military action."[86]

Such myopia fed into a subtle naturalization of the pattern of illiberal political order in the region. As the assistant secretary of state for inter-American affairs Edwin M. Martin opined in the New York *Herald Tribune* in October 1963, "In most of Latin America there is so little experience with the benefits of political legitimacy that there is an insufficient body of opinion, civil or military, which has any reason to know its value and hence defend it."[87] Similarly, a Department of Defense report asserted in 1965, "To the three typical roles of military forces, i.e., to protect the sovereignty of the nation, to preserve internal order, and to play a constructive part in national development, must be added, in the case of Latin America, a fourth one of special significance, namely, to act as political arbiter."[88] Latin America, the report concluded, "provides at best an alien soil for constitutional democratic government on the Anglo-Saxon model."[89]

Revealing a poorly disguised sense of North American superiority, such assertions obscured the role played by U.S. Cold War policy in strengthening politically ambitious military leaders at the expense of regional democracy. In addition to significantly enhancing security forces' repressive capacity in Central and South American nations ruled by anticommunist dictators like Nicaragua's Anastasio Somoza and Paraguay's Alfredo Stroessner, the U.S. emphasis on internal security contributed to the consolidation of bureaucratic-authoritarian rule in the Southern Cone: Brazil (1964), Argentina (1966), Chile (1973), and Uruguay (1973)—"a chain of governments," the State Department would later write, "whose origin was in battle against the extreme left."[90] Exporting a paradigm of internal security that extended the military's purview deep into the realms of social and economic policy, the United States made a decisive contribution to the rise of a generation of Latin American officers perceiving national security as "the yardstick by which all policies are measured, and the beginning and the end of politics."[91] Indeed, by 1973, more than 170 graduates of the School of the Americas were Latin American government leaders, cabinet ministers, military commanders, or intelligence directors. Such military training programs, admitted Adm. Gene LaRocque (Ret.), who served as director of the Inter-American Defense College from 1969–1972, paradoxically focused on "training people to more efficiently manage a government, without any encouragement for them to take over."[92]

Moreover, by significantly increasing security forces' repressive capacity, logistical efficiency, and technical expertise, the United States played a foundational role in the establishment of what the historian Greg Grandin aptly describes as "counterinsurgent terror states"—fiercely anticommunist regimes combining sophisticated intelligence-gathering technology with extralegal kidnappings, torture, and disappearances of political opponents.[93] Specifically, U.S. deliveries of light weaponry geared toward internal security operations, along with the provision of everyday tools of intelligence collection and analysis such as typewriters and computerized filing programs, combined with U.S. counterinsurgency instruction dramatically enhanced the repressive capacity of security forces vis-à-vis perceived antigovernment movements and served as a blueprint for harsh repression.

In the U.S. Army manual "Counterintelligence," for example, used in training Latin American soldiers during the 1960s as part of "Project X," the U.S. Army's Foreign Intelligence Assistance Program, potential targets were defined as "local or national political party teams, or parties that have goals, beliefs, or ideologies contrary or in opposition to the government." Similarly, the manual "Combat Intelligence" classified political demonstrations by minority groups and "civilians including children who don't want to associate with U.S. troops or their own country's troops" as indicating an impending guerrilla attack, as well as the "celebration of national or religious festivals, or the presence of strangers."[94]

Moreover, perceived subversives warranted harsh interrogation methods according to U.S. military doctrine. A 1963 CIA interrogation training manual outlined techniques of "arrest, deprivation of sensory stimuli through solitary confinement or similar methods, threats and fear, debility, pain, heightened suggestibility and hypnosis, narcosis, and induced regression," and included an "Interrogator's Check List" and descriptive bibliography. Implicitly condoning the use of electric shock in interrogations, the manual informed readers, "If a new safehouse is to be used as the interrogation site, it should be carefully studied to be sure that the total environment can be manipulated as desired. For example, the electric current should be known in advance, so that transformers or other modifying devices will be on hand if needed." Although admitting that "coercive manipulation" might "impair the subject's "ability to make fine distinctions," the manual asserted that it "will not alter his ability to answer correctly such gross questions as 'Are you a Soviet agent? What is your assignment now? [and] Who is your present case officer?'"[95] By the late 1960s, the School of the Americas was translating between twenty and thirty thousand pages of such manuals into Spanish every year for distribution in Latin America.[96]

The scale of such initiatives underscored the success of U.S. Cold War policies toward Latin America. After more than a quarter century of concerted efforts to cultivate close ties with Latin American militaries, by the end of the 1960s the United States could boast an unprecedented hemispheric alliance system predicated on U.S. hemispheric hegemony, fueled by mutual anticommunism, and sustained through extensive transfers of U.S. military equipment and training. Indeed, in few world regions was the imperial nature of U.S. Cold War foreign policy so starkly evident: with tens of thousands of Latin American soldiers passing through U.S. training centers every year, increasing standardization of security forces' weaponry and equipment along U.S. lines, and thousands of U.S. military personnel engaged in training and equipment procurement activities, the United States exerted immense political-military influence throughout Latin America. A core element in the effort to protect U.S.

national security, the militarized nature of U.S. policy toward Latin America heightened regional military leaders' political ambitions, accelerated the development of Latin American doctrines of national security, and increased armed forces' repressive capacity. Indeed, it was only a small step from the selective repression prescribed by U.S. counterinsurgency strategy to systematic state-sanctioned terrorism. As one former student at the School of the Americas candidly informed a journalist, the basis of military intelligence was to "capture a guy without the others finding out, interrogate him, kill him, eliminate him, [and] bury him—you understand?" Underscoring the United States' complicity in the formation of Latin America's worst human-rights-violating regimes, the SOA graduate concluded, "That is, to interrogate him while he can speak, and once the guy dies, to make him disappear so that the reds don't find out that we have the information."[97]

2

THE "THIRD WORLD WAR"
U.S.-Argentine Relations, 1960–1976

Counterrevolutionary training in Argentina was well under way by the time John F. Kennedy began promoting internal security as the primary Latin American military mission in the aftermath of the Cuban Revolution. In fact, Argentine training programs for regional military officers *preceded* the development of similar U.S. programs focusing on counterinsurgency. Although sharing Washington's anticommunist fervor, in the early 1960s Argentine military leaders looked to the French, rather than the Americans, for military assistance and training. Recognized as counterrevolutionary experts thanks to their participation in the brutal suppression of anticolonial revolutionary movements in Vietnam and Algeria, in 1957 French military advisers had been invited to assist in integrating counterrevolutionary warfare into the curriculum of the Argentine Superior War College. The cooperation proved fruitful, and in 1961 two French officers of the Organisation de l'Armée Secrète—a clandestine counterinsurgency force operating in Algeria—accepted invitations to offer courses in Buenos Aires, while French military treatises, notably Col. Roger Trinquier's *Modern Warfare* and Jean Larteguy's *Les centurions*, were translated and widely disseminated in Argentine military circles.[1]

By 1962, the Argentine military had established a "Counter-Revolutionary Course," the first session of which had been attended by students from fourteen Western Hemisphere nations. "The course covered the theory of communism together with strategy and tactics on guerrilla and antiguerrilla warfare," a U.S. assessment team reported. "Current advisors for the course were French officers who advocate the concepts used in Indo-China and Algeria. . . . The instruction is related primarily to the Argentine situation, but the international participation should serve to highlight the importance of internal security." Underscoring the agency of the Argentine military in the context of Latin America's Cold War, the report concluded, "The Armed Forces are definitely anticommunist."[2]

Remarkably, a small contingent of U.S. students also underwent instruction at the Argentine course, foreshadowing subsequent use of French counterinsurgency experts in military training courses in the United States, notably at the Army Special Warfare Center at Fort Bragg. While U.S. policymakers sought to utilize military assistance and training programs to induce Latin American militaries to standardize their arsenals and equipment according to U.S. models—thus achieving preeminence over Western European and potentially Soviet competition—the mutual objectives served by the French in Argentina did not go unnoticed. When a State Department report in mid-1962 recommended engaging in efforts to "minimize the present French advisor influence in [the] Argentine armed forces," the U.S. Embassy in Buenos Aires demurred. "While understanding [the] intent of [the] recommendation," the embassy cabled Washington, "... we [are] inclined to believe activities such as these (concentrated on antiguerrilla training) tend to complement rather than compete with our own efforts."[3]

Although recognizing the potential benefits of the Argentine-French anticommunist initiative, in the early 1960s U.S. policymakers set out to significantly increase U.S. ties with the Argentine military, enticing the armed forces more fully into the internal security role envisioned by the Alliance for Progress. As elsewhere in the hemisphere, the U.S. emphasis on Argentina's internal security ultimately outweighed support for constitutional development and economic growth, and despite a long-standing sense of rivalry with the United States, Argentina was no exception to the broader pattern of deepening U.S.-Latin American Cold War cooperation. Indeed, by the second half of the decade, the United States had displaced the French as the primary military influence on the Argentine armed forces and established a close relationship with the military government led by the army commander in chief Juan Carlos Onganía. As Cold War ties between the two nations solidified, U.S. military training and aid played a defining role in the formulation of the Argentine military's national security doctrine—the blueprint facilitating the systematic use of kidnapping, torture, and disappearance of tens of thousands of perceived subversives following the 1976 military coup d'état.

* * *

At the outset of the 1960s, the Kennedy administration looked to Argentina as a model for the democratic stability, economic growth, and internal security envisioned by the Alliance for Progress. The 1958 election of President Arturo Frondizi had marked the first democratic transfer of political power since the overthrow of Juan Perón, who had been forced into exile by the Argentine military in 1955 after maintaining near-dictatorial power for almost a decade. An army colonel of middle-class origin, Perón's participation in the successful 1943 military coup d'état against President Ramón Castillo had initially garnered the ambitious forty-eight-year-old an appointment as secretary of labor. Recognizing the political potential of Argentina's working class, Perón began systematically cultivating a strong following among Argentine labor unions, through worker-friendly government arbitration of labor disputes, increases in state-mandated worker benefits—including social security, vacations, and housing—and state support for the formation of new unions.[4] The initiative quickly bore fruit, and Perón's growing popularity translated into his appointment as vice president and minister of war in 1944. The following year, when leery Argentine military leaders forced Perón's resignation and deposited him in the island prison of Martín García, thousands of working-class Argentines occupied the Plaza de Mayo, successfully demanding Perón's release and stimulating the military's decision to hold presidential elections in 1946.[5]

The Argentine election corresponded with a surge of democracy that swept Latin America at the end of World War II. Ironically, U.S. efforts to promote democracy in Argentina by derailing Juan Perón's presidential aspirations played a key role in his sweeping 1946 election victory. U.S. policymakers correctly concluded that Perón had been deeply impressed with German and Italian fascism during a short military-training stint in Italy at the outset of the Second World War.[6] More contentiously, in 1945 the State Department believed Perón had maintained strong links with the Nazis throughout the conflict, and hypothesized that the Argentine leader sought to establish a fascist bloc throughout Latin America's Southern Cone; capturing the distrust—and hubris—underpinning U.S. policy toward Perón's political aspirations, the secretary of state Dean Acheson noted in his memoirs, "Perón was a fascist and a dictator detested by all good men—except Argentinians."[7] Accordingly, in a move indicative of both traditional hemispheric dominance and a newly acquired status as a global superpower, the United States openly attempted to defeat Perón's presidential campaign. Spearheaded by the newly appointed ambassador Spruille Braden, the U.S. Embassy became a center of political opposition, even going so far as to publish a damning account of Argentina's conduct toward the Axis powers only two weeks prior to the election. To the lasting detriment of U.S.-Argentine relations, however, Perón deftly turned the ambassador's campaign to his own advantage, handily winning the presidency after shrewdly marketing his candidacy as one of "Perón versus Braden."[8]

Over the next nine years, Perón's promotion of state corporatism transformed Argentina's political and socioeconomic landscape. Championing "economic independence," Perón deepened the government's management of the economy and enacted far-reaching regulatory legislation while simultaneously carrying out Latin America's most extensive nationalization program of industry, agriculture, and foreign investments.[9] Correspondingly, Perón advanced a unique social reform program designated *justicialismo*. Defined as a "third ideological position" in addition to capitalism and Communism, *justicialismo* sought to elevate the Argentine working class to a privileged position in political society by extending civil rights into the socioeconomic arena. Peronist discourse, writes the historian Daniel James, "explicitly challenged the legitimacy of a notion of democracy which limited itself to participation in formal political rights and . . . extended it to include participation in the social and economic life of the nation."[10] In practice, Peronism's effort to cultivate the support of Argentine workers translated into sweeping social welfare measures, expansive state-organized labor unions, and government arbitration of labor disputes.[11] In turn, Perón engendered enormous loyalty among Argentina's *"descamisados"* ("shirtless ones"), as he famously referred to members of the working class. Assisted by his wife, Eva ("Evita") Duarte—whose rags-to-riches experience, public tirades against the Argentine elites, and extensive charity on behalf of Perón created an almost-religious following—by 1948, Perón had achieved near-dictatorial control.

Notwithstanding Perón's landslide reelection in 1951, over the course of the decade his political fortunes declined in the face of a growing economic downturn. Because the country depended on agricultural exports as the primary source of foreign exchange, and had a limited capacity to expand production, the investment of state funds in one domestic sector inevitably occurred at the expense of other sectors. In a pattern that would continue to dog Argentine leaders in subsequent decades, Perón was unable to avoid cycles of economic expansion followed by violent contraction, in which government investment initiatives resulted in rising inflation, economic stagnation, and a balance of payments deficit. Combined with Eva Perón's death in 1952 and, in 1954, a bitter feud with the Catholic Church, Perón's inability to bring about sustained economic prosperity precipitated a military coup d'état in September 1955.[12]

Elected to office in the tense aftermath of Perón's ouster, Arturo Frondizi sought to carefully hew to a middle path between Argentina's competing constituencies. It was an unenviable challenge. Politically, Frondizi's plan to integrate the mass of unreformed Peronists—roughly 30 percent of the voting public—into the mainstream of Argentina's fragile democracy immediately raised the hackles of anti-Peronists. Economically, the president's effort to stabilize Argentina's volatile economy by implementing economic austerity measures prescribed by international lending agencies strained the pocketbook of the working class, while his accommodation of foreign investment drew sharp criticism from Argentine nationalists.[13]

Frondizi looked to the United States for political support and economic assistance in order to carry out his reform agenda. As the Argentine minister of economy informed Kennedy in May 1961, Frondizi needed "firm assurance, for political purposes," that the Alliance for Progress would provide loans to Argentina for fiscally sound projects, such as modernizing the nation's dilapidated railroad system.[14] Equally significant to Frondizi was U.S. political support for Argentina's unstable democracy. By exemplifying the democratic tenets of the alliance, Frondizi hoped to stay the insurrectionary designs perpetually percolating in the *circulo militar*—the Argentine officers' club.

Finally, Frondizi aimed to take advantage of Kennedy's obsessive animosity toward Fidel Castro's revolutionary regime by establishing Argentina as a mediator between the United States and Cuba. Successful mediation, the Argentine president hoped, would simultaneously confirm his anticommunist credentials in the eyes of Argentine military officers and belie accusations from across the Argentine political spectrum of kowtowing to the United States.[15] Accordingly, in January 1962, Frondizi ordered the Argentine delegation to abstain from a U.S.-backed resolution to exclude Cuba from the Organization of American States at the inter-American foreign ministers' meeting at Punta del Este, Uruguay. Shortly thereafter, reports surfaced of a secret meeting between Frondizi and Ernesto "Che" Guevara—the famous Argentine national who had served as one of Castro's top commanders during the Cuban Revolution and was acting minister of industry.[16]

The Kennedy administration supported Frondizi's aspiration to establish Argentina as a model of Alliance for Progress success. The Argentine president's reform agenda was a far cry from the corporatist Perón era, which had grated against the U.S. postwar vision of a global order based on limited government intervention in the economy, liberal capitalism, multilateral trade, and U.S. hemispheric hegemony. Frondizi's economic initiatives also found a receptive audience in Washington. By late 1961, the United States was supplying half of all foreign investment for Frondizi's industrialization program, and after a private meeting with Frondizi in Palm Beach, Florida, in February 1962, Kennedy promised an additional $150 million in loans for economic development.[17]

The United States was far less accommodating to Frondizi's effort to mediate between Kennedy and Castro, and quietly supported Argentine military leaders' inroads into the political arena in the name of anticommunism. In September 1961, the United States forced Frondizi onto the defensive by publicizing a collection of documents obtained by a member of the Cuban Embassy staff in Buenos Aires alleging Cuban involvement in subversive activities in Argentina, as well as close ties between Cuban and Argentine government officials.[18] Five months later, when Argentine military commanders—incensed by Frondizi's decision to abstain from the OAS referendum on Cuba—forced the Argentine president to break diplomatic relations with the Castro regime, U.S. policymakers quietly exulted. Referring to the sudden reversal in Argentine-Cuban relations, the State Department cabled the U.S. Embassy in Buenos Aires, "We welcome foreign policy changes brought about by internal pressures mainly from [the] military."[19]

While welcoming the Argentine military's anti-Castro initiatives, U.S. policymakers recognized the distinct limits to U.S. leverage. At the outset of the decade, U.S. military influence over Argentina was distinctly limited; a training mission existed for each of the three Argentine service branches, along with attachés charged with obtaining intelligence, but no U.S. police assistance program had been established, nor had the Argentines expressed an interest in a bilateral Military Assistance Agreement. While military assistance could be delivered through a credit assistance program, and the cost of U.S. training for Argentine soldiers could be offset by a grant aid program, as the State Department reported in January 1962, "The Army Mission has been unsuccessful in getting the Argentine Army to accept mobile training teams for assistance in counterguerrilla warfare training. It is difficult to determine whether nonacceptance is a matter of pride or lack of interest in this type of training."[20]

The U.S. effort to lure the Argentine military into accepting the subordinate status envisioned by the Alliance for Progress significantly influenced U.S. policymakers' response to the dramatic showdown between Frondizi and conservative Argentine military officers that followed the March 18, 1962, gubernatorial elections. Dashing Frondizi's hopes of a victory for his own Intransigent Party, the Peronists handily won nine provincial races, and significantly increased their representation in the Congress. Recognizing that the surge in Peronist political strength would solidify the military's desire to carry out his own ouster, Frondizi immediately ordered an interdiction barring the Peronist candidates from assuming office. Nonetheless, the president's credibility had been irreparably sullied in the eyes of *golpista* military officers, and in the chaotic ten days after the election, demands for Frondizi's overthrow gained momentum.

Ironically, by all accounts the election was clean and fair, and, as the recently appointed U.S. ambassador Robert McClintock incisively noted, the outcome was hardly a referendum on Frondizi's foreign policy. "These elections were largely determined by factors of purely domestic origin and concern," the ambassador cabled Washington. "The Alliance for Progress was not directly involved nor was Castro communism an essential factor in the outcome."[21] Nonetheless, McClintock, one of the Department of State's most experienced foreign service officers, consistently advocated avoiding U.S. involvement in preserving

Argentine democracy.[22] In the tense aftermath of the election McClintock assured Frondizi that the U.S. military delegation in Buenos Aires would not encourage the political aspirations of their Argentine counterparts. Despite Frondizi's entreaties that the U.S. ambassador actively work to dissuade coup-minded Argentine officers, however, McClintock refused to actively defend Argentina's democratically elected president.[23] "I am not winding up our own military on what is essentially an Argentine internal problem. At the same time I have given assurance to Frondizi . . . of my concern that Argentine constitutional safeguards be preserved," McClintock cabled Washington on March 18. The ambassador concluded, "I think this is a problem Frondizi will have to work out for himself. I want him, however, to think I am on his side."[24]

The Kennedy administration concurred with McClintock's recommendation to avoid U.S. involvement in Argentina's volatile political situation. "You were entirely right," the department responded on March 19, ". . . in refusing Frondizi request [that] you seek [to] exert influence on [Argentine] military in electoral situation created by Peronista victory [in] Buenos Aires Province."[25] Although the department surprised McClintock late on March 23 with a declaration that "it is our strong desire and policy that Frondizi not . . . be forced to resign by [the] military and nothing should be done that might in any way encourage the military to take such action," by March 26 Washington had concluded that the "best present course for U.S. in Argentina is let events take their course."[26]

Accordingly, in meetings with Argentine military leaders, McClintock encouraged the officers to find a constitutional solution to the crisis but did not openly oppose their impending decision to depose Frondizi. Moreover, when the armed forces finally removed Frondizi from office on March 29 and replaced him with the conservative Argentine politician José María Guido, McClintock praised the military for whitewashing the overthrow by having a new president sworn into office by the Argentine Supreme Court and he repeatedly encouraged the State Department to recognize the new administration. The military, McClintock cabled the State Department on April 6, "sincerely believed that they have acted with exemplary restraint and that they have leaned over backwards to maintain a constitutional regime," a theme he reiterated in subsequent cables.[27]

The ambassador's willingness to accept the military coup underscored the importance U.S. policymakers placed on strengthening U.S.-Argentine military ties. As McClintock pointed out in an April 13 cable urging Washington to recognize the Guido regime, the Argentine officers' political platform was highly compatible with U.S. national security concerns. "[The] only points up to now on which [the] military will definitely intervene are [the] threats of [an] increase in Communist strength or a return of [the] Peronists to power," McClintock wrote. "In this . . . their line of policy is identical to ours."[28] A few months later the ambassador went a step further. The Argentine military were "friendly to the United States at the present time and find it difficult to understand why we should look down our noses at the military who are as fervently anti-Communist as we." The Argentine military, McClintock concluded, "should be regarded as an asset by the United States (if rightly used) and not as a liability as some people in Washington seem to believe."[29]

The Kennedy administration agreed with McClintock's assessment, resuming relations with the military-backed government in Argentina on April 19, 1962. The decision marked the beginning of the administration's shift away from the emphasis on regional democracy that Kennedy had loftily proclaimed in the Alliance for Progress little more than a year earlier, and precipitated the spiral of Latin American militarization—and U.S. sanction—that would characterize the region during the remainder of the decade. Indeed, in early June the administration reopened the aid spigot to Argentina, announcing a grant of $50 million in standby credits in conjunction with similar credits of $100 million from the International Monetary Fund to Argentina's military-backed government.[30] The decision, taken only days before the presidential election in Peru, elicited a swift response from the politically ambitious Peruvian military. On July 18, the Peruvian president Manuel Prado was dragged out of bed by a U.S.-trained Peruvian special forces officer and deposed after a Sherman tank—provided to Peru by the U.S. Military Assistance Program—smashed through the gates of the presidential residence.[31] Moreover, although the United States initially severed diplomatic relations and canceled economic and military assistance, Kennedy's decision to restore relations with the Andean nation less than a month later, following the military's promise to hold free elections, did little to dissuade similar plans elsewhere in the hemisphere. As Robert McClintock cabled the State Department from Buenos Aires in August 1962: "In view of our recent recognition of [the] Peruvian junta, none of [the] would-be [Argentine] *golpistas* are at all concerned as to [the] U.S. attitude toward withholding recognition from a de facto regime here, it being regarded as inevitable that, to forestall an ultimate Castro-Communist take-over, [the] U.S. will eventually have to recognize and probably also to resume economic and financial support of whatever regime is in power in Argentina as long as it is anti-Communist."[32]

* * *

Although Frondizi's overthrow struck a serious blow to the Alliance for Progress, the United States succeeded in drawing Argentina more closely into a U.S.-led hemispheric anticommunist alliance. In October 1962 the Argentine Navy took the lead among Latin American nations participating in the Cuban Missile Crisis blockade, and the following month, the Argentine military requested U.S.

training for an elite brigade. Emphasizing the Argentine armed services' previous "reluctance even to contemplate hemispheric cooperation," the U.S. Embassy described the request as "a decisive turn in attitude." "In our opinion we have [a] unique opportunity not only to consolidate new lines of cooperation with [the] Argentine Army but to accomplish strategic and policy objectives," Ambassador McClintock enthused.[33] By January 1963, the United States had made significant progress in reversing the pattern of Argentine military resistance to U.S. hemispheric hegemony, and had made unprecedented gains in luring the Argentine military away from European—predominately French—influence. "U.S.-Argentine military relations are better now than they have been at any time during modern history," the Department of State exulted in January. "Argentine military leaders have indicated the belief that the national interests of the country are inextricably entwined with the efforts of the U.S. to combat communist imperialism."[34]

As elsewhere in the hemisphere, the Kennedy administration hoped that by facilitating the professionalization of Argentina's armed services, the United States could assist in establishing an apolitical military dedicated to internal security. Accordingly, over the course of 1963, the United States worked assiduously to cultivate a close relationship with the Argentine Army commander in chief Juan Carlos Onganía. Of humble origin, Onganía cut a less-than-charismatic figure; a confidential U.S. biographical report described the general as "somewhat austere and cold," who, out of uniform, "has the tweedy appearance of a British country squire."[35] Nonetheless, Onganía's opposition to an abortive coup attempt in August 1962 established his reputation as a staunch constitutionalist—a "legalist," in the patois of Buenos Aires military circles. As a Department of State memorandum made clear, "An important objective of our proposed military program in Argentina . . . is to help General Onganía and the constitutionalist military with their aim of turning the Argentine armed forces away from politics toward a normal role for the military in a democratic society."[36]

Onganía also impressed Washington with his perceived willingness to embrace the United States as the hemispheric leader—a welcome shift away from "the traditional neutral policy of Argentina in two World Wars and the vacillating and on occasion neutralist policy of the Frondizi regime."[37] Granted, practical considerations played no small role in the Argentine general's support for equipment modernization according to U.S. standards; in 1963 the Argentine Army arsenal offered a geography lesson in the major arms producers of Western Europe: rifles and carbines from Germany, Dutch machine-guns, Belgian automatic rifles and submachine guns, and mortars from France.[38] By the same token, the Kennedy administration's emphasis on the hemispheric threat posed by the Cuban Revolution resonated with the fiercely anticommunist Onganía. Aiming to strengthen control over Argentina's armed forces by establishing more vertical lines of command while simultaneously expanding the military's purview into the social and economic realms, the Argentine general looked to U.S. military assistance as a necessary step en route to the establishment of a uniquely Argentine doctrine of national security.[39]

Accordingly, Washington plied Onganía with offers of an expanded training program and the benefits of signing a formal U.S. military assistance agreement. In an effort to impress the Argentine general with U.S. military technology, in May 1963 Onganía was invited on an official visit to the United States for an inspection of army installations. At the end of the tour, U.S. officials decorated Onganía with the Legion of Merit Award, citing his support for "civil government, constituted by free elections in accordance with the constitutions of the country." Surprised by the unexpected decoration, Onganía, the U.S. Army chief of staff happily reported, was "touched with deep emotion."[40] Underscoring the importance Washington attached to expanding military ties with Argentina, despite a near-complete cutoff of U.S. economic aid in response to President Arturo Illia's refusal to compensate U.S. oil companies (whose contracts Illia had revoked in late 1963), military negotiations between the two nations continued uninterrupted through mid-decade.[41]

Critics of Washington's military policy were quick to question the depth of Onganía's respect for constitutional democracy, and worried that U.S. support would encourage praetorian tendencies. "Washington does not see in him what it does not want to see—the leader of fascist and brutal militarism which split a democratic regime, and ousted a legally and freely elected president and installed uniformed autocracy. But that is not important," the Brazilian newspaper *Diario de Noticias* complained when the Kennedy administration decorated Onganía with the Legion of Merit. "General Onganía is a friend," the editorial concluded, "which is to say that General Onganía proposes to mobilize all forces whenever the hour for the invasion of Cuba comes."[42] Arturo Illia—who had won the 1963 presidential election with only one-quarter of the electorate thanks to the military's ban on Peronism—expressed similar concerns.[43] In an October 1963 meeting with the assistant secretary of state for inter-American affairs Edwin M. Martin, the Argentine president asserted that the U.S. military had "perhaps oversold their Latin American counterparts on [the] one and only danger of communism," with the result that the "Latin American military seemed prone to exculpate their subsequent action[s] on [the] ground [that] they were working against communism." When Martin inquired whether this was the case in Argentina, Illia—no doubt highly cognizant of his own political dependence on the military—demurred.[44]

In the short run, U.S. policymakers could confidently dismiss such criticism as groundless. Given that Argentina was the last Latin American nation to agree to a Military Assistance Agreement, for U.S. policymakers the quiet signing ceremony on May 10, 1964, marked a defining step on the road to integrating Argentina into a U.S.-led hemispheric anticommunist alliance.[45] As elsewhere in the region, Washington anticipated that U.S. military assistance and training would cultivate a new generation of Argentine officers whose professionalism—a product of U.S. tutelage—would allow them to "find the new game more engrossing than the old one of 'throw out the president,'" in the words of a mid-1960s study of U.S. military policy toward Latin America, while also providing the tools to "successfully distinguish the revolutionary guerrilla (badly infected with alien ideology) from the protestor against injustice and oppression (a goodly agrarian reformer)."[46]

Early returns on the U.S. military investment in Argentina appeared highly promising. Under Onganía's leadership, professionalization of the Argentine armed forces continued apace, and as military relations between the United States and Argentina deepened, French counterrevolutionary doctrine was increasingly supplanted by U.S. military counterinsurgency manuals. The United States "has maintained its post-World War II position as the predominant foreign military influence in Argentina," a State Department report claimed in April 1966. "The Argentine armed forces have not turned away from us and toward third countries for their doctrine, equipment and training." Instead, the report continued, "they have concentrated on modernization and professionalization under U.S. guidance and have participated to a limited extent in combined multi-national exercises under U.S. auspices."

Although admitting that the Argentine military continued to refuse to make internal security their primary mission and citing limited counterinsurgency coordination between Argentine police and military forces, the department could nonetheless claim significant success in its policy toward the fiercely independent South American nation. "In brief, while the record is not earthshaking," the report concluded, "it is on the whole gratifying, especially when one compares it to situations elsewhere in the hemisphere and keeps in mind what it is reasonable to expect from Argentina."[47]

Two months later, on June 28, 1966, a bloodless military coup d'état swept President Illia f om power and installed General Onganía as head of the successor govern· lent. The new president proceeded to dismiss the Argentine Congress, the Supreme Court, and all provincial governments, including all appointed or elected officials.[48] Dispensing with the mechanisms of democracy, Onganía issued the "Statute of the Revolution," a decree superseding the constitution and providing the executive branch the power to rule by decree. Moreover, in an unprecedented break with the Argentine military's previous forays into the political realm, Onganía anticipated at least a decade of military rule.[49] "It is almost certain" the U.S. Embassy cabled Washington in the immediate aftermath of the coup, that the "Onganía government will not give assurances of free elections in near future."[50]

Anticommunism held a central position in Onganía's expansive notion of national security. Under presidential decree, activities interpreted as Communist resulted in severe penalties, and less than two months after assuming power, Onganía ordered a major intervention in the state-run university system to eradicate "communist penetration of classrooms and facilities." When students in Buenos Aires refused to vacate campuses, police quickly resorted to clubs and tear gas, resulting in nearly three dozen hospitalizations and more than two hundred arrests. In the aftermath of the "Night of the Long Batons," as the intervention became known, the president of the University of Buenos Aires, eight deans, and 184 professors resigned, leading to a prolonged academic crisis that remained unresolved two months later.[51]

Onganía also spearheaded an increasingly repressive government campaign of press censorship. Initially focusing on radio and television, rising popular discontent with the Onganía regime led to heavy-handed government control over the content of Argentine magazines and provincial newspapers, primarily by threatening editors, publishers, and reporters with disrespect for authority ("*desacato*"), a criminal offense. By 1970, Onganía's "strong bent to prudishness," as the CIA put it, resulted in the extension of government censorship to books, plays, and films deemed indecent.[52] Communist infiltration, however, remained the president's primary concern; "If a free press would make it possible for Communists to take over Argentina," Onganía told a representative of the Inter-American Press Association, "then I would be proud to say that there is no free press in Argentina."[53]

U.S. policymakers publicly lamented the setback to Argentine democracy precipitated by the 1966 military coup and immediately suspended diplomatic recognition of the military regime. Yet if the coup shattered the illusion that U.S. military assistance and training could inculcate respect among Argentine military leaders for constitutional democracy, it nevertheless illuminated the extent to which the U.S. emphasis on internal security had influenced the Argentine armed forces. By redefining the military's mission to encompass virtually all aspects of Argentine life, and elevating anticommunism to the center of his administration's agenda, Onganía's doctrine of national security bore the unmistakable influence of the U.S. military's imperial auspices.

Indeed, the deterioration of Onganía's constitutionalism corresponded with the rise in U.S.-Argentine military cooperation. At the fifth annual Conference of American Armies at West Point in August 1964, Onganía emphasized that the armed services "cannot passively nor blindly follow established authority."[54]

A few months later, the influence of U.S. counterinsurgency policy was unmistakable in Onganía's declaration of a doctrine of "ideological borders," extending the military's traditional role of defending against external attack to include defense against "exotic ideologies." Likewise, the Argentine general's decision to unveil the policy during a formal visit to Brazil shortly after the military's overthrow of President João Goulart served as an unmistakable display of support for the U.S.-backed authoritarian-bureaucratic regime.[55] Indeed, Brazil's subsequent decision to make a token troop contribution to the U.S.-led OAS military intervention in the Dominican Republic in April 1965 to prevent alleged Communist subversion decisively contributed to Onganía's disillusionment with Arturo Illia, whose refusal to participate in the operation catalyzed the Argentine general's decision to resign as commander of the army in November 1965.[56]

Handed the helm of state eight months later, Onganía grandly proclaimed the beginning of an "Argentine Revolution" in which he promised to carry out dramatic economic, political, and social development, while eradicating Communist efforts at subversion. Underscoring the significance of U.S. Cold War policy for Onganía, in the immediate aftermath of the coup he was reportedly perplexed by the U.S. decision to suspend diplomatic relations. "We thought the Pentagon favored a grand anti-Communist alliance between the military governments of Brazil and Argentina," an Argentine government aid blithely told reporters.[57]

Onganía need not have worried. The coup plotters had informed the United States of their intentions well in advance, and although Edwin Martin—appointed U.S. Ambassador to Argentina in early 1964—had consistently advocated respect for constitutional democracy in his meetings with Argentine military and political leaders, the Johnson administration had no intention of denying recognition to the staunchly anticommunist Argentine military regime.[58] Despite Onganía's refusal to provide a timetable for future elections, his "anti-communist leanings" the CIA later wrote, would "continue to be a force for close cooperation with the U.S."[59] After suspending diplomatic recognition for a mere seventeen days, Lyndon Johnson recognized the Onganía regime on July 15, 1966, and quietly resumed economic assistance to the South American nation the following month.[60]

The United States was not responsible for the 1966 Argentine coup; domestic considerations—spiraling inflation, increasing labor unrest, and the threat of a Peronist victory in the scheduled 1967 elections—were the primary catalysts of the military overthrow. Nor did the United States simply implant anticommunism onto the complex Argentine political landscape. Military involvement in modern Argentine politics dated to the early 1930s, as did police surveillance, control, and repression of perceived Communists, anarchists, and "foreign" subversives. Moreover, the Western European influence on Argentina's military evolution should not be overlooked; in addition to a legacy of German and Italian political and military influence in the first half of the twentieth century, beginning in the late 1950s, the French played an important role in the development of the Argentine military's counterrevolution strategy.[61]

Nonetheless, U.S. military assistance and training over the course of the 1960s significantly enhanced the Argentine military's repressive capacity against perceived subversives and facilitated the development of a distinctly Argentine doctrine of national security. In a 1967 Argentine Intelligence School guide on countersubversion, for example, U.S. military manuals and course materials constituted nearly one-third of the sources cited.[62] Likewise, by the end of the 1960s, dozens of federal police officers and nearly four thousand military officers had been trained at U.S. facilities in the Canal Zone or in the continental United States, and between 1963 and 1967, the United States supplied Argentina with $60 million worth of arms and equipment through grant and sales agreements.[63] The significance of U.S. Cold War policy toward Argentina was made clear by General Ramón Camps, who would emerge as a principal architect of dirty war tactics following the military's return to power in 1976: "in Argentina we were influenced first by the French and then by the United States. We used their methods separately at first and then together, until the United States' ideas finally predominated. France and the United States were our main sources of counterinsurgency training. They organized centres for teaching counterinsurgency techniques (especially in the U.S.) and sent out instructors, observers, and an enormous amount of literature."[64]

Argentina's integration into the U.S. Cold War alliance system also decisively contributed to the formulation of the distinctly Argentine doctrine of national security, emerging at the onset of the *Onganiato* and evolving over the following decade into a radically militaristic dogma with messianic overtones.[65] As elsewhere in South America, the United States' emphasis on internal security sharpened Argentine military officers' belief in their own capacity to resolve Argentina's complex political, economic, and social issues, while also providing justification for the bureaucratic-authoritarian designs of *golpista* military officers and their conservative political allies. U.S. efforts to professionalize the Argentine military, in other words, not only failed to steer the armed forces away from a deep engagement in national politics, but facilitated, as Guillermo O'Donnell asserted in a pioneering analysis, "a much more comprehensive military intervention directed toward the establishment of much more complete domination."[66]

As the United States became increasingly embroiled in the Vietnam War, U.S. policy toward Argentina—and Latin America as a whole—shifted increasingly away from even rhetorically supporting democracy and instead championed stability and anticommunism. As the Johnson administration entered its final year, the U.S. Embassy in Buenos Aires discarded outright the "return to

Constitutional government in the immediate future" as an objective of U.S. policy toward Argentina. "The GOA is making a serious attempt to correct some important distortions in the economic and social field," the embassy asserted, "and it should be given a chance to succeed."[67]

U.S. support for stable, anticommunist client regimes deepened under Richard Nixon, whose disinterest in the region led to an overriding effort to maintain the political status quo. "Long as we've been in it, people don't give one damn about Latin America," Nixon once told a staff member.[68] Henry Kissinger, who dominated U.S. foreign policy in the Nixon and Ford administrations, took an even more trivializing view of Latin America. A staunch believer in Realpolitik, Kissinger's tenure in the Nixon White House was defined by an emphasis on big power relations, particularly the effort to triangulate between the United States, the Soviet Union, and China. The developing world, in Kissinger's view, warranted sustained U.S. attention only when it impinged on the Cold War; with U.S. power in the international arena increasingly constrained in the face of an intractable war in Vietnam, growing balance of trade deficits, and the rising assertiveness of the Organization of the Petroleum Exporting Countries (OPEC), the Nixon administration relied heavily on pro-U.S., right-wing dictators to maintain regional stability. Accordingly, with the significant exception of extensive covert efforts to destabilize the democratically elected government of Chilean leftist Salvador Allende, Kissinger demonstrated an almost total disinterest in hemispheric affairs. "You come here speaking of Latin America, but this is not important. Nothing important can come from the South," Kissinger told a startled Chilean foreign minister in 1969. "History has never been produced in the South," he continued. "The axis of history starts in Moscow, goes to Bonn, crosses over to Washington, and then goes to Tokyo. What happens in the South is of no importance."[69]

With its foreign policy priorities elsewhere, the Nixon administration consistently worked to maintain strong relations with Latin American militaries. "U.S.-style democracy won't work here," Nixon maintained during an eleven-day tour of South America in mid-1967. "I wish it would."[70] After conferring with Onganía, Nixon described the Argentine president to reporters as "one of the best leaders I have known." Onganía, Nixon concluded, was "the right man for Argentina at this moment in its destiny."[71] When Nelson A. Rockefeller presented the president with a detailed report on Latin America, Nixon predictably ignored the recommendation for "reorganization of the United States government's foreign policy structure, fundamental changes of U.S. trade and lending policies, renegotiation of foreign debts, and a more realistic division of labor in the hemisphere." Instead, Nixon latched onto Rockefeller's low-key affirmation of the Mann Doctrine, which emphasized the need to avoid U.S. military interventions in the hemisphere and offered praise for the "new type of military man" that had emerged in Latin America, "prepared to adapt his authoritarian tradition to the goals of social and economic progress."[72]

In 1970, the National Security Council explicitly directed U.S. embassies to deepen ties with regional armed forces; in practical terms for the U.S. Country Team in Argentina, with the military occupying the Casa Rosada, the directive implied a strengthening of relations with the government. "In the case of Argentina," the embassy responded, "we are fortunate that at this critical juncture in Latin American affairs there is a government in Argentina increasingly disposed to perceive a mutuality of interests and to cooperate with us in hemisphere affairs."[73] The following year, although a decrease in MAP funding due to congressional opposition had prompted the Argentine military to resume buying arms from Europe, the U.S. Embassy described relations with Argentina's military government as "quite good," and in May 1973, the U.S. ambassador characterized U.S.-Argentine military cooperation as "reasonably unrestrained."[74] Indeed, although the Argentine military's reluctant decision in 1973 to retreat from the political stage in favor of a return to constitutional democracy clearly demonstrated the near-total failure of Onganía's "Argentine Revolution," Washington nonetheless continued to look to the military as a significant *political* ally. Emphasizing the importance of increased military sales to Argentina in order to draw the South American nation more fully into the U.S. orbit, for example, the U.S. Embassy maintained in mid-May 1973 that "the military are then far more likely to act as a brake on any inclinations the new GOA [Government of Argentina] may have to align itself with governments hostile to us."[75]

In fact, Washington's emphasis on stability in the final years of the 1960s translated into the maintenance of close U.S.-Argentine military ties despite the Onganía administration's exacerbation of Argentina's political, economic, and social problems. As early as 1966, many Argentines were bitterly complaining that the Onganía government "*no anda*" (is not getting anywhere), and only two months after Nixon's 1968 visit to Argentina, a public opinion poll indicated that the majority of Argentines felt Onganía had accomplished "nothing good."[76] Similarly, as early as December 1967 the CIA predicted that Onganía would not be able "to keep Argentine political problems on the shelf."[77] The agency's skepticism proved prescient; the military government was incapable of creating sustainable economic growth by reducing Argentina's economic dependence on agricultural exports, and failed to either co-opt or destroy the continued affiliation of the bulk of Argentina's working class with the Peronist political party. Instead, by cutting off the possibility of political reform, the Onganía dictatorship accelerated the rise of violent revolutionary movements, including distinctly Peronist groups as well as left-wing organizations inspired by Castro's Cuba.

Correspondingly, in mid-1969 popular disillusionment with stagnating wages and a rising cost of living boiled over in a wave of violent protests in a half dozen Argentine cities. Not only did the protests lead to Onganía's overthrow by a military coup d'état the following year, but they set in motion a clumsy transition to democracy that culminated in the triumphant return of Juan Perón to the presidency after eighteen years in exile.[78]

* * *

In the midst of Argentina's political upheaval, Robert C. Hill arrived in Buenos Aires as the newly appointed United States ambassador. A staunch Republican, Hill spent the Kennedy-Johnson years tending to his extensive investments and serving out a brief tenure in the New Hampshire legislature. Throughout the decade, he remained an inveterate cold warrior, denouncing both the Kennedy and Johnson regimes for diplomatic ineptitude and laxity in the battle against Communism, and keeping up a steady barrage of inflammatory rhetoric on Cuba. Fidel Castro was a "monster and a tyrant," in Hill's estimation. "I continue to attack his regime every time I have an opportunity to speak in the United States," Hill confided to an associate shortly before the Cuban Missile Crisis.[79]

Correspondingly, despite the increasing number of military coups d'état in the region, Hill continued to support U.S. military assistance and training programs for Latin American security forces. "Many of the new military leaders are conscious of social change and regard it as part of their military duty to guide their countries through the dangerous conflicts of disorder toward a better social, political, and economic level of living," Hill wrote in 1966 while serving as chairman of the Republican Coordinating Committee's task force on foreign policy. Staking out a position that was perhaps closer to the Johnson administration's than he would have liked to admit, Hill noted that while military juntas were not acceptable as permanent substitutes for democracy, in the short term they could be relied on to stamp out Communist inroads and establish stability. "We should not be quick to undermine," Hill concluded, "what is now often the one non-Communist element in Latin America responsive to the legitimate aspirations of the people."[80]

The 1968 election of Richard Nixon brought Hill back onto the diplomatic circuit. Not surprisingly, as rumors of a high-profile appointment circulated in the aftermath of Nixon's victory, the veteran *Washington Post* correspondent John M. Goshko reported Latin American progressives criticizing Hill for being an "ultra-conservative" with "one overriding interest—advocacy of a tough anti-communist and anti-Castro policy." Hill's appointment, Goshko concluded, "would be regarded all over Latin America as a negation of Nixon's own statement that the United States should offer 'a handshake to the dictators and an *abrazo* to the democrats.'"[81] Nonetheless, underscoring the pro-business, anticommunist fervor that characterized his administration's Latin America policy, Nixon pressed Hill into diplomatic service. After a brief stint as assistant secretary of defense for international affairs and nearly two years as U.S. ambassador to Spain, the Vermont native was appointed envoy to Argentina in November 1973.

The assignment, the fifty-six-year-old Hill declared, was "the climax of my career."[82] Hill's enthusiasm was tempered, however, when a human body was thrown into the road by left-wing terrorists directly in front of the ambassador's car less than a week after his arrival.[83] The grisly incident, along with biting attacks in left-wing Buenos Aires newspapers that greeted Hill's arrival, made brutally clear the extraordinary challenges the new ambassador would face.[84] On one end of the spectrum, Hill's arrival corresponded with the zenith of revolutionary terrorism, "a wild assortment," in the ambassador's words, ". . . of Maoists, Marxists, [and] Leninists, that would like to overthrow this government."[85] Led by the People's Revolutionary Army (ERP), the military arm of the Marxist-Leninist Revolutionary Workers Party, and the Montoneros, an offshoot of the Peronist Youth Movement, by 1973 left-wing revolutionary groups were engaged in a concerted and sophisticated campaign to destabilize the Argentine government. Estimates of the guerrillas' strength ranged from a few hundred to as many as 35,000 soldiers, while their finances—procured primarily through the kidnapping and ransom of multinational corporate executives—stood at over $100 million.[86]

On the other end of the spectrum, state-sanctioned violence in response to the guerrilla threat deepened the fissures in Argentine society. Thoroughly disgraced by its inability to resolve Argentina's pressing problems, the military had retreated from political power in 1973 and ended the electoral proscription on Peronism. In the subsequent national elections, the Peronist candidate Héctor Cámpora won 52 percent of the vote, then resigned after holding office less than two months to facilitate Juan Perón's return to the presidency on October 12, 1973. Having attained almost mythical status after deftly directing the Peronist movement from exile in Spain for nearly two decades, in the early 1970s Perón had played a key role in encouraging popular resistance against the Argentine military, describing the Montoneros in particular as "that marvelous youth that struggles against military dictatorship with weapons in their hands and who know how to give their lives for the fatherland." Once Perón was firmly ensconced in the Casa Rosada, however, he pursued a decidedly conservative agenda, and his support for radical youth groups quickly turned to harsh repudiation, culminating in his public dismissal of the Montoneros in May 1974 as "beardless wonders" and "pernicious elements." By summer many young Peronists had resolved to resume clandestine armed struggle against the government.[87] With political violence increasing and no end in sight to Argentina's economic crisis, Perón's death in July 1974 boded poorly for Argentina's future; not only was Perón's running mate (and wife), Isabel Martinez de Perón, politically inexperienced, but her dependence on advisers—particularly the social welfare minister José López Rega, an occultist referred to as "the Wizard"—was widely known.[88]

Officially, Isabel Perón's declaration of a state of siege following the murder of the federal police chief Alberto Villar in early November 1974 resulted in the incarceration of thousands of suspected subversives, held indefinitely and without charges "at the disposition of the executive power." Unofficially, reports quickly surfaced of widespread application of the "ley de fuga"—the killing of suspected left-wing terrorists by law enforcement officers who invariably claimed that the victims had resisted arrest.[89] Moreover, in late 1974, right-wing extremist organizations such as the Alianza Anticomunista Argentina (known as the Triple A, or AAA) began retaliating against perceived left-wing subversives. Linked to López Rega, complicity in Triple A violence reached the highest levels of the Argentine government.

The bloodletting pushed Argentina to what the U.S. State Department described as "near civil-war dimensions."[90] In the first 351 days of Isabel Perón's presidency, 503 political deaths were recorded. By early 1975, it was clear that far more violence was perpetrated by the Triple A than by their counterparts on the far left; of twenty-five political murders recorded throughout Argentina in the forty-eight-hour period of March 20 and 21, for example, two-thirds were victims of right-wing terrorism. "The bodies of young leftists turn up daily," Ambassador Hill cabled Washington in late March, "and are at least twice as frequent as the victims of left-ist terrorists."[91]

Not surprisingly, Argentina's political woes spilled over into the economic arena. The beleaguered nation's inflation rate—estimated to be as high as 700 percent—was considered the worst in the world, and in 1975 alone productivity declined by one-half.[92] Moreover, Argentine efforts to attract new capital, as the U.S. State Department bluntly asserted, "will be to little avail if the government cannot guarantee the security of lives and property."[93] Indeed, threatened by left-wing terrorist kidnappings, many business executives were operating under siege-like conditions. "Those firms that did not close up shop and leave Argentina," one journalist wrote, "surrounded their officials with squads of bodyguards armed with grenades and even flame throwers."[94]

Similar conditions existed at the U.S. Embassy, a fortified compound consuming roughly $1 million dollars per year, with the bulk earmarked for security.[95] In April 1975, the State Department warned that the ERP was initiating a terror campaign against U.S. government personnel as part of a broad effort to eliminate the U.S. presence in Argentina.[96] It was not a threat to be taken lightly; in 1973 left-wing terrorists attacked a U.S. Embassy residence with rockets, and in

February 1975 the U.S. consular agent John Patrick Egan was kidnapped and brutally murdered by left-wing terrorists in Córdoba.[97]

For Ambassador Hill the experience was especially difficult. With its historic neighborhoods and distinctively European ambiance, Buenos Aires boasted more than three hundred theaters and cinemas, and only Paris was said to have more art exhibitions.[98] Widely recognized among *porteños*, Hill, however, was rarely able to enjoy even a quiet dinner out. Indeed, on one occasion Hill and his wife, "tired of being cooped up in the Embassy residence," dismissed the objections of the security chief and decided to eat at a popular local restaurant. But, as the *Buenos Aires Herald* reported, "when they sat down, the other diners began to get up. And as they were recognized, people began leaving the restaurant, until it was almost empty. Realizing that the restaurant was emptying out because of the fear that the ambassador's presence might provoke a terrorist attack, Mr. and Mrs. Hill are said to have gone up to the restaurant proprietor and said, 'Don't worry, we'll go.'" The ambassador and his wife, the *Herald* sympathetically concluded, resigned themselves to yet another quiet repast at their residence.[99]

Security considerations also affected Hill's ability to carry out his professional duties. With dozens of bodyguards in tow, the U.S. ambassador was shuttled to diplomatic engagements in a $30,000 armored Chevrolet with the protection of five other U.S. government vehicles. In addition to limiting Hill's mobility, such extensive protection occasionally created a stir among less security-minded members of the diplomatic community in Buenos Aires. In the midst of one February 1976 cocktail party at a Western European embassy, for example, the host looked out the window and saw "20 or 30 horrible men with guns" moving quickly toward the entryway. Petrified, he turned to his wife and exclaimed, "My god, dear, we're being attacked by guerrillas." A nearby guest quickly put his fears to rest. "Don't worry," he told his hosts, "they're only Bob Hill's bodyguards." Informed of the mix-up as he entered the party, Hill responded with grim resignation, "That's the way one has to live these days."[100]

Significantly, Hill looked to the Argentine military as the best option for restoring political stability in Argentina. The U.S. ambassador was not oblivious to the potential human rights violations that might occur in the event of a military coup in Argentina. In the chaotic months leading up to the military takeover on March 24, 1976, however, Hill turned a blind eye to troubling evidence of impending state-sanctioned violence on the part of the Argentine military. On February 13, for example, Diego Medus, chief of the North American desk at the Argentine Foreign Ministry informed his counterparts at the U.S. Embassy that the Argentine Military Planning Group had requested that he prepare a study on how the future military government could avoid human rights problems with the United States. When Medus responded by saying, "They will have trouble if they start executing people," the officers openly admitted their intention to engage in illegal violence, telling Medus "they intend to carry forward an all-out war on the terrorists and that some executions would therefore probably be necessary." In his recapitulation of the incident in a subsequent cable to Washington, however, Hill nonetheless praised the Argentine military's apparent awareness of the significance of human rights in U.S. foreign policy. "It is encouraging to note that the Argentine military are aware of the problem," the ambassador commented at the bottom of the page, "and are already focusing on ways to avoid letting human rights issues become an irritant in U.S.-Argentine relations."[101]

Hill's support for the Argentine military's political aspirations went beyond a simple faith in the generals' ability to bring about political and economic stability, and tapped into the anticommunism that had guided his approach to U.S.-Latin American affairs since the Truman era. Like much of the Washington foreign policy establishment, Hill's abiding fear of leftist insurgencies in the aftermath of the Cuban Revolution led to a conception of U.S. national security rooted in the close cultivation of U.S.-Latin American military ties. Accordingly, by 1975, Hill considered the military the best hope for Argentina's future. "The Argentine military have changed," Hill wrote in September. "Either they are more democratically minded and dedicated to the Constitution than they were ten years ago, or they are more politically astute, or both."[102] Privately, Hill was more explicit. "At last the military are cracking down," he wrote an old friend in his native Vermont the following month. "Hopefully then Argentina can move forward."[103]

In fact, the Argentine military *had* changed in the ten years since the Onganía coup, though not in a moderate direction. The final stage in the development of the Argentine military's national security doctrine—evolving in tandem with the cataclysm of guerrilla violence and the return of Perón—culminated at mid-decade, with Argentine military hardliners openly asserting that Argentina stood on the front lines of the "Third World War" in which "Western civilization" was locked in a death struggle with global Communism. Combining U.S. internal security doctrine with lessons gained from the French antisubversive campaign in Algeria—along with a potent dose of Argentine nationalism and radically conservative Catholicism—by the early 1970s influential Argentine officers such as General Ramón Camps were extending the national security doctrine to facilitate the systematic use of kidnapping, torture, and disappearance of tens of thousands of perceived subversives.[104] After years of evolution under the influence of the U.S. counterinsurgency strategy, a distinctly Argentine national security doctrine "came of age" in 1975, as Camps later maintained, allowing the Argentine military to achieve "victory against the armed subversion."[105]

The systematic use of state-sanctioned terror lay at the heart of the doctrine. In early 1974, Argentine security personnel initiated contact with military representatives from Chile, Brazil, Uruguay, Paraguay, and Bolivia in the effort to

establish a covert transnational countersubversive organization, and the following September the Argentine military assisted Chilean agents in the assassination of General Carlos Prats, the exiled former commander in chief of Chile's
armed forces and a harsh critic of Augusto Pinochet. By mid-1975, cooperation
among the Southern Cone military regimes had evolved into Operation Condor,
a formal apparatus geared toward facilitating intelligence exchange and cross-
border operations in Latin America, Western Europe, and the United States.[106]
Correspondingly, in February 1974 the Argentine military launched Operation
Independence, a major counterinsurgency campaign in Tucumán province
of northwestern Argentina. Presaging the tactics that would become standard
operating procedure during the military dictatorship, Operation Independence
introduced the widespread application of abduction, secret detention, torture,
and clandestine murder of perceived subversives.[107]

     With plans for the Argentine military's return to political power solidifying,
in late 1975 top-ranking Argentine officers swore a secret oath of allegiance to
the national security doctrine—including the use of disappearances—and made
extralegal repression the centerpiece of their design to radically transform Argentine society.[108] The basic premise behind the "National Reorganization Process,"
however, was openly proclaimed: "If the Argentine situation demands it," the
army commander Jorge Videla declared in October 1975 at the eleventh annual
Conference of American Armies in Montevideo, "all necessary persons must die
to achieve the security of the country."[109]

     Indeed, less than two months after the Argentine military coup on March
24, 1976, Hill was beginning to have serious doubts regarding the validity of the
military junta's self-proclaimed "moderate line." Although the ambassador, along
with most Argentines, continued to view Videla as a moderate, Hill was disturbed
by reports of the three armed service branches operating independently of each
other and engaging in widespread arbitrary arrests. According to Perónist Party
estimates, over four thousand individuals had been imprisoned since the coup,
and many were being held incommunicado. The result, Hill cabled Washington,
"is [an] extremely confused and arbitrary environment in which many are beginning to wonder if they have any protection under the law."[110]

     Indications of systematic human rights violations left the U.S. ambassador
deeply conflicted. On the one hand, with anticommunist credentials dating
to the Truman administration, Hill fully backed the Argentine military's campaign to eradicate left-wing subversives. On the other hand, the ambassador felt
a deep sympathy for innocent victims of the military's counterinsurgency net.
Indeed, Hill's forays into the foreign service had been defined by a rare willingness to engage ordinary Latin Americans—as Hill's wife, Cecilia, once told
a journalist, his hobbies were "people and foreign affairs."[111] At the end of his

tenure as ambassador to Costa Rica in 1955, for example, Hill accepted then–vice president Richard Nixon's suggestion that he and Cecilia—along with their eighteen-month-old baby—return to Washington by car along the recently completed Pan-American Highway.[112] "We had been advised to carry firearms but we decided instead to fly a small American flag on our front bumper," Hill subsequently wrote in an op-ed piece in the *New York Times*. "This created considerable interest, and in the back country of Guatemala we received many a '*Viva los Estados Unidos.*' When we stopped for gas the car would be surrounded by curious, friendly Indians who asked many questions about our trip."[113]

Similarly, Hill's tenure in Mexico reflected an abiding interest in local people that was unusual in the insular culture of the U.S. Foreign Service. Hill made headlines, for example, by being the first U.S. ambassador to visit each of Mexico's thirty-one states. The ambassador also raised eyebrows among the diplomatic community by extending "open house" invitations to all embassy personnel—including Mexican citizens—resulting in an unusual mix of more than five hundred attendees ranging "from top diplomats to charwomen," as one journalist put it.[114] On another occasion, when a Mexican *campesino* family arrived at the U.S. Embassy with the gift of a hand-woven *serape* for the ambassador, Hill personally greeted the visitors, unwrapped the package, and subsequently invited them to a formal lunch with his own family.[115]

More than a decade later, from his vantage point at the U.S. Embassy in Buenos Aires, Hill was deeply disturbed by the growing number of reports of state-sanctioned kidnappings, the widespread use of torture, and clandestine murder. Although the embassy had little idea of the thousands of victims being swept up in the Argentine military's counterinsurgency campaign, a growing body of evidence indicated a concerted campaign of political repression. "They questioned me, but it was more just give it to her," Gwenda Mae Loken informed the U.S. Embassy after her release from a clandestine detention center. A U.S. citizen, Loken was abducted in April 1976 by Argentine security forces for distributing antigovernment pamphlets and subjected to electroshock torture. "They said they'd fix me so I couldn't have children," she later testified.[116] Similarly, Patricia Erb, the nineteen-year-old daughter of U.S. missionaries in Argentina, informed the U.S. Embassy of extensive torture and extreme privation at the hands of Argentine military personnel.

> I was conducted as were many others, to rooms which we called "the torture house." There, men dressed in civilian clothing would begin interrogations, using torture. . . . That torture took various forms: beating with clubs, fists, kicking, immersing in water or in fecal substances to almost the drowning point and applying "*La Picana*" (electric

machine) . . . to the most sensitive parts of the body, like [the] mouth, eyes, nose, ears, vagina, breast, penis, feet, and hands. . . . After these interrogations we were conducted again to the "barn." . . . By night our sleep was accompanied by rats that ran over and around our bodies. We were also at the mercy of being raped by the sub-officials.[117]

Confronted with a growing body of evidence indicating state security forces' systematic use of kidnappings, torture, and disappearances, in the months following the 1976 coup, Hill made a remarkable transition from staunch junta supporter to an adamant critic of the military junta's dirty war tactics. Throughout the second half of 1976 and early 1977, the ambassador led embassy efforts to protest, through private diplomatic channels, the Argentine military's incorporation of right-wing death squads and widespread utilization of illegal repressive measures. Not surprisingly, the embassy's efforts were most effective in the handful of cases in which U.S. citizens were illegally detained by military or paramilitary forces. Between September 1, 1976, and January 6, 1977, embassy officials made thirty-five human rights representations to the Argentine government, thirty-one of which dealt with U.S. citizens caught in the military's scattershot assault on perceived antisubversives.[118] After learning of the September 14 abduction of Patricia Erb, for example, Ambassador Hill immediately raised the case with the Argentine police and military on September 15, directed U.S. Embassy personnel to attempt to ascertain Erb's whereabouts by utilizing Argentine contacts, and made a formal appeal to the Argentine government.[119] Underscoring his growing involvement in human rights advocacy, Hill personally discussed the cases of Gwenda Mae Loken and Patricia Erb directly with President Jorge Videla on September 21.[120]

Through immediate and sustained communication with a wide range of contacts in the Argentine government, the U.S. Embassy could reasonably hope to procure the release of American nationals; one former kidnap victim of a self-described "combined police and military command" recalled her captors complaining that the U.S. Embassy was "driving us crazy trying to find out where she was being held." For Hill, the incident no doubt evoked a certain degree of grim satisfaction; having endured two days of interrogation, threats, and physical abuse, the woman "stated that her life was saved only by quick intervention of [the] Embassy and her relatives."[121]

Hill also spearheaded broader efforts to pressure the Argentine junta to curtail human rights violations. On May 28, 1976, the ambassador personally delivered a warning to the foreign minister César Guzzetti that U.S.-Argentine relations would be seriously impaired without improvements in human rights. Although he judged the meeting to be largely ineffectual, Hill was undeterred. "Though Guzzetti indicated his understanding of the problem, I did not have the impression that he really got the point," the ambassador cabled Washington. "We will keep working on him and others in [the] GOA [government of Argentina]."[122]

Ambassador Hill's attempts to pressure the Argentine junta to curtail human rights violations were stymied, however, by the secretary of state Henry Kissinger's Realpolitik approach to U.S.-Argentine relations. Recognizing the significant role top-level U.S. political pressure could play in curbing the Argentine dirty war, Hill made arrangements for a visit by the secretary of state to Argentina on seven separate occasions. Each time Kissinger canceled. Finally, at an Organization of American States meeting in Santiago, Chile, Kissinger met personally with Guzzetti. According to Hill, the Argentines "were very worried that Kissinger would lecture them on human rights."[123] To Guzzetti's surprise, Kissinger did not broach the issue. When the perplexed Argentines finally requested the secretary of state's opinion on human rights, Kissinger personally dismissed the issue as an obstacle in U.S.-Argentine relations. "Look, our basic attitude is that we would like you to succeed," Kissinger told the foreign minister. The secretary of state continued: "I have an old-fashioned view that friends ought to be supported. What is not understood in the United States is that you have a civil war. We read about human rights problems but not the context. *The quicker you succeed the better.*"[124] When Guzzetti asserted that the military government would "clean up the problem" by the end of the year, Kissinger gave his approval.[125]

Reflecting the significance of U.S. official sanction, after unexpectedly receiving Kissinger's blessing Guzzetti returned to Buenos Aires in what Hill described as a "state of jubilation." To the ambassador's dismay, the foreign minister was "convinced that there is no real problem" with the U.S. government over the human rights issue. Hill continued: "Based on what Guzzetti is doubtless reporting to the GOA, it must now believe that if it has any problems with the U.S. over human rights, they are confined to certain elements of Congress and what it regards as biased and/or uninformed minor segments of public opinion. While that conviction lasts it will be unrealistic and unbelievable for this embassy to press representations to the GOA over human rights violations."[126]

Undermined by his superiors in Washington, the effectiveness of Hill's human rights advocacy was dramatically constrained. Remarkably, Hill detailed his lonely efforts to protect human rights in Argentina to the assistant secretary of state for human rights and humanitarian affairs Patricia Derian on her first trip to Buenos Aires following Jimmy Carter's electoral victory over Gerald Ford. "Kissinger gave the Argentines the green light," the ambassador bluntly concluded.[127] In a 2008 interview, Derian remembered sensing that Hill's experience in Argentina had shaken his core political beliefs. "After that happened I think he realized the whole weight and horror of what was going on," she recalled, "and that we [in the United States] were complicit in it."[128]

Kissinger's support for the Argentine junta was hardly revolutionary; rather, the secretary of state's refusal to condemn widespread state-sanctioned human rights abuses was merely a continuation of a historical process rooted in the early years of the Cold War: U.S. support for anticommunist Latin American military establishments.[129] Hill's frustration, however, clearly revealed the fundamental flaw in Kissinger's "quiet diplomacy": with little or no accountability, the secretary of state could publicly pay lip service to the importance of human rights while secretly offering U.S. support for the junta's antisubversive terror campaign.

Months after finishing his ambassadorship, Kissinger's callous dismissal of state-sanctioned violence in Argentina continued to grate against Hill. When he read in the *Buenos Aires Herald* in July 1978 that the then–former secretary of state had blandly informed an Argentine journalist, "I'm supposed to be an expert in international affairs, but I hadn't been in touch with what's been happening in Argentina in the last 10 years," Hill highlighted the paragraph and angrily wrote "Really Bull," in the margin.[130] Yet despite his horror at the Argentine military's terror campaign and frustration with Kissinger's quiet complicity, as the budding human rights movement in the United States blossomed into a major political force following the 1976 election of Jimmy Carter, Hill could never fully reconcile diplomatic advocacy on behalf of the victims of state-sanctioned violence with his lifelong affiliation with the policy prescriptions of the Cold War.

It was a dilemma that would remain unresolved until Hill's untimely death in late 1978.[131] At times, Hill was still an unapologetic cold warrior, criticizing human rights as interfering with U.S. ties to an anticommunist ally. "As Americans we want to see the Carter Administration a success, yet in their desire to change the world—old relationships should not be trampled on," Hill told the Pan-America Society of New York in June 1977, shortly after concluding his ambassadorship in Argentina. "Human rights is a worthy objective," he continued, "but its orchestration and application have to be accomplished quietly to be effective."[132] Similarly, in an address to the Argentine-American Chamber of Commerce Hill emphasized the extent of the guerrilla threat in the early 1970s and counseled U.S. "patience" toward Argentina, advising the Carter administration to keep a tight rein on human rights advocacy "before it embarrasses itself further and humiliates a friend of the United States."[133]

Yet Hill could not escape the fact that his abiding frustration with Kissinger underscored the need for a strong U.S. commitment to human rights in foreign policy. Indeed, at the height of the dirty war, Hill had quietly embraced nascent U.S. human rights legislation—in an "eyes only" memorandum to Kissinger in September 1976, he recommended that the secretary vote against an Inter-American Development Bank (IDB) loan to Argentina, citing recently enacted congressional legislation that linked U.S. foreign aid to human rights. When Assistant Secretary Shlaudeman personally warned that if he sent the memo Kissinger "might fire Hill," the ambassador told Shlaudeman to send it anyway. (Kissinger ignored the memo and voted in favor of the loan.)[134]

The contradictory impulses guiding Hill's political thought were most clearly evident in an interview with William F. Buckley Jr. on *Firing Line* in January 1977. Asked if he supported sanctions on human rights grounds, Hill responded, "I believe that it should be discussed at the United Nations, and I believe it should be discussed by the powers, the powerful countries in the world—an exchange of ideas." When Buckley pointed out that the Security Council veto system made enacting UN sanctions practically impossible, Hill equivocated. "I think they should discuss it and I think that the United Nations should then try through their means, even facing the veto, to moralize the issue which you raised a short time ago, and hopefully some of the countries will do something about it," he awkwardly replied. Most important, the ambassador added, the United States and its allies should avoid unilateral human rights–based initiatives, "because all they'll do is create enemies for their countries."

Recognizing the inconsistency between advocating support for the protection of human rights yet refusing to take action, the ever-incisive Buckley pressed the ambassador. "This seems to be a counsel of despair," he told Hill. Unable to balance fierce anticommunism with a desire to protect the thousands of victims swept up in the Argentine military's terror campaign, Hill could only acquiesce. "*It is,*" the ambassador dejectedly concluded.[135]

3

"HUMAN RIGHTS IS SUDDENLY CHIC"

The Rise of *The Movement*, 1970–1976

News of Olga Talamante's kidnapping reached her parents by telephone in mid-November 1974. The call, dialed by a friend in Azul, Argentina, to the elder Talamantes' residence in Salinas, California, was brief, the details agonizingly vague. There had been a gathering, a classic Argentine *asado*, a daylong barbecue held as a kind of *despedida* for Talamante as she prepared to return to the United States and pursue graduate studies. Late in the evening, as Talamante and a group of friends started to leave, an unidentified car pulled up to the curb, and a man identifying himself as a policeman demanded that they accompany him for questioning. When Talamante refused, the individual forced them into the vehicle at gunpoint. Olga Talamante's whereabouts, the caller concluded, along with that of a dozen others who had attended the *asado*, were unknown.[1]

For *Don* Lalo and *Doña* Cuca, as Talamante's parents, Eduardo and Refugio, were known in the local Latino community, news of their daughter's disappearance came as a terrifying, debilitating shock. *What could be done?* Immigrants from Mexico, the Talamantes had raised Olga and her two brothers in an agricultural labor camp in Gilroy, California. For nearly a decade the family had lived in a single room with no furniture, stove, or refrigerator in an old warehouse that had been divided up among house laborers. From the long hours in the fields to the irregular pay to discourage worker transience, it was a hard, grinding existence rooted in exploitation emblematic of the immigrant experience in rural California. Having endured for years the weekly indignity of waiting in line with other farm laborers for the *patrones* to dispense a meager allotment of cash, the Talamantes felt the possibility of successfully lobbying on Olga's behalf, of harnessing enough political leverage in Washington to influence the Argentine government—if, indeed, she was held captive by the state—was an endeavor of extraordinary magnitude.[2]

Yet Olga Talamante was no ordinary young woman. After spending roughly the first decade of her life in Mexico, she had accompanied her parents to the United States in 1961. Unable to speak English, Talamante was initially classified as mentally retarded by primary school officials, and placed in a classroom with younger students.[3] After only one year, however, she had mastered the language sufficiently to move directly from fourth to sixth grade. In high school, Talamante's stellar performance in the classroom and participation in extracurricular activities set her apart from peers. She was elected president of her sophomore class, acted as both secretary and vice president of the honor society, led the local chapter of an international student exchange program, served as president of a student-run advisory council on school reform, and earned a letter in girls' hockey. Receiving the "Outstanding Student of the Year" award at her high school graduation, Talamante—whose parents had not completed elementary school—set her sights on a college education, and with the assistance of several academic scholarships she enrolled in the fall of 1969 at the University of California at Santa Cruz, where she majored in Latin American Studies.[4]

Talamante graduated from UC–Santa Cruz with honors in 1973, shortly after obtaining U.S. citizenship. She spent the summer working in the garlic fields of Gilroy until she had saved enough money to buy a plane ticket to Argentina, where she taught English and volunteered at a community center in Azul that offered basic social services such as legal aid and tutoring to the residents of a poor neighborhood.[5] In early November 1974, with political violence in Argentina increasing, Talamante wrote her family that she had purchased a return plane ticket and would be coming home on the twenty-fourth. Eduardo and Refugio's daughter, however, never arrived.

The Talamantes immediately began working to ascertain what had happened, frantically contacting elected representatives in California and Washington, DC, as well as Olga's associates and friends in Gilroy and at UC–Santa Cruz. Initially, it seemed a fruitless endeavor since the Department of State could provide no information on Olga Talamante's case. Officers in the Bureau of Inter-American Affairs (ARA) dutifully contacted the U.S. Embassy in Buenos Aires, however, and by the end of the month it was confirmed that Talamante had been arrested five days after President Isabel Perón had enacted "State of Siege" provisions—in which suspected subversives could be held indefinitely and without charges—to crack down on left-wing political violence. The U.S. Embassy further ascertained that Talamante was being held in a government prison in Azul for alleged possession of "subversive literature" and handguns, and that she would remain in detention until the case was adjudicated by the Argentine justice system.[6] Perhaps more important for her worried parents, a U.S. consular visit allowed Olga the chance to write her family. "What happened is that I have been arrested along with some friends, under the charge of having arms and of being in opposition to the government," Talamante wrote on November 27. She continued:

> I don't know if you remember, Mama, of the times I wrote you telling you that here the young men and women that I know help people a lot, especially the humble people, those in need. That is why I tell you there is confusion, because none of us attempted to do more than this.
>
> Mama, more than anything else what hurts me most is the pain I may have caused you and am causing you and Papa now. I would give anything to avoid this suffering, but the circumstances are not determined by us. I know that you will be strong and that together we will have faith in a rapid solution. You receive all my love. I love you very much.[7]

No doubt overjoyed to learn that their daughter was alive, Olga Talamante's parents also received word that their daughter had been tortured by members of the Argentine security services.

Recognizing that Olga's academic achievements and extracurricular activism had cultivated supporters in both the white and Latino communities, the Talamantes redoubled their efforts to generate support for her release. In early December they formed the Olga Talamante Defense Committee (OTDC) and began a grassroots campaign on her behalf, including vigils, letter-writing campaigns, and picket lines.[8] In subsequent months, the Talamantes' unflagging dedication to securing Olga's release transformed the OTDC into a full-fledged social movement. With support from Ed McCaughan and Peter Baird, editors at the North American Congress on Latin America (NACLA), a left-wing, nonprofit organization dedicated to social justice in hemispheric affairs, the committee eventually cobbled together a broad coalition of support from a diverse range of organizations, including the United Farm Workers Union, the National Council of Churches, the United Auto Workers, and the National Women's Political Caucus.[9] Although Talamante remained in prison throughout 1975, by mid-March, Norman Y. Mineta (D-CA)—House representative for the Talamantes' congressional district—informed the State Department, "It is rare that a day passes without an inquiry from a friend, relative, or school acquaintance regarding her trial's progress."[10]

The initial support garnered by the Olga Talamante Defense Committee was indicative of the widespread respect in Gilroy and at UC–Santa Cruz for Talamante's extraordinary success in overcoming linguistic, racial, and cultural barriers. The immense outpouring of solidarity the OTDC eventually generated, among both the thousands of petition signers in the San Francisco Bay Area and religious, church, and labor groups nationwide, reflected the rising support for human rights in U.S. society and politics.[11] Rooted in the struggle for civil rights and the anti–Vietnam War movements and gaining strength thanks to widespread disillusionment with U.S. support for repressive regimes, the effort to institutionalize human rights in U.S. foreign policy and improve the protection of human rights overseas blossomed in the early 1970s. Put broadly, grassroots organizers, human rights lobbyists in Washington, and sympathetic members of Congress consciously embodied a countermovement to the maintenance of close U.S. political, economic, and military ties to staunchly anticommunist, authoritarian governments—a defining feature of U.S. Cold War policy, particularly toward Latin America. Over the course of the 1970s, in other words, the idealism of the blossoming human rights movement vied for primacy with the realist policy prescriptions that had undergirded U.S.-Latin American Cold War relations since the late 1940s.

As a result, as state-sanctioned violence in Argentina increased, the South American nation moved to the center of the struggle between idealism and realism in U.S. foreign policy. Human rights advocates played a central role in raising awareness of state-sanctioned violence in Argentina, and, following the 1976 coup d'état, in pressuring policymakers to distance the U.S. from the Argentine military junta. The successful 1978 congressional cutoff of U.S. security transfers to Argentina was a clear indication of the human rights movement's evolution; by the end of the decade, human rights advocates enjoyed support from a broad grassroots base, maintained an influential lobby in Washington, and had established a reputation for effective mobilization on behalf of human rights issues.

* * *

Although human rights language was written into the United Nations Charter in June 1945 and the international humanitarian law enshrined in the Geneva Conventions gained near-universal acceptance four years later, over the course of the subsequent quarter century human rights took a backseat in U.S. foreign policy to the perceived exigencies of the Cold War. Divided into ideologically charged voting blocs and unwilling to accept criticism, from its founding the UN Human Rights Commission openly abdicated the power to "take any action in regard to any complaints concerning human rights." As the historian Geoffrey Robertson writes, "The best that can be said for Cold War law was that superpowers felt obliged to resort to such fictions, covering up as best they could the atrocities committed by their own allies in order to accuse more loudly the other side."[12]

By the late 1960s, however, increasing disaffection with the rising costs of U.S. military intervention in Southeast Asia among both nongovernmental antiwar advocates and their liberal allies in Congress stimulated a broad reevaluation of U.S. foreign policy. Latin America was widely seen as a particularly egregious illustration of the illiberal nature of U.S. Cold War policymaking. Less than a decade earlier, Kennedy's Alliance for Progress had cultivated enormous hope in the region for a flowering of representative democracy, enhanced internal security, and dynamic economic growth. Instead, by the late 1960s most of the region was ruled by U.S.-backed right-wing military regimes; as the former U.S. ambassador to Chile Ralph Dungan informed the U.S. Senate Foreign Relations Subcommittee on Western Hemisphere Affairs in mid-1969, "The basic defect in the stability counterinsurgency tactic as perceived by the U.S. military is that somehow stability is an end in itself and that it matters little in whose hands or under what condition stability exists—or what means are used to obtain it."[13]

Dungan's assessment received a warm reception from the subcommittee chairman Frank Church (D-ID), who, along with the Foreign Relations Committee chairman J. William Fulbright (D-AK), had emerged in the final years of the decade as one of the most outspoken critics of the prominent role accorded to the Pentagon in U.S. foreign policy. Indeed, for more than a decade, Church had worked to place restrictions on U.S. military assistance programs, albeit with little success. "Against the combined opposition of the State Department, the Pentagon, and most often the White House, it is not easy to accomplish," the Idaho senator bluntly responded when Dungan suggested stopping assistance programs to Latin American militaries. The Washington bureaucracy, Church wearily concluded, "is like a hydraheaded monster."[14]

Church's effort to rein in the role of military assistance in U.S. foreign policy was by no means the only crack in the Washington Cold War consensus, particularly in regard to Latin America. During the Kennedy administration, Senator Wayne Morse (D-OR), Church's predecessor on the Senate subcommittee, had adamantly resisted White House efforts to repeal the congressional prohibition on military assistance to Latin America for internal security purposes, out of a conviction that "aid to nondemocratic Latin American regimes to assist the maintenance of internal security will be equivalent to the maintenance in power of harsh and repressive regimes."[15] The following year, along with Fulbright, Morse expressed "great alarm" at the prospect of maintaining Alliance for Progress aid to Argentina following the Argentine military coup against Arturo Frondizi.[16] Although by no means representative of the legislative branch as a whole, such resistance forced the Kennedy administration to justify its approach to hemispheric affairs—undercutting the lofty rhetoric of the Alliance for Progress. As Secretary of State Dean Rusk asserted in a letter to Morse in September 1962, "The Latin American military have in general been a force for good and have played a leading and often decisive role in unseating dictators and helping to maintain political stability against revolutionary efforts to impose totalitarian regimes."[17]

Congressional resistance to the close maintenance of U.S.-Latin American military ties increased during the Johnson administration. Along with Senator Hubert Humphrey (D-MN), in 1964 Morse denounced the Mann Doctrine's shift away from democracy as a core U.S. policy goal in Latin America.[18] More concretely, following the 1966 Argentine coup, Senator Jacob K. Javits (R-NY) rattled White House officials by proposing an addition to the foreign aid bill prohibiting Alliance for Progress aid to Latin American countries run by military regimes.[19] The "mischievous amendment," in the words of the National Security Council staff member William G. Bowdler, threatened to put "the President personally and the U.S. government across a barrel." Foreshadowing future debates over human rights initiatives in U.S. foreign policy, Bowdler continued: "One thing is to tie aid to economic actions by the Latinos . . . which they understand even if they don't like it. Tieing [sic] aid to internal political developments is quite another matter. The President by omission or commission will be passing personal judgment on each coup."[20] Although the bill failed to pass muster, in 1967 Congress succeeded in placing a "ceiling" of $75 million on all arms grants or credit-term sales to Latin America (plus an additional $12 million for training), denied a Pentagon naval request for Latin America, and extended the revolving fund used by the Department of Defense for arms sales for only one year.[21]

The groundswell of opposition to the Vietnam War intensified congressional efforts to limit U.S. military assistance and training programs. By the time Richard Nixon entered the Oval Office, such initiatives were receiving unprecedented scrutiny on Capitol Hill. "Do you have no question in your mind that something is wrong with our relations with most of Latin America except for your favorite dictators?" Fulbright demanded of the assistant secretary of state for inter-American affairs Charles A. Meyer during the 1969 Church subcommittee hearings on U.S. military programs in Latin America. "Mr. Duvalier is the only one who seems to be enthusiastic about you," Fulbright acidly concluded, referring to recent newspaper photos of the Haitian dictator and presidential envoy Nelson Rockefeller.[22] A few minutes later, when G. Warren Nutter, assistant secretary of defense for international security affairs, described the amount of U.S. military assistance to Latin America as insignificant, Church responded by citing a study conducted for the subcommittee by the University of New Mexico professor Edwin L. Lieuwen, asserting that U.S. arms assistance supplemented the amount Latin American militaries spent on arms by "more than 50 percent, and by more than 90 percent in some of the smaller countries."[23]

In his refusal to accept the shibboleths of U.S. Cold War foreign policy, Church challenged the Nixon administration to redefine U.S.-Latin American relations. Dismissing Rockefeller's recommendation for the maintenance of U.S. military assistance to the region in his 1969 *Report on the Americas,* Church instead asserted, "We should bring home our military missions, end our grant-in-aid and training programs, and sever the intimate connections we have sought to form with the Latin military establishments." Noting that U.S. arms had been utilized by both sides in the 1969 conflict between El Salvador and Honduras, Church told his Senate colleagues, "This is a shabby business for us to mix in."[24]

With Church and Fulbright in the vanguard, during Nixon's first term in office the Congress took an increasingly active role in shaping U.S. foreign policy. Indeed, in the four-year period between 1968 and 1971, the Senate held an average of more than twenty roll call votes on defense bills each year—a dramatic increase from the previous decade's average of one vote every two years.[25] Moreover, successive congressional amendments placed increasingly stringent limits on U.S security assistance, particularly the grant-based Military Assistance Program (MAP). In 1970, the Congress limited the number of military trainees brought to the United States under MAP to the number of foreign students studying in the United States during the previous fiscal year under the Hayes-Fulbright Act.[26] Two years later, the Congress successfully terminated the presence of U.S. military groups overseas unless specifically authorized by the Congress, and by 1974, MAP had declined to $885 million from the $1.2 billion earmarked for the program in 1967.[27]

Seeking to maintain U.S. support for stable, anticommunist clients, in response to congressional restrictions on grant-in-aid military assistance Nixon significantly increased arms sales to U.S. allies abroad. Recognizing the relatively limited congressional oversight of the international arms trade, and aiming to offset a serious balance-of-payments problem, the president waived the Congress-imposed ceiling on arms transfers to Latin America and more than doubled arms sales to the region in fiscal year 1971 over the annual average of $30 million during the previous decade.[28] Yet as evidence emerged of Nixon's secret expansion of the Vietnam War into Cambodia in the spring of 1970, opposition to what Arthur M. Schlesinger Jr. famously referred to as the "imperial presidency" hardened.[29] The result, as Representative Robert F. Drinan (D-MA) declared in February 1971, was "a movement for a new Congress." "People sent me here to stop this war," Drinan asserted a few weeks after his election to the Ninety-Second Congress. "The essence of the whole movement for a new Congress is to restore the decency and the dignity of this House—to once again assert its constitutional power to declare war and to finance a war."[30]

During a visit to South Vietnam in mid-1969, Drinan had been horrified by the extent of U.S.-sponsored violence and destruction. The experience, he told his congressional peers, "caused me to change the whole course of my life." As the first Roman Catholic priest elected as a voting member to the House of Representatives, Drinan's personal austerity—he resided in a simple dormitory in Washington with a group of fellow Jesuits—and fiercely liberal brand of politics reportedly gained him the reputation in his native Massachusetts as "Our Father who art incongruous."[31] Drinan's tenacious determination to halt U.S. intervention in Southeast Asia and to insert a heavy dose of morality into U.S. foreign policy as a whole, however, exemplified the increasingly widespread rejection of the Cold War consensus on Capitol Hill. In April 1972, Drinan described Nixon's decision to bomb the North Vietnamese cities of Hanoi and Haiphong as "tactically disastrous and unspeakably immoral," and in May 1973, Drinan and four colleagues initiated impeachment proceedings against Nixon for ordering the covert U.S. military operation in Cambodia.[32] Although Drinan's impeachment effort failed, the Congress successfully passed the War Powers Resolution six months later, requiring congressional review of any attempt to deploy U.S. military forces overseas and providing the legislative branch with the authority to enact a troop withdrawal after deployment.[33] Praised by liberal supporters for his outspoken opposition to the Nixon administration, Drinan ruffled the feathers of cold warriors across the aisle. As the conservative Republican freshman Trent Lott (R-MI) griped to a journalist in mid-1973, "If he's a priest, I'm the Pope."[34]

If liberals such as Drinan set their sights on halting the U.S. military intervention in Southeast Asia, their efforts nonetheless paved the way for rising support of human rights advocacy. On Capitol Hill, the increasing significance of human rights was clearly evident in the Foreign Assistance Act of 1973. In a nonbinding "sense of Congress" declaration, legislators asserted that "the President should deny any economic or military assistance to the government of any foreign country which practices the internment or imprisonment of that country's citizens for political purposes." Additionally, Congress requested that Nixon encourage the recently installed Chilean military junta to protect the human rights of its citizens, and, more concretely, required that the foreign police training program operated by the Agency for International Development's Office of Public Safety (OPS) be shut down.[35]

More significantly, human rights advocacy took a major step at the beginning of August 1973, when Representative Donald M. Fraser (D-MN) utilized his chairmanship of the House International Relations Subcommittee on International Organizations and Movements to initiate an unprecedented series of hearings on the international protection of human rights.[36] In a four-month period, Fraser held fifteen hearings with more than forty witnesses, including U.S. government officials, Congress members, scholars, lawyers, and representatives from nongovernmental organizations.[37] The following March, Fraser published a landmark report on the hearings, *Human Rights in the World Community: A Call for U.S. Leadership.* Including twenty-nine specific recommendations for integrating human rights into U.S. foreign policy, Fraser notably called for the creation of a Department of State Bureau of Human Rights, as well as the assignment of a human rights officer to each regional bureau in the State Department. Fraser also lobbied for annual human rights country reports, and emphasized the need to link U.S. foreign aid to human rights conditions.[38]

Eventually conducting 150 hearings over five years on U.S. relations with governments across the globe, and involving more than five hundred witnesses, Fraser's subcommittee played a critical role in raising human rights awareness, integrating human rights NGOs into the policymaking process, and institution-alizing human rights in U.S. foreign policy. From the outset, the Fraser subcom-mittee hearings reflected a remarkable degree of coordination with the close-knit community of nongovernmental human rights advocates. Fraser aide John Salz-berg—the primary author of *Human Rights in the World Community*—joined the congressman after serving as representative of the International Commission of Jurists at the United Nations.[39] Salzberg not only played a key role in situat-ing Fraser's effort to make U.S. foreign policy consistent with the U.N. human rights covenants to which the United States was a signatory, but was also particu-larly influential in establishing a close working relationship with human rights–focused NGOs such as the Washington Office on Latin America (WOLA), a bridge organization linking Latin American solidarity groups, exiles, and human rights organizations with official Washington in the effort to raise awareness of human rights conditions in Latin America and influence U.S. policy toward the region.[40]

Indeed, the Fraser subcommittee hearings provided an unprecedented venue for groups such as WOLA to advocate on behalf of human rights in Latin Amer-ica. With direct access to John Salzberg, WOLA cofounder Rev. Joe Eldridge and his colleagues were able to recommend hearings as well as witnesses to give tes-timony, thus making a major contribution in the effort to raise awareness of the human rights situation in Latin American countries. Correspondingly, the hear-ings stimulated WOLA and its peer organizations to become increasingly effec-tive at collecting, analyzing, and distributing reliable human rights data, both as a means to generate wider participation in the human rights movement and to lobby members of Congress, while also encouraging the creation of additional region- and country-specific human rights organizations. "Congress became the critical point that brought it all together," recalled Roberta Cohen, who served as executive director of the International League for Human Rights (ILHR) throughout the first half of the 1970s. The Fraser subcommittee, she continued, "brought together all the different groups that were interested," thus facilitating the establishment of new human rights organizations and increasing coordina-tion among existing groups.[41]

Fraser's *Human Rights in the World Community* was also instrumental in setting the stage for an unprecedented wave of congressional human rights legislation. When the Nixon administration ignored a letter formally presented by Fraser and signed by more than one hundred members of Congress warning that congressional approval of the president's foreign policy decisions would be contingent on the promotion of human rights, in November 1974 Fraser successfully introduced a "sense of Congress" amendment (section 502B) to the Foreign Assistance Act. Patterned on the UN language in *Human Rights in the World Community*, 502B explicitly linked human rights to U.S. security assistance, asserting that "except in extraordinary circumstances, the President shall substantially reduce or terminate security assistance to any government which engages in a consistent pattern of gross violations of internationally recognized human rights, including torture or cruel, inhuman, or degrading treatment or punishment; prolonged detention without charges; or other flagrant denials of the right to life, liberty, and the security of the person."[42] Although the non-binding nature of 502B, along with vague terminology such as "gross violations," quickly proved problematic, Fraser's amendment nonetheless provided a foundation for subsequent efforts to institutionalize human rights in U.S. foreign policy, which gained momentum in late 1974 following the immense popular outcry accompanying the Watergate scandal.[43]

* * *

From the outset, congressional human rights initiatives were fiercely resisted by the Nixon and Ford administrations. With his close adherence to Realpolitik, Secretary of State Kissinger consistently downplayed human rights as a viable U.S. foreign policy goal, creating deep enmity between the White House and Capitol Hill. "Human Rights advocates in Congress accused the Administration of moving on human rights only in response to pressure," Kissinger recalled in his memoirs. "We, in turn, believed that Congress was reflecting single-issue ideological and political agendas, pushed to a point that the administration considered inimical to broader United States strategic or geopolitical interests, or oblivious to them." Reflecting on the issue more than two decades later, Kissinger conceded that "there was a measure of merit in both views."[44] In the mid-1970s, however, the secretary of state's near-total dismissal of human rights infuriated liberal members of Congress and their supporters. "To describe the relationship between Congress and the Executive Branch at that time as adversarial would be an understatement," one human rights advocate recalled years later. "It was an out and out war."[45]

Indeed, notwithstanding the rising chorus of human rights advocates in the House and Senate, Kissinger repeatedly ignored internal proposals by the State Department Policy Planning Staff on how to integrate human rights more fully into foreign policy. More remarkably, despite a unanimous recommendation from the Department of Defense, the State Department Latin America Bureau, and the Politico-Military Staff, in 1974 Kissinger reportedly refused to consider cutting military grant aid to Latin America. The secretary of state also sidestepped congressional requests the following year for human rights reports on individual countries receiving U.S. military assistance, sending instead a general report containing very little country-specific detail. The response, recalled one observer, was "sulfurous," with Senator Hubert Humphrey (D-MN) describing the document as "about as bland as swallowing a bucket of sawdust."[46]

Seeking to maintain executive branch primacy in the formulation of foreign policy, Kissinger was particularly opposed to congressional legislation binding U.S. actions in the international arena to human rights considerations. The secretary of state was "diametrically opposed to the viewpoint of Congress," Donald Fraser told listeners in a 1976 speech, and congressional human rights legislation "has not been faithfully executed by the Department of State, principally because Secretary Kissinger does not accept the arguments for the legislation."[47] The tension between human rights advocates on Capitol Hill and the secretary of state was especially evident on December 5, 1974, when a small group of congressmen led by Fraser held a tense meeting with Kissinger over the role of human rights in U.S. foreign policy. Having repeatedly pressed the Department of State on the human rights issue in written correspondence in previous months, Fraser went straight to the point.[48] "Basically we feel it's very difficult to continue to support foreign assistance programs to governments which oppress their own people," the congressman bluntly told the secretary. "We feel that the United States should be putting stronger emphasis on human rights issues in countries around the world."[49]

In response, Kissinger expressed a willingness to discuss human rights with Congress. Nonetheless, the secretary emphasized that "there are a number of problems." Quiet diplomatic discussions, Kissinger asserted, rather than congressional legislation, should constitute the core of U.S. human rights policy. "The thing that I'm most allergic to is the obligatory statutes," Kissinger declared. "I don't mind requirements for reports of periodic progress, but I feel very strongly that obligatory requirements are counterproductive." When Alan Cranston (D-CA) pressed Kissinger to discuss foreign aid, which the California senator described as frequently politically motivated, military focused, and "seem[ing] to serve the people who are already powerful," the secretary responded coldly. "This has been a very interesting session," he abruptly informed the assembled members of Congress. "Could we perhaps arrange a meeting again in late January?"[50]

Ironically, Kissinger's refusal to mollify congressional concerns over human rights strengthened legislators' resolve to enact binding legislation. According to Rev. Eldridge, Donald Fraser believed Kissinger's opposition played a key role in the movement's success. "If Henry Kissinger had been a little less arrogant and a little less haughty vis-à-vis the Congress," Fraser asserted, "and a little more willing to descend to the level of Congress he could have handed off all this legislation—it wouldn't have been legislation."⁵¹

Instead, by mid-decade, growing support for human rights in Congress forced a rearguard action in the State Department to head off further legislative action. In a classified memo summarizing a human rights meeting on September 12, 1974, the deputy secretary of state Robert Ingersoll informed Kissinger that "the general consensus, was that, if the Department did not place itself ahead of the curve on this issue, Congress would take the matter out of the Department's hands."⁵² Thus, despite Kissinger's antipathy toward the human rights initiative, the State Department named human rights officers to each of the five geographic bureaus, began requesting U.S. embassies in countries affected by congressional human rights legislation to prepare human rights reports, and, in 1975, established an Office of Humanitarian Affairs in the State Department with the career foreign service officer James M. Wilson at the helm.⁵³

Notwithstanding the Ford administration's tentative steps toward integrating human rights into the machinery of U.S. foreign policy, human rights advocates continued to press the issue. An amendment by Fraser in November 1975 added teeth to 502B, replacing the "sense of Congress" language with a legally binding stipulation denying U.S. security assistance to gross human rights violators. Although President Ford vetoed the foreign authorization bill in May 1976, human rights considerations nonetheless gained prominence in a watered-down version signed by the president in July.⁵⁴

More significantly, in September 1975 Representative Tom Harkin (D-IA) successfully offered an amendment to the International Development and Food Assistance section of the Foreign Assistance Act, stipulating that no U.S. aid be provided "to the government of any country which engages in a consistent pattern of gross violations of international recognized human rights," unless it could be shown that the aid would benefit the "poor and needy."⁵⁵ Particularly in Latin America, the Harkin Amendment, as the legislation quickly became known, inserted human rights considerations into nearly every foreign aid decision. As the Kissinger-appointed human rights coordinator James M. Wilson Jr. lamented to the secretary in an internal memo, "We will get no respite from the Harkin Amendment."⁵⁶

Like the broader human rights movement, despite Kissinger's resistance, the State Department could not ignore the Olga Talamante Defense Committee's intensive lobbying effort. In Washington, forced onto the defensive by the wave of human rights legislation on Capitol Hill, the secretary of state hoped to resolve human rights cases involving U.S. nationals as quickly and quietly as possible. Indeed, in a February 1975 cable to all U.S. embassies in Latin America, Kissinger directed U.S. ambassadors to give "Human Rights issues in Latin America, especially with respect to [the] treatment of U.S. nationals, host country nationals and others, . . . a high priority in U.S. policy formulation and implementation." In particular, the secretary highlighted cases involving U.S. citizens imprisoned overseas. Emphasizing the need for consular officers to immediately seek access to U.S. nationals held under such conditions, Kissinger instructed U.S. Foreign Service officers to determine prisoners' physical and mental health, document evidence of mistreatment, and provide "appropriate humanitarian assistance," and recommended that U.S. nationals be advised of their rights under international law.[57]

Underscoring the significance of the human rights movement in forcing the issue to the forefront of U.S. diplomacy, Kissinger further emphasized the need to respond quickly to human rights cases involving U.S. citizens to avoid unfavorable publicity. "Failure to act promptly in protection cases may not only endanger the rights of the American nationals involved but also can prove most detrimental to the Department's relations with the public, the information media and with the Congress." Finally, Kissinger warned that U.S. nationals alleging inadequate protection by the U.S. embassy could produce "explosive publicity." "Conversely," the secretary concluded, "quick and effective protection can be very helpful to all—the U.S. national, the Department and the field," and appended a transcript of a Fraser subcommittee hearing on human rights in Brazil, in which a U.S. national recently released from a Recife prison praised prompt U.S. diplomatic efforts on his behalf.[58]

From the outset, however, the Talamante case failed to fit the pattern of consular assistance for U.S. nationals imprisoned overseas. Indeed, human rights advocates and their congressional allies also targeted the U.S. Embassy in Buenos Aires, flooding ambassador Robert C. Hill with letters he described as "depicting Miss Talamante as being in a 'fascist' prison."[59] The embassy was heavily criticized by human rights advocates on Capitol Hill, notably the senators Edward M. Kennedy (D-MA) and Alan Cranston (D-CA), for failing to meet with Talamante until December 4, 1974—nearly a month after her arrest. Such criticism was an unwelcome irritant for Ambassador Hill; Talamante, the ambassador reported to Washington, had made no effort to contact the embassy, and when news of her arrest finally reached the ambassador on November 25, it came from the young woman's supporters in California by way of human rights advocates in Washington. Piqued by the bad publicity, Hill nonetheless dispatched consular officers to visit Talamante in Azul—nearly two hundred miles from Buenos Aires— more than a dozen times over the course of 1975, and took up the case himself with the Argentine foreign minister. "I emphasized the need to resolve this case quickly by having Miss Talamante leave Argentina as soon as possible before this case poisoned the good relations between the United States and Argentina," Hill cabled Washington in July.[60]

Once Talamante's case had been adjudicated, Hill hoped to secure the young woman's expulsion from Argentina regardless of the judge's ruling because of her status as a U.S. national. Conflicting reports on the case's progress, however, complicated the embassy's efforts. In September, Talamante and her codefendants were found guilty as charged and given a three-year prison sentence. Word subsequently reached the embassy that Talamante had initiated an appeal, then, a few days later, that she had dismissed her publicly appointed attorney. As congressional pressure on the State Department to secure Talamante's release continued unabated—in all, nearly three dozen members of Congress wrote the department on Talamante's behalf—in early October Secretary of State Kissinger signed off on a cable from the ARA Bureau chief William D. Rogers, instructing Ambassador Hill to "assume personal charge of this case in effort to obtain [the] earliest solution. . . . This will ensure that we are provided accurate and complete information on all pertinent developments as they occur in Talamante case."[61]

Frustrated by Talamante's seemingly erratic decision making and shocked by a threatening cable directed to him by one of Talamante's supporters, Hill reluctantly accepted responsibility for the case. In a meeting with the Argentine minister of interior on October 15, Hill reiterated the importance of Talamante's release, asserting that the young woman's expulsion would "avoid an orchestrated publicity campaign that could cause the GOA embarrassment if the Talamante case were allowed to become a cause célèbre."[62] The following month, however, Hill's efforts were stymied by Talamante's decision to continue to appeal the case, thus making it impossible for her to leave Argentina until a verdict was handed down.[63]

* * *

Olga Talamante's decision to maintain solidarity with her codefendants resulted in her continued incarceration for the duration of Isabel Perón's fraught presidency, which came to an abrupt end following the military coup on March 24, 1976. In a prepared statement broadcast over the radio the following evening, the three service chiefs solemnly declared the beginning of the National Reorganization Process. Promising to govern according to "clearly-defined standards" and fostering the "total observance of ethical and moral principles," the generals pledged harsh measures against subversives. "The armed forces have assumed control of the republic," the communiqué concluded. "And we want the entire country to understand the profound and unequivocal meaning of our actions so that the responsibility and the collective efforts accompanying this undertaking, which seeks the common good, will bring about, with the help of God, complete national recovery."[64]

Within a matter of months, it would become clear that the coup dramatically accelerated the unprecedented state-sanctioned terror campaign against perceived subversives carried out over the previous two years by right-wing paramilitary organizations and in the military's counterinsurgency campaign in Argentina's northern province of Tucumán. In the immediate aftermath of the military takeover, however, the Argentine military's effort to promote an image of protecting human rights, and, correspondingly, to cultivate U.S. support provided Ambassador Hill with a window of opportunity to resolve the Talamante case—the only known instance of a U.S. citizen incarcerated in Argentina at that time. The case had already dragged on for nearly a year and a half and—thanks to ongoing political pressure by the OTDC—threatened to sour the newly installed Argentine government's relationship with the United States.

Accordingly, only two days after the coup, a group of soldiers entered the cell occupied by the female political prisoners at the Azul prison. After an extensive search, the women were ordered to line up against a wall. "Who is the Talamante woman?" demanded one of the guards. "I stepped forward and identified myself," Talamante recalled years later. "The officer looked at me and spat out, 'So you're the one that Kissinger wants released.'"[65]

Less than forty-eight hours later a Pan American Airways jetliner touched down in New York with a stunned Talamante on board. Welcomed by members of the Olga Talamante Defense Committee, she immediately boarded a flight to California, where she was greeted by a teeming throng of supporters and journalists. Three years after departing for Argentina, including sixteen months as a political prisoner, Talamante—the first foreign national to be expelled by the Argentine military junta—was finally reunited with her family.[66]

The Talamantes' long-awaited reunion, however, would prove short-lived. For Olga, the suddenness of her release and the continued incarceration of close friends offered little peace of mind. Acutely aware of the extent of state-sanctioned violence in Argentina, Talamante felt incapable of remaining with her family in California. "Although we had always talked about how a political prisoner's first and foremost goal was to be free to continue doing political work and I knew that my comrades were cheering me on, I felt torn," Talamante would later recall. "Instead of relief, I felt like my heart had been split in two."[67]

Indeed, Talamante's arrest, interrogation, and incarceration served as a grim capstone in her extraordinary process of intellectual development, rooted in her experiences as an immigrant in rural California. For Talamante, growing up in the labor camp and working for local whites created a foundational understanding of the deep-rooted disparities endemic in rural California. "During the winter I babysat for the ranchers," Talamante remembered, "so I was poignantly aware of how our 'homes' did not have heat in the winter or air conditioning in the summer, as theirs did. It was my first awareness of class differences, you might say."[68]

As she passed through adolescence, Talamante's crude sense of racial and class inequalities developed into a nascent political consciousness. At the encouragement of her high school's only Latina teacher, in 1967 and 1968 Talamante attended an American Friends Service Committee summer program on nonviolence and civil disobedience, an experience that pushed her to situate the Latino experience within the broader context of civil rights activism in the late 1960s. "After hearing the description of the voter registration drives in the South," Talamante remembered, "I became convinced that if you wanted to effect change, you had to take action, you had to take a stand and be true to it."[69]

Enrolling at the University of California—Santa Cruz in 1969, Talamante was immediately swept up in the intense outpouring of New Left political activism that characterized the late 1960s. For a budding activist, it was a dynamic, exhilarating, and frightening moment, with the anti–Vietnam War movement nearing its apogee, stirrings of second-wave feminism, and, particularly in California, an outburst of Latino and Chicano political activism. Talamante quickly became deeply involved with the Movimiento Estudiantil Chicano de Azatlán (MeCHA), a Chicano student organization, and soon identified herself as a Chicana activist. She also served as a field organizer for the United Farm Workers (UFW) in the struggle to win higher wages for farm laborers working in the grape and lettuce industries, organizing picket lines, food drives, and awareness-raising events at UC–Santa Cruz. In the summer of 1973, having survived dangerous confrontations with thugs hired by teamsters, Talamante proudly introduced UFW leader César Chávez to a cheering crowd of more than one thousand people.[70] Such experiences instilled in Talamante a hard-nosed dedication to personal activism. "There was a growing realization on my part that if you are going to take action to create change, and you are going to take a stand, that's what you need to do if that's what you stand for," Talamante remembered, along with a recognition that, "there may be consequences and repercussions."[71]

Talamante's sense of political awareness expanded dramatically during a study-abroad program in Mexico during the summer of her junior year. Falling in with a pair of leftist Argentine documentary filmmakers and eventually traveling through much of Central America and Mexico, Talamante began to map her dedication to Chicana activism onto the broader pattern of hemispheric relations. After witnessing the repressive tactics of the Mexican security forces against left-wing activists, Talamante recalled feeling a sense of shock that "Mexicans in power are being just as brutal and just as repressive and just as autocratic as gringos were to *Mexicanos* in the U.S. So it doesn't only depend on the color of your skin and your origin, but it depends on who is in power."[72] Underscoring her growing sense of a broad-based struggle that transcended traditional boundaries, upon returning to UC–Santa Cruz in the fall Talamante worked to establish alliances between MeCHA and African American, Asian, and Native American student groups.[73]

Reunited with her filmmaker friends in Buenos Aires in August 1973, Talamante was swept up in the heady sense of expectation felt by many young Peronists following the return to civilian government in 1973. In addition to teaching English, the twenty-four-year-old Talamante began volunteering at a community center in Azul that offered basic social services such as legal aid and tutoring to the residents of a poor neighborhood.[74] In the aftermath of Perón's harsh repudiation of the Joventud Peronista (Peronista Youth Movement) and the Montoneros in the Plaza De Mayo on May Day in 1974, however, Talamante's work at the center became increasingly difficult as municipal funding dried up and political violence on both ends of the political spectrum increased, a trend that accelerated in the chaotic aftermath of Perón's death on July 1, 1974.[75] By early November, with daily reports of terrorist killings and a military coup widely anticipated, Talamante made the decision to return to California.

Arrested only days before her departure, Talamante was taken to a police station and forced to stand with her hands against a wall for more than twelve hours before being hooded and deposited, hands bound, in a holding cell. "The burlap bag felt rough and scratchy against my cheek, but it also smelled earthy and deceptively comforting. Thick tape already covered my eyes, so the bag's only purpose was to frighten me," Talamante later recalled. "And it worked. I knew I had entered another dimension." Accused of participating in a left-wing terrorist attack on an Azul police station the previous week, Talamante was subsequently stripped, bound, and subjected to electroshock torture.[76]

> All I could do was scream. The terror came after. They are going to do it again, I thought. Someone shoved a pillow over my face to muffle my screams. I panicked. To survive, I must be able to breathe and scream.
>
> After about the third time the electric current surged, I figured out a brilliant maneuver. Right before the hands holding the pillow pushed down again, I turned my head sideways and took a breath. The timing of this took complete focus. It was a project. New reasoning kicked in: As long as I could get the timing right, I would survive.[77]

Talamante arrived at the Azul prison physically and mentally weak but lucky to be alive. There, in a twenty-by twenty-five-foot cell with human waste leaking down one wall from a broken sewer pipe, crowded with two dozen female political prisoners, Talamante underwent a further stage in her intellectual maturation. Guided by a sense of alienation from the U.S. government, Talamante refused to call the U.S. Embassy for assistance, relying instead on her family and friends to agitate on her behalf. Counseled by her cell mates, increasingly cognizant of the unflagging efforts of her family and friends on her behalf in the United States, and witness to prisoners taken from their cells and never seen again, over subsequent months Talamante came to see her own experience as part of a far larger, transnational struggle. "I know that we are presently being punished for having the courage and determination to rise against the injustice and exploitation allowed by a system which feeds and survives on those things," she wrote to a supporter on January 29, 1975, "but I also know that your courage and hard work are the rewards of our efforts."[78] Her decision to maintain solidarity with her codefendants—baffling the harried U.S. ambassador—further embodied the culmination of a lifelong process of political radicalization. "At this moment I find myself surrounded by an acute sense of awareness," she wrote in mid-February. "I see everything around me in its full dimension, these walls in relation to centuries of exploitation, this bed in relation to the thousands of unknown graves, myself in relation to my countless hungry brothers and sisters. And I learn once more that my imprisonment is but a small part of this historical yearning for freedom."[79]

Unexpectedly released from prison in March 1976, and acutely aware of the extent of state-sanctioned violence in Argentina, Talamante felt incapable of remaining with her family in California. Transforming the Olga Talamante Defense Committee into the Argentine Human Rights Commission (Comisión Argentina por Derechos Humanos [CADHU]), Talamante established an office in Washington, DC, and set out to draw on the OTDC's infrastructure to raise awareness in the United States of political conditions in Argentina and lobby policymakers to curtail U.S. military assistance to the Argentine junta.

* * *

Talamante's arrival in Washington corresponded with a heady moment in the development of the human rights movement. On Capitol Hill, senators such as Edward Kennedy and Alan Cranston and representatives such as Donald Fraser and Robert Drinan had made major advances in the effort to institutionalize human rights in U.S. foreign policy. Revealing the dramatic rise in human rights awareness since the outset of the decade, in September 1976, 102 incumbent members of the House and Senate and more than two dozen contenders in the upcoming congressional election signed a statement encouraging candidates for public office to promote human rights in U.S. foreign policy. More concretely, over the course of 1976 Congress significantly strengthened human rights legislation, cutting off bilateral U.S. security assistance to Uruguay and Chile, and, through the Humphrey-Cranston Amendment, replacing the nonbinding "sense of Congress" language in section 502B with a legal obligation that the executive terminate security aid to gross violators of internationally recognized human rights, and providing congressional legislators with the right to overrule the president. Similarly, section 301 of the International Security Assistance and Arms Export Control Act of 1976 (PL 94–329) reiterated the restriction on security assistance to human rights violators, and also required the State Department to draw up human rights reports on every nation receiving U.S. security assistance.[80]

Finally, throughout 1976, Fraser's wide-ranging subcommittee hearings continued to frustrate Washington bureaucrats unwilling to embrace the call for an infusion of morality in U.S. foreign policy. As one foreign service officer wrote in a memo in mid-July, "there are some hearings coming up ... which will undoubtedly result in adverse publicity, possibly be embarrassing to Departmental officers who testify, and almost certainly will be the forerunner to adverse actions under the new Foreign Assistance Legislation."[81] Raising the hackles of the foreign service, Fraser's subcommittee thus continued to serve as a key point on the expanding human rights spectrum. As one human rights advocate asserted during the hearings on Argentina the following month, "It seems to me that the kind of attention, whatever it is, that is attributed to human rights today is partly a result of the hearings of this very committee, [and] that it does indicate a sustained interest in this question, that it will be weighed throughout the policy process."[82]

In addition to growing interest in human rights on Capitol Hill, by 1976 nongovernmental human rights advocacy had blossomed into a major political movement. Indeed, the 1970s witnessed a veritable explosion of newly formed nongovernmental human rights organizations. Consisting of perhaps one hundred organizations in the latter half of the decade, an "amorphous yet multifaceted aggregate" as one early study aptly put it, the movement ranged from faith-based groups (such as the National Council of Churches) to organizations dedicated to raising awareness (such as the Council on Hemispheric Affairs), as well as solidarity organizations advocating on behalf of particular nations, ranging from Chile to the Philippines.[83]

On one level, internationally focused human rights groups in the United States worked to raise public awareness and generate popular opprobrium of repressive regimes overseas. Drawing from the playbook of the civil rights and anti–Vietnam War movements, human rights groups utilizing the "populist" approach sought to elicit human rights improvements abroad through mass mobilization campaigns. Through petitions and letter-writing campaigns on behalf of political prisoners, they sought to shame the leaders of rogue nations into compliance with international norms. "We assumed that all governments wanted to be accepted in the family of civilized nations and that by publicizing information that was not generally known, we would bring the force of world opinion to bear on them," recalled Jeri Laber, who acquired a reputation as a hard-hitting human rights advocate in the early 1970s. "By shedding light on hidden atrocities, we would make governments sensitive to the image they projected to the outside world," Laber continued. "Publicity was our primary tool."[84]

On another level, a growing coterie of U.S. human rights groups focused their efforts entirely on influencing Washington's policymaking elite. In a novel "post-populist" approach that eschewed a mass base, human rights advocates focused their energies on lobbying for more stringent congressional control over foreign aid funding to halt U.S. support for human-rights-violating regimes. In turn, such efforts resulted in a close working relationship between the nongovernmental human rights community and sympathetic members of Congress. As Senator Kennedy informed a gathering of human rights advocates, "We are absolutely dependent on you for information. We are basically all generalists, and we depend upon you for information, for the trends, the movements, the opportunities for congressional action."[85]

The surge of popular interest also dramatically affected the handful of long-standing human rights organizations such as the International League for Human Rights. Founded during the Second World War by the American Civil Liberties Union (ACLU) director Roger Baldwin on the pattern of the French interwar International Federation of Human Rights Leagues, the ILHR's effort to implement internationally recognized human rights had languished in the postwar era.[86] At the dawn of the 1970s, the league consisted of a handful of dedicated advocates along with affiliations with more prominent civil liberties organizations, such as the ACLU and the National Association for the Advancement of Colored People (NAACP).

Less than half a decade later, the ILHR executive director Roberta Cohen was nearly overwhelmed by a wave of human rights volunteers. "Having been in this tiny office where it was so hard to find anybody to pay any attention, in the course of several years suddenly I began getting telephone calls and walk-ins . . . from so many people, many of them prominent writers and scientists and publishers," recalled Cohen in a recent interview. In a matter of months, some fifty lawyers had offered pro bono assistance on human rights cases, making it possible for Cohen to establish a parallel organization, the Lawyers Committee for International Human Rights.[87] "Human rights is suddenly *chic*," Cohen exuberantly told the *New York Times* in early 1977. "For years we were preachers, cockeyed idealists, or busybodies and now we are respectable."[88]

A similar development was taking place at the U.S. affiliate of Amnesty International. Founded in 1961 by the British lawyer Peter Benenson as a one-year campaign on behalf of two political prisoners in Portugal, Amnesty had subsequently developed into a full-time voluntary human rights organization focusing on obtaining the release of international prisoners of conscience and using popular pressure to encourage governments to adhere to international standards governing their treatment.[89] During the 1960s, however, Amnesty's global influence, as one journalist accurately put it, was "almost imperceptible."[90]

The following decade, however, Amnesty International underwent an extraordinary transformation—a development most clearly evident in the United States. Between 1970 and 1976, membership with Amnesty International USA increased by an average of roughly ten thousand new members per year, and by mid-decade, AIUSA boasted offices in Washington, DC, New York, San Francisco, and Los Angeles, and was operating on an annual budget of nearly $1 million.[91] "Our time has come," one research assistant told a journalist in December 1976. "The interest in Amnesty has just absolutely boomed."[92]

In addition to facilitating grassroots human rights advocacy, Amnesty International also developed into an effective lobby for human rights legislation on Capitol Hill. In 1973, Amnesty's groundbreaking *Report on Torture* solidified the organization's credibility as a global human rights watchdog, and by mid-decade, not only were AI representatives serving as frequent participants in congressional hearings, but the organization was continuously feeding information to between forty and fifty members of Congress, thus significantly enhancing legislators' ability to pressure the State Department to fulfill the requirements of the growing body of human rights legislation.[93] Underscoring the impact Amnesty International achieved on the policymaking process, following the completion of the first round of State Department human rights reports on nations receiving U.S. security assistance, in an internal memo to U.S. embassies in Latin America, the assistant secretary of state for inter-American affairs Harry W. Shlaudeman noted the "high credibility Amnesty and others have with Congress" and requested that embassy personnel "go rather carefully through recent Amnesty and other reports and extract the references to individuals or specific legal situations (e.g. 'fair trials are not available')," and provide Washington updated information on each issue. Shlaudeman further requested that embassies maintain detailed chronologies of conversations, diplomatic representations, and programs on human rights. Underscoring Amnesty International's political influence, he concluded, "We simply have to establish—to congressional satisfaction—that we are paying detailed attention, . . . that we are familiar with what Amnesty and others are reporting and that we are active."[94]

Since the March military coup, Amnesty International had kept a particularly close watch on the deteriorating human rights situation in Argentina. Over the course of the late spring and summer of 1976, grim reports of the military junta's campaign against perceived subversives had begun to filter into the United States media with increasing frequency. On May 11, Robert Cox, the courageous editor of the English-language *Buenos Aires Herald,* reported in the *Washington Post* that since the military coup, more than 204 persons had been killed in the government's antisubversive campaign (an estimate that would later prove far lower than the actual number slain by security forces).[95]

A few weeks later Cox reported that lines were forming at the entrance to the Government House as early as one o'clock in the morning to receive appointments when the building opened six hours later to inquire into the fate of missing or detained relatives. "Most Argentines expected that the death squads would be abolished by the armed forces after the military takeover," Cox wrote, noting that the military had assumed control of all security forces, including the police. "But this has not happened. Bodies have continued to appear, although many are not reported because of press self-censorship and police secrecy."[96] In late June, the veteran New York Times reporter Juan de Onís reported that federal courts in Buenos Aires had received more than six hundred habeas corpus petitions since April 1, many for persons who had disappeared after being arrested by security forces.[97]

Amnesty International's own coverage of Argentina corroborated the intrepid reporting of journalists like Cox and de Onís. Over the course of 1976, Amnesty published a series of press releases and short reports on human rights issues in Argentina including academic freedom, detained or missing refugees, and the number of political deaths reported in the international press since the military coup.[98] The scale of state-sanctioned violence against perceived subversives in the South American nation, however, inspired Amnesty to dramatically extend its reporting by taking the unprecedented step of organizing a "mission" to Argentina, with the explicit intention of documenting firsthand human rights violations committed by the Argentine military government.

Unwilling to risk the negative publicity a refusal would undoubtedly generate, the Argentine military government reluctantly accepted an AI delegation. On November 5, three dedicated human rights advocates arrived in Buenos Aires to conduct an eleven-day study: Amnesty International secretariat member Tricia Feeney, Lord Eric Avebury, and Rep. Robert F. Drinan. Quick to denounce Amnesty for intervening in their country's internal affairs, Argentine military officers were especially distrustful of Drinan, who had established himself in the House of Representatives as a fierce critic of Argentina's human rights situation. In fact, on July 2, Drinan had declared before Congress that "in recent months, right-wing 'death squads' have been murdering and terrorizing supposed leftists," a theme he reiterated the following month. In both instances, the Massachusetts congressman attempted to garner support for legislation to parole endangered South American refugees residing in Argentina into the United States.[99]

From the moment the group arrived in Buenos Aires on November 5, 1976, it was subjected to intense surveillance by Argentine military and police forces. Nearly two dozen plainclothes police officers shadowed the mission at all times, frequently detaining and questioning individuals with whom the delegation met. On the morning of November 15, the group received a desperate telephone call from the mother of twenty-five-year-old Josefa Martinez, a student who had gone missing after meeting with the AI group the previous evening in Córdoba. Martinez's disappearance, Drinan later wrote, "caused me anguish as if a member of my own family had met such a fate." Immediately alerting the U.S. Embassy, Drinan also made a personal appeal to the papal nuncio to intervene, and continued to advocate on Martinez's behalf after returning to Washington.[100] Like thousands of other Argentines swept up in what the *Buenos Aires Herald* editor Robert Cox plaintively described as a "terrible black night, that may well be getting blacker," Martinez failed to reappear.[101]

Despite the military's effort to deter cooperation with the Amnesty mission, more than one hundred Argentines met with the delegation to declare arrested or disappeared friends or relatives or to deliver personal testimony regarding violations of human rights at the hands of security service personnel. As a result, Amnesty's mission report, released in March 1977, revealed in unprecedented detail the extent of human rights violations in Argentina.[102] Estimating that more than fifteen thousand Argentines had disappeared or been abducted since mid-1974, the report asserted that the Argentine government had "permitted widespread torture of political prisoners, and engaged in abductions of its own citizens."[103] Setting a remarkably high standard in human rights reporting, the ninety-two-page document, as the social scientist Lars Schoultz asserted in a pioneering study of human rights shortly thereafter, constituted a "masterpiece of the genre, possibly the most comprehensive public evidence ever assembled by a NGO on human rights violations by any Latin American government."[104] Solidifying Amnesty International's reputation as a reliable and courageous human rights watchdog, and underscoring the extraordinary rise in human rights awareness, nine months after the report's release Amnesty was awarded the Nobel Peace Prize.

* * *

Arriving in Washington with little more than a suitcase, Talamante and CADHU cofounder Gino Lofredo "scraped by"—staying with friends and relying on donations to rent a tiny office in Washington's relatively inexpensive Dupont Circle district. "We lived very, very meagerly," Talamante recalled in a 2008 interview.[105] Limited resources notwithstanding, Talamante quickly established CADHU as a leading voice among nongovernmental human rights organizations engaged in U.S.-Argentine relations. In addition to working closely with the Washington Office on Latin America, CADHU established close ties with other Latin American national solidarity committees including Brazil, Chile, Nicaragua, and Peru. Talamante also became an outspoken member of the Coalition for a New

Foreign and Military Policy, an umbrella organization with roots in the Vietnam War protest movement representing thirty-five religious, political, trade union, and human rights organizations.[106] Congressional lobbying, however, remained CADHU's primary mission. "The first thing we started doing was documenting what was happening," Talamante recalled. "We put together information packets and walked the halls of Congress."[107]

It was a heady moment to be engaged in human rights work on Capitol Hill. By early 1977, the human rights movement had emerged as a defining feature on the U.S. political landscape. Indeed, it was a development most clearly evident in Jimmy Carter's electoral victory over the incumbent Ford administration. A Washington outsider, Carter had repeatedly emphasized the need for an infusion of morality in U.S. foreign policy during the campaign, and, underscoring how far human rights advocates had shifted the U.S. political debate since the outset of the decade, in his inauguration address Carter asserted that "our commitment to human rights must be absolute," and "there can be no nobler nor more ambitious task for America to undertake on this day of a new beginning than to help shape a just and peaceful world that is truly humane."[108] Cognizant of Carter's political inexperience and embrace of the human rights issue late in the presidential campaign, human rights advocates nonetheless welcomed the opportunity the new administration presented for dramatically accelerating the institutionalization of human rights in U.S. foreign policy. Indeed, in comparison with the Nixon and Ford administration's fierce resistance to human rights initiatives, the Carter team initially demonstrated a remarkable willingness to engage the nongovernmental human rights community. In early February 1977, for example, the International League for Human Rights convened a conference on implementing human rights in U.S. foreign policy at the Washington-based Carnegie Endowment for International Peace. More than fifty human rights experts attended—unmistakable evidence, the league director Jerome J. Shestack subsequently wrote Carter, "of the widespread support your advocacy is generating throughout the world."[109] Underscoring his support for human rights, after receiving a copy of the extensive report, Carter sent a handwritten letter of thanks and subsequently offered Shestack the position of U.S. delegate to the United Nations Human Rights Commission.[110] Capturing the ebullient mood among human rights advocates, the ILHR *Annual Review* praised Carter's support and declared, "These are days of hope for human rights."[111]

Similarly, congressional human rights supporters relished Secretary of State Cyrus Vance's recognition of human rights as a U.S. foreign policy goal, and his willingness to engage nongovernmental advocates. In April 1977, for example, the deputy secretary of state Warren Christopher emphasized the importance of meeting with members of the human rights community in an internal memorandum to Vance. "Since there is an increasingly active, vocal, and influential human rights lobby operating on the Hill, the Department should complement its efforts with the Congress with efforts to meet and talk with representatives of the more important human rights organizations in town," Christopher wrote, emphasizing in particular WOLA, the National Catholic Conference, and the Coalition for a New Foreign and Military Policy.[112] To be sure, human rights advocates quickly recognized that Secretary Vance's conception of the role of human rights in U.S. foreign policy was far from "absolute"; few, however, could deny the dramatic shift in congressional relations with the State Department. When a newly elected member of Congress asked Rep. Tom Harkin's opinion of Vance following a meeting between the secretary and a group of Congress members, the veteran human rights advocate responded drily, "You should have been here when Kissinger was Secretary of State." Kissinger, Harkin continued, "would never have come down here to meet with us," or "condescended to answer our questions, except in only the most general and non-committal way." Secretary Vance, Harkin concluded, "is indeed a breath of fresh air in that position."[113]

If the Carter administration's apparent interest in human rights in the opening months of 1977 raised hopes among human rights advocates, it did not stop nongovernmental groups from continuing to actively lobby liberal members of Congress to expand the existing body of human rights legislation. As the hemisphere's worst human rights violator, at the outset of the Carter presidency Argentina took center stage in the debate, and Olga Talamante became a leading voice in the effort to convince congressional lawmakers to curtail U.S. security transfers to the South American nation. As Talamante told participants at a symposium on U.S. foreign policy in April, "For the past 15 years the United States has explicitly supported the role of the Armed Forces in Argentina as in the rest of Latin America." Notwithstanding the Argentine military junta's "apparent strength, fervent anti-communism and identification with the United States," Talamante continued, "the current military regime in Argentina is actually deeply vulnerable, unstable and weak." Faced with an "embarrassing and undesirable ally," Talamante concluded, the United States "must have the courage to recognize its past mistakes and firmly disassociate itself from the Argentine Military."[114]

Human rights advocates were heartened by the Carter administration's February decision to reduce Foreign Military Sales (FMS) credits to Argentina for fiscal year 1978 from $30 to $15 million on human rights grounds. Although the Argentine military junta subsequently rejected the remaining FMS quota, the U.S. government reduction did not affect $750,000 in International Military Education and Training (IMET)—a credit program for foreign soldiers to train at U.S. military institutions—and Argentina retained access to U.S. government and commercial cash sales of military hardware.[115] Accordingly, in the late spring nongovernmental human rights advocates' lobbying efforts for a complete arms cutoff to Argentina intensified. "I visited office after office of every Senator or Representative for a period of three months," recalled Patricia Erb, a U.S. citizen who had survived abduction and torture by Argentine security forces in 1976.[116] Similarly, capturing the sense of urgency that guided her efforts, in a three-page letter detailing the extreme brutality of the Argentine military government to Jimmy Carter in early June, Talamante quoted General Ibérico Saint Jean, the governor of Buenos Aires Province. "First we will kill all the subversives," the general had recently asserted, "then we will kill their collaborators; then . . . their sympathizers; then . . . those who remain indifferent; and, finally, we will kill those who are timid." In light of such brutality, President Carter, Talamante concluded, should "join the United States Congress on this issue and support its initiatives to terminate all forms of military aid to Argentina."[117]

The debate over U.S. policy toward Argentina culminated in September 1977. In deliberations over the Senate's military aid authorization bill, the staunch human rights supporter Edward Kennedy introduced an amendment cutting off all U.S. military and commercial sales to Argentina. With the support of Senator Church (D-ID), and strong backing in the House of Representatives—a similar proposal by Representative Gerry Studds (D-MA) had been defeated by a mere thirteen votes—the amendment appeared destined to pass.[118] At the eleventh hour of negotiations, however, the Carter administration entered into the debate. Fearing the bill's passage would prevent the president from offering the Argentine military junta incentives for improvements in human rights, Carter asked Senator Hubert Humphrey to negotiate a postponement of the cutoff date. Incensed by Carter's apparent unwillingness to enforce tough human rights sanctions, Kennedy nonetheless pragmatically agreed to postpone the cutoff until September 30, 1978.[119]

In spite of the delayed implementation date, the successful passage of the Kennedy-Humphrey Amendment constituted a defining moment in the effort to institutionalize human rights in U.S. foreign policy. The amendment, combined with broader congressional legislation binding U.S. foreign policy to human rights considerations, provided Patricia Derian—the Carter administration's newly installed assistant secretary of state for human rights and humanitarian affairs—with the ability to use delayed or denied transfer applications earmarked for the military junta in Buenos Aires as leverage to demand improvements in the protection of human rights. Indeed, by mid-1978, the Department of State had blocked an estimated $800 million in U.S. transfers to Argentina on human rights grounds.[120] With the total cutoff mandated by the Kennedy-Humphrey Amendment looming, the extensive backlog of U.S. sales to Argentina played an important role in convincing the military junta in mid-1978 to accept a formal visit by the Inter-American Commission on Human Rights Commission (IACHR), an organ of the Organization of American States. In the months leading up to the September 1979 visit, state-sanctioned violence in Argentina decreased markedly as the military junta sought to avoid an embarrassingly negative report—disappearances dropped dramatically, prison conditions improved, and the government made unprecedented steps toward confronting the issue of the disappeared.[121]

More broadly, as the Kennedy-Humphrey Amendment made clear, by 1978 the human rights movement could cite major achievements in promoting human rights in U.S. foreign policy. A countermovement to the maintenance of close U.S. ties to anticommunist, right-wing military regimes, since the late 1960s human rights advocates had worked to uproot the policy prescriptions that had undergirded U.S. Cold War policy over the previous quarter century. A decade later, nongovernmental human rights advocates and their sympathizers in Congress had created a strong grassroots base, established a powerful presence in Washington, and could effectively mobilize on behalf of human rights issues.

For Olga Talamante, in particular, the successful congressional cutoff was a defining triumph in her own fierce struggle to cast international opprobrium on the Argentine military junta. Having personally experienced the horrors of state-sanctioned violence in Argentina, Talamante had developed into a tenacious advocate on behalf of human rights, and following the successful passage of the arms cutoff, Talamante shifted from CADHU to a position with the American Friends Service Committee focusing on global human rights–related issues. Yet as state-sanctioned violence continued in Argentina, Talamante would find little peace of mind. Capturing the lasting imprint of her experiences in Argentina, in a poem inspired by the annual round-trip migration of swallows from Argentina to California, Talamante later wrote:

> I, swallow,
> my tears on the shores of a new ocean
> I am no longer a swallow
> I will not make the 6,000-mile trip
> every other beat of my heart
> I will no longer swallow my tears and smile unhappily
>
> I will now cry happily in my sadness[122]

4

"TOTAL IMMERSION IN ALL THE HORRORS OF THE WORLD"

The Carter Administration and Human Rights, 1977–1978

Three days after the first anniversary of the Argentine military coup against Isabel Perón, a passenger jet carrying Patricia Derian touched down on the tarmac at Ezeiza International Airport. Met by U.S. officials and ushered into an embassy car, President Carter's newly appointed Department of State coordinator for human rights and humanitarian affairs was whisked to the United States Embassy, where ambassador Robert C. Hill was awaiting her arrival. Sparing Derian a long-winded greeting, Hill went straight to the point. "I'm going to tell you a secret, you have to promise not to tell anyone," he began. Secretary of State Kissinger, the ambassador confided, "came down and he said that they didn't need to worry about human rights issues anymore."[1] Despite his insistent efforts to convince Kissinger to make a strong statement on behalf of human rights in Argentina, Hill continued, the secretary had personally informed the Argentine foreign minister in mid-1976 that he hoped Argentina would "finish its terrorist problem" by the time Congress reconvened in January 1977. Appalled at the rising number of extralegal killings, by September Hill sensed that the architects of Argentina's dirty war against perceived left-wing subversives were following the secretary of state's advice. "Kissinger gave the Argentines the green light," the ambassador bluntly concluded.[2]

It was a remarkable introduction for the untested human rights coordinator into the legacy of U.S. support for anticommunist Latin American military establishments over the previous quarter century. Not surprisingly, although Derian found an unlikely ally in Hill, her visit to Argentina also starkly demonstrated that the ambassador's quiet support for human rights was by no means shared by all U.S. Embassy personnel. To the contrary, Derian sensed almost complete op-position to Carter's nascent human rights policy among the U.S. Foreign Service officers posted in Buenos Aires. Underscoring the long-standing military ties that had largely defined U.S.-Argentine relations over the course of the Cold War, in one well-attended meeting at the embassy, Derian's discussion of the Carter ad-ministration's commitment to the promotion of human rights was interrupted by the U.S. defense attaché, who stood up and loudly demanded, "What the hell does that mean?"[3] "Well, we're not going to sell them thumbscrews anymore, if that's what you mean," Derian responded.[4]

Similarly, Argentine foreign ministry officials brooked no criticism of state repression, dismissing Derian's human rights concerns as a peripheral consid-eration in their struggle against left-wing extremists. Derian's meetings with Ar-gentine officials, Fred Rondon wrote Ambassador Hill, were "almost beside the point." On the one hand, Derian was uncompromising, emphasizing that the nature of Argentine relations with the United States would henceforth be contin-gent on the government's protection of human rights. On the other hand, even Rondon—a thirty-year veteran of the foreign service currently serving as ARA deputy director, Office of East Coast Affairs—was shocked by the extremism of the foreign ministry, who seemed to be "in another world." "I really sympathize for those on your staff who deal with this Alice in Wonderland character," Ron-don confided to Hill, presumably referring to the Argentine foreign minister, Vice Admiral César Guzzetti.[5]

By far the most significant moment in Derian's visit to Buenos Aires, however, was the glimpse into the terror of the Argentine dirty war provided by human rights advocates and relatives of victims of state-sanctioned violence. The situ-ation in Argentina was "barbaric," ninety-year-old Alicia Moreau de Justo told Derian during a meeting with the Permanent Assembly for Human Rights. Less than two weeks before, de Justo asserted, a group of armed men had invaded the home of an elderly grandmother, mother, and daughter, ransacking the house and kidnapping the mother and daughter. Blindfolded and transported to a clan-destine detention center, where she was forced to listen to her daughter being tor-tured in an adjacent room, the mother was subsequently released. "To this day," de Justo concluded, "she is desperately trying to locate her daughter, who, to her knowledge, is guilty of no subversive activity."[6] Encouraged by de Justo's outrage, other participants weighed in, flooding Derian with stories of the thousands of habeas corpus petitions gathering dust in government files; of the disappear-ance of journalists who reported on state-sanctioned violence; of the body of a daughter, recovered with great difficulty from secret detention, an autopsy of which later revealed that "two live rats had been sewn into the girl's vagina and had torn her body apart as they tried to get out."[7]

Derian left the meeting profoundly shaken and filled with moral outrage. Coupled with her meetings with embassy officials and Argentine military leaders, Derian's March 1977 visit to Argentina served as an exhausting introduction to the challenges of international human rights advocacy, which the former civil rights activist would pursue with remarkable zeal over the subsequent four years. Horrified by the extent of the Argentine military's human rights violations, on her return to Washington, Derian set out to make the South American nation a defining test case for the Carter administration's human rights policy. Utilizing the power and leverage of her office, Derian worked, in effect, to dramatically redefine the U.S. Cold War relationship with Argentina by publicly denouncing dirty war violence and consistently opposing U.S. economic and security assistance.

More broadly, Patricia Derian's determination to promote human rights reflected a watershed moment in the struggle between human rights advocates and cold warriors over the nature of U.S. foreign policy. As I illustrate in this chapter, the competition between idealists and realists culminated in the Jimmy Carter presidency. Following Carter's inauguration, the administration set out to institutionalize human rights in the policymaking process, and as a result, over the course of 1977 the locus of human rights advocacy shifted from Capitol Hill and the nongovernmental sector to the White House and the Department of State Human Rights Office. Correspondingly, however, the administration's efforts ignited a bitter internal debate centering on which human rights the U.S. should promote, where the policy should be deployed, and what approach would most effectively advance the human rights agenda.

* * *

Ironically, although Patricia Derian's human rights advocacy would make her one of the most widely recognized—and in many instances reviled—Carter administration appointees, she had been a late convert to the Carter campaign. In fact, Derian's decision to support the Georgia governor's presidential bid had not been based on a desire to promote human rights abroad, but rather on regional political considerations linked to her long-standing civil rights activism in Mississippi. Trained as a psychiatric nurse in Virginia, in 1959 Derian had accompanied her husband—an orthopedic doctor—to Jackson, Mississippi, where she quickly established a reputation in the local community for helping African American acquaintances confront the quotidian inequalities of southern segregation.[8] It was an unlikely pursuit for a white woman in the Deep South, but Derian refused to abide practices such as the local telephone company's use of courtesy titles on white customers' bills but not on those of blacks. "I got into it at the beginning on a one-to-one basis," Derian told an interviewer years later. "I'm no hero. They were just people I cared about."[9]

Yet as the civil rights movement increasingly took national stage in the early 1960s, Derian's involvement in the struggle blossomed into a dynamic leadership role. By the time Freedom Riders protesting interstate bus segregation were unceremoniously delivered to the Jackson City Jail, Derian had begun touring Mississippi prisons to assess the facilities, treatment of prisoners, and adherence to due process, and was working to bring about improvements through conferences with sheriffs, local and state legislators, and the press. When National Guardsmen forced the University of Mississippi to accept its first African American student in 1963, Derian was in the vanguard of efforts to integrate Mississippi's schools, having founded Mississippians for Public Education, a grassroots organization promoting school desegregation.[10] Derian was also active in registering African American voters, and, in 1964, organized the campaign to have Lyndon B. Johnson's name on the Mississippi presidential ballot.[11]

At the epicenter of southern resistance to black integration, civil rights work enjoyed few successes and was always dangerous; the brutal murder of three young activists less than two hours from Jackson in early August 1964 made starkly evident the risks of undermining the racial status quo. Yet Derian was not one to back down from a challenge. Born on the eve of the Great Depression as the only child of liberal, socialite parents who, in her description, "were almost totally absorbed in their own lives," Derian developed into a self-sufficient, fiercely independent youngster. By the time she entered adolescence, Derian had little regard for the confining gender mores of the mid-twentieth century. "I'm 13, I smoke, and I'm not going to curtsey anymore!" she bluntly informed her parents on one memorable occasion. Far from rebuking their precocious daughter, the Derians were delighted; as Patt Derian recalled in a recent interview, "My father's lifetime message to me was 'You live your life so that you can look any man in the eye and tell him to go to hell!'"[12]

It was a lesson that guided Derian's civil rights activism. Despite threats from the Ku Klux Klan, Derian increased her political activity in the aftermath of the 1964 presidential election, in which the Republican Party candidate Barry Goldwater swept Mississippi with almost 90 percent of the vote.[13] After four years of unsuccessful efforts to convince the all-white Mississippi Democratic Party to accept participation by African Americans, in 1968 Derian played a central role in founding the "Loyalist" Mississippi Democratic Party, organizing an alternative delegating system at the precinct, county, regional, and state levels. With the African American civil rights activist Charles Evers as national committeeman and herself as national committeewoman, Derian successfully challenged the seating and recognition of the Mississippi "Regulars" at the 1968 Democratic Convention in Chicago.[14]

Despite their success in drawing national media attention to the Regulars' intransigence on the race issue, for Derian and her Loyalist colleagues the prospect of a perpetually divided Democratic Party in Mississippi boded poorly for their goal of making concrete advances in the field of civil rights. Scorned by their Democratic colleagues, the stunned Regulars had cast their ballots for the Independent candidate George Wallace, whose unabashedly racist views and vitriolic diatribes against the New Left were well received among prosegregationists in the Magnolia State.[15] Accordingly, during the Nixon and Ford administrations, Derian spearheaded efforts to unite the Mississippi Democratic Party, a feat that was finally achieved through a cochairman arrangement in early 1976. Derian's decision to support Jimmy Carter's bid for the Democratic nomination a few weeks later reflected similarly local concerns: with Wallace yet again vying for president—and this time on the Democratic ticket—Derian gambled that Carter's southern roots, fiscal conservatism, and progressive stance on race could unite the divided Mississippi Democratic Party and edge out Wallace in the upcoming state primary. It was, Derian later told a journalist with characteristic candor, "really the first, cold decision I have ever made for strictly pragmatic reasons," since in her view Carter initially appeared to be "soft on race and bad on women."[16]

The strategy was a success, and after finishing a distant third in the Mississippi Democratic primary Wallace officially endorsed Carter in mid-June, bringing his delegates to the Carter camp and papering over the rift that had divided the Mississippi Democratic Party for more than a decade. More significantly, as the campaign progressed Derian became an avid backer of Jimmy Carter, particularly citing his support for racial integration in the south. In March, Derian became a full-time Carter campaign worker, and, following Carter's successful nomination at the Democratic Convention in July, she accepted the position of deputy director of the Carter-Mondale campaign.

In turn, the Carter campaign found a valuable asset in Patricia Derian. Although in subsequent years journalists would almost invariably define Derian as a "former civil rights activist," the breadth of her leadership on behalf of racial equality, education, and health care defied a shorthand definition. By 1976, Derian had established herself not only as a key player in Mississippi politics but as a leading liberal voice in the south. In addition to serving as president of the Southern Regional Council, a multimillion dollar foundation dedicated to racial justice with operations in eleven states, Derian sat on the board of directors at the American Civil Liberties Union, the National Prison Project, and the Democratic Forum. She also served as a consultant to more than a hundred organizations ranging from the Council on Negro Women to the Carnegie Council on Children, and oversaw the management of a twenty-five-county educational pilot project in Mississippi. Indeed, the editors of the exclusive "Who's Who" register included Derian not only on the "American Politics" and "American Women" lists, but on their global inventory of the "World's Who's Who of Women" as well.[17]

Recognizing Derian's political experience and contribution to the campaign, in the hectic weeks following Carter's electoral victory, the president-elect's transition team hit on a political appointment that seemed a nice fit given her experience in the civil rights arena: the recently established position of Department of State coordinator for human rights and humanitarian affairs. By her own account, Derian knew relatively little about the effort to institutionalize human rights in U.S. foreign policy; indeed, she had not been aware that the coordinator position even existed.[18] After a long talk with the newly appointed deputy secretary of state Warren Christopher, however, Derian accepted the position, in part since "it was a job that really had never been done," and partly on the assumption that her experiences as a civil rights activist would provide a foundation for human rights advocacy.[19] "After all," she later told the *Washington Post*, "it is my line of work."[20]

* * *

Like Derian, to a considerable extent Jimmy Carter viewed the human rights issue through the lens of the civil rights movement. Although the promotion of human rights in U.S. foreign policy would arguably constitute the centerpiece of Carter's presidential legacy, the one-term Georgia governor discovered the issue late in the 1976 campaign. The previous year, Carter had opposed the Helsinki Accords with the Soviet Union on the basis of nonintervention, despite the agreement's unprecedented human rights guarantees, and in early 1976, the Carter campaign barely mentioned human rights in the lead-up to the Democratic National Convention.[21] It was not until the second presidential debate, in San Francisco on October 6—less than a month before Election Day—that the majority of U.S. voters first associated Jimmy Carter with the effort to institutionalize human rights in U.S. foreign policy. In a heated give-and-take, Carter castigated the incumbent administration for "supporting dictatorships" and "ignoring human rights," and asserted that because of such policies, "we are weak and the rest of the world knows it."[22]

Overshadowed in the press by Ford's infamous gaffe denying the Soviet Union's control over Eastern Europe, Carter's unexpected invocation of human rights nonetheless electrified Americans searching for an alternative to the perceived immorality of the Nixon and Ford administrations. "I still remember hearing Carter talk about human rights in one of his televised preelection debates with Gerald Ford," the Amnesty International activist Jeri Laber recalls in her memoirs. "*Is he talking about what we're doing?* I asked myself, incredulous."

Underscoring the significance of the San Francisco debate, "Within a short time," Laber concludes, "the words 'human rights' seemed to be on everyone's lips."[23]

To be sure, the role of morality in U.S. policy—both at home and abroad—was a founding principle of the Carter campaign. On one level, Carter's embrace of the human rights issue was a clear outgrowth of his support for the civil rights movement. Institutionalized racial inequality, Carter had asserted in his 1975 campaign booster *Why Not the Best?*, "hung like a millstone around our necks under the label of 'separate but equal.'"[24] Similarly, sounding a theme he often used on the campaign stump, in a town hall meeting in Yazoo City, Mississippi, Carter declared the civil rights movement "the best thing that ever happened to the South in my lifetime." Asked whether his "southern heritage" contributed to a concern for human rights overseas, Carter responded, "I would not be here as President had it not been for the Civil Rights Act," and further asserted that the civil rights struggle had "made the human rights issue very vivid for me."[25]

On a deeper level, Carter's call for more government transparency, less intrusion into the lives of its citizens, and a return to the ethical principles of an idealized American past was a savvy recognition of the national mood in the post-Vietnam, post-Watergate era. "Disgruntled Americans sought new ideas, fresh faces, and a style of leadership predicated on openness, truthfulness, and public responsiveness," the historians Burton Kaufman and Scott Kaufman write. "Indeed, morality was the emerging keynote of the campaign—a desire to restore a sense of purpose, trust, fairness, and civic responsibility to American life."[26] Correspondingly, in the realm of foreign policy, although Carter's limited experience led him to rely heavily on his fellow Trilateral Commission member Zbigniew Brzezinski, the Georgia governor's personal philosophy nonetheless set the tone. Jimmy Carter, Brzezinski concluded in his memoirs, "came to the Presidency with a determination to make U.S. foreign policy more humane and moral."[27]

In fact, Carter recognized to a remarkable extent the illiberal nature of U.S. policy toward much of the developing world and he refused to blindly adhere to the Cold War shibboleths that had guided U.S. foreign policymaking over the previous quarter century. As a result of U.S.-Soviet competition, "a dominant factor in our dealings with foreign countries became whether they espoused an anti-communist line," Carter wrote in his memoirs. "There were times when right-wing monarchs and military dictators were automatically immune from any criticism of their oppressive actions."[28] Instead, Carter emphasized that the need to balance support for authoritarian allies with the promotion of human rights reflected a major shift in U.S. foreign relations.[29] "I was familiar with the widely accepted arguments that we had to choose between idealism and realism, or between morality and the exertion of power; but I rejected those claims,"

Carter later maintained. "To me, the demonstration of American idealism was a practical and realistic approach to foreign affairs, and moral principles were the best foundation for the exertion of American power and influence."[30]

Carter's ardent denunciation of the lack of morality during the Nixon-Ford era, epitomized by what he referred to as Henry Kissinger's secret, "Lone Ranger" diplomacy, was a common refrain over the course of the campaign.[31] "There has been a deep sense of alienation of people from our government and a sense of disappointment, a sense of embarrassment—sometimes even a sense of shame," Carter told listeners in August 1976. Pointedly referencing the Vietnam War, CIA covert operations, and U.S. involvement in Angola, Carter described himself—as a populist political outsider—as having a distinct advantage over the Washington establishment. "I have always felt that, to the extent that government in all its forms can equal the character of the American people—to that extent, our wrongs can be redressed, our mistakes corrected," he asserted.[32]

Although Carter repeatedly championed the need for an infusion of morality in U.S. foreign policy during the presidential campaign, his invocation of human rights in late 1976 served more as shorthand for his own broadly conceptualized reform agenda than a clear show of support for either grassroots human rights organizations or the legislative initiatives of the so-called human rights lobby and their liberal supporters in Congress. Whereas since the early 1970s human rights advocates led by Rep. Donald R. Fraser (D-MN) had worked to legally bind U.S. foreign aid to the human rights protections enshrined in *international* covenants to which the United States was a signatory, Carter's foundation for moral leadership invoked an idealized *national* past. The shortcomings of U.S. policy during the Cold War, he intoned in his memoirs, were the failure "to exhibit as an American characteristic the idealism of Jefferson or Wilson," leading the United States to forfeit "one of our most effective ways to meet threats from totalitarian ideologies and arouse the spirit of our own people."[33] It was a notion shared by Carter's top advisers. Secretary of State Cyrus Vance would later describe the administration's human rights policy as "one of the fundamental values that is our heritage," and on the thirtieth anniversary of the Universal Declaration of Human Rights, Brzezinski rather ironically struck a decidedly exceptionalist tone, describing the United States as "the first country ever in the history of mankind to consciously come together and shape itself around a central philosophical idea, namely the freedom and independence of man."[34]

If Carter's promotion of human rights through the lens of Wilsonian exceptionalism exhibited few links to the internationalist focus of the U.S. human rights movement, Carter was nonetheless able to reap significant political dividends by utilizing the lexicon of human rights. In the aftermath of the San Francisco debate, Carter campaign managers were elated by an unexpected outpouring of support for his human rights initiative, and Carter pounced on the theme in the final countdown to Election Day. It was "a beautiful campaign issue," a Carter foreign policy adviser told the veteran political commentator Elizabeth Drew, "an issue on which there was a real degree of public opinion hostile to the [Ford] Administration. That's actually how it started for Carter."[35]

In fact, the effectiveness of human rights in the 1976 campaign was its appeal to both liberal internationalists and cold warriors. For liberals, Carter's open criticism of U.S. Cold War policymaking represented an extraordinary opportunity in the ongoing struggle to weave human rights into the fabric of U.S. foreign policy. By 1976, the wave of interest in human rights that had swept across the nation during the decade was nearing its peak; at the grassroots level, membership with the U.S. affiliate of Amnesty International, for example, had increased by an average of roughly ten thousand new members per year between 1970 and 1976, facilitating the expansion of branch offices in San Francisco, California, Chicago, Illinois, Colorado, and Washington, DC.[36] Likewise, by late 1976, more than one hundred human rights lobby groups had taken up residence in the nation's capital, and sympathetic lawmakers had succeeded in passing nearly a dozen pieces of legislation binding U.S. actions in the international arena to the promotion of human rights.[37] Finally, although recognizing that Carter's moralism bore little resemblance to their own increasingly sophisticated legal expertise in linking U.S. foreign aid to the protection of human rights, many liberal human rights sympathizers in Congress nonetheless welcomed the possibility Carter presented for shifting the locus of human rights advocacy from Capitol Hill to the White House.

Carter's jump onto the human rights bandwagon was also welcomed by cold warriors such as the senators Henry M. "Scoop" Jackson (D-WA) and Daniel Patrick Moynihan (D-NY) as a means to indict the Communist world for its oppression of subject peoples. Jackson's successful cosponsorship of the Jackson-Vanik Amendment in 1974—placing limits on U.S. trade with nations with restrictive emigration policies and command economies—coupled with his fierce opposition to the second round of the Strategic Arms Limitation Treaty (SALT II), had constituted a major impediment to Henry Kissinger's effort to deepen détente with the Soviet Union.[38] By contrast, Carter's newfound willingness to broach the human rights issue in U.S.-Soviet relations—particularly evident in his open criticism of Gerald Ford's refusal to meet with the Soviet dissident Alexander Solzhenitsyn in 1975—won plaudits from Jackson and his fellow congressional hawks. Jackson and Carter, the senator from Washington told the press in mid-1976, had the "same approach" on human rights, since both believed that "over the long pull there must be more freedom in the world."[39]

In sum, human rights was "the perfect unifying principle" for the Carter campaign, as the historian Arthur M. Schlesinger Jr. concluded in an early assessment, which tapped into "the most acute contemporary concerns as well as the finest American traditions."[40] Appealing to a broad, bipartisan constituency—albeit for very different reasons—Carter effectively utilized the rhetoric of human rights to distance himself from the Ford administration, narrowly edging out his opponent on Election Day by a mere 2 million votes.[41] Indeed, the significance of Carter's human rights rhetoric in the 1976 campaign became increasingly clear in the aftermath of his slim victory. "Judging from news articles and direct communications from the American people to me during the first few months of my administration, human rights had become the central theme of our foreign policy in the minds of the press and public," Carter later wrote. "It seemed that a spark had been ignited, and I had no inclination to douse the growing flames."[42]

* * *

Exactly how the new administration intended to implement human rights in U.S. foreign policy, however, was far from clear in early 1977. After loftily declaring in his inauguration speech that "our commitment to human rights must be absolute," Carter maintained a steady emphasis on the issue in the initial weeks of his presidency, criticizing political repression in Czechoslovakia and Cuba, informing the startled Soviet ambassador that he would "not back down" from defending human rights abroad, and personally responding to a letter from the Soviet dissident (and Nobel Peace Prize laureate) Andrei Sakharov.[43] Carter also revealed a willingness to discuss human rights beyond the boundaries of the Communist world; at a press conference in mid-February the president expressed concern for political prisoners in South Korea and several Latin American nations.[44] Given the president's constant stream of human rights commentary in early 1977, few political observers could deny Carter's personal commitment to making the United States "the focal point for the preservation and protection of human rights."[45]

A far greater challenge facing the Carter administration, however, was how to convert the president's human rights rhetoric into practical policy initiatives. Having picked up the banner of human rights late in the presidential campaign, the Carter administration, as one adviser later admitted, entered the White House with "no specific planning for a particular human rights campaign or program."[46] Indeed, two weeks after Carter's inauguration, the newly appointed national security adviser Zbigniew Brzezinski told the National Security Council (NSC) the administration needed to find a "constructive way to infuse human rights into foreign policy."[47] Two days later, the State Department director of policy planning Anthony Lake informed Cyrus Vance that successful implementation of a human rights policy "depends on our designing an overall strategy—with a coherent set of goals, sense of priorities, and assessment of U.S. leverage." The State Department, Lake observed, "now lacks such a strategy." Emphasizing the lack of intradepartmental coordination on pending human rights problems, Lake continued, "There is no focal point for considering future initiatives or establishing a general context that could reduce the need for tough decisions in other areas under crisis conditions."[48]

In the following weeks, the policy planning team scrambled to generate a foundational human rights strategy. By February 18, however, little concrete progress had been made, with top U.S. policymakers merely agreeing on scheduling a formal review of human rights and U.S. foreign policy.[49] As the NSC staff member Jessica Tuchman admitted to *U.S. News and World Report*, "I think it must be fairly obvious that we hadn't got our act together in those first few weeks."[50] Nonetheless, by the end of the month, Vance had taken a handful of ad hoc steps toward creating a policy framework for the promotion of human rights, establishing an informal Human Rights Coordinating Committee at the deputy assistant secretary level to synchronize human rights policymaking within the State Department, requesting the geographic bureaus to develop human rights strategy papers, and, in the first week of March, appointing Patricia Derian as the department's human rights coordinator.[51]

By far the most contentious initiative, however, was Vance's announcement of reductions in Foreign Military Sales (FMS) credits to three U.S. allies on human rights grounds: Argentina, Ethiopia, and Uruguay.[52] A watershed moment in Carter's presidency, the decision was a clear, public disavowal of Henry Kissinger's Realpolitik approach to foreign affairs and, more generally, of the overarching U.S. approach toward the developing world since the onset of the Cold War. Moreover, the public airing of the decision—solemnly announced by the secretary of state during a February 25 press conference—was a clear shift from Kissinger's much-touted "quiet diplomacy"—a practice human rights sympathizers in Congress had accurately criticized as a none-too-subtle means of evading legislative initiatives.

Predictably, although mollifying complaints from Moscow that Carter was using human rights to publicly pillory the Soviets in the international court of opinion, the aid reduction sparked heated criticism from U.S. Cold War hawks determined to maintain close ties to anticommunist allies, repressive domestic policies notwithstanding. "On Argentina and Uruguay aid, Carter made a mistake," the ultraconservative North Carolina Republican Jessie Helms groused to a journalist. "I've visited those countries and they are absolutely anti-Communist. It is wrong to try to undermine those governments."[53] The decision also raised the hackles of liberal human rights advocates. Citing the administration's unwillingness to cut U.S. aid to authoritarian allies with greater geostrategic significance for the United States, such as South Korea, the Philippines, and Iran, Cold War doves such as Representatives Tom Harkin (D-IA) and Herman Badillo (D-NY) were quick to criticize Carter's perceived inconsistency.[54]

In fact, in the absence of a clearly defined human rights policy, the State Department's deliberation over which nations to sanction on human rights grounds had been a disorganized and unsystematic affair. "What happened," one State Department official admitted, "was that if anyone, including one of the regional Assistant Secretaries . . . put up a strong argument against zapping any of these countries, he won."[55] As a result, the administration settled on what the *New York Times* dismissively categorized as "the easy ones."[56] Regarding Ethiopia and Uruguay, the administration was especially hard-pressed to deny the validity of such criticism. The reduction in aid to the socialist regime ensconced in Addis Ababa was a mere $1.1 million since the U.S. Congress had already legislated a full military aid cutoff to take effect at the end of September. Likewise, sanctioning the extraordinarily repressive right-wing military regime in tiny Uruguay was "a throwaway case," as one official put it, since congressional lawmakers had informed the White House shortly after the inauguration that any efforts to earmark U.S. foreign aid—which had been banned since 1976—would be fiercely resisted.[57]

Finally, Foreign Military Sales credits constituted a relatively small portion of the total U.S. foreign aid, and in the case of Argentina, only four out of fifteen channels for U.S. aid fell into the category of "U.S. foreign assistance" affected by the aid reduction—a mere 7 percent in fiscal year 1976 of the $518.5 million in U.S. military assistance, Export-Import Bank financing, and loans from the Inter-American Development Bank (IDB) and International Monetary Fund (IMF). In light of the fact that the United States supplied more capital to both the IDB and the IMF than any other nation, the FMS credit reduction was hardly a major economic blow to the Argentine military junta.[58]

Nonetheless, to Carter's credit, Argentina was a far more challenging case than either Ethiopia or Uruguay. As successive U.S. Embassy cables demonstrated in grim detail, as many as twenty thousand people had been disappeared in the horrific wave of state-sanctioned violence that followed the military coup d'état the previous March.[59] Yet with its advanced nuclear technology program, substantial agricultural export sector, and extensive reserves of crude oil, Argentina had the potential—as Ambassador Hill pointed out in late January—to be "a major force for stability in the Southern Cone, and in the rest of Latin America."[60] Economically, in addition to $1.4 billion in U.S. investment, the United States enjoyed a $250 million annual trade surplus with Argentina, and the South American nation owed U.S. banks roughly $3 billion.[61] Finally, Argentina was a long-standing U.S. Cold War ally, and the fiercely anticommunist military junta unmistakably sought to maintain strong ties with Washington. With the administration "caught between its desire to support Argentina's struggle for economic recovery, while disassociating ourselves from human rights abuses," Carter's decision to slash FMS credits to Argentina from $32 to $15 million thus constituted an unprecedented—albeit limited—executive initiative that would serve as a defining test case for the development of the administration's human rights policy as a whole.[62]

* * *

Patricia Derian arrived at the Department of State in early March to find an atmosphere highly charged by the Carter administration's opening human rights initiatives. From the outset, despite her almost total lack of experience in the formulation and implementation of U.S. foreign policy, Derian was determined to spearhead a dynamic human rights policy. Indeed, Derian had accepted the position as Department of State coordinator for human rights and humanitarian affairs only after securing Deputy Secretary of State Warren Christopher's assurances that she would wield a good deal of political clout vis-à-vis other department bureaus. "I don't want to come here if you want a magnolia to make it look good," Derian told the deputy secretary. "I'm not going to come here if I'm going to lose every time." When Christopher asked if she had to win every battle, Derian responded, "No, . . . but I have to win most of them."[63]

Simply mastering the topography of the human rights landscape, however, proved a daunting task. On one level, Derian had to familiarize herself with the State Department's unique institutional culture, in which career foreign service officers typically looked askance at political appointees, and human rights advocacy in particular was widely considered peripheral—if not antithetical—to the interests of the U.S. diplomatic corps.[64] As one foreign service officer bluntly put it in February, "It doesn't help in the State Department to be for human rights. If you're concerned about it, you sort of get labeled a bleeding heart."[65] Recognizing that any significant exertion of influence within the department would require access to information, Derian began working to link her office into the flow of correspondence running between U.S. embassies overseas and the geographic and "functional bureaus" on the sixth floor of "New State," as political insiders referred to the lackluster, two-block building a short walk from the Washington Mall.[66] The department's seemingly myriad back channels and unwritten rules, however, proved an enduring obstacle, and in the opening months of the Carter presidency the Human Rights Office repeatedly became aware of foreign policy decisions with human rights implications only after a position had been drafted by the geographic bureaus and delivered to the secretary.[67]

On a deeper level, at the outset of her tenure Derian had little idea what activities the State Department human rights coordinator was supposed to perform, and as a result, much of her first month was spent in intensive study. Working fifteen hours a day, at times Derian struggled to maintain a healthy sense of perspective; on one occasion, after staying up late reading an Amnesty International report detailing electroshock torture of the gums, in the early hours of the morning Derian awoke terrified. "I ran my tongue over my teeth and they felt like they were all broken and fractured," she recalled years later. "I knew it was a dream but I couldn't shake the feeling." Later, thinking back on her first weeks as human rights coordinator, Derian concluded, "It was really total immersion in all the horrors of the world."[68]

From the outset of Derian's grim *tour d'horizon* of human rights violators, Argentina stood in the foreground. As Derian later remembered, "One of the first things I started learning was about Argentina and the unbelievably calamitous events there."[69] Moreover, as a result of Secretary Vance's reduction of FMS credits, from the outset of Derian's tenure at the department tension between Washington and Buenos Aires was high. The decision to reduce U.S. foreign aid had left Argentine military leaders "shaken, disappointed, and angry," Ambassador Hill reported, and in the face of the perceived threat of left-wing terrorism, Argentine military leaders deeply resented the U.S. refusal to accept their justification for "special tactics" and "final solutions."[70] The reduction rankled still further given the State Department's near-simultaneous refusal to reduce U.S. aid to South Korea and the Philippines—despite state-sanctioned human rights abuses—on geostrategic grounds. As the British Embassy in Buenos Aires noted, "Argentines concluded that their military aid had been cut not simply because of human rights violations, but because the Carter administration considered that Argentina was unimportant to boot."[71] Accordingly, less than a week after the announcement of the U.S. aid reduction, the military junta rejected the remaining $15 million earmarked for Argentina, on the grounds that "no state, whatever its ideology or power, can set itself up as a court of international justice, interfering in the domestic life of other countries."[72]

For Derian, such complaints rang hollow in the context of the military junta's systematic campaign of kidnapping, torture, and murder—a sentiment reinforced by the Amnesty International report on Argentina, released shortly after she arrived at the State Department.[73] With her extensive civil rights experience utilizing public criticism to shame transgressors into enacting improvements, Derian fully concurred with Rep. Robert. F. Drinan's call for a strong U.S. stance on human rights vis-à-vis the Argentine military junta. "By speaking out forcefully and consistently, we risk the temporary loss of influence in certain nations. But by failing to speak out, we risk the permanent betrayal of our most cherished principles," Drinan—who had served as a member of the Amnesty mission the previous November—told his congressional colleagues following the

report's release. Couching the issue in moralistic terms that Derian would subsequently echo almost verbatim, Drinan concluded, "Our human rights policy
must always concern itself with the question, 'What is most effective?' But we
must not permit that concern to obscure the even more important question,
'What is right?'"[74]

Accordingly, when the newly appointed assistant secretary of state for inter-
American affairs Terence Todman invited Derian to make an informal visit to
Argentina a mere three weeks after her appointment, Derian perceived the offer
as a personal challenge. A twenty-year veteran of the foreign service, Todman's
appointment had been heatedly opposed by liberal activists focused on Latin
America, who cited his limited experience in the region (two years as ambassador to Costa Rica) and scant evidence of an abiding concern for human rights.[75]
Moreover, Todman's subsequent resistance to human rights initiatives in Latin
America quickly garnered the assistant secretary a reputation for protecting
right-wing U.S. "clients" in Latin America; from the outset of the Carter administration, Todman's stewardship of ARA led the bureau to oppose Derian "on
almost every human rights issue affecting Latin America," recalled the policy
planning director Anthony Lake.[76]

In fact, Todman was *not* opposed to the notion of improving human rights
protection in Latin America, particularly Argentina. Rather, like many career
foreign service officers, although concerned by the reports of state-sanctioned
violence, Todman conceptualized the human rights policy as simply one of a
number of diplomatic issues under consideration by Washington and Buenos
Aires. "Our policy was not based on whether we approved or disapproved of the
Argentine government," recalled Fred Rondon, who worked closely with Todman
from his position as ARA deputy director, Office of East Coast Affairs. "ARA did
not accept the thesis that a single issue should govern all relationships with a
particular country," Rondon continued, since "there were other issues that had
to be discussed with Argentina."[77]

Moreover, like much of the Foreign Service Corps, Todman was also deeply
skeptical of both the stridency of Derian's human rights advocacy and her use of
the public arena to cast opprobrium on repressive regimes. "There were a number of people around who believed that the answer to everything was a great deal
of shouting. And it seemed to me that the consideration was what was going
to make them feel good," Todman recalled in a 1995 interview. He continued:
"And, quite frankly, I resented that, because my concern was suffering people
and I wanted to see things done that would ease the suffering. I recognized that
sometimes this is a whisper in the ear, sometimes it's a poke with your finger, it's
different things. And I don't think that it's possible to say that the same kind of
approach would work in every situation. And I found that in many cases there

were people who were not willing to be nuanced in dealing with the issues."[78] Thus although Todman considered himself a quiet supporter of human rights, his opposition to Derian's public approach and her overriding emphasis on human rights issues, combined with his strongly held belief that existing U.S. military and economic programs in Latin America should be maintained, made a confrontation with the human rights office all but inevitable.[79]

Indeed, for Derian, the extreme nature of state-sanctioned violence in the South American nation, coupled with her own struggle to gain institutional standing in Washington, overrode all other foreign policy considerations. Accordingly, despite feeling ill prepared to undertake a high-profile visit to Argentina, Derian immediately accepted Todman's invitation. "I didn't want to go because I didn't think I was ready," the human rights coordinator recalled years later, "but I realized that if I didn't I would make a terrible mistake within the bureaucracy."[80]

If Todman calculated that a visit to Buenos Aires would dilute the human rights coordinator's moralistic fervor, the plan backfired almost immediately. Derian's secret meeting with Ambassador Hill, clashes with U.S. military personnel, and the horrifying accounts of state-sanctioned violence voiced by relatives of *desaparecidos* galvanized the former civil rights activist. As a result, when she returned to Washington Derian played an active role in the State Department's April 1977 disapproval of a series of small arms sales to Argentina on human rights grounds, and by the end of May, the Human Rights Office was holding up virtually all new arms transfer applications earmarked for the military junta in Buenos Aires.[81]

* * *

As Derian's struggle to promote human rights in U.S.-Argentine relations intensified over the spring of 1977, Carter administration officials were hammering out an overarching policy framework for Latin America. The priority accorded the process no doubt reflected Jimmy Carter's personal interest in the region—arguably greater than any Cold War president since John F. Kennedy. In a striking shift from the anticommunism that had guided his predecessors' approach to Latin America, Carter recognized that U.S. Cold War policymaking had wrought damage throughout the region, and from the outset of his presidency he looked to Latin America as a potential showcase in his effort to chart a new path in North-South relations.[82] "The people of the Western Hemisphere share a common past and a common future," Carter told listeners in Caracas on Pan American Day in March. "As friends and neighbors we have an obligation to help one another, in order to promote our common good and to solve the problems of each nation, and advance our mutual interest in global solutions to problems that confront all of mankind."[83]

Carter's interest in Latin America was welcomed by Robert Pastor, the director of Latin American and Caribbean Affairs at the National Security Council. Not quite thirty years old when he was tapped by Zbigniew Brzezinski to join the NSC, Pastor was the former staff director for the Linowitz Commission, a bipartisan group founded in 1974 with the aim of integrating U.S. policy toward Latin American into a general North-South framework.[84] Echoing the commission's recommendations, "the idea of Latin America as a region is a myth [... because it is] composed of diverse nations with diverse economies," Pastor wrote Brzezinski in mid-March. "In terms of the objective realities," he continued, "we do not need a Latin American policy, and I hope that in the future, we will not have one."[85] Brzezinski concurred with Pastor's assessment, and at a top-level Policy Review Committee meeting on Latin America three days after Carter's Pan American Day speech, the National Security Adviser rejected the notion of a "special relationship" between the United States and Latin America as "ahistorical."[86] Underscoring the administration's commitment to redefine U.S.-Latin American relations along a less interventionist framework, Brzezinski asserted, "In the past, it has done nothing more than lock us into a cycle of creating unrealistic expectations and then having to live with the subsequent disappointments." The Monroe Doctrine, Brzezinski continued, "is no longer valid. It represents an imperialistic legacy which has embittered our relationships."[87] To promote healthier U.S.-Latin American relations, the National Security Adviser concluded, the United States needed to put its southern neighbors "on a more equal footing."[88]

The majority of the gathered assembly concurred with Brzezinski's call for a more global approach to Latin America, including top U.S. policymakers from State, Defense, the Joint Chiefs of Staff, the CIA, Treasury, the Arms Control and Disarmament Agency, Commerce, and the NSC—although both the Department of Defense and ARA openly lamented the decline of the U.S. "special relationship" with the region. Equally significant was the shared belief that the promotion of human rights could play a major role in shaping U.S. bilateral relations with the nations of the region. The consensus, Brzezinski subsequently wrote Carter, was to cultivate "warm relations with civilian and democratic governments, normal relations with nonrepressive military regimes, and cool but correct relations with repressive governments." The human rights policy, the group concluded, should be projected toward Latin America in the same manner as any other geographic region.[89]

Underscoring the importance Carter accorded U.S.-Latin American relations, the president detailed the committee's conclusions in a major foreign policy address at the Organization of American States on April 14. The United States, Carter asserted, would henceforth adhere to three guiding policy principles for the hemisphere: U.S. nonintervention; a willingness to work with Latin American leaders on global economic issues; and a commitment to promoting human rights and an expansion of democracy throughout the region.[90] Proudly mentioning that both he and his wife, Rosalynn Carter, were Spanish-language speakers and had visited Mexico and parts of Central and South America, Carter loftily concluded, "Simón Bolívar believed that we would reach our goals only with our peoples free and our governments working in harmony. I hope the steps I have outlined will move us toward those goals."[91]

Less than three months into the Carter presidency, the administration had thus laid the groundwork for a dramatic reshaping of U.S.-Latin American relations. Granted, the relative absence of pressing Cold War threats toward the region allowed Carter considerable diplomatic leeway; with the waning of Cuban attempts to foster *foco*-style agrarian revolutions in the hemisphere in the late 1960s, the muzzling of democratic socialists in the aftermath of the Chilean president Salvador Allende's brutal overthrow in 1973, and little chance of an alliance between any of the fifteen military regimes in the hemisphere and the Soviet Union, the Carter administration had a relatively free hand to formulate a new approach to hemispheric affairs.[92] Nonetheless, the unfurling of Carter's Latin America policy in 1977 reflected a degree of engagement in the region arguably unrivaled since the Alliance for Progress.[93] As one State Department official exulted, "We have dealt ourselves back into the game, politically, in the Western Hemisphere."[94]

Unlike the relatively rapid formulation of the Latin America policy, the Carter administration struggled through the late spring of 1977 to generate an overarching human rights policy. Following the precedent set by congressional human rights legislation, by mid-March the administration began augmenting exceptionalist rhetoric defining traditional U.S. heritage and traditions as the basis for the promotion of human rights overseas with an emphasis on upholding international agreements. "All the signatories of the U.N. Charter have pledged themselves to observe and to respect basic human rights," Carter told the United Nations General Assembly on March 19. "Thus no member of the United Nations can claim that mistreatment of its citizens is solely its own business. Equally, no member can avoid its responsibilities to review and to speak when torture or unwanted deprivation occurs in any part of the world."[95] Underscoring the importance the president attached to human rights, Secretary of State Vance subsequently cabled the text of Carter's UN speech to all U.S. diplomatic posts overseas.[96]

Throughout early 1977, however, Carter's emphasis on promoting human rights seemed to raise more questions than answers. "The world now knows that Jimmy Carter thinks human rights are important," Deputy Secretary of State Christopher wrote Cyrus Vance a few weeks after Carter's UN speech. Nonetheless,

Christopher continued, "Many—not just representatives of foreign governments and journalists, but also our own personnel—*do not* know what he means by 'internationally recognized human rights,' which human rights are to get priority U.S. attention, and what criteria we plan to apply in individual cases." Christopher recommended embracing more fully the internationalist—rather than exceptionalist—approach to the human rights issue by connecting Carter's policy more concretely within the protections afforded by articles 1, 55, and 56 of the UN Charter and the UN Universal Declaration of Human Rights.[97]

If Carter hoped to alleviate criticism of U.S. intervention in the domestic affairs of sovereign nations by linking the U.S. promotion of human rights to widely accepted international human rights charters, the administration would nonetheless need to articulate exactly which rights the United States should—or could—effectively encourage overseas. Indeed, the very elasticity of the phrase "human rights"—which had served Carter well during the 1976 presidential campaign—impeded the effort to formulate a clear and manageable policy in the first half of 1977. A general consensus on both sides of the political spectrum recognized that torture, political imprisonment, and murder constituted violations of individual human rights; defining—and defending—political liberty and socioeconomic rights, however, proved far more contentious. On one side, congressional hawks such as Senator Henry M. "Scoop" Jackson fiercely denounced the Communist world for political repression—particularly the Kremlin's refusal to provide emigration rights to Russian Jews. On the other, for decades the Soviets themselves had publicly censured the United States for failing to protect the social welfare of its citizens, a criticism not infrequently echoed in the 1970s by left-wing U.S. human rights groups. Having boldly set out to promote human rights abroad, in the tangle of competing demands the Carter administration now struggled to find its way; as one administration official grumbled, "You get into arguments about trade-offs: liberty versus having a job."[98]

Finally, the Carter administration faced a difficult decision regarding how far to cast the human rights net. As the discussions leading up to the March FMS credit reductions to Argentina, Ethiopia, and Uruguay had made clear, attempting to project a strident human rights policy beyond the world's worst offenders would garner fierce resistance throughout Washington's policymaking bureaucracy. Nonetheless, focusing solely on a country "hit list" would undoubtedly generate criticisms of inconsistency both at home and abroad. "It would not reflect the *universal* dimension of our policy—i.e., general concern for all rights everywhere and working with all nations," Christopher asserted to Secretary Vance. "And, it might be counterproductive—i.e., needlessly antagonize some nations, while giving others a free ride." Underscoring the challenges inherent in the issue, however, Christopher somewhat contradictorily admitted that the United States "would inevitably focus on some nations more than others."[99]

Compounding the Carter administration's difficulties were congressional efforts to extend human rights conditionality to U.S. votes on international financial institution (IFI) loans. In late March, during the House floor debate over a $5.2 billion authorization bill to the World Bank and the Asian and African Development Banks, human rights advocates Tom Harkin and Herman Badillo sponsored an amendment that would require U.S. representatives to vote against loans to any nation engaging in "a consistent pattern of gross violations of internationally recognized human rights."[100] Recognizing that the bill's passage would significantly limit the president's flexibility in the IFIs, the Carter administration quickly voiced its opposition, actively lobbying lawmakers on Capitol Hill that the amendment presented too "wooden an approach to the problems it addresses," and was inconsistent with Carter's belief "that the means for dealing with specific human rights issues must vary depending upon the circumstances of each particular situation."[101]

The Carter administration's effort to derail the congressional amendment stemmed at least in part from a belief that rigid legal constraints on the executive would limit the effectiveness of the human rights policy. As Warren Christopher advised Cyrus Vance in an interdepartmental memorandum, "Flexibility is in order—both for defining the *continuum* of countries of most concern to us and in discerning what approaches (public or private, bilateral or multilateral, symbolic or substantive, positive or reactive, etc.) could be most useful."[102] Nevertheless, on Capitol Hill and in much of the elite media, Carter's opposition to the measure seemed uncomfortably similar to Henry Kissinger's emphasis on "quiet diplomacy," generating scuttlebutt in the press that the Carter administration was backing away from a central campaign promise. "It may be unintentional, but with all the President's talk about human rights," Harkin griped to the *Wall Street Journal*, "the first time the measure comes up the administration's trying to retreat."[103]

Far worse than none-too-subtle comparisons with the Ford administration, despite the Carter team's efforts the Badillo amendment successfully passed in the House on April 6. By all accounts, it was an ugly defeat for the president; after initially opposing any human rights provision in the IFI bill, the administration had belatedly supported a less-stringent alternative authored by the House Banking Committee chairman Henry Reuss (D-WI), who proposed replacing the mandatory vote in the IFIs with a requirement that the United States merely seek to direct assistance to regimes with positive human rights records. In the lead-up to the vote, no fewer than four top administration officials—Zbigniew Brzezinski, Warren Christopher, Terence Todman, and Patricia Derian—were drafted into lobbying on behalf of the Reuss amendment, and President Carter himself appealed to lawmakers in a personal letter.[104] House members, however, refused to yield—in fact, adding insult to injury, Badillo invoked Carter's own human rights rhetoric to support the bill's passage: "If we should now retreat," he asserted during the two-hour floor debate, "it would be a signal to the world that the words of President Carter have no meaning."[105]

Strong executive lobbying ultimately resulted in Senate passage of a significantly watered-down version of the original bill. The bruising battle in the House, however, clearly demonstrated the limits of Carter's influence over a Congress adamantly resurgent in the realm of U.S. foreign policymaking. Indeed, although Carter's "outsider" status had contributed in no small part to his successful bid for executive office, by largely eschewing traditional party politics, the former Georgia governor arrived in Washington with relatively little clout over congressional Democrats—a situation made more difficult thanks to intraparty rivalries and an increasing dispersal of legislative power beyond the once-dominant committee heads.[106] More to the point, the Carter administration's rearguard effort to head off the Badillo amendment revealed the lack of a clear executive policy that could shift the momentum of human rights promotion from Capitol Hill to the White House. As Zbigniew Brzezinski informed the president on April 13 regarding the upcoming IFI debate in the Senate, "We face a real dilemma: while we don't like any of the amendments, we must voice support for the more flexible amendments . . . or we will appear to be weakening our strong human rights position."[107]

Accordingly, in an effort to bolster his human rights credentials, Carter significantly ratcheted up the human rights rhetoric in a commencement speech at Notre Dame University on May 22. Evocatively dressed in the traditional cap and gown, complete with the purple and gold cowl symbolizing an honorary doctor of law degree, and accompanied by human rights leaders from Rhodesia, Brazil, and South Korea, the president explicitly rejected previous administrations' Realpolitik approach to Cold War policymaking.[108] The United States, Carter declared, was "now free of that inordinate fear of communism which once led us to embrace any dictator who joined us in that fear." Having lost its moral bearings in the struggle to contain Soviet expansionism, Carter continued, the United States had adopted "the flawed and erroneous principles and tactics of our adversaries, sometimes abandoning our own values for theirs," an approach painfully evident in the "intellectual and moral poverty" of the Vietnam War.[109] By contrast, Carter asserted that his own administration had "reaffirmed America's commitment to human rights as a fundamental tenet of our foreign policy." As a result, "we can already see dramatic, worldwide advances in the protection of the individual from the arbitrary power of the state," Carter concluded. While ignoring this pattern would result in the dissipation of U.S. global influence and moral authority, "to lead it will be to regain the moral stature that we once had."[110]

Hailed by human rights advocates as a watershed moment in the effort to institutionalize human rights in U.S. foreign policy, Carter's Notre Dame speech constituted an eloquent rhetorical rejection of the Cold War consensus that had dominated U.S. foreign policymaking over the course of the previous quarter century. Compared to its predecessors, the Carter administration, the journalist Bernard Gwertzman asserted shortly after Carter's Notre Dame speech, was "more idealistic, more open, more moralistic, and more willing to compromise with the developing countries."[111] And, underscoring Carter's assertion that "in the life of the human spirit, words are action," the text of the president's speech was sent by cable to all U.S. diplomatic posts accompanied by a message from Secretary of State Vance requesting that U.S. ambassadors "continue to give human rights matters your personal attention."[112]

If Carter's lofty rhetoric at Notre Dame successfully regained moral high ground lost in the fracas surrounding the Badillo amendment, it did little to settle the debate over which human rights the United States intended to promote, and how the effort would be integrated into U.S. foreign policy. That task fell to Secretary Vance. Having served for nearly two decades in the upper echelons of Washington policymaking, Vance emerged as a staunch supporter of Carter's emphasis on human rights as a centerpiece of the administration's effort to reconnect with traditional U.S. values in foreign policy—particularly as part of the effort to reshape relations with the Third World.[113] A consummate diplomat, Vance preferred avoiding the public spotlight when engaging in human rights diplomacy. "We will speak frankly about injustice both at home and abroad," he told reporters in January 1977. "We do not intend, however, to be strident or polemical," he continued, "but we do believe that an abiding respect for human rights is a human value of fundamental importance and that it must be nourished. We will not comment on each and every issue, but we will from time to time comment when we see a threat to human rights, when we believe it is constructive to do so."[114]

Spurred on by the president, Vance offered a more comprehensive definition of the U.S. human rights policy in a commencement address at the University of Georgia School of Law on April 30. Echoing the recommendations of the Department of State Policy Planning team, Vance outlined three basic human rights that the Carter administration intended to promote: first, the right to be free from government violation of the integrity of the person—i.e., torture, arbitrary arrest or imprisonment, and denial of habeas corpus; second, economic and social rights, including food, shelter, health care, and education; and third, civil and political rights, including "freedom of thought, of religion, of assembly; freedom of speech; freedom of the press; freedom of movement both within and out-side one's own country; [and] freedom to take part in government."[115] Although Vance admitted that the most significant human rights advances would most likely be achieved in combating violations of personal integrity, the secretary emphasized that all three rights were recognized by the Universal Declaration of Human Rights, and would all be included in the Carter administration's human rights policy.[116]

Significantly, in sharp contrast to Carter's declaration at his inauguration that the administration's commitment to human rights would be "absolute," in his Law Day address Vance emphasized the need for a case-by-case approach to human rights issues. Underscoring the need to "be realistic," the secretary me-thodically listed no fewer than sixteen questions that would need to be addressed in each human rights case in order to accurately assess the nature of the human rights violations, the prospects for successful U.S. action, and how that action would fit within the broader pattern of U.S. diplomacy. "In the end, a decision whether and how to act in the cause of human rights is a matter for informed and careful judgment," Vance pragmatically concluded. "No mechanistic formula produces an automatic answer."[117]

Although it established a rough foundation for the Carter administration's human rights advocacy, Vance's Law Day speech left the final shape of the policy far from clear. As the *Washington Post* noted shortly after Vance returned from Georgia, "We read the Secretary's words as the attempt of a good lawyer to refine and focus a presidential position. That position is a courageous and valuable one but, at the moment, it seems to mean something a bit different to each person who hears it."[118] Indeed, a lack of consensus in Washington on how the United States should approach the human rights issue continued to impede the formula-tion of a clearly defined policy throughout the second half of 1977. Underscoring the challenge human rights presented U.S. policymakers, after reviewing a draft of a Policy Review Memorandum (PRM) on human rights authored by Warren Christopher's special assistant Steven Oxman, Anthony Lake complained to the deputy secretary in late June that the document failed to provide "a clear consen-sus on what we mean by human rights or a clear sense of where differences exist." Citing a cleavage within the department between those who favored Vance's em-phasis on promoting all three basic human rights and supporters of a policy focusing entirely on crimes against the security of the person, Lake emphasized the need to clearly identify "that philosophical and practical divergence."[119]

Moreover, U.S. policymakers struggled to outline the relationship between human rights policy and broader foreign policy goals. "What will pressing for [the] promotion of human rights mean in the short- and long-term for cer-tain bilateral relations, security interests, dealings with the Congress, etc.?" Lake wrote Christopher after reviewing the PRM draft. "Conversely, how might a well-managed human rights program in fact reinforce goals in the North-South dialogue?"[120] If Oxman left such key questions unanswered, it was not due to the PRM's brevity—underscoring the challenge human rights posed for U.S. policymakers, by the end of June the draft version had already ballooned to 127 pages. "Whew! Why hadn't I signed up for the President's speed reading course?" the policy planning staff member Sandy Vogelgesang quipped to Lake after she finished reading the draft. Noting that the PRM's original goal was to formulate "specific programs for action," Vogelgesang concluded, "The document has grown like Topsy—to the extent many may never read what should be considered a significant point of policy reference."[121]

The lack of consensus among policy planners at State and at the NSC on the role human rights should play in U.S. policy proved a major obstacle in the effort to establish a clear set of guidelines. It was not until February 17, 1978—more than a year after entering the Oval Office—that Carter issued a presidential directive (NSC-30) mandating human rights as a "major objective of U.S. foreign policy."[122] Underscoring the lack of policy guidelines, shortly before Carter signed NSC-30, Zbigniew Brzezinski informed the president that the human rights policy "lacks the necessary solid intellectual base." The "frustration" of the PRM exercise, Brzezinski continued, "provided excellent evidence of the need for basic research on the varieties of human rights and on the most effective means of promoting human rights in diverse social and cultural contexts."[123] More concretely, without a clearly defined human rights policy, in the latter half of 1977 U.S. policymakers came to rely on the general outline of the U.S. human rights policy presented by Cyrus Vance in his Georgia Law Day speech; Carter's presidential directive on the subject was little more than a reiteration of the secretary's broadly construed emphasis on promoting the protection of individual integrity, economic and social rights, and political liberties. As the congressional staffer on arms control and foreign policy Caleb S. Rossiter later asserted, "Rather than acting as a starting point for the formulation of policy," Vance's speech "came to represent the policy itself."[124]

* * *

The absence of a detailed set of policy guidelines impeded Patricia Derian's effort to institutionalize human rights in U.S. foreign policy and contributed to mounting resistance to the Human Rights Office throughout the Washington bureaucracy. Given that the primary mission of the geographic bureaus was to maintain a close working relationship with their foreign counterparts, from the outset an assertive human rights office was bound to raise the hackles of career diplomats. As an early congressional study pointed out, "Rather than offering to the regional bureaus potential benefits that could facilitate bilateral relations—such as economic or security assistance programs or food aid—the human rights operation promoted a series of efforts that would, for the most part, complicate and strain bilateral and multilateral relations."[125] Dubbed "clientitis syndrome" by human rights advocates, the geographic bureaus' resistance to Derian's human rights initiatives had shifted into high gear by mid-1977. "The desk officers think of their countries as clients," one Senate staff member griped to a journalist, "and their attitude is: 'Don't insult my client.'"[126]

The initial tension between the Human Rights Office and the geographic and functional bureaus was exacerbated by Derian's nonconformist style of leadership and the uncompromising nature of her human rights advocacy. Derian's office, recalled Laurent E. Morin, a career foreign service officer who worked with Derian, "was the most relaxed one I have ever been in." Morin continued, "She was very informal. Everyone was approachable, you just walked in the door. Everyone was on a first name basis."[127] On one occasion, the EA assistant secretary Richard Holbrooke inadvertently sent a response to a human rights memo to "Patrick Derian." "With great enthusiasm," remembered the foreign service officer Kenneth Rogers in a 1997 interview, Derian took a green pen and wrote on the memo, "Try the Irish embassy. No Patricks here," and returned it to Holbrooke. "I thought that was a great show of charm and good humor," Rogers concluded.[128]

If Derian's management style garnered extraordinary loyalty from her subordinates in the human rights office, her strident advocacy on behalf of human rights engendered intense antipathy throughout the department. Derian was described as a "bully" and "idiotic," and her efforts to promote human rights "blunt, undiplomatic, and even hysterical."[129] More concretely, Derian was widely perceived by the Foreign Service Corps as a liberal activist rather than a diplomat. As John Bushnell, then serving as the senior deputy secretary in the Latin America Bureau, recalled in a 1997 interview:

> The problem I had with Derian and with the other human rights activists was that they were driven much more by making sure that our human rights actions were seen by their domestic constituencies and that strong human rights precedents were set than with progress in a particular country. I had sort of a foreign constituency that I was focused on, trying to get progress on human rights performance. They were much more domestically focused in making sure that their domestic constituency saw that human rights was driving our policy toward Country A, so visibility drive became more important than accomplishment drive.[130]

Similarly, the foreign service officer Paul M. Cleveland described Derian as a "strong liberal, if not a radical," who was "well remembered for the fervor with which she pursued human rights violations—actual and alleged." According to Cleveland, Derian's approach was so polemical as to hinder effective decision making. "I can remember meetings chaired by Warren Christopher," Cleveland recalled, " . . . when he would have to ask Derian to restrain herself, particularly when she advocated actions that may have seemed justified from her human rights' point of view, but would have caused severe damage to US interests in some foreign country."[131]

Derian's status as a Washington outsider further exacerbated tension with career foreign service officers, who accused the human rights coordinator of projecting a one-dimensional view of foreign affairs that failed to account for the multiplicity of U.S. interests abroad. On one level, Derian's limited knowledge of Latin American history and culture were roundly criticized. News correspondents covering one of Derian's visits to Argentina were "struck somewhat dumb by her unique analogies," the syndicated columnist Georgie Ann Geyer asserted in a representative critique. According to Geyer, Derian told the assembled group that the United States was going to "force" the Argentines to observe human rights, "just like we did in Mississippi." When one of the journalists skeptically asked Derian, "And where is the Supreme Court?" Derian admitted that it was a "good question," then proceeded to draw questionable comparisons between the Argentine working class and blacks in South Africa living under the apartheid system. "Virtually all of the strengths and weaknesses of Carter's human-rights policies in Latin America are incorporated in that all-too-typical exchange," Geyer subsequently wrote, "idealism, total self-confidence, self-righteousness, an absence of any historic understanding and . . . an appalling ignorance."[132]

On a deeper level, foreign service officers recoiled from Derian's abrasive approach to human rights advocacy, which was widely interpreted in Foggy Bottom as detrimental to the overarching effort to maintain close working relations with foreign governments. Instead, career diplomats such as Bushnell advocated the use of "quiet diplomacy"—raising the human rights issue with foreign leaders in private—as the most effective means of eliciting human rights improvements and maintaining diplomatic ties. By contrast, Derian, Bushnell recalled, preferred the "bully pulpit."

> It was impossible to convince her that one would get better human rights improvements . . . by quiet diplomacy than with going public and making a lot of noise and condemning the leadership. She said to me once, "You can't get anywhere negotiating with the devil." I pointed out that I had spent years at the NSC with Kissinger who spent a majority of his time negotiating with North Vietnam, China, and Russia. All I thought qualified as devils, even on human rights grounds. I thought

> Kissinger had made quite a bit of progress although not every negotia-
> tion was a success. She replied that human rights was not what he was
> negotiating.[133]

Like the majority of U.S. Foreign Service officers, Bushnell thus criticized Derian's strident rhetoric and preference for public forums to cast opprobrium on
human-rights-violating regimes as antithetical to the maintenance of smooth
diplomatic relations and rarely successful in eliciting policy changes.

For Derian, such criticism sidestepped the central issue: that Kissinger's "quiet
diplomacy" was in effect shorthand for U.S. diplomatic silence on human rights
issues. Without question, Derian's understanding of Latin American history was
limited. Regarding Argentina, for example, on one occasion Derian admitted to
having no knowledge of Spruille Braden's 1946 effort to prevent Juan Perón's election as president—arguably the nadir of U.S.-Argentine relations prior to Jimmy
Carter's election.[134] That Derian would have benefited from a stronger sense of
Latin American history and culture is undeniable; it is worth noting, however,
that in the late 1970s the same could be said for the bulk of the State Department—and the Washington bureaucracy in general—in regard to the international human rights charters to which the United States was a signatory. Indeed,
one former staff member of the Bureau of Human Rights recalled feeling a sense
of shock during a conversation with a career foreign service officer when she realized that the individual had never heard of the Nuremberg war crimes trials.[135]

More to the point, for Derian, criticism of her approach to the promotion
of human rights as overly assertive failed to address the central issue: that it was
her congressionally mandated responsibility to demonstrate U.S. concern over
human rights violations. In this endeavor, there was no room, in Derian's view,
for the cautious, discrete lexicon of traditional diplomacy. "All countries say that
they are great defenders of and believers in human rights," Derian asserted at
a 1978 congressional conference. "Refusing to admit a systematic violation of
human rights," Derian continued, "they explain their crisis, which threatens their
society, and next say that as soon as they get on the other side of this crisis they
will begin to observe human rights again, but during this interval it is necessary
for them to take extraordinary measures." Derian continued:

> Then I talk respectfully about what they mean by extraordinary mea-
> sures. There is ordinarily a great breakthrough because I use the word
> "torture" in places where this is applicable and it is applicable in far too
> many places. I talk about the specific kinds that they do, the names of
> places where people are detained, the names of people who are missing,
> the names of people who are no longer in detention . . . who have suf-
> fered various kinds of abuses and mistreatment.

Then we come to a kind of reality facing. Mostly an explanation that they are not responsible, that we have to understand things are so terrible and intense in the place that people at a lower level are moved by their own overriding emotions to take these actions on their own. Then I talk about responsibility. If you hold high office you must take the full responsibility and the blame. Then we generally start all over again and go through the whole thing again. That is generally the end of the first encounter.[136]

From Derian's perspective, the fulfillment of the responsibilities vested in her position thus necessarily entailed eschewing "quiet diplomacy" and instead adopting a forthright approach that unmistakably indicated U.S. awareness and condemnation of human rights violations.

By mid-1977, the focal point for bureaucratic infighting between the Human Rights Office and the geographic bureaus centered on the Interagency Group on Human Rights and Foreign Assistance. Commonly referred to as the Christopher Group, the body was an outgrowth of informal meetings between Warren Christopher and representatives from the geographic and functional bureaus—particularly the Human Rights Office—that began in February 1977 to discuss specific actions on foreign aid proposals.[137] Recognizing that the administration would face many issues involving the "interrelationship between human rights and our foreign assistance program," in early April Zbigniew Brzezinski had suggested that Vance formalize the process by establishing an interagency group "to examine our bilateral and multilateral aid decisions as they relate to human rights, to provide guidance regarding specific decisions on bilateral and multilateral loans and to ensure proper coordination of a unified Administration position."[138] Concurring with Brzezinski's request, Vance promptly asked the deputy secretary to serve as coordinator.[139] Christopher agreed—though not without some reservations: "The answer is yes—(but I am not sure an inter-agency group is necessary or desirable, but will be glad to head up if Secy [Secretary] thinks it is inevitable)," he responded.[140] Accordingly, in early May the Christopher Group convened with representatives in attendance from numerous State Department offices and bureaus, as well as the departments of Treasury, Defense, Agriculture, Commerce, Labor, the NSC, and the Export-Import Bank.[141]

With its focus on human rights and foreign assistance—rather than U.S. foreign policy as a whole—the Christopher Group's impact on the broader contours of U.S. policy planning was constrained from the outset. With little U.S. foreign assistance directed to the Communist world, the Human Rights Office necessarily focused its efforts on sanctioning right-wing authoritarian regimes with reprehensible human rights records. The Carter administration's geostrategic considerations further constrained the office's room to maneuver, effectively insulating most of the Middle East from U.S. foreign assistance limitations on human rights grounds and providing fodder for the assistant secretary of state for East Asian and Pacific affairs (EA) Richard Holbrooke's fervent resistance to human rights sanctions toward South Korea or the Philippines.

As a result, in addition to limited initiatives in sub-Saharan Africa, the majority of the Human Rights Office's advocacy on the Christopher Group came to focus on Latin America, a region dominated by repressive right-wing military regimes that, at the outset of the Carter presidency, appeared unlikely to move into the Soviet camp. Predictably, the seemingly inordinate emphasis on hemispheric affairs brought swift protest from the Latin America Bureau. "There's certainly an argument that if you have a human rights policy that's dominant it ought to be decisive in all countries," John Bushnell recalled. "But of course it can't be decisive in all countries, because in some countries you have other interests that are much more dominant and therefore you're not going to pay as much attention to human rights." The Human Rights Office emphasized Latin America, Bushnell concluded, "because they couldn't get anywhere with Eastern Europe or the Middle East."[142]

Corresponding with the narrowing of the Human Rights Office's geographic scope, fierce bureaucratic resistance over the course of 1977 led to a dramatic reduction of the Christopher Group's purview. Perceiving the group as infringing on her bureaucratic turf, by threatening to resign the undersecretary of state for security assistance Lucy Benson successfully gained exemption from the Human Rights Office's oversight for the two largest U.S. aid programs: military assistance (cash, credit, and grant transfers of arms and training) and Security Supporting Assistance (cash, grants, and loans geared toward nations facing major economic challenges). Although the Human Rights Office could appeal military aid and security decisions to Warren Christopher by way of its membership on the Arms Export Control Board and its subsidiary, the Security Assistance Advisory Group, Benson's success in limiting the purview of the Human Rights Office established a precedent that was successfully emulated by the Department of Agriculture regarding food export programs. More significantly, thanks to the lobbying efforts of the assistant secretary of the treasury G. Fred Bergsten, the International Monetary Fund (IMF)—the largest and most powerful international financial institution—won exemption from the Christopher Group as well.[143]

The activities of the Export-Import Bank (Exim) and the Overseas Private Investment Corporation (OPIC) also eluded regular appraisal by the Christopher Group. Both agencies were designed to assist U.S. corporations, the former by insuring commercial transactions that would otherwise deter private sector investors and providing low-interest export financing, and the latter by insuring

U.S. corporations in the developing world against expropriation, currency in-convertibility, and loss due to political unrest.[144] Although congressional human rights law required the Eximbank to take human rights into account beginning in October 1977, and covered OPIC the following year, Warren Christopher in-terpreted the law "to allow programming in countries violating human rights if it either benefited the needy or was not channeled through the government of that country." Accordingly, only in exceptional cases would the Christopher Group review programs involving the two agencies.[145]

The spate of exemptions left only one major channel of U.S. assistance within the Christopher Group's purview: the multilateral development banks (MDBs), an assortment of international financial institutions (IFIs) that had been a focal point of congressional legislation during the Ford administration linking U.S. votes in the institutions to human rights.[146] In a bitter irony for the Human Rights Office, in the overall spectrum of U.S. foreign aid, the United States had the least amount of control over the MDBs; although voting power was distrib-uted according to economic strength, the United States had only marginal sway over other voting members.

Finally, Christopher's decision-making process impeded the establishment of a clear set of guidelines on which human rights cases would be decided. A quiet supporter of the human rights initiative, Christopher had worked closely with Cyrus Vance during the Johnson administration and enjoyed the full trust and confidence of the secretary of state. Christopher "was strong and imperturbable under pressure," Vance later wrote, "with a keen, analytic mind and a selflessness all too rare in government."[147] In particular, Christopher's willingness—and ability—to examine complex issues from multiple perspectives quickly garnered the reserved North Dakota–native a reputation in Washington. Christopher was "the kind of lawyer you'd like to be your wife's divorce lawyer," Representative Charlie Wilson (D-TX) would later tell a journalist with his usual aplomb, "al-ways seeing the other side, always going the extra mile."[148]

When the task of coordinating foreign assistance and human rights unexpectedly fell into his lap, Christopher characteristically established a case-by-case decision-making approach, allowing the deputy secretary to decide each case on its own merits. Correspondingly, Christopher elected to open the Group to a broad constituency of interested parties, including State Department geographic and functional bureaus and the National Security Council, as well as the Departments of Agriculture, Commerce, Defense, Labor, and Treasury.[149] Despite the unwieldy number of participants, Christopher placed a premium on the ability to hear a variety of opinions. "I have a lot more confidence in my own judgment after I've heard a disparate group of people," he later asserted.[150]

Although demonstrating the deputy secretary's desire to examine the complexity of each case individually—and earning Christopher the nickname "Mr. Human Rights" in the process—significantly, the case-by-case approach failed to establish human rights precedents that could be integrated into subsequent policymaking. As Patricia Derian succinctly put it, "I never really understood Christopher's mode of decision."[151] Indeed, the inability to predict Christopher's rulings, coupled with the size of the body—between twenty-five and forty participants convened at each meeting—accentuated intra- and interdepartmental tension and hamstrung cooperation between competing bureaus; in the resulting "tennis match" the Human Rights Office and the geographic and functional bureaus came to rely on almost-identical arguments at successive meetings, leading one weary participant to wryly suggest that the opposing factions "save time by simply numbering their standard arguments and calling them out during deliberations."[152]

Despite the Christopher Group's shortcomings, reviews of the IFIs provided the Human Rights Office with an important venue for advancing human rights in U.S. foreign policy. By September 1, the Christopher Group had reviewed fifty-six loans over the course of five meetings, and had recommended six U.S. abstentions, along with twenty-three démarches emphasizing the need for human rights improvements to avoid U.S. censure. Moreover, the prospect of a U.S. "no" vote resulted in ten additional loans being withdrawn or delayed by human rights violators.[153] Without question, such victories for Patricia Derian's office constituted very small steps in the effort to institutionalize human rights in U.S. foreign policy. By the same token, the very existence of the Christopher Group constituted a major shift from the almost-total dismissal of human rights that had characterized the Kissinger era; and, more broadly, the deputy secretary's willingness to sanction human-rights-violating regimes overseas—although indisputably limited—nonetheless indicated an emphasis on human rights unprecedented in U.S. foreign policy during the post–World War II era.

In the face of widespread bureaucratic resistance, such piecemeal victories for the Human Rights Office underscored the support Derian enjoyed in the White House and on Capitol Hill in the opening months of the Carter presidency. First, Jimmy Carter's own advocacy over the course of 1977 demonstrated a clear commitment to human rights. In mid-June, Carter decided to hold the swearing-in ceremony for Derian at the White House, an unmistakable show of support for her efforts on behalf of human rights. "It's a bit unusual to have a White House ceremony for that level appointment," the veteran foreign service officer Frank Sieverts told a journalist. "I think it is a testament to the President's commitment to human rights."[154] Indeed, during the ceremony, Carter described the human rights coordinator as "a very major position" in the U.S. government. The president also praised Derian's civil rights activism, asserting that "there were just a few people in our part of the country in years gone by who had the deep commitment and the intense demonstration of courage to be almost alone in a community and say the time has come for the black people of our region to have a chance to vote, to own property, to hold a job, to go in public places, to be educated on an equal basis with whites." Patricia Derian, the president concluded, "was one of those very rare people who had the commitment and the courage to do so."[155]

More concretely, although Carter's closely watched efforts to promote human rights in U.S. relations with the Soviet Union during his first six months in office failed to bear fruit, the president achieved notable, if largely symbolic, successes in Latin America.[156] On June 1, Carter signed the Inter-American Convention on Human Rights at a gathering of the Organization of American States, and, thanks to the administration's lobbying efforts, the convention went into effect in July.[157] A corresponding high-level trip to Latin America by the First Lady reflected a clear preference for regional democracies—including Jamaica, Costa Rica, Venezuela, and Colombia—or, as in the case of countries such as Peru and Ecuador, nations recognized as undergoing a transition from military rule to democracy.[158] Additionally, by early fall the president had expressed strong support for congressional ratification of the Genocide Convention and the Covenant against Racial Discrimination, and had signed both the International Covenant on Civil and Political Rights, and the International Covenant on Economic and Social Rights—international documents that the United States had refused to endorse for almost a decade.[159]

Second, Derian benefited from strong allies on Capitol Hill and among nongovernmental human rights advocates. Nine months after the human rights coordinator arrived at the Department of State, congressional human rights advocates led by Donald M. Fraser (D-MN) successfully passed legislation elevating the Human Rights Office to the bureau level, promoting Derian to the position of assistant secretary of state at the Bureau of Human Rights and Humanitarian Affairs (HA). Mandating an increase in Derian's staff and resources and requiring full-time human rights officers be appointed in each of the State Department bureaus, the legislation dramatically enhanced Derian's clout in the department and integrated the Human Rights Office more fully into the diplomatic information flow.[160] Most significantly, the congressional legislation provided HA with the bureaucratic "standing" to partake in all decisions on U.S. security assistance and, in the event of a disagreement with the geographic or functional bureaus, to use the human rights provisions of the Harkin Amendment (section 502B) as a legal basis to elevate the issue to Secretary of State Vance, who made a decision based on "action memoranda" drafted by all interested bureaus.[161] "HA is continuing to approach most human rights disputes with the bureaus as negotiations in which it pays to go high so that when the dispute is resolved by 7th floor principals, HA at least gets half a loaf which is better than none," Steven Oxman later wrote Warren Christopher. "This approach," he added, "drives the bureaus up the wall."[162]

Corresponding with strong congressional support, Derian found a particularly valuable ally in Mark Schneider, whom she hired as deputy coordinator. A former Peace Corps volunteer in El Salvador, Schneider had acquired extensive experience in human rights advocacy as a staff member for Senator Edward Kennedy (D-MA). Brushing aside his disappointment at not being chosen for the coordinator position, Schneider proved an invaluable member of the fledgling Human Rights Office, balancing Derian's hard-nosed advocacy with an insider's knowledge of the policymaking process and extensive contacts on Capitol Hill among the press and within the nongovernmental human rights community.[163] Indeed, in the face of fierce bureaucratic resistance, Schneider viewed such "backstairs lobbying" as a necessary tactic to ensure the Human Rights Office's continued existence. Not surprisingly, utilizing informal channels to advance HA's interests only added to the geographic bureaus' antipathy toward Derian's office. Backstairs lobbying, combined with HA's aggressive emphasis on action memorandums, Oxman wrote Christopher, "drives the regional bureaus from the wall to the ceiling."[164]

Finally, at the State Department, the effort to institutionalize human rights received support from Cyrus Vance. "Vance was a great help to me," Derian recalled. "I met with him pretty regularly and he was wonderful."[165] Although preferring private rather than public negotiations over human rights, and emphasizing the need for a case-by-case decision-making process, the secretary believed that "a nation that saw itself as a 'beacon on the hill' for the rest of mankind could not content itself with power politics alone. It could not properly ignore the growing demands of individuals around the world for the fulfillment of their rights." As Vance later recalled in his memoirs, he felt strongly that "These aspirations were producing new or strengthened democratic institutions in many nations, and that America would flourish in a world where freedom flourishes." Underscoring his commitment to human rights, by October 1977 Vance had reportedly broached the human rights issue with more than eighty leaders.[166]

* * *

By the fall of 1977, the Carter administration had made the promotion of human rights in U.S. foreign policy a core objective. Indeed, Jimmy Carter's embrace of human rights had played a decisive role in the one-term Georgia governor's successful bid for the White House, and Carter's continued association with the issue bolstered the president's popularity throughout his first year in office. "Of our numerous foreign policy initiatives," his adviser Hamilton Jordan wrote the president in December, "it is the only one that has a broad base of support among the American people and is not considered 'liberal.'"[167]

More significantly, Carter could claim notable successes in the effort to institutionalize human rights in U.S. foreign policy. The administration's high-profile advocacy on behalf of human rights had created an enormous impact on popular and governmental awareness of the relationship between human rights and foreign policy. As Amnesty International's David Hawk later asserted, "Anyone who worked in the field of human rights before Carter became president can appreciate the difference he makes." Carter's approach, Hawk continued, "made human rights a front-ranking issue in international affairs. That in itself is Carter's primary contribution to the promotion of international human rights."[168] Similarly, in testimony before the House Subcommittee on International Relations in late October, Mark Schneider asserted that the promotion of human rights "is no longer a stranger to the front pages of newspapers across the globe," with the result that repressive governments were beginning to "weigh the costs of repression for the first time." Underscoring the dynamic shift from the Cold War focus of previous administrations embodied by Carter's human rights policy, Schneider concluded, "For too long we had become identified with regimes which denied human rights, rather than with the victims whose rights were violated. Now I believe this new policy helps to return us to a position of leadership, one which is in conformity with a more traditional perception of the United States as a nation that received and welcomed two centuries of dissidents."[169]

By the same token, the lack of a clear set of guidelines on the role human rights should play in U.S. foreign policy, coupled with the intense resistance HA's initiatives generated throughout the Washington bureaucracy, made it clear that the struggle to institutionalize human rights would be long and bitter. Ten months after the Carter administration took office, Derian was still clamoring for greater involvement in high-level meetings with foreign officials. "I think she is feeling a bit frozen out," Steven Oxman wrote Warren Christopher in October 1977. "My impression is that HA needs about all the bureaucratic help it can get."[170] A few months later, the veteran diplomat Lars Holman Hydle captured the mood at the annual awards presentation of the American Foreign Service Association by informing the assembled listeners that the members of the Human Rights Bureau regarded "criticism of the human rights policy or caveats about its implementation as bordering on immorality or disloyalty to the Administration." In an unmistakable allusion to McCarthyism, Hydle acidly concluded, "It is difficult to have a serious conversation with someone who thinks you are immoral, and we hoped we had seen the last of demands, implicit or explicit, for 'positive loyalty.'"[171]

For Derian, such criticism masked the geographic bureaus' close ties with human-rights-violating regimes. By autumn, the assistant secretary had established a firm foothold within the State Department, and had no intention of retreating. "It boils down to an intra-building struggle," Derian told the Washington Post in late October. "Some parts of the bureaucracy say our concern for human rights will pass," Derian continued. "But they are going to have to think again."[172]

In the coming months, Argentina, in particular, would serve as the defining test case for Derian's effort to promote human rights in U.S. foreign policy. In a fitting denouement to the intense period of learning and adjustment that characterized Derian's initial months at the State Department, the human rights coordinator returned to Argentina for a second visit in mid-August. With a new-found knowledge of human rights advocacy forged in hundreds of internecine bureaucratic struggles over the previous five months, Derian's meetings with Argentine officials pushed the boundaries of diplomatic propriety. Fred Rondon, who accompanied Derian on her visit, recalls having to physically restrain Derian during her August 10 conversation with the minister of interior, General Albano Eduardo Harguindeguy:

> I will never forget the moment during the conversation when Patt and the Minister [of Interior] . . . seemed about ready to stand up to trade blows when both interpreters put their hands on their respective boss' shoulders; it was an instinctive reflex action by both of us to try to stop matters before they really got out of hand. Then the conversation continued. I must say that Derian was not afraid to call "a spade a spade"; she was very clear about her views—even to the point of being undiplomatic. There was no question about her dedication to human rights.[173]

Derian was similarly unequivocal in her meeting with the de facto president and junta member General Jorge Rafael Videla.[174] "He told me years later that he'd never been spoken to by anybody, let alone a woman, like she spoke to him," John Bushnell recalled. "Had it been a man, he would have challenged him to a duel on the spot."[175]

By far the most heated exchange, however, occurred during Derian's meeting at the Escuela Mecánica de la Armada (Naval Mechanics School [ESMA]) with the junta member Admiral Emilio Eduardo Massera, a known "hardliner" linked to extensive extralegal violence. Dismissing Massera's claim that Argentina was in the process of normalization, Derian bluntly changed the subject. "Let's talk about the bottom floor of this building," she began. "Yes, it's a big building," the admiral responded blandly. "It's also a place of torture," Derian bluntly asserted. Taken aback, Massera quickly denied the charge, but Derian was undeterred. "I know that you are torturing people there, downstairs," she repeated, and when

Massera continued to deny any complicity in extralegal violence, the human rights coordinator upped the ante. "Well, you give me a piece of paper and I'll draw a diagram," she told Massera. "I'll outline every room and what happens in it." It was a brazen gamble; in mid-1977 Derian had little knowledge of the inner workings of the ESMA. Yet Massera was apparently taken in; after a pause, the admiral smiled and gestured as if washing his hands. "Well, you remember the story of Pontius Pilate," he concluded.[176]

After meeting with Argentine officials, U.S. Embassy personnel, and Argentine human rights advocates, Derian returned to Washington with an unshakeable certainty that stronger U.S. economic and military sanctions on the Argentine military junta were needed in order to curtail extralegal violence. Whether HA's highly visible advocacy could induce improvements in the protection of human rights in the South American nation, however, was by no means clear. On the one hand, for much of Washington's policymaking elite and the business community, the policy shift represented by Derian's well-publicized human rights advocacy reflected a major—and unwanted—rupture with the previous three decades of U.S. Cold War foreign policy toward Latin America. Indeed, less than a week after Derian's visit to Argentina, the ARA bureau chief Terrence Todman made his own official visit to the South American nation. After a round of talks with Argentine officials and human rights groups, Todman emphasized the progress the military junta had achieved—an unmistakable divergence from Derian (and a development widely publicized in the Argentine press).[177] Todman returned to Washington advocating strong U.S. support for Argentina's perceived military moderates, led by Jorge Videla.[178]

Similarly, exemplifying the widely felt skepticism regarding the Carter administration's human rights policy rooted in three decades of close U.S.-Argentine military ties, when the Argentine delegate to the Inter-American Defense Board (IADB) asserted in mid-March that the initiative threatened to drive a wedge between the United States and its allies and thus create opportunities for Communist expansion in the hemisphere, U.S. Lt. Gen. (Ret.) Vernon Walters agreed wholeheartedly, responding, "Let's hope that this will not last long." Although conceding that the intentions of the human rights advocates were "understandable," Walters, who had served as deputy director for Central Intelligence for most of the Nixon and Ford administrations, nonetheless asserted that "reality is reality. And the idea that friends can be changed into enemies is for them [the Communists] a very attractive concept."[179]

On the other hand, the Carter administration's limited leverage over the Argentine military junta ensured that eliciting human rights improvements from Buenos Aires would be no easy task. Without question, the military junta exhibited a "strong desire for understanding from the U.S. and a sense of frustration and confusion as to why the U.S., whom they regard as the leader of the free world, does not openly applaud Argentina's efforts against Marxist expansion," reported Lt. Gen. Gordon Sumner, chairman of the IADB, following a formal visit to Argentina in mid-April. Nonetheless, Sumner ominously concluded, "It was equally clear, that the GOA is determined to continue its fight against subversion with or without U.S. support."[180]

5

ON THE OFFENSIVE

Human Rights in U.S.-Argentine Relations, 1978–1979

In the fall of 1977, a tall, gregarious junior foreign service officer hailing from west Texas arrived at the U.S. Embassy in Buenos Aires. Selected to serve as the embassy's external affairs officer, Franklin A. "Tex" Harris had attended briefings in Washington, DC, on issues such as nuclear proliferation, Argentine actions in the United Nations, and the disputed Falkland/Malvinas Islands. Shortly after his arrival in Argentina, however, Harris was asked if he would switch positions with the embassy's internal affairs officer, whose basket of assignments centered on monitoring the status of human rights. Lacking expertise on the issue, Harris agreed to the change on one unprecedented condition: that ordinary Argentines be allowed to enter the U.S. Embassy to report acts of political violence. Recognizing the importance of firsthand testimony, the ambassador approved the request, and Harris soon found himself at the forefront of the embassy's effort to penetrate the layers of secrecy surrounding the Argentine military junta's dirty war against perceived subversives.

Operating in the Western Hemisphere's worst human rights violator, Tex Harris had little guidance on how to fulfill the responsibilities of a largely untested position. Consequently, he focused his energies on meeting three overarching goals: "to know what is going on, to be responsive, and to report accurately." It was a task to which the convivial diplomat was uniquely suited. As the embassy's political counselor later wrote, "Harris meets people easily, impresses them indelibly, seeks them repeatedly—all the while expanding his circles of friendship and acquaintance to the point that his professional and personal contacts are enormous."[1] Indeed, in succeeding months, Harris would establish an extraordinary web of sources, including hundreds of relatives of victims, members of the international press, and human rights advocates in Argentina and the United States.

As a result, the volume and incisiveness of Harris's human rights reporting made the U.S. Embassy in Buenos Aires unique among U.S. diplomatic posts overseas, and constituted a crucial element in Assistant Secretary of State for Human Rights and Humanitarian Affairs Patricia Derian's struggle to curtail U.S. economic and security assistance to the Argentine military junta. Indeed, in late 1977 and 1978 the Human Rights Bureau (HA) spearheaded an extensive U.S. effort to convince the military junta to end its brutal campaign of extralegal violence. Culminating in the successful U.S. orchestration of a formal visit to Argentina by the Inter-American Human Rights Commission (IACHR), Derian's advocacy constituted a remarkable shift from the previous quarter century of U.S. Cold War policy.

Advances in the human rights arena, however, came at a heavy cost. Although Harris's willingness to investigate Argentine state-sanctioned violence and his irrepressible energy in documenting grim discoveries endeared him to human rights advocates, from the outset of his tenure in Buenos Aires Harris encountered fierce resistance from his foreign service colleagues. In the face of accusations that he was "grandstanding" and failing to be a "team player," by mid-1978 Harris had become a virtual pariah in the embassy. Similarly, in Washington, Patricia Derian's effort to cast international opprobrium on the Argentine military junta confronted enormous opposition from much of Washington's byzantine bureaucracy, U.S. business leaders, and top-ranking members of the Carter administration.

* * *

Of the thousands of Argentines who passed through one or more of the 364 clandestine concentration camps, the U.S. Embassy in mid-1977 was aware of only a tiny fraction. Nonetheless, by the time Harris took up residence in Buenos Aires, the basic characteristics of the military's countersubversive campaign were clear to U.S. Embassy personnel. Thousands of *desaparecidos*—"disappeared persons"—were being "sucked up" (*chupado*) by the ruling military junta's unbridled campaign to eradicate perceived subversives.[2] Kidnapped by groups of heavily armed men, victims were driven bound and blindfolded in one of the Argentine security forces' ubiquitous Ford Falcons to a clandestine detention facility. At such sites, the torturers and guards operated with almost total impunity, and detainees endured frequent torture sessions and extreme privation. "You don't exist," one victim recalled his torturers repeating on a daily basis. "We are everything for you. We are justice. We are God."[3]

Few *desaparecidos* reappeared, and for thousands of Argentines the extraordinary cruelty of the military government's dirty war was the simple inability to determine the fate of victims. Police and military officials refused to provide information regarding abductions, and writs of habeas corpus were scrupulously ignored by government officials. Moreover, with the exception of the English-language newspaper the *Buenos Aires Herald,* a combination of government repression and self-censorship stifled press reporting on military human rights abuses. More broadly, in the immediate aftermath of the March 1976 coup, the military had emasculated the legislative and judicial branches of government—disbanding the Congress, purging the Supreme Court, and replacing the prosecutor general and the majority of federal judges.[4] Denied the pillars of civil society, relatives of *desaparecidos* had little legal recourse. "In less than one year a whole family has disappeared," one Argentine mother grieved in late 1977. "Nobody has told me what they are accused of, or where they are. I don't know if they are sick, if they are being tortured, if they are alive or dead." Capturing the peculiar sense of anger and helplessness felt by family members of *desaparecidos,* she concluded, "If they are prisoners, I know that this horror of misinformation and doubts is one of the weapons employed by the government of my country in this so called 'war' in which the lists of arrested people are not made public."[5]

At a political level, it was clear to U.S. Embassy officials that for Argentine military hardliners, the National Reorganization Process—referred to by Argentines simply as *el Proceso*—was predicated on a radical vision of Argentina's role in the Cold War. Rooted in a deep tradition of nationalism and conservative Catholicism, combined with French and especially U.S. Cold War doctrine, by the mid-1970s military leaders had developed a radical vision of Argentina's central role in the global anticommunist struggle. As the navy commander (and junta member) Admiral Eduardo Emilio Massera told listeners on May 15, the roots of left-wing terrorist violence in Argentina lay in the thirty-year third world war against the "destructive gospel of totalitarianism." Rising moral indolence had left the Western world, "intoxicated with indifference," Massera continued, leaving Argentina on the front line of a grim struggle with global ramifications. The following day the Argentine Marine Corps commandant took a similar, albeit less colorful approach. "It's either them or us," he bluntly declared to a U.S. Embassy official.[6]

Moreover, it was evident that the members of the Argentine military junta were united in their support for harsh counterterrorist tactics.[7] Although the postcoup division of political power between the armed service chiefs had exacerbated a decades-long intraservice struggle—particularly between the army and the navy—in the fight against left-wing terrorism, "there appears to be no dispute," the U.S. Embassy concluded in June. Granted, the de facto president and army commander Jorge Rafael Videla had acknowledged "excesses in repression by the forces of order," in the local press, leading the U.S. Embassy to speculate that the general imparted a restraining influence that was ameliorating human rights abuses by security forces.[8] Such thinking was tempered, however, by clear indications of Videla's own expansive notion of counterterror; in December 1977, the characteristically taciturn general informed journalists that "a terrorist is not only someone who kills with a gun or plants bombs, but anyone who encourages their use by others through ideas contrary to our Western, Christian civilization."[9]

Most significantly, by the time Harris arrived U.S. Embassy officials clearly recognized that the quotidian horror of the National Reorganization Process was proceeding unabated. "In general, the methods adopted by the security forces in the anti-subversive campaign remain arbitrary and harsh," an embassy cable asserted in June 1977. "Persons continue to be abducted by armed men claiming to be police and military officials. Families are rarely or only belatedly informed about the whereabouts and status of their detained relatives." Although the military junta's decision to divide the nation into military zones had created dozens of mini-fiefdoms run by local commanders with significant autonomy, extralegal repression was no longer being carried out by right-wing terrorist cells operating without official oversight. "The security forces appear to have assumed complete control of the counter-terrorism effort," the embassy concluded, "and the military government must be considered fully responsible for internal security efficiency and practices."[10]

As the embassy liaison for human rights issues, Harris immediately set out to establish a broad base of contacts. Able to deal with people "with extraordinary skill and without tiring," as a State Department evaluation later asserted, Harris expanded his pool of sources dramatically over the summer and fall of 1977.[11] In addition to establishing a strong working relationship with the official organs of the Argentine government—particularly the Argentine Ministry of the Interior, the Ministry of Foreign Affairs, and the navy—Harris met regularly with members of the international press and organized lunch gatherings with representatives from other embassies. Meeting in a cavernous Portuguese restaurant named the Basque, where the limited risk of eavesdropping Argentine security personnel compensated for mediocre cuisine, the diplomats traded information on human rights cases of international interest and worked to keep abreast of the evolving political situation on the ground.[12]

Significantly, Harris also established strong ties with Argentine human rights advocates, particularly Emilio Fermín Mignone, whose daughter Monica had been abducted by state security forces the previous May. A lawyer by training,

Mignone had spent half a decade in the United States while working at the Organization of American States and later served as founding rector of a university in Lujan, Argentina.[13] Like many relatives of *desaparecidos,* for months following their daughter's disappearance, Mignone and his wife had desperately sought to ascertain her whereabouts through official channels. Outraged by continuous bureaucratic stonewalling, Mignone joined the Permanent Assembly for Human Rights, where by mid-1977 he had risen to a position of leadership. From his vantage point at the Permanent Assembly, Mignone was thus in a unique position to gauge the extent of human rights violations in Argentina, and he quickly became one of Tex Harris's most trusted sources.

Harris also made contact with the Madres de Plaza de Mayo (Mothers of the Plaza de Mayo), a group of Argentine women whose children were among the *desaparecidos.* Despite the Argentine military's ban on political organizing, at great personal risk the Madres had begun weekly marches in the plaza—directly in front of the presidential palace—in April 1977, both to share information with one another and to draw public attention to the military junta's human rights violations. Dismissed by the Argentine military officials as *las locas* (the madwomen), the Madres were one of the few visible signs of popular protest against the military's campaign of state-sanctioned violence. "When everyone was terrorized we didn't stay at home crying—we went to the streets to confront them directly," Madres member Aída de Suárez recalled. Capturing the women's irrepressible courage, Suárez concluded, "We were mad but it was the only way to stay sane."[14]

With government repression stifling nearly all forms of civil dissent, blanket censorship of the press, and an emasculated judicial system, Harris immediately recognized the importance of obtaining testimony from members of the Madres. Visiting the plaza during the Mothers' weekly gathering, Harris handed out dozens of business cards carrying his name and embassy office number and informed the women that the U.S. Embassy would offer assistance in petitioning the Argentine government to disclose the whereabouts of their children.[15]

The effort to obtain data from relatives and friends of *desaparecidos* quickly bore fruit, and the corridor outside Tex Harris's office was soon crowded each afternoon from two to four o'clock with Argentines waiting to offer testimony on disappeared loved ones.[16] Within a few months, Harris was receiving dozens of reports. "The number of people who will actually come to the American Embassy to report a disappearance must be fairly small," Harris acknowledged in a missive to Washington in mid-1978. "However," he continued, "it does speak well as an indication that our policy is really understood and known to the population here in Argentina."[17]

Extensive firsthand testimony also provided Harris with a unique source of data with which to gauge the extent of state-sanctioned violence in Argentina. To manage the rising influx of cases Harris implemented a system in which his assistant, Blanca Vollenweider—an Argentine citizen working at the embassy—would meet with victims' family members to record personal information and the circumstances surrounding the disappearance, after which Harris would enter to discuss the case in greater detail. In this manner, "each of the innumerable visitors are seen," Harris later wrote, describing himself as "shuttling back and forth between rooms like a busy dentist."[18] Expediting his meetings with Argentine visitors not only increased the number of individuals from whom Harris could receive testimony; drawing on Vollenweider's eye for organization, Harris established a card-file system on each human rights case, thus creating a unique data set with which to analyze the breadth and depth of state-sanctioned human rights violations in Argentina.[19]

Simply responding to human rights inquiries arriving on a daily basis from Washington, however, required a daunting amount of Harris's attention. "The congressional letters were absolutely flooding the Department and each letter had to be answered," recalled Fred Rondon, then serving in the State Department as the Bureau of Inter-American Affairs (ARA) deputy director, Office of East Coast Affairs. "Often there was a stock answer because you could only say so many things about an individual who had disappeared, but very often you also had to acknowledge receipt of the letter and send an inquiry to the Embassy in Buenos Aires. And of course we were flooding them with requests for information."[20] As a result, in his first nine months in Buenos Aires, Harris answered hundreds of "special interest" inquiries from U.S. citizens regarding Argentines caught up in the military junta's counterinsurgency net, as well as roughly 150 pieces of congressional correspondence pertaining to human rights.[21] "It is an impossible position in terms of workload—the 'in-box' has become the 'in-drawer,'" Harris later admitted in a State Department evaluation. "Lack of time and energy—physical and emotional—become daily tests of self."[22]

Nonetheless, Harris managed to churn out a prodigious volume of human rights reporting, drafting dozens of cables to Washington each month. Moreover, drawing on a growing array of contacts, Harris was able to provide Washington with near–real time reporting on human rights unrivaled among U.S. embassies. In the effort to track the flow of violence, daily testimony from relatives of *desaparecidos* proved particularly valuable. "We were producing weekly 'temperature charts,' as we called them," Harris recalled years later, " . . . showing to Washington a graphic depiction of the repression, based on what the people who came to the Embassy told us." By late 1977, Harris's remarkable understanding of the human rights situation in Argentina made his policy recommendations into the foundational reference for deliberations on bilateral and multilateral aid decisions on Argentina by Deputy Secretary Warren Christopher's interagency group—including decisions on international financial institution (IFI) loans to Argentina, Export-Import Bank transactions, and security transfer requests. "As usual I reiterate my request for more frequent human rights roundups," Rondon wrote Harris in early 1978. Underscoring the importance of Harris's reporting, Rondon concluded, "There's no other way to inject order into the human rights information monster."[23]

* * *

By the time Tex Harris's memorandums on human rights began to filter into the State Department in the fall of 1977, the bureaucratic struggle to define the nature of U.S. policy toward the Argentine military junta was in full swing. With the United States required by congressional legislation to take human rights factors into consideration on votes in the Inter-American Development Bank (IDB) and the International Bank for Reconstruction and Development (IBRD), throughout the late spring and summer of 1977 Patricia Derian's Human Rights Office had looked to the IFIs as a key source of leverage for eliciting human rights improvements in Argentina. Indeed, the Argentines' acute sensitivity to U.S. IFI actions appeared to demonstrate that a carefully calibrated U.S. voting policy could advance U.S. interests in the human rights arena; when Ambassador Hill informed the Argentines in September 1976 (without then-Secretary of State Kissinger's approval) that the Harkin Amendment's human rights provisions made it unlikely that the U.S. could support future loans to Argentina in the IDB that did not support the needy, the military junta quietly withdrew certain loans, including a $30 million loan for industrial credits in December.[24] Three months later, the U.S. representative to the World Bank board elicited an "angry reaction" from the Argentine delegate by making a statement on human rights regarding a $105 million highway project in the IBRD. Underscoring the Argentines' sensitivity to U.S. economic sanctions, despite the U.S. vote in favor of the loan, the Argentine official bitingly accused the United States of politicizing the IFIs.[25]

Despite apparent Argentine responsiveness to initial U.S. economic actions on human rights grounds, Derian's effort to harness the IFIs as a means to systematically sanction the military junta elicited sharp resistance from her colleagues on the Christopher Group. Notwithstanding a consensus that the situation in Argentina was deplorable, along with a "grudging agreement that something should be done," according to Steven Oxman, the group's meeting on May 18 revealed an "undercurrent of great dissatisfaction with the whole idea of seeking to implement human rights through the IFIs." Underscoring the key position of Argentina in the overall development of the administration's human rights policy, Oxman, Warren Christopher's special assistant for human rights issues, emphasized that the question of how to deal with economic assistance to Argentina brought the United States to "the Rubicon on the question of whether we really mean to seek to implement our human rights policy in part through the IFIs."[26]

In the resulting debate, battle lines were drawn in the State Department between HA and the geographic and functional bureaus that would remain largely unaltered for the duration of the Carter administration. The Latin America Bureau—like the vast majority of the State Department as a whole—sought to avoid a major showdown over human rights with any of its foreign counterparts, including Buenos Aires. In late May, for example, an ARA memorandum admitted that "we may wish to oppose these loans if the Argentines force them to a vote." Revealing the diplomatic corps' overriding emphasis on maintaining smooth relations abroad, however, the memo added, "It is not in our or the GOA's interest to provoke an open confrontation. Rather our approach should be to attempt to persuade the Argentines to postpone those loans which give us the most difficulty."[27]

By contrast, for Derian, the IFIs provided a key means to cast international opprobrium on the Argentine military junta, potentially extracting human rights concessions in the process. Warren Christopher's decision on a June IBRD industrial credits loan seemed to substantiate Derian's position; when the Argentine political counselor was informed that the United States intended to abstain on the loan based on the human rights situation in Argentina, he immediately "asked if it was too late for Argentine developments to influence [the] U.S. vote." The U.S. response—emphasizing the need to halt disappearances, end the use of torture, publish a list of all government-held prisoners, implement habeas corpus, and reinstate the "right of option" allowing individuals held without charges under the state-of-siege provisions to opt for voluntary exile—revealed just how far the Carter administration had moved away from the traditionally warm U.S. Cold War policy toward anticommunist Latin American military regimes. And although the military junta balked at U.S. demands for political normalization, Buenos Aires *did* enact a small number of much-publicized steps to improve its human rights image abroad. While "the initiative is hollow from the substantive side," the U.S. Embassy noted the following week, it was nonetheless "interesting and encouraging in what it demonstrates about rising Argentine bureaucratic sensitivity concerning the seriousness of the U.S. human rights position."[28]

Nonetheless, Christopher's decision to abstain on the IBRD loan raised hackles throughout the foreign service bureaucracy. "The human rights people are getting pretty uppity these days, and they're sitting on a bunch of things," one unnamed U.S. official told the *Christian Science Monitor* in late June. Imbued with a moralistic zeal antithetical to the art of diplomacy, the official continued, Derian and her supporters "live in a sort of separate world from the rest of the State Department."[29] Such resistance to linking human rights to the IFIs was not limited to Washington bureaucrats. The U.S. decision to abstain on the June IBRD loan to Argentina garnered sharply critical responses from nearly all the voting members of the World Bank board. IBRD decisions, the Dominican Republic's representative hotly asserted following the U.S. statement of abstention, "is not the appropriate forum for the discussion of issues other than economic and financial ones." The Dutch, Indian, and Egyptian delegates concurred; capturing the mood, the Egyptian delegate informed his U.S. counterpart that "although human rights are important, discussing them could lead the Board into an unhelpful debate."[30] As anticipated, despite the U.S. abstention the loan was approved. Nonetheless, the board members' criticism of the decision clearly demonstrated the limits to U.S. moral suasion in the international sphere, raising the ire of human rights sympathizers at the State Department. "By their 'rationale,' loans to Nazi Germany would have received *pro forma* approval so long as they were economically viable," Oxman angrily wrote Christopher. "Somewhere the line has got to be drawn."[31]

Exactly where the line should be drawn in U.S.-Argentine relations, however, proved an enduring challenge for U.S. policymakers over the course of 1977. Corresponding with the debate over U.S. votes in the IFIs, a hotly contested dispute flared up in the summer between Patricia Derian's office and the geographic and functional bureaus over U.S. military assistance to the Argentine junta. The previous year, congressional lawmakers had successfully added section 502B to the Foreign Assistance Act of 1961, asserting that "except in extraordinary circumstances, the President shall substantially reduce or terminate security assistance to any government which engages in a consistent pattern of gross violations of internationally recognized human rights."[32] Whereas the Ford administration had offered almost-total resistance to the legislation, under Carter the Human Rights Bureau was included in all decisions on security assistance, primarily through membership on the Arms Export Control Board and its subsidiary, the Security Assistance Advisory Group. Significantly, HA could formally oppose security assistance transfer cases, thus elevating the case in question to Secretary of State Vance's office for resolution based on action memorandums drafted by each interested party.[33]

From the outset of Carter's tenure, Argentina was recognized as a particularly egregious human rights violator. Indeed, less than two months after entering the Oval Office, Carter had made a clear showing of disapproval of the military junta in Buenos Aires by slashing Foreign Military Sales credits to Argentina from $32 million to $15 million, and by mid-1977, nearly all arms transfer requests from Buenos Aires were being rejected on human rights grounds. Nonetheless, to avoid locking the executive into a restrictive policy framework, the administration avoided formally designating Argentina—or any other nation—as a gross violator of internationally recognized human rights under section 502B. Accordingly, like the Christopher Group's review of IFI proposals, security assistance transfer cases were reviewed by the deputy secretary on a case-by-case basis—resulting in a series of clashes between Derian's office and both the Bureau of Inter-American Affairs and the Security Assistance Bureau, and leaving the administration vulnerable to criticism that the human rights policy lacked consistency and coherence.

The contentious nature of security assistance cases was particularly evident regarding a proposed $15 million sale of eight Bell-Textron UH-1H helicopters to the Argentine military junta. According to Bell-Textron, a division of the Fort Worth–based Textron Corporation, the sale was purely commercial, with two of the helicopters intended for use by the Argentine executive and the other six for Antarctic exploration. Accepting Bell-Textron's emphasis on the commercial nature of the transaction at face value, ARA offered strong backing for the sale, while also opining that in light of the growing number of recently denied security assistance transfer cases to Argentina, "a limited goodwill gesture will demonstrate a token of faith that the Argentine armed forces will turn the human rights situation around." Likewise, the Bureau of Political and Military Affairs (PM) gave the proposal a green light, noting that although the helicopters would be equipped with machine-gun mounts and armor plating, "almost any helicopter can be armed, but this does not make it an efficient weapon in an urban environment."[34]

At the Bureau of Human Rights and Humanitarian Affairs Patricia Derian strongly objected to the sale, arguing that the Argentine government's human rights violations warranted an unconditional U.S. refusal. Barring an outright rejection, HA recommended authorizing only two armor-plated helicopters (to be used by the Argentine executive) and removing the machine-gun mounts from all eight. Additionally, in light of evidence from the U.S. Embassy that Argentine security services were utilizing helicopters in antisubversive operations, Derian proposed making the sale contingent on the military government's assurance that the vehicles would not be used for internal security.[35]

HA's strident resistance to the sale brought the under secretary of state for security assistance Lucy Benson into the debate. Citing nuclear nonproliferation as the most important U.S. objective vis-à-vis Argentina, Benson recommended that the United States sell the helicopters according to HA's prescription, minus the assurances. "We do not need assurances for what amounts to a commercial transport helicopter to justify the sale on the Hill," Benson wrote Cyrus Vance. "And we risk a good deal, particularly on non-proliferation, for a marginal return, since we have no way of verifying compliance of any assurances we might be given."[36]

Caught in the cross fire of competing demands, Warren Christopher struggled to reach a compromise that would be consistent with the broader human rights policy. As Stephen Oxman noted on August 20, "To urge the Argentines to withdraw IFI loan applications, while at the same time permitting them to buy American helicopters without making any commitment to us as to their intended use, sends very mixed messages." By the same token, denying the sale would have little more than symbolic value; similar aircraft were readily available on the European market, and an Argentine delegation's conspicuous attendance at a Paris aircraft exposition in June clearly indicated that the South American nation was not dependent on U.S. imports. Moreover, lobbying by Senator Lloyd Bentsen Jr. (D-TX) and Representative Jim Wright (D-TX) ensured that an outright rejection of the proposed sale would spark criticism on Capitol Hill that the Carter administration's human rights policy was hurting U.S. manufacturers.[37]

Seven weeks after the State Department began reviewing the proposed sale, on September 3, 1977, the Argentine ambassador Jorge A. Aja Espil received Warren Christopher's decision: the Bell-Textron sale would be approved. No machine-gun mounts would be included, however, only two helicopters would include armor, and assurances that the machines would not be used in counterinsurgency operations would be required.[38] Despite reflecting the deputy secretary's best effort to find a middle ground between the competing voices on the case, the Argentine government's response—curtly informing the United States that it could "forget the sale"—elicited a predictably angry reaction from proponents of the transfer.[39] "While I understand and applaud the Administration's concern with human rights, I sincerely question whether the six aircraft in question would be used to infringe [on] the rights of the Argentine people," Senator Bentsen asserted to Cyrus Vance in early October. Not only were the majority of the aircraft intended for use in the Antarctic, Bentsen concluded, but the very premise of the Carter administration's attempt to link the sale to human rights was flawed. "While it is theoretically possible that the helicopters could be used to transport political prisoners," Bentsen concluded, "the same arguments could be used to bar the sale of a truck or taxicab to Argentina."[40]

For Patricia Derian, Christopher's decision—and the subsequent Argentine refusal—marked a small yet not insignificant victory for the embattled Human

Rights Bureau. Indeed, not only had Derian's office played a critical role in linking the proposed transfer to section 502B, but there was strong evidence belying Bell-Textron's claim to the U.S. government that the majority of the helicopters would be utilized in the Antarctic. At the eleventh hour of deliberations on the case, Stephen Oxman came across a previously overlooked cable from Bell-Textron noting that all eight helicopters were expected to spend a considerable amount of time flying over Buenos Aires. More disconcerting for human rights advocates was the provision, buried in the proposed contract, that Bell-Textron "assist the Buyer in making ammunition boxes, support mounts and electrical connections needed for the installation immediately of a flexible machine gun on each side of the [six non-executive] Helicopters," as well as deliver detailed plans on the helicopters' armament electrical system.[41]

Nonetheless, repeated lobbying by the Human Rights Bureau to institute a full embargo on U.S. sales to Argentina failed to bear fruit. Despite being sympathetic with Derian's effort to institutionalize human rights in U.S. foreign policy, Warren Christopher concurred with the undersecretary of state for security assistance on the impracticality of across-the-board sanctions on the Argentine military junta. "An embargo is strong medicine—if applied to Argentina, why not others?" Benson asserted in a memorandum to the deputy secretary on September 20. "Consistency may be the hobgoblin of small minds," Benson concluded, "but there will be strong domestic political pressure to be even-handed."[42]

More broadly, despite the weeks of wrangling over the proposed Bell-Textron sale, Christopher's case-by-case approach ensured that the decision would not provide a precedent for subsequent arms transfer proposals. Instead, the absence of a clearly defined set of ground rules for decisions on U.S. security assistance to Argentina opened the administration to domestic political pressure of a different kind: special-interest lobbying on behalf of U.S. manufacturers. In September, the Speaker of the House Thomas P. O'Neil Jr. (D-MA) and Representative Silvio R. Conte (R-MA) wrote Secretary Vance emphasizing the importance of a proposed $4.4 million sale of submarine periscopes to the Argentine Navy from the Massachusetts-based firm Kollmorgen. The sale, the congressmen asserted, "will mean a great deal to the local economy which is suffering from high unemployment. Kollmorgen is a vital key to the recovery of the area."[43] Moreover, submarine periscopes were hardly tools of internal security, Edward W. Brooke (R-MA) informed Undersecretary Benson. Since the submarines would not be delivered for five years, Brooke added, "it is difficult to envision the nature of the regime that will be in power in Argentina then."[44]

Similarly, a proposed $24 million sale of three Boeing Vertol helicopters to the Argentine Air Force also brought heavy, bipartisan lobbying from the

Pennsylvania contingent on Capitol Hill, including the Republican senators Richard S. Schweiker and Henry J. Heinz III, and House Democrats Robert W. Edgar and Gus Yatron.[45] Noting the high unemployment affecting Pennsylvania's Delaware County, and emphasizing that two recently lost bids on Department of Defense contracts had resulted in layoffs of two thousand employees over the past year and a half, the Pennsylvania Congressional Delegation Steering Committee informed Cyrus Vance that "if approval of the Argentine orders is not forthcoming, Boeing Vertol will be forced to suspend its helicopter production line, and to lay off more highly skilled workers who would be difficult to rehire because of their job opportunities in other sections of the country."[46]

In both the Kollmorgen and Boeing Vertol cases, concerted lobbying efforts had a major impact on State Department decision making. As one department official admitted to the *Washington Post* regarding the proposed Boeing transfer, "You have no idea of the pressure."[47] Indeed, Warren Christopher alluded to the influence of the domestic political lobby in his recommendation to Secretary Vance that both cases be approved. "They are non-concessional, they are arguably 'non-lethal,' and they have considerable Congressional support from sensitive quarters," Christopher wrote.[48] Vance concurred with his deputy secretary, approving the sales on November 3.[49]

Despite such concessions to domestic political interests, top officials in the Carter administration took an active role in promoting human rights in U.S.-Argentine relations over the fall of 1977. During consultations with Latin America leaders in Washington regarding the impending Panama Canal Treaty, Jimmy Carter personally emphasized the importance of human rights with the de facto president and junta member General Jorge Rafael Videla. Although human rights advocates subsequently criticized Carter for meeting with the heads of the hemisphere's worst human-rights-violating regimes, in fact, in his meeting with Videla, Carter firmly sought to elicit promises from the Argentine leader of pending advances in the protection of human rights.[50] In a particularly dramatic show of support for the work of nongovernmental human rights advocacy groups, Carter informed Videla that a list of roughly 3,500 human rights cases had been compiled by the Argentine Committee on Human Rights in Washington. Although admitting that the U.S. government could not vouch for the accuracy of the list, Carter nonetheless asserted that "it was of concern to the U.S." and would be delivered to the Argentine foreign minister the following month.[51]

In addition to emphasizing human rights concerns, by meeting with Videla, Carter hoped to send a clear message of support for perceived military "moderates" in Argentina who seemed to hold the promise of eventual political liberalization. Although U.S. intelligence analysts recognized that Videla brooked no opposition to severe measures against alleged leftist subversives, in comparison with strident advocates of indefinite military rule guided by harsh repression, such as Generals Carlos Suárez Mason and Luciano Menéndez, or military populists such as Admiral Massera, Videla appeared to U.S. policymakers as cautiously working to conciliate fierce inter- and intraservice strife while charting a moderate path.[52] Indeed, in a meeting with President Carter shortly after Videla's departure, Secretary Vance's handwritten notes underscored the U.S. effort to support Argentina's military moderates. "Hope that strength of V[idela]'s gov[ernmen]t will lead to action in H.R. [human rights] field," the secretary scribbled on White House stationery.[53]

Carter's meeting with Videla initially appeared to be an important step toward Argentina's normalization. In what Carter described as "one of the most productive and most frank discussions I've had with any leader," the Argentine leader promised to accept a formal fact-finding visit from an international human rights group. Videla also pledged that Argentina's detainee problem would be resolved by Christmas.[54] "President Videla was very frank with me about pointing out the problems that have existed in Argentina and his commitment to make very rapid progress in the next few months," Carter told reporters after the meeting. "He wants Argentina to be judged not on his words alone, but on the demonstrable progress that he stated would be made."[55]

Moreover, by the end of month, Videla's meeting with Carter seemed to have bolstered the Argentine leader's institutional standing vis-à-vis Argentine hardliners. In a White House memo to the president on September 29, the national security adviser Zbigniew Brzezinski asserted that the visit to Washington had "enhanced the image of Argentina, as well as Videla." According to U.S. intelligence, Brzezinski continued, "one result of Videla's diplomatic success is that it will permit him to continue with his policy of a slow, but sincere, effort to reestablish human rights in Argentina."[56]

Finally, Carter's meeting with Videla facilitated a series of subsequent top-level diplomatic communications regarding human rights. In addition to the delivery of the list of human rights cases on October 12, Carter personally wrote Videla on November 3 to remind the Argentine leader of his promise to achieve significant progress by the end of the year. Carter also sought to engage Videla in personal diplomacy; when the Argentine leader sent Carter a selection of recordings by the Buenos Aires chamber ensemble La Camerata Bariloche, Carter responded with a personal thank-you note.[57]

More concretely, the Panama Canal meeting paved the way for a formal visit to Argentina by Secretary of State Vance in November. On a tour of South America that included stops in Brazil and Venezuela, Vance arrived in Buenos Aires flanked by Patricia Derian and the ARA chief Terrence Todman.[58] In separate meetings with the members of the Argentine military junta, Secretary

Vance clearly underscored the importance the Carter administration placed on the protection of human rights; speaking with Admiral Massera, for example, Vance firmly asserted that "the only way to restore [U.S.-Argentine] military cooperation would be to resolve the human rights problem."[59] In an unmistakable show of support for the State Department's Human Rights Bureau, Vance also presented his hosts with an expanded list of individuals allegedly missing or imprisoned by state security personnel.[60] Although the secretary of state informed the Argentine military leaders that he could not verify the accuracy of the list—containing 7,500 names compiled by the Argentine Commission on Human Rights and signed by representatives of numerous nongovernmental human rights organizations—he informed his hosts that "excesses committed in combating terrorism cannot be justified."[61] Last, Vance reiterated U.S. support for human rights advocates in Argentina by hosting representatives from the Permanent Assembly for Human Rights at the U.S. Embassy.[62]

Over the course of fall 1978, top U.S. policymakers thus took an active role in promoting human rights in Argentina. In comparison with preceding administrations' Cold War policy toward the South American nation—and indeed, Latin America as a whole—Carter's attention to human rights in Argentina embodied a dynamic policy shift. In particular, the president's decision to submit lists of *desaparecidos* to the Argentine military junta constituted a signal moment in the evolution of the U.S. human rights policy; although the United States had little recourse in protecting the lives of foreign citizens, by giving the lists its formal imprimatur the Carter administration clearly indicated that the United States sought to promote the rights not only of U.S. citizens but Argentines as well.

* * *

The brutal kidnapping by Argentine state security personnel of nearly a dozen members of the Madres de la Plaza de Mayo, along with two French nuns assisting in human rights advocacy, in early December 1977 dispelled Carter administration officials' optimism that the Argentine human rights crisis would be resolved by the end of the year. In fact, the raid had been carefully orchestrated by Argentine security personnel to disrupt the Madres's plans to pressure Videla to fulfill his promise of curtailing hostilities by Christmas through two major demonstrations and a prominent advertisement in the Argentine daily *La Nación*. Although Videla publicly professed no knowledge of the perpetrators of the raid, and notwithstanding the emergence of a highly implausible press package blaming the left-wing Montoneros, the grim undertaking bore all the hallmarks of state-sanctioned violence.[63]

Indeed, weeks earlier, the navy captain Alfredo Astiz had successfully infiltrated the Madres by posing as a relative of a *desaparecido* under the pseudonym

Gustavo Niño. Known by his peers as the "Angel of Death," thanks to his youthful appearance and extraordinary brutality, Astiz led Task Force 3.3.2, one of several contingents of dirty war operatives based at the Naval Mechanics School (ESMA).[64] On Thursday, December 8, as the Madres filtered onto the street after meeting to collect signatures and funds for the advertisement in a church in the heavily populated Buenos Aires neighborhood of San Cristóbal, a half dozen unmarked cars swarmed the exit and the women were set upon by plainclothes security personnel. As Madres member María del Rosario later recalled:

> Suddenly two men appeared and took one of the Mothers in front. They dragged her to the side and when she began to shout other men appeared and took the Mother beside me. . . . They threw me against the wall and told me not to move, saying it was a drugs raid. So I screamed to the other Mothers walking behind, "They're taking us! They're taking us!" and they [the Mothers] came towards us, thinking someone wanted to give us a lift in a car. Another man appeared, in shirtsleeves, and he pushed us away shouting "Move on! Move on!" and we ran and hid in the church. The people were beginning to leave the mass so we mingled in with them, scared to death.[65]

Ten women were abducted from Santa Cruz; three others were picked up shortly thereafter, including, on December 10, Azucena Villaflor de Vicenti, the founder of the Madres de la Plaza de Mayo.[66]

Word of the kidnappings reached the U.S. Embassy in Buenos Aires almost immediately. In addition to coverage of the event in the local media, on Sunday, December 11, a group of distraught Madres made a personal appeal to the U.S. ambassador Raúl Castro, who sent a hurried cable to Washington the following morning.[67] The news shocked State Department officials, who recognized that the Madres and French nuns had been peacefully engaged in civil protest, and Secretary Vance immediately ordered Castro to raise the matter with top-ranking Argentine military officials. In subsequent weeks, the ambassador repeatedly discussed the abductions with members of the military junta, as well as the minister of economics, the defense minister, and Videla's second-in-command, General Roberto Viola.[68] The whereabouts of the thirteen women remained undetermined, however, and although Videla reportedly ordered the Argentine Army and federal police to locate the women and "cough them up," the U.S. Embassy offered Washington few details. "Our findings are contradictory and inconclusive," Castro cabled Washington on January 20. "Our sources agree that the operation was carried out by some arm of the security forces," the ambassador continued, "but which specific group and the level of responsibility is unclear."[69]

Steady U.S. pressure on the Argentines regarding the women's disappearance throughout the month of February was equally unproductive. On February 1, Castro informed the deputy foreign minister that "this episode could be the straw that breaks the camel's back" in U.S.-Argentine relations.[70] Two weeks later, underscoring the importance the State Department placed on the women's abduction, Secretary of State Vance ordered the ambassador to "make known to all levels of the Argentine government and to the public the seriousness with which the U.S. views continuing human rights violations, making clear that an improvement in our relations, particularly the provision of military and economic assistance, depends upon improvements in the Argentine human rights situation."[71] The women, however, remained *desaparecidas*.

In fact, the Madres and the two nuns had been quickly killed and disposed of by Argentine Navy personnel—most likely before the end of December. Like thousands of Argentines who passed through the Naval Mechanics School, under a shroud of official secrecy the women had been transported to the ESMA, tortured, and eventually thrown from a navy airplane into the South Atlantic.[72] It was a grisly practice increasingly recognized by residents of the coastal areas bordering Buenos Aires. "They are convinced that they have been thrown into the sea by aircraft of the Navy from the nearby bases, which they see frequently from the area," Emilio Mignone, the vice president of the Permanent Assembly for Human Rights, wrote in March after three dozen bodies were tossed by the ocean onto a stretch of beach just south of the capital. "Some neighbors," Mignone continued, "affirmed having seen bundles falling from the aircraft."[73] Along with two of her fellow advocates, Azucena Villaflor's mutilated body washed up on the Atlantic coastline in early 1978 and was buried in an anonymous grave.[74]

Villaflor's remains would not be positively identified for more than three decades; information did surface, however, regarding the fate of the two French nuns and five of the disappeared Madres. More than three months after the women's disappearance, on March 30 Ambassador Castro reported that a reliable source in the Argentine government had confidentially confirmed to the U.S. Embassy that Argentine security forces had indeed abducted the women. The mutilated bodies of the Madres and the two nuns, Alice Doman and Leonie Duquet, the source revealed, had washed ashore weeks earlier on the Atlantic coast near Mar Del Plata.[75]

Confirmation of the kidnapping and murder of the Madres and the French nuns sparked a major shift in U.S. policy toward Argentina. Despite the December abductions, in the first three months of 1978, the U.S. approach had continued to reflect the hope that Jorge Videla was slowly pushing a moderate agenda; although at the end of the year Videla had publicly denied his September promise to Jimmy Carter that state-sanctioned violence would be curtailed by Christmas, the Argentine government made small yet not insignificant advances in the first three months of the new year: restoring the "right of option" (allowing prisoners held under state-of-siege provisions to petition for exile), publishing a list of 3,600 prisoners held under executive privilege and releasing 387, and showing an increasing responsiveness regarding U.S. high-interest cases.[76] In response, in February Warren Christopher had switched from "no" votes to abstentions on international financial institution loans to Argentina and approved the sale of a limited amount of military equipment.[77]

The tragic denouement of the Santa Cruz kidnapping arrested the tentative warming of relations between the United States and Argentina. Ordered to explicitly express U.S. "outrage" over the incident, Ambassador Castro met with Videla on April 10, accompanied by the head of U.S. Southern Command, General Dennis P. McAuliffe—an unmistakable display of U.S. military support for Carter's human rights policy.[78] More significantly, the episode hardened top Washington policymakers' attitude toward Jorge Videla. Since the previous year, Washington intelligence analysts had been struggling to ascertain whether the army commander was genuinely a cautious moderate beleaguered by military hardliners, or if he was adeptly masking his own fealty to the military's terror campaign by paying lip service to the liberal concerns of the international community. No consensus had been reached: while the State Department's Latin America Bureau strongly supported Videla as Argentina's best hope for eventual political liberalization, far less optimistic analyses were also aired, primarily, but not exclusively, by the Human Rights Bureau. Prior to Secretary Vance's November 1977 visit to Argentina, for example, the Treasury Department's Office of the Assistant Secretary for International Affairs submitted an intelligence analysis entitled "President Videla: An Alternative View." In addition to detailing Videla's ties to the austere economic policies of the minister of economy Martínez de Hoz, the memo contended that although Videla and other moderates had probably prevented military hardliners from extending the counterinsurgency net to include "intellectual and economic subversion," the number of victims was "so high as to have directly touched a large percentage of Argentine families."[79]

In fact, although a veil of secrecy effectively insulated Videla's role in overseeing state-sanctioned violence from outside scrutiny, the taciturn commander was a central architect of the Argentine military's terror campaign. Unlike fellow junta member Emilio Massera, Jorge Videla did not personally participate in operations against perceived subversives, nor did he actively engage in torture sessions.[80] And as the debate in U.S. policymaking circles in 1977 and 1978 made clear, to a remarkable degree, the decentralized nature of the *Proceso* allowed Videla to appear disassociated from the systematic abduction, torture, and murder of thousands of Argentines: a cautious, well-intentioned leader unable to curb the abuses of extremist subordinates. As Videla declared to the journalists María Seoane and Vicente Muleiro in an interview many years later, "I never killed or tortured anyone."[81]

In the aftermath of the military dictatorship, however, a growing body of evidence would belie Videla's claims of noninvolvement. The discovery of secret orders bearing Videla's signature, such as the "Directives from the Commander-in-Chief of the Army No. 504/77" issued on April 20, 1977 and providing procedural information on clandestine actions, conclusively linked Videla to the orchestration of the dirty war. As the Argentine general Santiago Omar Riveros later attested, "We waged this war with our doctrine in our hands. With the written orders of each high command."[82] More broadly, revelations regarding the enormous bureaucratic structure that undergirded Argentine military repression made Videla's claims of noninvolvement thoroughly unbelievable. "Orders came down through the chain of command until reaching those entrusted with carrying out the actions, the so-called Task Groups—principally young military officers, along with some noncommissioned officers, civilians, and off-duty police—who also had their own organization," the historian Luis Alberto Romero writes. He continues:

> The execution of their acts required a complex administrative apparatus because they were supposed to follow the movement—the entries, moves, and departures—of a vast array of people. Anyone arrested, from the moment he or she entered the list of suspects, was assigned his or her own number and file, with a follow-up, an evaluation of the case, after which a final decision would be taken, which always was the preserve of the highest levels of the military. The repression was, in sum, a systematic action carried out by the state.[83]

Further underscoring Videla's complicity in extralegal repression, the former commander in chief would be sentenced to life in prison at the trial of the military junta in 1984.[84]

In the spring of 1978, however, U.S. policymakers were only beginning to recognize the hollow nature of Jorge Videla's "moderate line." "Videla's response, while sympathetic, is like the responses he always gives," Stephen Oxman wrote Deputy Secretary of State Christopher following Castro's April meeting with the Argentine leader regarding the Santa Cruz abductions, "and it does not really change anything."[85] Noting that the trend since the previous fall had been characterized by "modest improvements punctuated by major retrograde developments such as the murder of the nuns," and with the congressionally mandated arms cutoff to Argentina due to take effect in six months, Oxman argued for increasing pressure on the military junta by tightening restrictions on U.S. transfers to Argentina. Oxman continued:

> Specifically, I think we should tell them that unless they curtail the irregular detention practices routinely used by the security forces, and begin to charge and try—or to release—those held under executive authority, we will be unable to approve most of these transfers. If there were solid steps in these directions, we would be prepared to be responsive in a "calibrated and sequential" fashion, but if there are only minor improvements, then the *status quo* will persist.

Militating in favor of U.S. success in eliciting Argentine human rights improvements, Oxman contended, was the growing backlog of sales that had been held up by the Christopher Group over the past year. In fact, by March 1978, more than one hundred applications from U.S. firms for sales to Argentina had been frozen by the State Department, including $48 million in U.S.-approved but undelivered military equipment purchased through the Foreign Military Sales (FMS) program and $510,390,000 in outstanding Export-Import Bank (Exim) credits, along with $23.8 million in pending loan applications.[86] Citing the importance of sending a clear message regarding the administration's human rights policy to both the Argentine government and U.S. domestic interests, Oxman advocated making the sales contingent on significant evidence of Argentine political normalization. "When all is said and done, we have, through this backlog of cases, built up a very considerable amount of leverage over the Argentines, and I think it would be a pity to squander it," Oxman wrote. "In general, it is preferable to avoid *quid pro quo* arrangements in the human rights context," he concluded, "but given the gravity of the human rights problems and the strength of our leverage, I think it would be worth making an exception."[87]

Strengthening Oxman's appeal to increase U.S. pressure on Argentina in the spring of 1978 was the departure of the Latin America bureau chief Terrence Todman. Over the course of his short tenure at ARA, Todman had developed a reputation among human rights advocates and sympathetic members of Congress for near-total opposition to Patricia Derian's initiatives in the hemisphere. Regarding U.S.-Latin American military ties, for example, Todman strongly viewed the maintenance of U.S. assistance as an essential means of retaining leverage over Latin American armed forces. "Our military ties are now so curtailed . . . that we have few means available to induce Latin American military leaders and institutions to cooperate with us in achieving these or other goals,"

Todman wrote Secretary Vance in March 1978. Noting that Indonesia alone was slated to receive nearly as much FMS financing for fiscal year 1979 as all the nations of Latin America and the Caribbean combined, Todman concluded, "Our responses to individual military requests of all kinds are so erratic that most of the continent's influential military leaders no longer consider the United States a reliable ally."[88]

Similarly, in regard to U.S.-Argentine relations, throughout 1977 Todman had set the tone for the U.S. emphasis on Jorge Videla as the nation's best hope for political liberalization.[89] Capturing the flavor of ARA's consistent efforts to dilute Patricia Derian's repeated call for a more punitive human rights policy, in response to a proposed Inter-American Development Bank loan to Argentina shortly before Secretary Vance's November visit to Buenos Aires, Todman asserted that "diplomatic nuances are important. The explicit strategy in the Secretary's trip involves a judgment that in the tragic Argentine situation, Videla is the best and only hope, however uncertain, in the near run, for some progress on both the human rights and nuclear issues as exemplified by his restoration of the right of option and his interest in the Tlatelolco Treaty [on nuclear nonproliferation], both anathema to Argentine hard-line military." In sum, Todman concluded, "If we accept the consequences of that strategy, prudence dictates abstention."[90]

By early 1978, however, Todman seemed increasingly out of step with the Carter administration's human rights policy. After giving a public address to a New York business association on Valentine's Day, the ARA chief was hammered by human rights organizations—with Lawrence Birns at the Council on Hemispheric Affairs (COHA) leading the attack—for defending right-wing dictatorships.[91] In fact, Todman's speech, centering on ten broad practices the United States should avoid in its dealings with Latin America, hardly constituted a revanchist assault on Carter's human rights policy. In addition to emphasizing the need to learn the facts in each case before taking action, for example, Todman warned against "being so concerned with declaring the rightness of our course that we lose sight of our true objective—to alleviate individual suffering."[92] Nonetheless, COHA used the address as an opportunity to highlight Todman's resistance to prioritizing human rights in U.S.-Latin American relations. "Todman is systematically undermining Christopher's efforts for a coherent human rights policy," COHA declared, "and is apparently winning his struggle to maintain normal relations with Latin American dictatorships because of Christopher's preoccupation with other regions of the world."[93]

If the row over Todman's speech was somewhat overblown, there was little doubt that the ARA director nonetheless was proving a serious obstacle for

Patricia Derian's efforts to promote human rights in Argentina. And as Stephen Oxman and Warren Christopher began moving toward tightening human rights restrictions toward Argentina in the aftermath of the Santa Cruz abductions, Todman's stance toward the Argentine military junta began to appear increasingly obstructionist. "I can plot several possible plans which would be superior to this hit or miss pulling and tugging we have now," a frustrated Derian wrote Christopher in April. "We could do the same for each troublesome country in that region and at the same time have a regional, coherent policy with a great many positive aspects." Derian continued: "At present, this would simply be a paper exercise because our human rights efforts are being subverted by the bureau's leader. Instead of bona fide efforts to work on the problem, we have bureaucratic game playing which is entirely negative." In a remarkable display of candor, the human rights bureau chief concluded, "There is no hope for an effective policy in Latin America under these circumstances."[94] Christopher apparently concurred with Derian's assessment; on April 8, Todman was quietly reassigned as ambassador to Spain.[95]

In the weeks following the bureau chief's departure, Stephen Oxman's proposal for increasing U.S. pressure on the Argentine military junta moved to the center of U.S. policy toward the South American nation. Hoping to stimulate "a serious exchange with the Argentine government as to where our relationship is heading in view of the human rights situation in Argentina," the State Department arranged for a formal visit to Buenos Aires in late May by the under secretary of state for political affairs David Newsom.[96] A top-ranking thirty-year career foreign service officer, Newsom was charged with pressing the Argentines to try, release, or send into exile the more than three thousand prisoners held without charge under the executive authority, as well as establishing an official procedure to account for the *disaparecidos*.[97] Most important, the United States hoped to convince the Argentine military junta to make a formal invitation to the Inter-American Human Rights Commission (IACHR), an autonomous organ of the Organization of American States (OAS). As part of Carter's effort to promote multilateralism and U.S. nonintervention abroad, at the OAS General Assembly the previous year, the administration had signed the Inter-American Convention on Human Rights, supported the decision to increase the IACHR budget, and encouraged member states to invite the commission for a formal visit.[98] Throughout 1977 and early 1978, however, the Argentine military junta had refused to admit the IACHR on the grounds of defending national sovereignty. Faced with Argentina's intransigence, Newsom's primary objective was thus to convince the Argentine military junta "that if they implement the kinds of human rights improvements he will be talking to them about, we will be in a position to be forthcoming on a variety of fronts, including arms transfers[,] EX-IM as well as other programs."[99]

* * *

At the U.S. Embassy in Buenos Aires, Tex Harris welcomed the rising tide of State Department pressure on the Argentine military junta. Over the course of late 1977 and early 1978, Harris had positioned himself in the vanguard of diplomatic efforts to promote human rights in Argentina, gaining recognition by tracking the costs of the Argentine military's dirty war with irrepressible energy. In particular, Harris's successful petition to invite non-U.S. victims of state-sanctioned violence into the U.S. Embassy inaugurated what the *Buenos Aires Herald* editor and steadfast human rights advocate Robert Cox would later describe as "an incredible change, an extraordinary change" from previous U.S. foreign policy.[100] Capturing the unique challenges of Harris's position vis-à-vis victims of extralegal repression, in April 1978 the embassy political counselor William H. Hallman wrote, "Mr. Harris has counseled and consoled, and though there was little hope he could offer he has comforted many with the belief that the United States is aware of dramatic personal needs."[101]

Combined with Harris's close engagement with Argentine organizations such as the Permanent Assembly for Human Rights, the opening of the embassy ingratiated the young diplomat into the local human rights community. In June 1978, for example, the Madres de la Plaza de Mayo wrote Harris to "express all the gratitude that your humane and consistent actions deserve." The letter continued: "As a diplomat of a friendly country, we acknowledge your cordial and sincere assistance to our painful demands. For this, and especially your abundant humanity that has strengthened our spirits, we would like to recognize your efforts and express how much we value them."[102] Underscoring the sea change in Argentine human rights advocates' perception of the U.S. Embassy that occurred during the Carter administration, at the end of 1977 the country team cited the embassy's transformation over the previous twelve months into a "beacon of hope" for the Argentine human rights community as a major achievement. "For the guy who puts the oil in the beacon," Harris noted wryly in a subsequent self-evaluation, "that is progress."[103]

Harris was also heralded by U.S. human rights advocates concerned with military repression in Argentina. After the American Association for the Advancement of Science completed a fact-finding visit to Argentina in late 1977 to gauge state-sanctioned violence against doctors and scientists, for example, Bruce Allan Kiernan, the organization's human rights coordinator, expressed admiration for the U.S. Embassy's internal liaison. "The reason for the effectiveness of our human rights policy in Argentina is due, in large measure, to the work of F. Allen

Harris," Kiernan later wrote Deputy Secretary of State Christopher. "The position of human rights officer in Argentina is a full-time job," he continued. "Hundreds of family members of the disappeared look to the American Embassy, and in particular Tex Harris, for understanding and compassion." Harris, Kiernan concluded, "has shown himself, in my view, to be an exemplary representative of this government."[104]

Most important, Harris's weekly "temperature charts," drawing on an ever-expanding pool of sources that included journalists, diplomats, and human rights advocates, as well as the daily meetings at the U.S. Embassy with relatives of *desaparecidos,* provided Washington policymakers—particularly the Human Rights Bureau—with unprecedented insight into the scale of Argentine human rights violations. Indeed, by debunking the Argentine military's claim that the targets of counterinsurgency operations were confined to violent left-wing terrorists, Harris's human rights reporting and policy recommendations formed the evidentiary base for Patricia Derian's efforts to curtail U.S. security and economic assistance to Argentina.[105] The human rights officer added "a new and well-rounded dimension to our understanding of developments and trends in that country," Derian would write at the end of Harris's tenure in Buenos Aires. "This information and analysis have been of invaluable assistance to the Department," she continued, "in monitoring events in Argentina and in developing policies to further U.S. human rights objectives."[106]

If the zeal with which Harris carried out his mandate was welcomed by human rights advocates in Buenos Aires and Washington, his military hosts were far less accommodating. On one occasion, a reception for members of the human rights community held by Harris and his wife, Jeanie, was interrupted by a group of heavily armed men, who—after Jeanie unwittingly answered the door—stood menacingly for a moment, then dubiously claimed that they had the wrong address and departed. The message was clear: Harris's reporting was ruffling feathers among the military—a dangerous enterprise in the capital of Latin America's most egregious human-rights-violating regime.

Worse was yet to come. Driving home from a human rights meeting late one night in his unmistakable Chevrolet Caprice station wagon, Harris was suddenly pinned at a stoplight by unmarked military vehicles. As plainclothes state security personnel swarmed around his car, Harris remembered having read that forensic autopsies could determine whether the victim had resisted arrest according to the body's posture at the instant of death. Cracking the window, he slipped his U.S. diplomat's passport to one of the security officers, and then waited, awkwardly holding his arms as high above his head as possible. "At the time I was very calm," Harris recalled years later. "But afterward I just completely broke down."[107]

Resistance to Harris's human rights reporting was not limited to Argentine dirty warriors. Indeed, by mid-spring 1978 Harris had become a virtual pariah within the U.S. Embassy. With his ties to the Argentine human rights community, coupled with the close professional relationship he had established with Patricia Derian's Human Rights Bureau, Harris was "regarded as 'grandstanding' and not being a 'team player,'" recalled the labor attaché Anthony G. Freeman. "The extreme reaction within the embassy bordered on the ridiculous," Freeman asserted, with Harris "virtually treated as a subversive."[108]

In particular, Harris clashed with Ambassador Raúl Castro, whose appointment as U.S. envoy to Argentina had roughly corresponded with Harris's own arrival. A charismatic former ambassador to El Salvador and Bolivia, Castro's appointment to Argentina by President Carter stood as a testament to a life of assimilation and hard work in the face of deeply entrenched racial discrimination in the American Southwest. Born in Sonora, Mexico, as the second youngest of fourteen children, Castro emigrated with his family to Pirtleville, Arizona, a tiny hamlet on the outskirts of the bustling border town of Douglas. Despite the death of his father when Castro was twelve, he nonetheless excelled in his adopted nation, particularly in athletics, winning a football scholarship to the Arizona State Teachers College in Flagstaff, where he also led the track team and was the undefeated Border Conference Boxing champion.[109]

Although Castro became a naturalized U.S. citizen shortly after graduation in 1939, as a Mexican American his efforts to obtain a teaching position in Douglas were repeatedly rejected. Unable to find work, Castro eventually became an itinerant prize fighter. "I was boxing on the road for a couple of years—New Orleans, Pennsylvania, New York," Castro recalled in a recent interview. "I would fight at carnivals, wherever, get $50 or $100."[110] When his youngest brother threatened to follow a similar path, however, Raúl Castro returned to Arizona and eventually found work overseeing immigration and accounting services at the American consulate in Sonora.

The position marked the beginning of Castro's hard-won rise to national prominence. Shortly after the end of World War II, Castro was hired to teach Spanish at the University of Arizona and he quickly enrolled in the institution's law degree program. Rejected on racial grounds—Castro recalls being told by the university dean that "Mexican-Americans just did not graduate"—he was accepted into the program only after threatening to cancel his teaching contract, which the university sorely needed.[111] Four years later, Castro was a senior partner in the law firm Castro and Wolfe, and after serving successive terms as district attorney and a juvenile court judge in Pima County, Castro was widely recognized as a rising star in Arizona, winning the Naturalized Citizen of the Year award in 1963.[112]

Having achieved extraordinary success in his adopted nation, Castro none-theless retained a strong cultural, class, and racial identity. Selected by the John-son administration to serve as U.S. ambassador to El Salvador (1964–1968) and reappointed by Richard Nixon as envoy to Bolivia (1968–1969), Castro brought a dynamic, rough-and-tumble approach to diplomatic affairs. When asked by a group of Bolivians of mixed European and indigenous ancestry if he, too, was a *mestizo,* Castro responded, "Hell no," and raised eyebrows by describing himself as "pure *indio.*" A few months later, in the immediate aftermath of the October 1969 nationalization of Gulf Oil's concessions in Bolivia, Anthony Freeman over-heard Castro brazenly inform a Bolivian caller over the telephone, "We've just landed the Marines in Valparaíso and they'll be up here by tomorrow." Unsure whether Castro was attempting to give Bolivian wiretappers a scare or simply "venting his macho side," Freeman was impressed. "You can't help but like a guy like this," he concluded.[113]

Appointed U.S. ambassador to Argentina in mid-1977, Raúl Castro proved willing to go to bat for the Carter administration on behalf of human rights—dutifully carrying out dozens of representations and demarches to Argentine leaders over the following months. "I am constantly pressing [the] GOA [Gov-ernment of Argentina] for improvement in the field of human rights," Castro wrote in February 1978. "It isn't that we aren't pressing," he concluded. "We do that seven days a week."[114] Testifying to Castro's loyalty to the human rights agenda, in August 1978 the U.S. Embassy would present the Argentine govern-ment with its five hundredth human rights case inquiry.[115]

Yet by early 1978, Castro had become a strong supporter of the perceived "moderate" military faction led by Jorge Videla. Quietly snubbed by aristocratic Argentines for his Mexican ancestry and humble origins, Castro formed a close friendship with General Roberto Viola, who had also overcome a humble back-ground by rising through the ranks of the army to become Videla's second-in-command.[116] As a result, Castro increasingly viewed Washington's economic and military sanctions against Argentina as counterproductively playing into the hands of military hardliners, and, by the end of 1977, his initial support for Tex Harris's human rights reporting had soured as Washington overruled his own policy recommendations on human rights grounds with increasing frequency. For Castro, in other words, by supplying the State Department Human Rights Bureau with evidence of the Argentine military's human rights abuses (resulting in political decisions antithetical to the ambassador's wishes), Harris was acting outside the embassy chain of command—a subversion of Castro's leadership that the ambassador would not abide. "God damn it Harris, . . . this is crap," Castro told the human rights officer on one occasion after his favorable recommenda-tion of a sale of pilot helmets to the Argentine Navy had been rejected by the

Christopher Group—in part due to Harris's reporting on navy counterterror teams operating out of the ESMA. Bluntly informing Harris that it was the ambassador's job to direct U.S. policy, Castro concluded, "That's not happening and it's because of your reporting, and we've got to change that."[117]

Castro's frustration with Tex Harris reverberated throughout the U.S. Embassy, and by mid-1978, the human rights officer had become the target of intense antipathy from his foreign service colleagues. As with the ambassador, much of the animosity directed toward Harris—particularly from the Economic/Commercial Section, the Military Group, and the defense attaché's Office—stemmed from the impression that his human rights reporting constituted the impetus behind Washington's increasingly stringent delays, cutbacks, and cancellations of U.S. programs and product transfers to Argentina. Given the traditional mandate of the foreign service, and especially representatives of the Department of Defense, such a response was perhaps predictable.[118] Rather than holding the Argentine military's terror campaign responsible for eliciting U.S. sanctions, in other words, many embassy officials blamed the Carter's administration's human rights policy for interfering in the preservation of close U.S.-Argentine relations—with Harris at the point of the lance.[119]

Opposition in the embassy to Harris's human rights advocacy dramatically curtailed his ability to influence embassy reporting on human rights developments in Argentina. Following the December 1977 abduction of the Madres and French nuns at Santa Cruz, for example, Ambassador Castro repeatedly responded to State Department requests for human rights updates by asserting that the embassy was "puzzled" by the disappearances. In fact, by the end of the year Harris had presented the embassy country team with a full description of the Argentine security forces' role in the kidnappings drawn from his web of local contacts. The report, however, was "voted down as mere speculation," by top-ranking embassy personnel; in his missives to Washington, Ambassador Castro professed ignorance as to the perpetrators of the raid until the bodies of the nuns were recovered in late March. It was no small coincidence that during this same three-month period, lacking critical information regarding military operations in Argentina, the Christopher Group switched from "no" votes to abstentions on international financial institution loans and approved a limited U.S. military equipment transfer to the Argentine military junta.[120] As Harris complained in a one-way recorded telephone message to Patricia Derian, "I have done a number of cables which tied in reported events to targeting by the Argentine security forces of individuals for intellectual subversion. This has been taken out of all messages going out."[121]

Opposition to Harris's human rights reporting also threatened to derail his chances for career advancement. In the annual officer evaluation report, the deputy chief of mission (DCM) Maxwell Chaplin criticized Harris for failing to draft reports "rapidly and clearly" as well as experiencing "difficulty in producing the volume of reporting required." Most important, Harris needed to direct his energy, Chaplin contended, "at the objectives of the organization of which he is a part."[122] Privately, embassy officials were more direct; as one foreign service officer pointedly informed Jeanie Harris, "The State Department needs good, grey men."[123]

For Tex Harris, such criticism obscured the real issue at stake: his superiors' unwillingness to embrace the Carter administration's human rights policy. "The Country Team would greatly prefer that the Embassy's 'Human Rights Attache' maintain a lower profile, concentrating on political reporting," Harris wrote in response to Chaplin's evaluation. He continued: "However, such a policy does not respond to the real demands made on the Embassy by this Administration, the Congress, and the American and Argentine publics. . . . A great number of my Human Rights reports either have not been sent or were deferred by the DCM who later complains that there was not enough reporting." During the nine months covered by the evaluation report, Harris concluded, "I sent in over 200 cables to the Department on human rights."[124]

* * *

By mid-April 1978, as the State Department's increasingly hard line toward the Argentine military junta sent a deep chill through U.S.-Argentine relations, tension between Tex Harris and the country team at the U.S. Embassy in Buenos Aires neared a fever pitch. On the one hand, led by the U.S. ambassador, top embassy officials chafed against the increasingly stringent approach to the Argentine military government emanating from Foggy Bottom. "I consider this policy poorly timed as regards U.S. trade and aviation interests in Argentina," Raúl Castro angrily cabled Washington regarding delays in Exim Bank loan approvals to Argentina on human rights grounds, "and irrelevant to the end sought."[125]

On the other hand, despite his superior officers' none-too-subtle demands that he moderate his reporting, Tex Harris continued to push his brief as internal liaison to the limit, playing a central role in the Buenos Aires human rights community and serving as Patricia Derian's eyes and ears at the center of the military junta's terror campaign. Death threats from Argentine security personnel and substandard FSO evaluations notwithstanding, Harris remained resolute. "I will close with my best regards and a *bon mot*," he wrote the Human Rights Bureau after detailing ongoing efforts to discover the locations of clandestine military detention sites. "Argentina is the only country in the world where you are safe in the streets, but not in your home."[126]

The failure of Under Secretary Newsom's attempt to make significant headway on the human rights issue during his diplomatic visit to Buenos Aires in late

May further accentuated diplomatic tension. After an exhausting series of talks with top Argentine policymakers, along with a small sample of human rights advocates, Newsom had departed confident that a major diplomatic breakthrough was in the offing.[127] In addition to convincing the under secretary that the military junta's ultimate goal was restoring civilian democracy, in a confidential meeting, President Videla informed Newsom that the IACHR would be invited to Argentina in June. Clearly impressed, Newsom cabled Washington that the military junta had demonstrated a "clear desire to improve [the] situation," and that U.S. pressure had "clearly raised the consciousness of human rights concerns, and has, I believe, had [a] positive impact." Accordingly, Newsom recommended that once the junta extended an invitation to the IACHR, Washington should release military training credits to Argentina and match subsequent human rights improvements with the staged release of the backlog of U.S. transfer cases.[128]

On the seventh floor of the Department of State, Secretary of State Vance concurred with Newsom's recommendation, and Ambassador Castro was dispatched to inform Jorge Videla.[129] The news reportedly exhilarated the characteristically taciturn commander; Videla, Castro reported, "smiled, gave a sigh of relief and said, 'Your news gives me the spirit to absolutely insist on a tremendous improvement in the field of human rights.'"[130] The stringent conditions attached to the foreign ministry's invitation to the Inter-American Human Rights Group the following month, however, merely resulted in a predictable rejection by the IACHR, and thus propelled U.S.-Argentine relations closer to a historic nadir.[131]

The rebuff corresponded with the culmination of tension within the U.S. Embassy between the country team and Tex Harris. During his lunch break on a Friday in mid-June, Harris borrowed the file on a pending Exim Bank decision for Allis-Chalmers, a Milwaukee-based manufacturing firm seeking a U.S. government loan guarantee for the construction of a hydroelectric turbine factory. Once completed, the plant would be turned over to Astilleros Argentina, an Argentine shipyards company intending to produce nearly two dozen turbines, governors, and generators for Entidad Binacional Yacyretá, a binational Argentine-Paraguayan commission charged with constructing a massive, long-delayed dam on the Paraná River near the Argentine city of Ituzaingó in Corrientes Province.[132] Given the significant cost of the project—roughly $270 million—Harris had a hunch that it would be worthwhile to review the details; fortunately for the human rights officer, the chief of the embassy's Economic/Commercial Section was out of the office and the administrative assistant handed over the file without question.

Reading over the details of the proposed sale while eating a sandwich at his desk, Harris stumbled on an internal "memo to the files," an information brief not distributed outside the embassy. To his amazement, the memorandum indicated

that Astilleros Argentina was a wholly owned subsidiary of the Argentine Navy—
a fact that the embassy country team had failed to report to Washington.[133] It
could hardly have been an accidental omission; over the past nine months, Harris's consistent reporting on kidnappings, torture, and clandestine killings linked
to the ESMA had led to an almost-total curtailment of U.S. transfers to the navy.

Quickly finishing his meal, Tex Harris drafted an urgent missive to Washington according to the format recently facilitated by Under Secretary Newsom.
During his visit to Buenos Aires in May, Newsom had recognized the antagonism
Tex Harris faced within the embassy. Thanks to strong support from the Human
Rights Bureau, the under secretary had brokered an unprecedented arrangement
between the embassy country team and Harris, allowing the human rights officer
to transmit information to the State Department that the embassy did not wish
to send through formal channels by using "official-informal" letters carried by
diplomatic pouch to Washington. Although Harris was obligated to send a copy
of each letter to the ambassador, under the agreement he was at liberty to provide
human rights information to HA and ARA without the threat of censorship by
his superiors.[134]

Accordingly, Harris drafted three copies of an official-informal letter on the
Allis-Chalmers project—one addressed to Patricia Derian, another to the Latin
America Bureau, and a final copy for Ambassador Castro. After delivering Castro's copy to the ambassador's office, Harris walked the remaining two letters to
the embassy pouch room, where they would be secured in a large bag with wax
seals and sent to Washington by airplane that evening. The letter was short and
direct: "Did you know that the beneficiary of the EXIM loan to Argentina was
the Argentine Navy?"[135]

The reaction to Harris's communiqué was swift. Late in the afternoon, the
human rights officer was stopped in the embassy hallway by his superior officer,
the political counselor William H. Hallman, who began to lecture Harris on the
value of "working for those who had more experience and wisdom." Never one
to back down on a point of principle, Harris fervently defended his actions and
a heated discussion ensued. Finally, Hallman abruptly ended the conversation by
handing Harris the two letters that he had delivered to the pouch room earlier
that day. "Well, at least you won't get it in the pouch this week," Harris remembers
Hallman concluding.[136]

For Harris, the episode constituted a flagrant breach of the informal rules on
human rights communications established during Under Secretary Newsom's
visit in May. Indeed, although Ambassador Castro was away from the embassy,
DCM Chaplin had read the ambassador's copy of Harris's official-informal letter.
According to Harris, Chaplin recognized that the revelation in Washington that
Astilleros Argentina was owned by the Argentine Navy would almost certainly

result in a disapproval of Exim guarantees for Allis-Chalmers. Unbeknown to Harris at the time, however, was the fact that the deliberations for the Allis-Chalmers Exim loan were slated for the following Monday. Chaplin, Harris later concluded, calculated that if the human rights officer's letters were delayed, by the time the next flight carrying U.S. diplomatic correspondence from Argentina arrived in Washington, the Exim decision would already be concluded.[137]

Outraged at his superiors' apparent duplicity, Harris refused to concede defeat. Although it was late in the afternoon, Harris hurried back to the pouch room, arriving moments before the office closed for the weekend. The clerk, however, had already affixed the wax seals on the diplomatic pouch. It was, Harris would recall years later, "a tough negotiation." Nonetheless the tenacious human rights officer eventually succeeded in convincing the clerk to break the seals and place the two letters once again into the pouch. Three days later, the Christopher Group denied the $270 million Exim bank loan to Allis-Chalmers.[138]

The Exim rejection brought U.S. relations with the Argentine military junta to a historic low. Indeed, the Argentine government considered the Allis-Chalmers case to have "profound political significance," as the deputy foreign minister Gualter Allara told State Department officials on June 24.[139] Required by law to take human rights considerations into account on Exim Bank loan proposals, and recognizing that the Argentine government "sought approval of such financing as [an] indication of U.S. acceptance," two days later Deputy Secretary of State Warren Christopher ordered Ambassador Castro to inform the military junta that, barring significant improvements in the protection of human rights, the United States was withholding financing for Allis-Chalmers, as well as the pending military-training package.[140]

In Buenos Aires, news of the rejection stirred shock and outrage among Argentine military leaders and their supporters. When Raúl Castro informed Roberto Viola, the general "looked like a ghost and his lips were quivering," the ambassador reported. Predictably, the formal rejection of the credits on July 17 sparked a fervent outburst of reactionary Argentine nationalism. Capturing the mood, President Videla gravely intoned, "As the Armed Forces of the nation, we must, permanently, spiritually and materially remain on guard against any type of aggression jeopardizing our territorial integrity or the full exercise of our sovereignty which may be launched against us in order to divide us from within or from without."[141] Two weeks later, the Argentine government issued a formal note of protest to the United States, specifically citing the Allis-Chalmers rejection as an "intrusion into the affairs of a sovereign government."[142]

Argentine indignation notwithstanding, from his vantage point at the White House, President Carter supported the State Department's decision. Indeed, during the summer of 1978, Carter kept an eye on developments in Argentina; in mid-June the president personally wrote Jorge Videla to encourage steps in the protection of human rights and nuclear nonproliferation, and when he learned of the Exim rejection in a brief memorandum from Cyrus Vance at the end of the month, Carter wrote in the margin, "My slight inclination would be to find an excuse to approve training—and hold back EXIM deal."[143] Two weeks later Carter requested additional information on developments in Argentina from the national security adviser Zbigniew Brzezinski, and at the end of July a further update was included in the president's evening reading.[144] The national security adviser's prognosis was grim: "While we are eager to build good relations with Argentina, the current human rights situation is so dismal that our relations may be reaching a breaking point," Brzezinski informed the president. Although the Argentines had not cut off negotiations with the IACHR, Brzezinski concluded, "we fear that if they don't reach agreement soon—i.e., before the October 1 deadline of the Kennedy-Humphrey amendment to bar military sales and training—our relations may be set back irreparably."[145]

Adding Allis-Chalmers to the long list of delayed or denied U.S. transfer cases had sent an unmistakable signal of U.S. censure to the Argentine military junta. Coupled with the looming congressionally mandated arms cutoff, in the summer of 1978, it was clear to Argentine leaders that rapprochement with the United States would require at least limited concessions on human rights. And although Argentina's stunning victory over the Netherlands in the championship match of the Fédération Internationale de Football Association World Cup in late June ushered in a frenzy of nationalistic euphoria among much of the Argentine population, Patricia Derian's extraordinarily frank explanation of the rationale behind the Exim decision in August brought the human rights issue once again to the fore. "The reason for our advice was the continuing violation of basic human rights by Argentina," Derian told the Congressional Subcommittee on Inter-American Affairs. Such violations, Derian continued, included "the systematic use of torture, summary execution of political dissidents, the disappearance and the imprisonment of thousands of individuals without charge, including mothers, churchmen, nuns, labor leaders, journalists, professors and members of human rights organizations, and the failure of the government of Argentina to fulfill its commitment to allow [a] visit by the Inter-American Commission on Human Rights."[146] Widely reported in the Argentine press, Derian's comments elated human rights advocates.[147] For military leaders, however, the human rights advocate's statement stoked U.S.-Argentine tensions that had festered since the beginning of the summer. "I do anticipate that when the whole affair is better digested all hell will break loose," Ambassador Castro glumly cabled Washington.[148]

U.S. pressure eventually succeeded, however, in convincing Argentine leaders to invite the IACHR. At the end of August, the Argentines quietly proposed a meeting between Jorge Videla and the vice president Walter Mondale, both of whom would be attending the coronation of Pope John Paul I in Rome the following month. It was, as the NSC Latin America expert Robert A. Pastor wrote Zbigniew Brzezinski, "the opportunity we have been waiting for": in a private meeting in Rome on September 13, Videla assured Mondale that Argentina would "seriously consider" an IACHR visit in exchange for Exim Bank approval.[149] Returning with Mondale's assurance that the United States would give the Allis-Chalmers sale a green light if Buenos Aires would provide an unconditional invitation to the IACHR, Videla successfully orchestrated the invitation the following month.[150]

The military junta's invitation to the Inter-American Commission on Human Rights constituted a signal victory in the Carter administration's effort to curtail state-sanctioned violence in Argentina. In comparison with the previous three decades of bilateral relations between the United States and Argentina, the Carter administration's emphasis on human rights constituted an extraordinary shift away from the policy prescriptions of the Cold War; in addition to reducing Foreign Military Sales (FMS) credits to Argentina in early 1977, the Christopher Group's review of Argentine arms transfer requests had resulted in dramatic cutbacks in the export of U.S. military equipment to the South American nation. Moreover, by the end of 1978, the United States had abstained or voted no on eleven IFI loans to Argentina, a number that would rise to twenty-eight by the end of 1980—the highest number of U.S. negative votes for any single nation. Although U.S. censure did not prevent the loans from being delivered, in each instance the United States capitalized on the negative publicity to press Argentine military leaders to make advances in the protection of human rights.

Throughout 1977 and the first half of 1978, the United States had also made repeated diplomatic representations on behalf of human rights in Argentina. In fact, by the fall of 1978, human rights had been raised in conversation with Argentine leaders by a remarkable number of top U.S. policymakers including President Jimmy Carter, Secretary of State Cyrus Vance, Deputy Secretary Warren Christopher, Under Secretary David Newsom, and Assistant Secretaries Patricia Derian and Terrence Todman. Correspondingly, human rights had dominated the U.S. Embassy's relationship with the Argentine Foreign Ministry.

Nonetheless, the Carter administration's success in eliciting human rights improvements in Argentina over the course of 1977 and the first half of 1978 was decidedly limited. Repeated U.S. representations on behalf of victims of state-sanctioned violence no doubt forced the Argentine military junta to consider international opprobrium as the necessary price for its use of dirty war tactics. Perhaps more significantly, Carter's human rights policy—and particularly Tex Harris's vigorous application of the policy—provided an unprecedented mantle of U.S. government legitimacy to Argentine human rights groups, thus providing a modicum of protection as well as a much-needed sense of solidarity. Such developments did little, however, to curtail the Argentine military's campaign to eradicate perceived subversives. In fact, dirty war violence remained at peak levels during Carter's first year in office: an estimated 80 percent of disappearances occurred during 1976 and 1977, and the number of *desaparecidos* dropped only marginally in the spring and summer of 1978.[151]

The Carter administration's failure to curtail political repression in Argentina stemmed in part from the challenges of transforming lofty human rights ideals into practical policy prescriptions. As elsewhere in the hemisphere, in its effort to harness U.S. economic and military leverage to pressure the Argentine military junta, the administration faced fierce pressure from Washington bureaucrats and the Department of Defense, as well as strong lobbying by the U.S. business community and its sympathizers on Capitol Hill. On a deeper level, despite its political, military, economic, and cultural power, the Carter administration found itself with relatively little leverage with which to pressure the Argentine military junta. Throughout 1977 and 1978, Argentina's access to non-U.S. economic and military suppliers, particularly in Western Europe and Israel, rendered U.S. sanctions largely symbolic. "Put simply," a State Department report on U.S.-Argentine relations asserted in November 1978, "the U.S. is trying almost single-handedly to encourage a basic policy reorientation on a sensitive matter in a country where its leverage is limited and competing policy objectives (nuclear) might be endangered."[152] More important, Argentine military leaders' radical belief in the National Reorganization Process superseded any fealty to U.S. hemispheric leadership. The Carter administration's human rights initiatives, in other words, failed to dramatically alter the convictions of Argentine military leaders who saw themselves as engaged in a historic conflict of global proportions.

The administration's success in pressuring the military junta to accept an IACHR visit, however, marked a turning point for the Argentine dictatorship. Hoping to avoid a deeply embarrassing and politically damaging report, in the months leading up to the September 1979 visit Argentine military leaders made substantial progress toward political normalization. As General Roberto Viola informed Ambassador Castro, "All of the GOA is being geared for [the] IACHR visit resulting in virtually no disappearances, no torture and no irregular arrests."[153] Indeed, disappearances dropped dramatically from the 1978 average of fifty per month; in June 1979 the U.S. Embassy reported only twenty-two confirmed *desaparecidos* over the previous six months.[154] Underscoring the significant role the IACHR visit played in the decline in state-sanctioned violence, one top-ranking Argentine officer told DCM Maxwell Chaplin, "It would be inconceivable to have disappearances taking place when the IAHCR was visiting."[155]

Correspondingly, the number of clandestine prisons decreased precipitously from more than three hundred at the peak of the military's terror campaign in 1976–1977 to forty-five by the end of 1978. When the IACHR arrived in Buenos Aires, only seven camps remained in operation, and by 1980 all but two had been shuttered.[156] Prison conditions and prisoner treatment also improved for individuals held under executive authority (Poder ejecutivo nacional, or PEN) declining from more than three thousand at the beginning of 1978 to roughly 1,600 in the months leading up to the IACHR visit, and in the first half of 1979 hundreds of PEN prisoners received formal charges.[157] Although such improvements were, as Tex Harris fittingly put it, little more than "apple-polishing" in light of the previous three years of intense state-sanctioned violence, the Argentine military junta's preparations for the IACHR nonetheless constituted a success for U.S. human rights policy.[158]

Perhaps most important, the IACHR's visit to Argentina in September 1979 provided an unprecedented opportunity for members of the human rights community to raise national and international awareness of the extent of human rights violations perpetrated by the military government. The visit received an enormous amount of coverage in Argentine press, radio, and television reporting, and despite a blanket of self-censorship regarding dirty war tactics, the human rights issue received widespread domestic scrutiny. Correspondingly, the image of thousands of Argentines waiting in lines stretching five blocks through the center of Buenos Aires to give testimony regarding the disappearance of loved ones shocked onlookers and electrified human rights advocates.[159] "For the first time the nation 'sees' our reality," one human rights pamphlet subsequently asserted. "'There are so many?' they ask. 'Yes, we are, and we are not afraid to publicly testify in front of the IACHR, destroying the expectations of the Dictatorship that had counted on the terror that enveloped the population to keep us quiet.'"[160] Underscoring the significance of the visit in raising awareness of the human rights issue, Ambassador Castro cabled Washington shortly after the commission's departure: "There can hardly be an Argentine alive who is now unaware that human rights are an issue of significance."[161]

Finally, the IACHR's 374-page report on Argentina, delivered to the Argentine Embassy in Washington in December 1979 and published in a shorter form in April 1980, was immediately recognized as a landmark condemnation of the Argentine military junta's systematic use of abduction, torture, and murder. Backed by the formal imprimatur of the Organization of American States, and based on testimony from 5,580 Argentines, the commission produced a scathing denunciation of the military junta's draconian violations of personal liberty and security, habeas corpus, freedom of expression and religion, and political and labor rights.[162] And although the military leaders publicly dismissed the report's findings and banned its distribution in Argentina, its publication was nonetheless highly significant. "An impartial, official hemispheric body had now laid the facts on the public record and had recommended specific improvements," wrote Patrick J. Flood, who served in the State Department Human Rights Bureau. "The hemisphere would be watching Argentina's compliance with these recommendations," Flood continued. "Argentine policymakers were beginning to accord more weight to the country's international reputation, and the visit was a factor in stimulating a trend toward better observance of human rights."[163]

The successful orchestration of the IACHR visit thus constituted a historic victory for the Carter administration's human rights policy. In the summer of 1978, however, the administration's decision to deny the $270 million Allis-Chalmers Exim loan to Argentina on human rights grounds did not go unnoticed by the U.S. business community and their supporters on Capitol Hill. In fact, in subsequent months Carter would face sharp criticism from U.S. business leaders, conservative media pundits, and sympathetic members of Congress over the perceived detrimental effects the administration's policy toward Argentina was having on the U.S. economy. Exacerbated by a ballooning balance of payments deficit and a resurgence of Cold War tension, over the second half of the Jimmy Carter's presidency the human rights agenda would increasingly move to the back burner as a U.S. policy priority. Indeed, notwithstanding the successful IACHR visit, setbacks in the struggle to institutionalize human rights in U.S. foreign policy pushed Patricia Derian to the brink of resignation so many times in the second half of the Carter presidency that by 1980 her packing boxes were permanently stacked along one wall of her office.[164]

6

"TILTING AGAINST GRAY-FLANNEL WINDMILLS"

U.S.-Argentine Relations, 1979–1980

Patricia Derian's frustration was palpable. "Unless things change I'll probably resign in a few days, over a major policy disagreement," the assistant secretary of state for human rights and humanitarian affairs informed the *New York Times* reporter Ann Crittenden in late May 1980. Having spearheaded U.S. efforts to promote human rights in Argentina for the previous three years, Derian was outraged when she returned from a brief vacation to discover that the Carter administration had decided to initiate "a major policy shift" toward the South American nation that aimed, in her view, to "normalize relations and end our official criticism of the regime." Barring a reversal of the decision, Derian told Crittenden with characteristic candor, "I'm leaving, and I won't say it's for 'personal reasons.'"[1]

It was a remarkable announcement, particularly in light of the publication only a month earlier of the Inter-American Commission on Human Rights (IACHR) report on its visit to Argentina in the fall of 1979. In the months leading up to the visit, the protection of human rights in Argentina had improved significantly, and the report itself constituted a landmark condemnation of the Argentine military junta's terror campaign against perceived subversives. Nonetheless, by the spring of 1980, it was increasingly evident at the State Department Human Rights Bureau that the Carter administration's success in orchestrating the Argentine military junta's invitation to the IACHR had come at a heavy political cost.

Indeed, the administration's July 1978 decision to make Export-Import (Exim) Bank approval of the $270 million Allis-Chalmers sale of a hydroelectric turbine factory to Argentina contingent on the junta's invitation to the IACHR sparked a firestorm of criticism from U.S. business leaders and conservative journalists, who accused the Carter administration of obstructing profitable bilateral trade relations in the interest of a poorly defined and badly executed human rights policy. Sympathetic members of Congress quickly followed suit, ratcheting up the pressure on the administration to delink U.S. commercial transfers to Argentina from the human rights policy. Underscoring the political power of the U.S. business community, opposition to the economic dimension of the human rights policy forced the Carter team onto the defensive, threatening to reverse the limited gains Derian's Human Rights Bureau had achieved over the previous nineteen months.

Corresponding with rising domestic resistance to the human rights policy, a resurgence of Cold War tension in the second half of the Carter administration hardened the president's outlook in foreign affairs, a development that reverberated with particular intensity in the developing world. As the Carter team grew increasingly concerned with Soviet adventurism in the Horn of Africa, rising popular unrest in Iran, and the deteriorating political situation in Nicaragua, human rights increasingly moved to the back burner as a U.S. policy priority. Most significant for U.S.-Argentine relations, in the immediate aftermath of the Soviet invasion of Afghanistan in December 1979, Argentina's strategic significance for the United States increased dramatically, and in the opening months of 1980 the fear that Argentina would offset the U.S. grain embargo on the Soviet Union had rapidly accelerated rapprochement between Washington and Buenos Aires. "The decision will probably result in Mrs. Derian's resignation early next week," Ann Crittenden wrote, "for if Patt Derian was identified with any single issue while in office it was her constant, and generally successful battle to distance the United States from the military regime in Argentina." That fight, Crittenden concluded, "now seems to have been lost."[2]

* * *

To a considerable extent, tension between the Carter administration and the U.S. business community was rooted in the contradictory impulses that emerged from Jimmy Carter's self-avowed social liberalism and fiscal conservatism.[3] On the one hand, Carter's inaugural declaration that the U.S. commitment to human rights would be "absolute" honestly reflected the president's religious beliefs and moralism, coupled with a keen political sense of the national mood in the post-Vietnam, post-Watergate era. Although the protracted struggle to transform Carter's lofty rhetoric into concrete policy prescriptions over the course of 1977 made it clear that the pursuit of human rights would necessarily be conditional on a wide range of additional foreign policy considerations, Carter remained dedicated to infusing U.S. foreign policy with a heavy dose of morality. "My personal commitment to human rights is very strong," Carter observed during

Human Rights Week in December. "The American people feel as I do," he continued. "Our government will continue to express that commitment and not ever hide it. And we will always encourage other nations to join us."[4]

On the other hand, Jimmy Carter's economic policies were fundamentally conservative. In what became known as the "locomotive strategy," Carter sought to expand the U.S. economy—particularly by increasing trade with Western Europe and Japan—thereby increasing U.S. production, lowering unemployment, and strengthening the dollar.[5] The thirty-ninth president also came to office committed to balancing the national budget deficit—more than $66 billion when Carter entered to the Oval Office—and lowering inflation, which was averaging roughly 6 percent per year.[6] Finally, the president supported traditionally Republican issues such as the deregulation of major industries; as Carter later wrote in his memoirs, "For more than three and a half years, my major economic battle would be against inflation, and I would stay on the side of fiscal prudence, restricted budgets, and lower deficits."[7]

Significantly, in the realm of foreign policy, Carter saw no contradiction between promoting both human rights and U.S. economic expansion overseas. During an official visit to Brazil in March 1978, Carter informed journalists that "it would be inconceivable to me that any act of Congress would try to restrict the lending of money by American private banks . . . under any circumstances." More broadly, there was "no conflict," Carter asserted, "between human rights . . . and the free-enterprise system."[8]

Carter's statement came as a shock to members of the nongovernmental human rights community in Washington. It was "an enormous gaff," recalled Larry Birns, the director of the Council on Hemispheric Affairs (COHA). Human rights advocates were not unaware of the limits to Carter's dedication to human rights, Birns asserted, "but the illusion was that the human rights factor affects everything."[9] More concretely, the growing body of congressional legislation linking U.S. foreign assistance to human rights considerations constituted a legal barrier to unfettered foreign aid, trade, and investment; by 1978, congressional human rights advocates had successfully passed legislation prohibiting U.S. foreign assistance, security transfers and police training, and agricultural commodity sales to gross violators of human rights, as well as legally binding requirements that human rights be taken into consideration in the Exim Bank and the Overseas Private Investment Corporation (OPIC).[10]

The apparent contradictions in Jimmy Carter's avowed support for both human rights and market capitalism also raised the hackles of the U.S. business community, particularly in regard to U.S. policy toward Argentina. Less than a year into Carter's presidency, the growing backlog of delayed or denied U.S. transfers to the South American nation was generating increasingly sharp criticism from business leaders, who regarded the administration's human rights policy as inconsistent, capricious, and counterproductive in the effort to curtail state-sanctioned violence. As a representative from the American League for Exports and Security Assistance bluntly informed a congressional committee, Carter's export policy was a "costly failure." Citing the administration's human rights policy toward Argentina as a particularly egregious example of the failed "export of morality," the league—a business lobby representing thirty-four U.S. aerospace corporations—emphasized the need to move beyond "principles of high moral purpose" and focus instead on "the reality of American national interest."[11]

To a considerable extent, such resistance reflected a combination of expanding trade and investment opportunities available to U.S. firms in Argentina and the military junta's savvy self-promotion. Following the March 1976 coup d'état, the military junta had assumed leadership of a nation on the brink of total economic collapse; during the chaotic presidency of Isabel Martinez de Perón inflation had reached 700 percent, productivity had fallen by 50 percent, and international investors had fled the threat of left-wing terrorist kidnappings in droves.[12] To reverse the nation's precipitous financial decline, the military junta's newly installed minister of the economy, José Alfredo Martínez de Hoz, immediately implemented tough market-based austerity measures: devaluation of the peso, elimination of price controls, and a freezing of wages. A staunch opponent of excessive government intervention in the economy, the economy minister also set out to reduce state spending, privatize government-owned enterprises, and deregulate banking. Finally, seeking to encourage the influx of foreign capital and increase trade, Martínez de Hoz offered tax incentives, freed exchange rates, and lowered tariffs.[13]

The viability of Martínez de Hoz's economic strategy was inextricably linked to attracting foreign investment and expanding trade, and with U.S. investment in Argentina at $1.395 billion in 1976—roughly 40 percent of total foreign holdings—the Argentine military junta placed special attention on enticing additional U.S. capital. Accordingly, in August 1976 the junta paid the New York-based public relations firm Burson-Marsteller (BM) $1.1 million to "assist in promoting confidence in and good will toward the country and its government" in eight countries, with $590,000 earmarked for the United States.[14] With experience representing repressive regimes—BM's clientele included the Soviet Union and Hungary—the firm's subsequent thirty-five-page report offered a blueprint to "project a new, progressive and stable image throughout the world." Focusing on three target audiences—"those who influence thinking," including government officials, the press, and academics; "those who influence investments"; and "those who influence travel," particularly in the tourist industry—BM offered a comprehensive series of steps to project a national image of economic stability, political security, and financial opportunity. On BM's recommendation, for example, more than fifty foreign journalists identified as particularly influential were plied by the Argentine government with all-expense-paid visits to Argentina, including entertainment, extensive tours of Buenos Aires, and the opportunity to meet Argentine government and business leaders.[15] BM further advocated the creation of training courses for Argentine government personnel focusing on how to respond to "international groups such as Amnesty International which carry out local anti-Argentina campaigns."[16]

In the United States, with Burson-Marsteller's oversight, the security of Argentina's political climate and the nation's extensive investment opportunities were touted in newspaper advertisements and radio and television slots.[17] In print media alone, the Argentine military junta took out seventeen pages in the *Nation's Business*, two pages in the *New York Times*, nineteen pages in *Time*, five pages in the *Wall Street Journal*, and two pages in the *Washington Post*. State funding of such ads was often obscured; when members of a nongovernmental human rights organization investigated the Maryland address provided by the group of "Concerned Argentine Women" who purportedly paid for an ad in the *Washington Post*, for example, they discovered a private house rented by the Argentine naval attaché at the Argentine Embassy in Washington.[18]

The Argentine military junta's economic policy, coupled with its savvy public relations campaign, quickly garnered support from U.S. business lobbies, led by the Council of the Americas (COA), a nonprofit business association funded by more than two hundred corporations with investments in Latin America. With direct access to top U.S. policymakers, legislators, and business leaders, along with extensive financial resources and a reputation for expertise in U.S.-Latin American economic issues, COA had emerged in the mid-1970s as the preeminent U.S. lobby on U.S.-Latin American affairs.[19] Shortly after the 1976 military coup d'état, COA sponsored a meeting between the president of the U.S. Chamber of Commerce in Argentina, a group of Argentine business leaders, and representatives of nearly three dozen COA-affiliated corporations. Similarly, in June the organization facilitated a gathering of three hundred U.S. business leaders to hear Martínez de Hoz discuss the Argentine military junta's economic policy, and when the Argentine economy minister visited the United States to attend the board of governors meeting of the World Bank and International Monetary Fund in September 1978, COA organized investment workshops focusing on Argentina as well as radio and television interviews in five U.S. cities on investment opportunities in the South American nation.[20]

Such lobbying, combined with the military junta's austere economic policies and harsh repression of organized labor, initially proved effective in reversing

Argentina's economic decline. Inflation fell to 176 percent in 1978, and dropped under 100 percent in early 1979.[21] Moreover, with financial backing from the Gerald Ford administration and multinational lending institutions, including the World Bank and the International Monetary Fund, Martínez de Hoz successfully renegotiated Argentina's $9 billion foreign debt; by the summer of 1977 the military junta had built up foreign currency reserves of $2.4 billion, with economists optimistically predicting a 4 percent rate of annual economic growth.[22] Correspondingly, thanks in no small measure to BM and COA, the Argentine military junta's pro-business policies and eradication of the left-wing terrorist threat to foreign investors succeeded in increasing the influx of U.S. private investment in Argentina, particularly in oil exploration. In November 1977, *U.S. News and World Report* asserted that "slowly, almost secretly, American businessmen are returning to Argentina," a theme echoed a few months later in *Business-Week*.[23] "They are cautious, still not entirely assured by the apparent economic and political stability there," the latter asserted, "but within the last year they have proposed deals worth some $400 million to the government, half of which have already been approved."[24]

* * *

Not surprisingly, the Carter administration's efforts to promote human rights in Argentina through delaying or denying U.S. trade and economic assistance sparked sharp criticism from the U.S. business community. In fact, many multinational firms that had weathered the storm of left-wing terrorist kidnappings in the first half of the decade openly praised the Argentine military junta's success in reestablishing security.[25] "American business has shown little inclination to involve itself on behalf of human rights in Argentina," a State Department memorandum asserted in March 1978. "On the contrary, American businessmen resident there have been the targets of leftist assassinations and many therefore support the Argentine government's harsh tactics." Tightening U.S. government restrictions on private U.S. businesses and banks operating in Argentina, the memo concluded, "would be seriously resented."[26]

Indeed, the increasing backlog of delayed or denied U.S. transfers to Argentina in late 1977 and early 1978 generated strident complaints from the U.S. business community. Private executives affected by the sanctions, such as E. B. Fitzgerald, the chairman of the Milwaukee-based Cutler-Hammer, Inc., dismissed government restrictions on U.S. trade and investment abroad as politically counterproductive and economically detrimental. When a proposed $8 million sale of Cutler-Hammer's AN/PPS-5 battlefield surveillance radar to the Argentine military was denied by the State Department, in late 1977 Fitzgerald fired off an angry letter to Rep. Clement J. Zablocki (D-WI). "I . . . am seriously concerned about our nation's interest in the face of what appears to be inconsistent and whimsical application of government authority on a tenuous premise," Fitzgerald wrote, "which denies to our country sorely needed export trade in an era of overwhelmingly unfavorable balance of trade and which denies to American workers employment in an era of significantly high unemployment." Noting that the Argentine military government had subsequently purchased a similar radar system for $11 million from a French company, Fitzgerald acidly concluded, "Thus, the U.S. government did not succeed in denying Argentina anything; but it did succeed in depriving the U.S. economy of sorely needed income and jobs."[27]

As Fitzgerald's letter made clear, at the heart of U.S. business leaders' frustration with the Carter administration was the apparent lack of a clear set of human rights policy guidelines. In the course of 1977, State Department policy planners had struggled to generate an overarching human rights policy framework; by the time Jimmy Carter delivered Presidential Directive/NSC-30 in February 1978—a formal ukase defining human rights as a "major objective of the United States"— the locus of human rights decision making had centered almost by default on the Inter-Agency Group on Human Rights and Foreign Assistance, chaired by Deputy Secretary Warren Christopher (and referred to as the Christopher Group).[28] Instituting a case-by-case decision-making process, Christopher examined each proposal for U.S. economic or security assistance to human rights violating regimes individually, thus consciously avoiding the establishment of human rights precedents that could be interpreted as guiding policy principles.

It was an approach that underscored the State Department's recognition that the multiplicity of competing considerations in each bilateral relationship made achieving across-the-board consistency in the promotion of human rights impossible. Indeed, in response to the question of whether U.S. human rights policy was consistent, the director of policy planning Anthony Lake candidly responded, "No. And we should not try to be completely so." In a remarkable illustration of challenges inherent in the effort to link human rights to U.S. foreign aid, Lake continued:

> There are times when security considerations, or broader political factors, lead us to be "softer" on some countries' human rights performance than others. Moreover, it often is a close call just what action is most likely to produce improvement in a human rights situation. We sometimes, for instance, approve a loan in recognition of a positive trend—even though the overall situation in the country remains as bad or worse than that in countries whose loans we oppose. One of the most difficult questions in the human rights business is what actions on our

part are most likely to encourage a government to believe that further progress is worthwhile, without leading it to think we believe its human rights problem is solved.

In sum, Lake concluded, "This can only be done on a case-by-case basis, and some of our decisions will turn out to have been wrong."[29]

If the Christopher Group's approach to human rights reflected a concerted effort to avoid applying narrow policy prescriptions to multifaceted political realities, it nonetheless accentuated the Carter administration's vulnerability to domestic political criticism. Indeed, when Carter quietly backed away from promoting human rights in U.S.-Soviet relations after representations on behalf of dissidents threatened to derail the second round of the Strategic Arms Limitation Treaty (SALT II), a bipartisan collection of congressional cold warriors loudly complained that the administration was unfairly targeting right-wing allies while soft-pedaling human rights in its relations with the Communist world. Capturing the mood, Rep. Larry T. McDonald (D-GA) declared, "We roar at our friends and whisper accusations at the Communist nations. In fact we even ignore human rights violations in Communist China entirely. This policy has failed."[30]

Correspondingly, as Carter's human rights policy became increasingly focused on Latin America over the course of 1977, the administration was roundly criticized from both sides of the political spectrum. While liberal internationalists such as Senator Edward Kennedy (D-MA) and Rep. Donald M. Fraser (D-MN) advocated equally tough U.S. sanctions toward right-wing human rights violators with higher geostrategic importance to the United States—such as South Korea, the Philippines, and Iran—Cold War hawks pressed for the maintenance of close U.S. ties with anticommunist military regimes in the hemisphere. Ideological differences notwithstanding, both groups associated the problems of the Carter administration's human rights policy with its inconsistent application; as Earl C. Ravenal asserted in the January 1978 issue of *Inquiry,* "When it comes to human rights, the very essence of what we should be doing is to draw a firm, straight line—a constraint—across all our diplomatic relations, and accept the consequences." Rather than creating a flexible, pragmatic human rights policy, Ravenal continued, "the administration's flexibility has degenerated into hypocrisy, and its attempted policy has remained just noise."[31]

As a defining test case for the Carter administration's human rights initiative, Argentina held a central position in the increasingly raucous domestic political debate. While congressional liberals complained that the administration was doing too little—culminating in Senator Kennedy's successful amendment eliminating all U.S. military transfers to Argentina on September 30, 1978—a growing chorus of conservatives criticized Carter for doing too much. "The people in the United States are going to hear a lot about the Argentine from old Hollings," Senator Ernest Hollings (D-SC) told a group of U.S. business leaders operating in Argentina in August 1977 after an official visit to Buenos Aires. Emphasizing Argentina's "free government," Hollings criticized the Carter administration for engaging in "too much moralizing." Rep. Eligio de la Garza Jr. (D-TX) was equally dismissive of Carter's human rights initiatives. "I expected to see tanks in the street," de la Garza asserted. "I expected oppressed people without civil rights, but I have found something completely different." Elating his Argentine hosts, de la Garza concluded, "I wish each member of Congress could come here and see the truth."[32]

It was the U.S. business community, however, that emerged in the spring of 1978 as the foremost critics of the Carter administration's effort to promote human rights in Argentina. In the face of widespread state-sanctioned violence punctuated by uneven responses to U.S. pressure—"promises of progress, short term progress then regression, a forward and back pattern repeated over and over," in the words of the National Security Council staff member Jessica Tuchman Mathews—Warren Christopher's attempt to reward indications of Argentine political normalization and punish retrograde violence was perceived by many U.S. business leaders as unpredictable and capricious.[33] Concessions to domestic political lobbying—such as the State Department's November 1977 approval of submarine periscopes to the Argentine Navy from the Massachusetts-based firm Kollmorgen and Boeing Vertol helicopters to the Argentine Air Force—further aggravated business leaders. E. B. Fitzgerald, for example, described as "disquieting" the fact that the Kollmorgen and Boeing sales had been approved at roughly the same period that Cutler-Hammer's proposed sale of battlefield radar to Argentina was denied. His unease turned to irritation, however, when the State Department subsequently approved the sale of an AN/PPS-15 battlefield radar system to Argentina—a model nearly identical to Cutler-Hammer's AN/PPS-5. "It is inconceivable to me how one sale can be contrary to government policy and the other is not," Fitzgerald complained.[34]

By midsummer 1978, as the backlog of delayed and denied U.S. transfers to Argentina deepened, tension between the Carter administration and the U.S. business community reached a fever pitch. When the State Department delayed a $1.6 million sale of a Swearingen Merlin 4A air ambulance to the Argentine military, despite having previously sold a similar model to the Argentine Ministry of Public Health, the General Aviation Manufacturers Association openly criticized the Carter administration. "If they would define what countries have human rights problems, and what it will require to sell aircraft to those countries, we would establish the mechanism and attempt to comply," the vice president

William R. Edgar asserted. "Our frustration revolves around the fact that we don't know the ground rules."[35]

Such complaints reverberated across the Washington bureaucracy and were echoed with increasing frequency by pro-business agencies within the U.S. government. In the same month as the air ambulance denial, Julius L. Katz, the assistant secretary of state for economic and business affairs, recommended that President Carter sign an executive order stipulating that the Departments of State, Defense, and Commerce should avoid controlling exports for "non-strategic reasons" if the withheld goods could be purchased from other countries. "The harmful effect of current practice on our trade is already apparent and the potential for further harm is great," Katz asserted. Not only did delayed and denied U.S. transfers based on human rights considerations total several billion dollars, the assistant secretary contended, the indirect effects of the human rights policy would have long-term negative implications for the U.S. economy. As a result, "The U.S. is coming to be regarded as an unreliable supplier," Katz wrote, with the effect that "U.S. companies are losing market positions which have taken years to develop and cannot be regained quickly."[36]

Echoing Katz's concern, aviation expert Robert Hotz—who had edited the trade journal *Aviation Week and Space Technology* since the Eisenhower era— illustrated the intense frustration Carter's human rights policy was generating among U.S. firms operating in police and military exports. "The Carter disarmament coterie includes some of the most naïve people to operate in the capital city during the 30 years we have observed the scene," Hotz editorialized in mid-1978. With bureaucratic obstacles hamstringing government clearance "on even the most routine export sales," Hotz asserted, the Carter administration was "eroding an industry that over the past eight years contributed $52 billion in exports for a nation that had a $53-billion trade deficit for the same period." Rather than inserting morality into U.S. foreign policy, Hotz concluded, the Carter team was merely "transferring jobs from Wichita, Dallas, Cincinnati, St. Louis and Hartford to Paris, Toulouse, Bordeaux, London, Bristol and Manchester."[37]

The accumulated tension between the Carter administration and the U.S. business community exploded following the State Department's July denial of the $270 million Allis-Chalmers sale. The sheer size of the transaction, combined with the questionable effect its rejection would have on the human rights situation in Argentina sparked fierce outcry from business leaders, members of Congress, Washington bureaucrats, and conservative media pundits. At the center of the controversy, David Scott, the chief executive officer at Allis-Chalmers, captured the mood. Angrily dismissing the decision as "arbitrary," Scott predicted that it would not "have any effect upon human rights policies in Argentina." In a revealing admission, Scott added that "most importantly" the Exim denial "was severely damaging to his company, audits, [and] shareholders."[38] Similarly, after a September meeting intended to cover a broad range of foreign policy issues with nearly two dozen senior U.S. business executives, Paul H. Kreisberg reported that "the only subject *they* were interested in was human rights." Deeply concerned over the inability to predict how the Carter administration's human rights policy would affect their businesses overseas, the group expressed "great skepticism that the State Department really cared much about U.S. exports and trade."[39]

Adding fuel to the controversy, conservative media pundits pounced on the Allis-Chalmers denial as a golden opportunity to pillory the Carter administration's human rights policy. Leading the attack were the *Washington Post* columnists Rowland Evans and Robert Novak, whose influential editorials served as staple reading for much of Washington's policymaking elite. Praising the Argentine military junta for having squashed an impending Communist takeover, Evans and Novak savaged Patricia Derian for her harsh criticism of the military regime in congressional hearings in early August. Dismissing the Human Rights Bureau's estimate of the number of Argentines killed and missing as having "dubious reliability," the columnists hinted that the human rights agenda was being used "to support revolutionary forces in the hemisphere."[40] More significantly, in a subsequent column two weeks later, Evans and Novak directly linked Carter's human rights policy toward Argentina to the sputtering U.S. economy. According to the columnists, delayed or denied U.S. transactions based on human rights considerations had resulted in $1.4 billion in lost business with the South American nation. "Excess zeal," Evans and Novak concluded, had resulted in "overstress on human rights at the cost of U.S. jobs during high unemployment and record trade deficits."[41]

In fact, such criticism exaggerated the stringency of the Carter administration's human rights policy. The lack of consensus among top policy planners at the State Department on how the human rights policy should be applied over the course of 1977, combined with resistance from Washington bureaucrats and the U.S. business lobby, had resulted in a highly limited application of human rights constraints on the U.S. private sector. First, the Carter administration approved the vast majority of U.S. assistance, trade, and investment abroad. By the Christopher Group's own account, of the more than five hundred international financial institution (IFI) loans that were voted on during the Carter administration's first sixteen months, the United States voted against only ten and abstained on seventeen (all the loans were approved despite the U.S. show of censure).[42] Similarly, in 1978, the State Department reported that it denied fewer than 350 out of fifty thousand applications for exports, and only twenty-three of the one thousand license applications reviewed on human rights grounds were subsequently refused.[43] Finally, out of 169 countries served by the Exim Bank, only four were subject to human rights denials.[44]

Second, the State Department consistently refused to "lobby" the private sector in regard to human rights considerations, instead projecting an image of neutrality regarding commercial transactions—a position that was thoroughly undermined in practice by extensive commercial promotion by U.S. government officials at both the department and embassy level. In regard to a pending $150 million sale of Boeing aircraft to the Argentine national carrier Aerolineas Argentinas, for example, Ambassador Raúl Castro strongly argued that a department denial would not be perceived by the Argentine military junta as an official sanction on human rights grounds. Instead, emphasizing his own extensive involvement in the case, Castro argued that the decision would almost certainly rekindle a bitter dispute dating back to 1972 between Aerolineas Argentinas and Pan American and Braniff Airlines over a proposed route expansion. Similarly, Castro argued against State Department action in the Exim Bank on a General Telephone and Electronics (GTE) project to expand telecommunication infrastructure in Argentina, a long-term contract that U.S. investors hoped would ultimately garner nearly $1 billion. Noting his own active lobbying on behalf of GTE, Castro asserted that "our competition from the Japanese, Germans, and the Swedes can probably count on official credit or guarantee assistance, and if the contract goes to one of them our gesture in removing GTE from the field will go unnoticed in Argentina."[45] Such pro-business lobbying was not an isolated case; underscoring the traditionally close relationship between the State Department and the U.S. business community, to Patricia Derian's frustration, more than a year after Carter entered office State Department responses to potential investors' queries regarding particular U.S. bilateral relationships failed to include any mention of U.S. human rights actions.[46]

Finally, even toward Argentina the Carter administration's constraints on U.S. trade and investment were far less stringent than critics alleged. By 1978, U.S. banks—led by David Rockefeller's Chase Manhattan—had lent Argentina almost $3 billion, with $1.2 billion earmarked for government- or state-owned companies.[47] In the same year, arguably the nadir of U.S.-Argentine relations, U.S. exports to the South American nation equaled nearly $700 million.[48] Indeed, U.S. private sector trade with the Argentine military junta was so extensive that Steven Oxman, Warren Christopher's special assistant for human rights issues, proposed issuing a set of informal guidelines emphasizing that notwithstanding the lack of U.S. government constraints on the vast majority of transfers to Argentina, U.S. business leaders should not "believe they are freed from the necessity of moral choice." Underscoring the limited nature of U.S. sanctions toward Argentina, Oxman continued, "The fact is that a manufacturer who sells, say, a computer to the Argentine Navy is making an important *moral choice*: he is choosing to conduct business as usual with people who condone the torture of human beings. Nothing would prevent him from choosing not to do so, and I think it is important that he be reminded of that fact."[49]

If the human rights policy was far less restrictive on U.S. assistance, trade, and investment overseas than critics alleged, the furor surrounding the Allis-Chalmers denial nonetheless brought to the fore the incongruity at the heart of Jimmy Carter's self-described social liberalism and fiscal conservatism. In the face of a $16.4 billion trade deficit in the first half of 1978, Carter advocated a substantial increase in U.S. exports. Yet the Allis-Chalmers denial brought the total amount of lost U.S. business with Argentina to an estimated $800 million according to the State Department Bureau of Inter-American Affairs (ARA); although substantially less than the figures touted by critics of the human rights policy, the denials nonetheless primarily affected a military-industrial complex that employed seven hundred thousand U.S. workers.[50] Moreover, the Exim Bank's supplier credits and discount loans were primarily geared toward medium-sized U.S. manufacturers, precisely the kind of firms that the president needed to mobilize in order to substantially increase exports of manufactured goods.

Not surprisingly, pro-business agencies within the U.S. government were far less conflicted regarding the balance between promoting human rights and market capitalism abroad. Less than a week after the Allis-Chalmers decision, the under-secretary of state for economic affairs Richard N. Cooper pointed out to Warren Christopher that discouragement from the U.S. government based on political considerations would inhibit medium-sized U.S. producers from entering the export market. "The costs in this dimension," Cooper argued, "seem to me potentially greater than the incremental gains with respect to human rights from prohibiting this class of transactions."[51] Underscoring Cooper's point, the following day a cabinet-level National Export Policy Task Force led by the commerce secretary Juanita Kreps delivered a set of recommendations to President Carter for stimulating the nation's flagging export sector. The Carter administration needed to eliminate obstacles inhibiting potential exporters from entering the market, the task force asserted, not least by substantially increasing the lending capacity of the Exim Bank.[52]

Caught between the competing demands of the human rights policy and the imperatives of U.S. economic growth, Christopher tried to chart a middle path that would placate both human rights advocates and the U.S. business leaders. When Julius L. Katz criticized the Christopher Group for denying exports of nonlethal manufactured goods to human-rights-violating regimes, Christopher wrote in the margin of Katz's memo, "This was the Argentine case. Should work gloves go to torturers?"[53] Similarly, when apprised of the Allis-Chalmers CEO David Scott's livid reaction to the Exim Bank decision, Christopher's frustration was unmistakable. "Does Scott understand that a Congressional statute requires us to give our advice to Ex-Im?" he wrote at the bottom of the memo. "I challenge anyone to objectively review the Argentine human rights picture and give advice different from ours."[54] Nonetheless, continuous resistance to the human rights policy took a toll on the deputy secretary—indeed, in at least one instance, Christopher approved a transfer to Argentina against his own better judgment in order to avoid a bureaucratic battle; "I would vote no," he noted to Steven Oxman in a 1978 memo, "but it is not worth a battle with the Treasury."[55]

More broadly, by the end of the July 1978, pro-business criticism of the human rights policy had placed the Carter administration squarely on the defensive. Indeed, Carter's top advisers warned in the president's evening reading on July 28 that "there is mounting pressure on us from business and some Members of Congress to modify our advice to Ex-IM, since it may well result in the loss of considerable business for American firms."[56] Rising dissention within the ranks of the Carter team itself regarding the efficacy of the Allis-Chalmers decision further complicated matters. In a remarkable memorandum to Warren Christopher on August 10, the director of policy planning Anthony Lake asserted that "the human rights policy, and American interests in general, ultimately will benefit if we do not seem to be using economic pressure to bring down a particular government." Economic sanctions, Lake argued, risked poisoning relations with the target government and eroding domestic support in the United States for the human rights policy. Conspicuously absent from the analysis was the fact that congressional legislation specifically linked U.S. economic actions to human rights; instead, in an extraordinary display of how far the backlash against the Allis-Chalmers decision had shifted the human rights debate, Lake went so far as to compare the Carter administration's use of economic sanctions on behalf of human rights to Richard M. Nixon's attempts to sow economic crisis in Chile at the outset of the decade. "The strongest argument seems to us to be one of principle," Lake wrote. "To deny a country access to international financial support in order to try to force political change on it is not qualitatively different from the Nixon Administration's efforts to 'destabilize' the Allende government."[57]

A similar theme was sounded by Andrew Young, the outspoken U.S. representative to the United Nations and a well-known supporter of the human rights policy. In mid-August, Young criticized the Exim denial as attempting to promote human rights at the expense of economic and social development. In Young's view, if a development project was soundly planned and would be administered efficiently, it deserved U.S. support—even if the beneficiary was an authoritarian government. "I think we should avoid using our economic power in a way that impedes development in the recipient country," Young wrote, "while denying jobs to U.S. workers and weakening our own economy and balance of payments situation."[58]

Finally, the Allis-Chalmers controversy brought the National Security Council (NSC) into the debate over U.S. policy toward Argentina. During the 1976 presidential campaign, Carter's hawkish NSC adviser Zbigniew Brzezinski had recognized the potential of the human rights issue to bridge the ideological divide between liberal internationalists and cold warriors. Although he later claimed intellectual authorship of core components of the Carter administration's human rights policy, in practice, Brzezinski envisioned human rights as first and foremost a means to weaken the Soviet Union, and his support for the application of sanctions toward right-wing U.S. allies was tepid.[59] As early as March 1977 the national security adviser had warned that U.S. human rights sanctions might lead to "a kind of coalition of Latin American countries against us," a position that hardened in the aftermath of the Allis-Chalmers decision. As a result of the department's punitive human rights actions, Brzezinski informed Jimmy Carter on August 7, 1978, the United States was "running the risk of having bad relations simultaneously with Brazil, Chile, and Argentina."[60]

Brzezinski was particularly concerned about the impact of the U.S. human rights policy for U.S.-Argentine relations. According to the NSC Latin America expert Robert A. Pastor, "About halfway through the Administration . . . he was persuaded that perhaps we had gone far enough, that we should allow more space for the [Argentine] regime."[61] Two weeks after warning Carter of deteriorating relations with the Southern Cone, the national security adviser personally forwarded Andrew Young's critique of the Allis-Chalmers decision to Warren Christopher. Concurring with Young's negative assessment, Brzezinski staked a claim on future decisions regarding U.S. policy toward Argentina by pointedly noting that the "counter-productive" decision had not been cleared by the NSC.[62] The national security adviser's most candid assessment of U.S.-Argentine relations, however, was reserved for Secretary Vance. "We have a large economic relationship with a relatively prosperous middle-income developing country," Brzezinski wrote. "We want to expand, not contract that."[63]

* * *

The intense outcry over the Allis-Chalmers decision, coupled with top U.S. policymakers' focus on stimulating the economy effectively curbed the State Department's use of economic leverage to promote human rights overseas. The increasingly dour mood in Washington was unmistakably evident when congressional lawmakers repealed the legislation linking the Exim Bank to human rights considerations only two months after the Allis-Chalmers denial.[64] Although the Carter administration refused to reverse the Exim ruling until the Argentine military junta offered an unconditional invitation to the Inter-American Commission on Human Rights in November, by the end of the year the Human Rights Bureau had largely lost its influence over U.S. economic policy. "The department leadership was reluctant to invest the necessary political capital and energy in

future battles with domestic interests and their supporters in Washington," recalled Patrick Flood, who served as HA desk officer for the Southern Cone. "The
Human Rights Bureau continued to review EXIM cases and to set forth our objections for the record," Flood continued, "but as a policy instrument the EXIM
lever had effectively fallen from our hands."[65]

More broadly, although the Allis-Chalmers denial successfully elicited the
Argentine military junta's invitation to the IACHR, ironically, the decision constituted the high-water mark in the Carter administration's effort to promote
human rights in Argentina. In fact, the State Department began caving to domestic pressure almost immediately; in the lead-up to the congressionally mandated
cutoff date for U.S. sales to Argentina on September 30, the Christopher Group
authorized nearly $120 million in military transfers to the military junta. In addi-
tion to approving the export of two Boeing helicopters to the Argentine Army in
mid-August, only days before the cutoff went into effect, Deputy Secretary Christopher authorized clearing all the military and safety-related items in the Foreign
Military Sales (FMS) "pipeline," and tentatively approved more than thirty slots
for Argentine officers at U.S. military training facilities.[66]

Reviewing the issue in a series of memorandums to Brzezinski, Robert A. Pastor captured the fundamental challenge at the heart of the Carter administration's
human rights policy. Following Patricia Derian's harsh congressional testimony
in August, Brzezinski had dispatched Pastor to assess the State Department's policy toward Argentina and take an active role in developing a long-term strategy.[67]
Yet despite the ARA assistant secretary Viron P. Vaky's promise to include him in
the planning process, by the end of August Pastor had developed a deep skepticism regarding the State Department's decision-making approach, particularly
regarding the question of consistency in the application of the human rights
policy. "Decisions are beginning to be made in a haphazard, uncoordinated manner," he warned Brzezinski on August 31.[68]

Pastor was particularly concerned by Warren Christopher's approval of the Boeing helicopters to the Argentine Army less than a month after the Allis-Chalmers
Exim denial. Without a coherent strategy, he maintained, the human rights policy
would be misunderstood domestically and lack leverage abroad; specifically, when
U.S. business leaders learned that the Carter administration had approved the
sale, "the President and our policy will look foolishly inconsistent."[69] By the time
the State Department approved the FMS pipeline and training slots, Pastor's frustration was manifest. "This is just the latest set of decisions in a disastrous policy,"
he wrote Brzezinski on September 25. "We are exactly back where we hoped we
wouldn't be: dribbling out decisions rather than agreeing to a strategy."[70]

The flurry of transfer approvals, however, signified more than mere inconsistency. In subsequent months, the Carter administration's efforts to rebuild relations with the U.S. business community resulted in a dramatic increase in U.S.

transfers to Argentina. As a result, despite the moratorium on security transfers, U.S. trade and investment soared, with U.S. exports to the South American nation topping $1.7 billion in 1979, a 140 percent increase over the previous year.[71] Similarly, Argentina's debt to international private banks—with U.S. firms leading the pack—grew from $4.139 billion to $9.074 billion during the same period.[72]

The Carter administration's effort to accommodate the U.S. business community hamstrung Patricia Derian's ongoing struggle to maintain pressure on the Argentine military junta. In fact, although the number of kidnappings and killings by state security forces declined precipitously in 1979, the human rights situation in Argentina remained dire. First, the infrastructure for dirty war violence was largely intact, and the threat of state-sanctioned violence against perceived "intellectual subversion" remained high. As General Omar Rubens Graffigna, the recently installed commander of the air force and a member of the ruling junta, declared in September, "The war continues. The enemy will change his tactics and terrain. He will appear to be in retreat . . . only to reappear in the most remote places, in classrooms, universities [and] in all the areas of the nation's life that can be used as a base."[73]

Second, despite significant preparations for the IACHR visit, throughout 1979 the Argentine military junta categorically refused to provide an accounting of the untold thousands of *desaparecidos*. They were "absent forever" (*los ausentes para siempre*), General Roberto Viola asserted in an Army Day address in May.[74] Four months later, the military junta approved law 22.068, effectively insulating the military from judicial investigations regarding *desaparecidos* by mandating that anyone who disappeared between November 1974 and September 1979 could be declared legally dead.[75] In a particularly Orwellian turn of phrase, outgoing President Jorge Videla dismissed the issue as beyond the government's control. Nothing could be done for the *desaparecidos*, Videla contended in late 1979, since they were "neither dead nor alive."[76]

Such denials were undermined, however, by a growing body of evidence regarding the web of clandestine military detention centers. After an official visit to Buenos Aires in April, Patrick Flood, HA's desk officer for the Southern Cone, returned to Washington certain that hundreds, if not thousands, of Argentines were being held in what he described as the "Gaucho archipelago." "The evidence of secret interrogation/transit and prison facilities is too strong to be put down to wishful thinking by families of the disappeared," he wrote Patricia Derian. "There are too many first-hand accounts, too many cross-references and corroborating testimonies, too many verifiable details to deny the existence of these facilities."[77] Estimates of the number of detainees held at such sites varied considerably (in fact, by mid-1979, most clandestine prisoners had been killed); strong evidence did indicate, however, that at least partial records of the prisoners who had passed through clandestine centers existed.[78] The U.S. Embassy reported in July, for example, that the Argentine minister of interior had allegedly confided to a diplomatic colleague, "We know who is dead, but saying this to anyone is impossible. So many officers ... simply must be protected against reprisals at some future date."[79]

Finally, beginning in 1979 the Argentine military junta began actively exporting dirty war tactics to assist in the stabilization of embattled right-wing regimes in Central America. Following the overthrow of the Nicaraguan dictator Anastasio Somoza Debayle by the left-wing Sandinista revolutionaries in July 1979, Argentine military leaders sent advisers to oversee the mobilization and training of counterrevolutionary forces in Honduras. During the same period, Argentine military interrogation and intelligence-analysis experts were dispatched to El Salvador to help the fiercely anticommunist regime of General Carlos Humberto Romero fend off a growing leftist insurgency, and the following year, an Argentine counterinsurgency training team began operating in Guatemala. By assuming a leadership role in what the historian Ariel Armony describes as a "transnational counterrevolutionary network," the Argentine military thus actively sought to extend the practice of systematic kidnapping, torture, and clandestine murder throughout the region.[80]

The grim human rights situation in Argentina notwithstanding, the Carter administration's effort to rebuild relations with the U.S. business community over the course of 1979 edged human rights into the background of U.S.-Argentine relations. In January, despite news that nearly forty mutilated corpses had recently washed onto Argentina's South Atlantic coastline, Derian's recommendation that the U.S. tighten restrictions on commercial sales and deny Exim Bank financing for Argentina was ignored by Secretary Vance.[81] Instead, for human rights advocates closely attuned to developments in U.S.-Argentine relations, the Carter administration appeared to be listening more closely to U.S. business leaders such as the Chase Manhattan Bank chairman David Rockefeller, who, in a February address, dismissed efforts to link U.S. trade to human rights considerations as "ill-conceived, misguided and often counterproductive."[82] Indeed, by mid-May, nongovernmental human rights leaders were openly complaining that the policy was being quietly shelved. "Their impression is that the President 'put his hand in the fire,' got burned, and at present is backing away now that he 'understands the realities,'" wrote the HA staff member Roberta Cohen.[83]

Accelerating the Carter administration's shift away from human rights as a top policy priority was a resurgence of Cold War tension between the United States and the Soviet Union, and the rising influence of Carter's hawkish national security adviser Zbigniew Brzezinski. In what U.S. policymakers feared was an expanded version of Cuba's successful military intervention in Angola during the

Ford administration, by early summer 1978 the Soviets had delivered approximately $1 billion in weapons to help the pro-Soviet regime in Ethiopia fend off an attack by Somalia. Moreover, in what the historian Odd Arne Westad describes as the most significant non-European Soviet military operation since the Korean War, Moscow deployed more than eleven thousand Cuban and six thousand Soviet military personnel in Ethiopia to assist in the defense of Mengistu Haile Mariam's fledgling Marxist-Leninist regime.[84]

U.S. policymakers' anxiety regarding the apparent surge of Soviet adventurism in the Horn of Africa was heightened by the implosion of longstanding U.S. client regimes in Iran and Nicaragua. Installed by a U.S.-led coup in 1953, the Iranian shah Mohammad Reza Pahlavi's rampant corruption, repressive internal security apparatus, and abortive modernization efforts had engendered near-total opposition among the Iranian people by the late 1970s. As popular unrest intensified and the influence of the radical exiled cleric Ayatollah Ruhollah Khomeini deepened, the Carter administration was forced to contemplate the possibility of a political vacuum in a leading oil-producing nation with a 1,500-mile border with the Soviet Union. Although recognizing the indigenous origins of the crisis, the prospect of the shah's overthrow was nonetheless daunting; as Brzezinski wrote Carter in late 1978, "The disintegration of Iran would be the most massive American defeat since the beginning of the Cold War, overshadowing in its real consequences the setback in Vietnam."[85]

Corresponding with the Iranian crisis, Nicaragua descended into civil war in 1978, with the widespread brutality of the Somoza regime's security forces pushing thousands of ordinary Nicaraguans into the ranks of the left-wing Frente Sandinista de Liberación Nacional (FSLN) revolutionaries. The assassination of the moderate opposition leader Pedro Joaquín Chamorro in January brought the full extent of Nicaraguan instability to the Carter administration's attention: thirty thousand Nicaraguans took to the streets in protest, and a subsequent general strike achieved a 50 percent closure in the capital and 80 percent in most provincial cities.[86] By the time tepid U.S. efforts to orchestrate a moderate political transition broke down twelve months later, the first successful leftist insurgency in the hemisphere since the Cuban Revolution in 1959 was imminent.[87]

In the face of aggressive Soviet initiatives in Africa and the deepening crises in Iran and Nicaragua, Jimmy Carter increasingly shifted toward the more traditional U.S. Cold War posture advocated by Zbigniew Brzezinski. In January 1978, Carter recommended 3 percent increases in defense spending for all North Atlantic Treaty Organization (NATO) members, and he approved the expanded use of theater nuclear weapons by NATO-members four months later.[88] Underscoring the deepening chill in U.S.-Soviet relations, in a widely publicized address at Wake Forest University in mid-May, Carter asserted that the administration had completed a "major reassessment" in response to an "ominous inclination on the part of the Soviet Union to use its military power—to intervene in local conflicts, with advisers, with equipment, and with full logistical support and encouragement for mercenaries from other Communist countries."[89]

More significantly, in March 1978 Carter approved Brzezinski's proposal to visit China, paving the way for normalization of relations between the two countries at the end of the year. The trip's timing was an unmistakable indication of U.S. preoccupation with Soviet assertiveness in foreign affairs; as Brzezinski informed the president in April, "We have failed to use the China card against the Soviets."[90] Further underscoring U.S. efforts to exacerbate tension between the two Communist giants, in 1979 the Carter administration granted China "most favored nation" status (a concession denied to the Soviet Union) and initiated an intelligence-sharing program with the Chinese military.[91]

Brzezinski's influence on Jimmy Carter's foreign policy increased in 1979 as the administration struggled to respond to the deepening crises in the Middle East and Central America, along with increasing Soviet interventionism in central Asia. Following the shah's humiliating departure, in February the Ayatollah Khomeini returned to Iran in triumph, presenting U.S. policymakers with a successor regime whose political orientation centered on a visceral anti-Americanism. Six months later, as tens of thousands of ecstatic Nicaraguans crowded the central plaza of the largely destroyed capital to celebrate the overthrow of the Somoza dictatorship, U.S. intelligence analysts warned that the political sea change could lead to revolutionary upheaval throughout the region. "A key U.S. security interest," the NSC's Robert Pastor later wrote, "was to try to prevent the FSLN from pouring gasoline on its increasingly combustible neighbors."[92] Finally, reports of deepening Soviet support for the recently installed Marxist-Leninist government in Afghanistan further accentuated the Carter administration's fear that the Soviet Union was engaged in a concerted effort to foster Third World revolutionary unrest.

With U.S. power in the international sphere facing unprecedented challenges, Brzezinski repeatedly pushed Carter to adopt a hard line in U.S.-Soviet relations. In the effort to orchestrate a hard-nosed U.S. response to global turmoil, the national security adviser, writes the historian Melvyn P. Leffler, was "unrelenting."[93] The Carter administration had been "excessively acquiescent," Brzezinski warned the president in September. "I believe that both for international reasons as well as for domestic political reasons you ought to deliberately toughen both the tone and the substance of our foreign policy."[94] Carter agreed. U.S. defense spending for fiscal year 1979 increased by 10 percent, and in June Carter announced the development of the MX nuclear missile. The following month, plans for removing U.S. troops from South Korea were indefinitely postponed, and Carter's initial promises to restore U.S. diplomatic relations with Vietnam and Cuba were quietly shelved.[95] More significantly, at Brzezinski's request, in July the president authorized the Central Intelligence Agency to begin supplying covert nonlethal support to Afghan insurgents.[96]

* * *

The ascendance of Zbigniew Brzezinski's hard-line approach to foreign affairs corresponded with a marked decline in the Carter administration's emphasis on promoting human rights overseas. From the outset of his tenure as national security adviser, Brzezinski's support for the human rights policy had been contingent on whether he perceived it to be enhancing U.S. power abroad. Accordingly, "when a choice between the two had to be made, between projecting U.S. power or enhancing human rights, . . . I felt that power had to come first," Brzezinski later wrote in his memoirs. "Without credible American power, we would simply not be able either to protect our interests or to advance more humane goals."[97] In other words, for Brzezinski, the historian Gaddis Smith writes, "power was the goal and morality was an instrument to be used when appropriate, abandoned when not."[98]

By mid-1978, Brzezinski's support for the active promotion of human rights had been largely supplanted by traditional Cold War policy prescriptions. On the one hand, in the face of rising Cold War tensions and a spate of Third World revolutions, Brzezinski was concerned that the human rights policy was "in danger of becoming one-sidedly anti-rightist."[99] On the other hand, Brzezinski's shift away from human rights was indicative of a broader trend among the U.S. electorate. In a national poll conducted in late 1978, only 14 percent of respondents felt the United States was stronger than the Soviet Union, compared to 40 percent who emphasized Soviet strength.[100] Although Carter's human rights policy remained popular, rising Cold War anxiety was clearly evident in the congressional election of November 1978, which resulted in a string of defeats for outspoken supporters of human rights, including Rep. Donald M. Fraser (D-MN).[101] Arguably the most influential human rights advocate on Capitol Hill, Fraser's defeat not only silenced his own consistent support of human rights, but also closed off one of the primary channels for nongovernmental human rights advocacy.[102]

By the end of 1978, Brzezinski's ability to frame foreign policy issues according to his own prescriptions through tight control over the NSC staff and direct access to President Carter had spearheaded a widely recognized policy shift to a more traditional Cold War posture at the expense of human rights. Indeed, in an article entitled "Is Carter Abandoning His Policy on Human Rights?" a reporter for U.S. News and World Report bluntly asked Patricia Derian if "political and economic realities" in nations such as Iran, Nicaragua, and Argentina, were "forcing the administration to switch to a less vigorous and public approach to human rights."[103]

Derian demurred. In private, however, the human rights bureau chief was highly critical of the Carter administration's flagging support for human rights. Although the Carter team had "done more in human rights than any other administration and have some positive results to show for the policy," Derian wrote Secretary Vance the following October, "we have done less than we could or should have." Derian continued: "Our policy is erratic and confusing. We send a mixed message; in the past we sent a consistent one (e.g. it's business as usual), so a mixed message is an improvement. But we should be striving for a *consistent message*. We could achieve that goal." Nonetheless, in an unmistakable indication of her increasing pessimism, Derian concluded, "I don't see the will to do it or to do more than coast along."[104]

In particular, Derian blamed Brzezinski for the drop-off in support for human rights. The NSC, Derian asserted in an internal memorandum to Secretary Vance, was "frequently an obstacle." Underscoring Brzezinski's control over information that reached Carter, Derian maintained that "it does not serve the President to present him papers so sanitized that there are no real choices in the human rights field."[105] Brzezinski, Derian concluded in a subsequent memo, "talks beautifully on the topic, but there's no follow through."[106] Similarly, by mid-1979, nongovernmental human rights organizations were openly complaining of an "absence of anyone in the White House or National Security Council strongly supportive of human rights."[107]

The increasingly cold reception Derian's human rights initiatives received at the White House quickly translated into deepening resistance to the Human Rights Bureau from the State Department's geographic and functional bureaus. Indeed, there was a "widespread perception" in the State Department that "the emphasis given earlier to human rights has gradually taken a backseat in Administration concerns to security factors, and therefore that neither human rights considerations nor HA need be given as much attention as formerly," Paul Kreisberg informed Warren Christopher in October 1979. Not only were career foreign service officers paying less attention to the human rights issues, Kreisberg asserted, but the apparent drop-off in executive support for Derian "may have increased the sense of an adversarial relationship between HA and the rest of the Department on both sides of the issues."[108]

* * *

Combined with the Carter administration's emphasis on increasing U.S. exports, the president's shift away from human rights was particularly significant for U.S. policy toward Argentina, and by mid-1979, Derian's relentlessly harsh criticism of the Argentine military junta—such as a blistering May address at Florida

International University—sounded increasingly out of step with White House policy.[109] In fact, relations between Derian and Brzezinski had deteriorated to the point of obstructing the normal flow of information regarding the South American nation; when Derian forwarded a copy of the recently published report on human rights violations in Argentina by the Lawyers Committee for International Human Rights, the NSC staff member Thomas Thornton wrote Brzezinski, "I gather that there is a considerable amount of history to your relations with Ms. Derian on the subject of Argentina and don't have any idea of how you want this handled." Underscoring the NSC's limited receptivity—and notwithstanding the unimpeachable credentials of the Lawyers Committee—Thornton dismissed the seventy-page report, informing Brzezinski, "Frankly, I haven't mustered the courage to read it yet."[110] By the end of the year, the declining visibility of the Carter administration's human rights policy toward Argentina was clearly evident. As Juan de Onís perceptively reported in the New York Times in early December, "The Carter Administration continues to press for respect for human rights in Argentina, but the strident tone has disappeared."[111]

The momentum toward rapprochement between Washington and Buenos Aires accelerated dramatically following the Soviet invasion of Afghanistan in late December 1979. Already struggling to find a diplomatic solution to the November 4 takeover of the U.S. Embassy in Tehran, Jimmy Carter responded to the Afghanistan crisis with alacrity. The invasion, Carter told NBC's Meet the Press on January 20, 1980, was "the most serious threat to peace since the Second World War."[112] In his state of the union address three days later, Carter presented himself as a tough-minded cold warrior by laying out an updated version of containment doctrine that media pundits quickly dubbed the "Carter Doctrine." "An attempt by any outside force to gain control of the Persian Gulf region," the president gravely intoned, "will be regarded as an assault on the vital interests of the United States of America, and such an assault will be repelled by any means necessary, including military force."[113] To further demonstrate U.S. resolve, Carter enacted a series of punitive sanctions against the Soviet Union, including revoking the Soviet national airline's landing rights in the United States, restricting U.S. high-technology transfers to the Soviet Union, restricting Soviet fishing rights in U.S. waters, and, most significantly, curtailing the 17 million metric tons of U.S. grain earmarked for export to the Soviet Union.[114]

As one of the world's leading producers of grain, Argentina's geostrategic significance for the United States surged following Carter's enactment of the grain embargo. Ironically, according to Brzezinski, when the decision to enact the embargo was taken on January 4, no one in the administration had seriously considered Argentina's ability to step into the void, leading to a subsequent "acrimonious" internal debate.[115] It was a significant oversight; in 1979, the Soviet

Union had purchased 19 percent of its grain needs in Argentina, and with the export capacity of the upcoming harvest estimated at 12 million metric tons, the South American nation suddenly emerged as a key player in U.S. Cold War policymaking.[116]

Having belatedly recognized Argentina's potential for offsetting the U.S. embargo, the Carter administration quickly moved to accelerate rapprochement with the military junta. On January 25, General Andrew J. Goodpaster was dispatched to Buenos Aires to discuss the grain issue as Carter's special emissary. The former supreme commander of NATO, Goodpaster's brief—to "exchange views on the full range of U.S.-Argentine relations, including Argentina's role in Western security, human rights, technical cooperation, and bilateral consultations"—was an unmistakable indication that human rights had ceased to hold a virtual monopoly on U.S.-Argentine relations.[117] In addition to a personal letter from Carter to Videla thanking the Argentine leader for his "cordial reception of General Goodpaster" and encouraging Argentine participation in the Olympic boycott, subsequent high-level diplomatic U.S. visits to Argentina further demonstrated the Carter administration's downgrading of the human rights issue.[118] In February, the under secretary of commerce Luther H. Hodges Jr. visited to assure the military junta that the United States would approve Exim guarantees for projects earmarked for Argentina, and in mid-March, Gerard C. Smith, Carter's head negotiator on nuclear disarmament, arrived to discuss Argentina's plans to construct the nation's third nuclear reactor.[119]

Widely perceived in Buenos Aires as a "U.S. courtship" after three years of tension regarding the human rights issue, Argentine military leaders relished Washington's unexpectedly conciliatory tone. Argentina, Videla told reporters at the end of January, "had never been in a stronger position in its relations with the U.S."[120] Similarly, in March the U.S. Embassy reported that the Argentine military junta was savoring the "spirit of Goodpaster." The regime, the embassy concluded, "no longer feels itself under global siege as a human rights pariah, [and] has faced the prospect of better Argentine-U.S. relations with a combination of hope and rising self-confidence."[121]

The Carter administration's effort to improve U.S.-Argentine relations culminated in a Policy Review Committee (PRC) meeting on May 14. With the explicit intent to "counteract alleged Soviet influence," the PRC recommended that the administration normalize U.S.-Argentine relations.[122] Accordingly, in the effort to increase U.S. leverage over the Argentine military junta, the committee recommended initiating a series of security consultations focused on the South Atlantic, inviting an Argentine guest military instructor to the School of the Americas, and coordinating a high-level U.S. military visit to Argentina.[123] Significantly, underscoring the extent to which Carter had moved away from the human rights issue, the president not only concurred with the PRC's proposal but noted that he was "inclined to move faster" than the committee had recommended.[124]

At the Human Rights Bureau, the PRC decision came as a shock to Patricia Derian. In fact, in a remarkable display of administrative disregard for the human rights assistant secretary, Derian was on a vacation in Maine with her husband Hodding Carter III when the PRC meeting transpired.[125] Apprised of the event on her return to Washington, Derian attacked the decision with characteristic fervor, situating herself at the center of an "intense controversy," as the veteran journalist John Goshko subsequently reported in the *New York Times*, between "officials who see the policy shift as a retreat from the administration's international advocate of human rights and those whose primary concern is to deter what they see as a Soviet bid for greater influence with the third largest country of Latin America."[126] For human rights supporters, however, it was a rearguard struggle; although Derian's public threat to resign over the proposed normalization demonstrated an ongoing commitment to promoting human rights in U.S.-Argentine relations, it was also an unmistakable indication of the assistant secretary's declining influence in the Carter administration.

Derian did not resign. Instead, less than two months after the PRC meeting, the U.S. normalization initiative ground to a halt following the Argentine military junta's participation in the Bolivian military's July coup d'état. Revealing Argentine military leaders' continued adherence to a national security doctrine situating Argentina on the front lines of the "Third World War" against global Communism, the junta not only assisted in planning the coup—"The Argentine military did everything but tell Gen. García Meza the day to pull it off," a U.S. military adviser confided to the journalist Ray Bonner—but more than two hundred Argentine military personnel were estimated to have actively participated in the takeover.[127] And although the Carter administration delivered a clear show of disapproval by canceling all military and economic aid to Bolivia and recalling the ambassador, in subsequent months Argentina continued to raise U.S. policymakers' ire by actively exporting dirty war tactics to the Andean nation via the Bolivian ministry of interior.[128] Combined with the military junta's unwillingness to support the U.S. grain embargo, Argentina's adventurism in Bolivia effectively halted the momentum toward normalization with the United States. As the secretary of state Edmund S. Muskie wrote to Carter in mid-October, "It would be inappropriate to proceed this year with some of the steps earlier contemplated."[129]

If the Bolivian coup d'état sent a chill through U.S.-Argentine relations, the Carter's human rights policy would nonetheless remain in the background for the remainder of the administration's tenure. Preoccupied by the ongoing hostage crisis in Iran, the newly installed revolutionary government in Nicaragua, and the one hundred thousand Soviet troops stationed in Afghanistan, in the fall of 1980 the Carter administration resigned itself to maintaining a holding pattern in regard to U.S.-Argentine relations, an approach that continued following Carter's decisive defeat to Ronald Reagan in the November 1980 presidential election. "To the extent that we have cards to play, let's leave them for the next administration, who might get something in return for them," the National Security Council member Thomas Thornton advised shortly after the election. "The Carter Administration certainly won't."[130]

Two months later, nearly one hundred human rights advocates gathered at the Rayburn Office Building for a luncheon to honor Patricia Derian, whose tenure as assistant secretary of state for human rights and humanitarian affairs was drawing to a close. The atmosphere was grim; a staunch cold warrior, Reagan's vituperative criticism of the Carter administration's human rights sanctions against right-wing U.S. allies led many advocates to predict the incoming president would dismantle the entire Human Rights Bureau. "This is my graveside suit," a somberly attired Lawrence Birns of the Council on Hemispheric Affairs told a reporter. "I've been wearing it a lot these days."[131]

In fact, as U.S. policy toward Argentina made clear, the political tide had turned against the human rights movement long before Reagan's sweeping election victory in November. In the aftermath of the Carter administration's July 1978 decision to make Exim Bank approval of the $270 million Allis-Chalmers sale of a hydroelectric turbine factory to Argentina contingent on the junta's invitation to the Inter-American Commission on Human Rights, fierce resistance from the U.S. business community, coupled with top U.S. policymakers' focus on stimulating the economy, dramatically constrained the State Department's use of economic leverage to promote human rights overseas. Correspondingly, the resurgence of Cold War tension in the second half of the Carter administration, combined with Zbigniew Brzezinski's hard-headed approach to U.S.-Soviet relations, had precipitated Jimmy Carter's embrace of a more traditional U.S. Cold War policy, relegating human rights to the back burner as a U.S. policy priority.

Throughout, Patricia Derian had kept up the struggle to institutionalize human rights in U.S. foreign policy, and at the January luncheon in her honor, one human rights advocate after another offered heartfelt praise. When one individual waxed poetic, describing the assistant secretary as "tilting against gray flannel windmills," Derian responded with characteristic irony. "Well, here I am in my gray flannel suit," she told the assembled gathering. "Actually," Derian continued after a moment's pause, "I always had a gray flannel suit. It's good camouflage."[132]

CARTER, REAGAN, AND THE HUMAN RIGHTS REVOLUTION

In the opening months of Ronald Reagan's tenure in the White House, human rights advocates' fear that the new administration would systematically uproot the hard-won advances to institutionalize human rights in U.S. foreign policy appeared to be borne out. Reagan's vehement anticommunism and determination to reverse perceived Soviet advances harkened back to the uncompromising rhetoric of the early Cold War. Capturing the strident tone that would guide Reagan's foreign policy approach, an influential 1980 monograph by the right-wing Committee of Santa Fe asserted that "containment of the Soviet Union is not enough. Détente is dead."[1] Determined to stem the spread of Communism in the developing world, the administration exacerbated local conflicts, particularly in Central America, where Sandinista revolutionaries had consolidated political power in Nicaragua and a leftist guerrilla threat in neighboring El Salvador was gaining strength. "The Caribbean is rapidly becoming a Communist lake in what should be an American pond," Reagan declared at the outset of his tenure, "and the United States resembles a giant, afraid to move."[2]

Corresponding with its aggressive posture in the international arena, the Reagan administration set out to dramatically downgrade the promotion of human rights as a U.S. foreign policy goal. During the electoral campaign, the Reagan team had sharply criticized Jimmy Carter's perceived inability to differentiate between "traditional authoritarian governments" and the totalitarianism of "revolutionary autocracies," resulting in U.S. destabilization of right-wing allies in an era of deepening Cold War tension. As the Reagan adviser Jeane Kirkpatrick wrote in an influential article in *Commentary*, "In the thirty-odd months since the inauguration of Jimmy Carter as President there has occurred a dramatic Soviet military build-up, matched by the stagnation of American armed forces, and a dramatic extension of Soviet influence in the Horn of Africa, Afghanistan, Southern Africa, and the Caribbean, matched by a declining American position in all these areas. The U.S. has never tried so hard and failed so utterly to make and keep friends in the Third World."[3] Concurring with Kirkpatrick's assessment, in early 1981 Reagan nominated Ernest Lefever as assistant secretary of state for human rights and humanitarian affairs. A conservative political theorist and founder of a right-wing think tank, Lefever had openly encouraged dismantling the bureau during the 1980 presidential campaign.[4]

The Reagan administration's repudiation of Jimmy Carter's human rights policy was particularly evident in U.S.-Argentine relations. Echoing Kirkpatrick, during the presidential campaign Reagan had sharply criticized the Carter administration's opprobrium toward the Argentine military junta. "There is an old Indian proverb: Before I criticize a man, may I walk a mile in his moccasins," Reagan declared in a late-1978 radio broadcast. "Patricia Derian and her minions at Mr. Carter's human rights office apparently never heard of it. If they had, they might not be making such a mess of our relations with this planet's seventh largest country, Argentina, a nation with which we should be close friends."[5] Under Reagan, the candidate's foreign policy team made clear, human rights would be conducted through "quiet diplomacy"; as the adviser Roger Fontaine asserted in a forum on U.S. policy toward the Southern Cone in June 1980, "The general belief is that you get more political mileage conducting things in private."[6]

The Reagan team was more direct in its initial communications with the Argentine military regime. Carter's human rights policy has had "disastrous effects on our relations with Latin America," the retired U.S. Army general and Reagan adviser Daniel Graham told Argentine officials in late June. Reagan, he promised, "will abandon the policy of throwing our old friends to the wolves to get along with Peking and Moscow."[7] Such favor was not lost on the Argentine military. In August, for example, a reliable source informed the U.S. Embassy in Buenos Aires that the minister of interior General Albano Eduardo Harguindeguy believed Reagan would "applaud the Argentine government tactics in the 'dirty war' and encourage such tactics in Argentina and elsewhere."[8]

The interior minister's prediction proved prescient. Two months after entering the Oval Office, the Reagan administration announced plans to convince congressional legislators to lift the ban on military sales to Argentina, and in July the administration ended the Carter administration's policy of voting against international financial institution loans to Argentina on human rights grounds.[9] Moreover, in an unmistakable show of presidential favor, General Viola was invited on an official visit to Washington in mid-March. Underscoring the buoyant mood among military leaders in Buenos Aires following Reagan's victory, in a press conference during the visit, Viola dismissed the possibility of an inquiry regarding the whereabouts of the thousands of Argentine *desaparecidos*. "I think you are suggesting that we investigate the Security Forces—that is absolutely out of the question," he asserted. "This is a war and we are the winners. You can be certain that in the last war if the armies of the Reich had won, the war crimes trials would have taken place in Virginia, not in Nuremberg."[10] Illuminating the extremism at the heart of the Argentine military's national security doctrine, Viola's statement nonetheless came as a shock to even close observers of the Argentine dictatorship. As the *Buenos Aires Herald* subsequently pointed out, "Viola after all is supposed to be a moderate, and if the moderates think the only thing the Nazis did wrong is to lose, the normal mind will find it hard to imagine what the view of the hardliners must be."[11]

It was not an issue that troubled the Reagan administration. Indeed, the fanatical anticommunism that underlay the Argentine dirty war dovetailed nicely with the Reagan team's plan to orchestrate a "low-intensity" conflict with Nicaragua's recently installed revolutionary government. Aware that since mid-1979 the Argentine military had been quietly exporting dirty war tactics through counter-revolutionary training programs in Nicaragua and El Salvador, in early 1981 the Reagan administration invited the armed forces chief of staff General Leopoldo Galtieri to Washington and secretly agreed to provide a stepped-up Argentine advisory program with military aid and financial support.[12] The details of the agreement were finalized by the former deputy CIA director Vernon Walters—whose harsh criticism of the Carter administration's human rights policy was well known in Argentine military circles—during a quiet visit to Buenos Aires in May.[13] As one U.S. official later asserted, "It was convenient to run the operation through the Argentines. We didn't have to ask questions about their goals that we couldn't escape asking about our own goals when we took over."[14]

* * *

If the Reagan administration's opening moves—particularly in regard to U.S.-Argentine relations—seemed to confirm human rights advocates' worst fears, the administration's subsequent setbacks revealed the human rights movement's resilience, and underscored the rationale, if not the success, behind Patricia Derian's opprobrium toward the Argentine military. In May, the White House encountered unexpectedly stiff congressional resistance to Ernest Lefever's nomination as human rights assistant secretary, a development influenced in no small degree by the attendance at the hearings of the Argentine journalist Jacobo Timerman. The founder of the influential Argentine daily *La Opinión*, Timerman had discussed U.S.-Argentine relations with Derian in a private meeting on her first visit to Argentina in March 1977.[15] Less than a month later, Timerman was abducted by state security personnel and deposited in a clandestine detention center, where he endured torture and extreme privation.[16]

News of the kidnapping quickly reached the State Department, and in subsequent months Derian spearheaded efforts to secure Timerman's release. By the time military leaders transferred Timerman from clandestine detention to house arrest in October 1977 he had become an international symbol of Argentine political repression, and in subsequent months, Timerman's imprisonment was repeatedly raised by top U.S. policymakers, the U.S. Embassy in Buenos Aires, human rights advocates in Congress, and nongovernmental human rights organizations such as Amnesty International.[17] Derian's own advocacy was particularly significant—on one occasion, the assistant secretary was so adamant to Harguindeguy regarding the case that after the meeting concluded the interior minister personally summoned Timerman to his office and demanded to know if he and Derian were related.[18] Underscoring the depth of U.S. human rights efforts on Timerman's behalf, when the journalist was finally expelled from Argentina in September 1979 after twenty-nine months in captivity, Jimmy Carter sent a personal letter of congratulations.[19]

Two years later, Timerman's attendance as a spectator at the Senate Foreign Relations Committee hearings on the Lefever nomination galvanized human rights advocates' effort to derail the confirmation. With the English translation of his extraordinary memoir, *Prisoner without a Name, Cell without a Number,* newly released in the United States, during the hearings Timerman was asked to stand by the committee chairman Charles H. Percy (R-IL) to be acknowledged for his efforts on behalf of human rights. The audience, John Goshko reported in the *Washington Post,* "burst into a thunderous applause." More significant, although Timerman did not officially testify, during an informal press conference following the day's hearings, he offered strong praise for the Carter administration's human rights policy. "I know positively how many lives were saved because Patt Derian was making a great scandal. She was always outspoken. There is no other way," Timerman asserted. Quiet diplomacy, he concluded, "is surrender."[20] The Senate Foreign Relations Committee agreed; feeling as though "they were choosing between Timerman and Lefever in casting their votes on the latter's confirmation," in the words of the Human Rights Watch founder Aryeh Neier, a majority of the committee members voted against confirmation.[21]

The Lefever fiasco forced the Reagan administration to reevaluate its approach to human rights. Indeed, by the fall of 1980, the president had eschewed the harsh criticism of human rights in U.S. foreign policy that had characterized the electoral campaign. Instead, taking a page from congressional cold warriors' use of human rights in the early 1970s as a weapon to batter the Communist world, the Reagan team initiated a concerted effort to fold the human rights policy into the administration's overarching Cold War objectives—an approach clearly evident in Reagan's decision to nominate Elliott Abrams for the human rights assistant secretary position. A former aide to Senator Henry M. Jackson (D-WA) and Senator Daniel Patrick Moynihan (D-NY), and son-in-law to the neoconservative stalwarts Norman Podhoretz and Midge Decter, the thirty-three-year-old Abrams was an outspoken proponent of U.S. support for "pro-democracy" forces fighting to stave off Communist advances in the developing world.[22] "To prevent any country from being taken over by a Communist regime," Abrams later asserted, "is in our view a very real victory for the cause of human rights."[23]

With Abrams at the helm, the Reagan administration's human rights policy would subsequently serve as rhetorical justification for U.S. military and financial aid to repressive right-wing clients in the developing world, particularly Central America, with appalling human and material costs. Indeed, over the course of the decade, more than three hundred thousand Central Americans were killed by military and paramilitary forces supported by the United States, and millions more were displaced. U.S. intervention also had crippling effects on the Central American economy; by one estimate, the region suffered $30 billion in economic losses.[24] Significantly, the Reagan administration adopted the human rights idiom to shield the abuses perpetrated by U.S. clients. According to Reagan, Efraín Ríos Montt, the architect of the Guatemalan military's genocidal campaign in the Western Highlands, was "totally committed to democracy."[25] When four U.S. nuns were raped and murdered by the U.S.-backed Salvadoran military, Jeane Kirkpatrick disingenuously told members of the press, "The nuns were not just nuns. The nuns were also political activists."[26] Perhaps most horrifying was Reagan's description of the Contras—the U.S.-financed guerrilla army waging an extraordinarily brutal war of attrition against Nicaragua's revolutionary government—as the "moral equivalent of our founding fathers."[27]

The administration's use of the human rights policy to justify U.S. support of repressive regimes outraged liberal human rights advocates. Nonetheless, the administration's decision to utilize—rather than uproot—the Human Rights Bureau had significant long-term ramifications. In part due to Reagan's conflation of human rights with the export of democracy, and partially as a result of what the political scientist Clair Apodaca describes as "the bureaucratic tendency toward policy inertia and entrenchment," during the 1980s the fierce bureaucratic opposition to the very concept of pursuing human rights in U.S. foreign policy largely dissipated.[28] As a result, HA increasingly became accepted as a legitimate player in the foreign policymaking process, thus enjoying greater access to the flow of information and, in a dramatic shift from the late 1970s, a growing reputation as a vehicle for career advancement in the foreign service. Correspondingly, human rights reporting—both by members of HA and foreign service officers charged with reporting on human rights at U.S. embassies—underwent a slow professionalization, a process particularly evident in the rising quality of the congressionally mandated *Country Reports*.[29]

Over the course of the 1980s, in other words, the Human Rights Bureau became increasingly entrenched in the byzantine web of Washington bureaucracy. "You can imagine how difficult it was in the beginning," recalled George Lister, who worked on human rights at the State Department throughout the Carter and Reagan administrations. Nonetheless, he continued,

> I soon discovered this work is like pushups—the more you do, the more you can do. . . . When Ronald Reagan became President in 1981, many assumed our human rights policy was over and our Bureau would be closed down. But it soon became clear the human rights policy had become institutionalized. There was widespread support in the Congress, and we were still required by law to get the annual Human Rights Reports up to Congress by January 31 of every year. So our performance continued to improve, like pushups.

Human rights, Lister concluded, had been "injected into the State Department's bloodstream."[30]

If human rights advocates in the United States found some solace in the Reagan administration's inability to dismantle the State Department Human Rights Bureau, the Argentine military junta's implosion following the disastrous decision in 1982 to invade the Malvinas/Falkland Islands clearly validated the human rights movement's effort to censure the military dictatorship over the previous seven years. With the economy in a shambles—Argentina's external debt reached $46 billion in 1983—and facing increasingly assertive demands for an accounting of human rights violations, in April 1982 the military junta dispatched an expeditionary force to wrest the long-disputed Malvinas Islands from the United Kingdom.[31] A desperate effort to garner popular support by playing to Argentines' nationalist sympathies, the Malvinas adventure illuminated not only the military junta's moral and financial bankruptcy but a remarkable lack of diplomatic aptitude and military prowess. In a predictable decision that nonetheless came as a shock to Argentine leaders, the Reagan administration promptly offered material and intelligence assistance to the British retaliatory force, which in turn routed the poorly trained Argentine conscripts defending the islands.[32]

Coupled with the deteriorating economic situation, the defeat eviscerated popular support for Argentina's military leaders. In the face of deepening divisions within the armed forces and intense popular outcry led by Argentine human rights organizations—one hundred thousand protesters gathered in one rally in December 1982—the Argentine military hastily declared a "self-amnesty law" before withdrawing from the political stage in favor of national elections in late October 1983.[33] The subsequent electoral victory of the Radical Civic Union Party candidate Raúl Alfonsín underscored the widespread support the human rights issue enjoyed in Argentina; during the campaign, Alfonsín repeatedly called for an investigation into the *desaparecidos* and pledged to prosecute those responsible for crimes committed during the period of military dictatorship.[34] Accordingly, less than a week after entering office on December 10, 1983, the new president announced the creation of a National Commission on the Disappeared (Comisión Nacional sobre la Desaparición de Personas, CONADEP) to investigate the victims of state-sanctioned violence during the Argentine dirty war.

CONADEP's subsequent report, *Nunca Más* (Never Again), was immediately recognized as a landmark contribution to the struggle for human rights in Argentina. Chaired by the prominent writer Ernesto Sábato, the commission methodically cross-checked testimonies, visited detention centers, and drew heavily on the assistance of the Argentine and international human rights community. Eventually compiling fifty thousand pages of testimony on seven thousand cases over a nine-month period, the CONADEP report, as the legal scholar Ronald Dworkin aptly put it, was a thickly documented narrative with two themes: "ultimate brutality and absolute caprice."[35] Detailing the military's systematic use of abduction, torture, and clandestine murder of perceived subversives—along with corresponding practices such as theft, sexual violence, and the stealing of victims' babies—the report documented nearly nine thousand cases of known victims of state-sanctioned violence and estimated that the actual number was far higher.[36] "Thus, in the name of national security," the report concluded, "thousands upon thousands of human beings, usually young adults or even adolescents, fell into the sinister, ghostly category of the *desaparecidos*, a word (sad privilege for Argentina) frequently left in Spanish by the world's press."[37]

An immediate best seller, more than a quarter million copies of *Nunca Más* were sold during the Alfonsín administration. Underscoring the report's extraordinary success in promoting popular awareness of human rights violations during the military dictatorship, the political scientist Alison Brysk recalled seeing *Nunca Más* "in settings ranging from a remote farmhouse in Entre Rios to supporting a heraldic crest on the bookshelf of a member of the Buenos Aires elite."[38] More concretely, the report facilitated the legislative abrogation of the outgoing military junta's self-amnesty law. After an unsuccessful attempt to have dirty war–era military leaders prosecuted by military justices, Alfonsín transferred the cases to the Buenos Aires Federal Appellate Court. In the subsequent trial, after hearing the testimony of more than eight hundred individuals and compiling 29,000 pages of records, the court convicted the leaders of the 1976 coup d'état. General Jorge Videla and Admiral Emilio Massera received life sentences, and Brigadier Orlando Ramón Agostí was sentenced to four and a half years in prison. Additionally, Lieutenant-General Roberto Viola received seventeen years in prison and Admiral Armando Lambruschini received eight; all those punished were permanently banned from holding public office in the future.[39]

Given the increasingly vocal criticism from Argentine military circles, the trial was an extraordinary achievement on behalf of human rights. Granted, in light of the enormity of the crimes committed, the sentences meted out to the military leaders were extraordinarily lenient, eliciting harsh criticism from human rights advocates.[40] Nonetheless, the CONADEP report and the closely followed judicial proceedings against the former military leaders served as a landmark repudiation of the illegality and immorality of the Argentine dirty war, establishing a precedent for future human rights trials in Argentina, as well as providing a model for subsequent truth commissions in nearly three dozen nations across the globe.[41]

* * *

Significantly, Argentina's postdictatorship strides in the human rights arena offered unmistakable validation for U.S. human rights advocates' struggle to curtail long-standing U.S. Cold War ties to anticommunist, right-wing military regimes in Latin America. In fact, the penultimate chapter of the CONADEP report expressly indicted the United States for its role in facilitating the Argentine military's national security doctrine. Consisting of a series of short statements by U.S. and Argentine political and military leaders over the course of the Cold War—ranging from the U.S. secretary of defense Robert McNamara's call for increased U.S. military instruction for Latin American soldiers in 1963 to the Argentine general Ramón Camps's admission in 1981 that the United States had served as the predominate source of Argentine counterinsurgency training—*Nunca Más* outlined the foundational role of U.S. military training and aid in facilitating the dirty war.[42]

Correspondingly, Patricia Derian's tireless advocacy on behalf of human rights in U.S.-Argentine relations received a significant degree of validation when she was invited by Raúl Alfonsín to participate as an honored guest in the presidential inauguration ceremony.[43] Along with then-former Rep. Robert F. Drinan (D-MA), Derian returned to Buenos Aires in 1985 to testify at the much-publicized trial of the military junta. Underscoring the extent to which the former human rights assistant secretary's efforts had ruffled the feathers of Argentine military leaders, as Derian assumed the witness stand the defense lawyers left the courtroom in protest. Undeterred, with characteristic candor Derian contributed to the prosecution's case by describing her meetings with Argentine military leaders, including Videla's repeated assertions that it was "difficult to control the lower rank personnel," and Massera's macabre allusion to Pontius Pilate when pressed to halt human rights violations carried out by navy operatives.[44]

More significantly, the restoration of democracy in Argentina marked the end of Argentina's participation in the Cold War. Since the late 1940s, U.S. relations with Argentina—and Latin America as a whole—had been defined by an overriding emphasis on protecting U.S. national security against the perceived threat of global Communism. By the mid-1960s, the United States had succeeded in enticing Argentina into a hemispheric alliance system predicated on U.S. hegemony and sustained through extensive transfers of military equipment and training. Heightening military leaders' political ambitions, accelerating the development of a distinctly Argentine doctrine of national security, and enhancing the armed forces' repressive capacity, the United States played a decisive role in the formulation of the counterinsurgency doctrine that guided the Argentine dirty war.

Despite Reagan's efforts to reestablish close U.S.-Argentine military ties, the chain of events leading from the Malvinas invasion to the election of Alfonsín forced the White House to make a historic policy shift toward Argentina. In a remarkably rapid transition, democracy promotion moved to the center of U.S. policy toward Argentina. Indeed, only four months after Alfonsín's inauguration, Ambassador Frank Ortiz told a reporter that "the absolute bottom line" of U.S. policy "is to fortify, support and see democracy flourish here."[45] Ortiz's successor, Theodore E. Gildred, who arrived in Buenos Aires in 1986, received a similar mandate. "Basically, my mission was to help the Argentine government consolidate its democracy and to help the institutions that needed to become more democratic continue on that path," Gildred later recalled.[46] Indeed, a 1987 State Department Policy Review Group memorandum bluntly declared, "Our most vital interest in Argentina is the consolidation of democracy."[47]

As a result, although the Reagan administration's policy of supporting the region's representative governments "by applause" offered almost no economic benefits, Washington nonetheless provided Alfonsín with an added dose of political clout in his bid to consolidate civilian rule in Argentina.[48] More broadly, by the end of Reagan's second term in office, the administration had thus distanced itself from Jeane Kirkpatrick's realist template and embraced instead a version of Cold War idealism with democracy promotion at its core. Far from disappearing, human rights became increasingly institutionalized in U.S. foreign policy over the course of the 1980s, resulting in subtle U.S. support for young democracies such as Argentina, and, by the end of the decade, assertive efforts to elicit democratic transitions, notably in the Philippines, South Korea, and Chile. The Reagan administration, in other words, demonstrated that the United States "could withdraw support from a dictator and support democratic change without producing another Iran or Nicaragua," writes James Mann, a policy shift that "represented a dramatic reversal from the 1970s."[49]

In particular, the cessation of close U.S.-Argentine military ties that accom-panied the Reagan administration's belated support for Argentine democracy clearly validated the abiding efforts of U.S. human rights advocates. A hetero-geneous mix of grassroots organizers, Washington-based lobbyists, and sympa-thetic members of Congress, the human rights movement had emerged in the late 1960s and early 1970s in opposition to the maintenance of close U.S. ties to anticommunist, right-wing military regimes. Notwithstanding intense opposi-tion by the Nixon and Ford administrations, by the middle of the 1970s, human rights advocates had succeeded in making significant inroads into the policy-making process, including more than a dozen pieces of congressional legislation binding U.S. foreign policy to human rights considerations, and had established a broad base of popular support—a key factor in Jimmy Carter's 1976 electoral victory.

Indeed, Carter's election constituted a defining moment in the effort to in-stitutionalize human rights in U.S. foreign policy. At the outset of his tenure in the White House, Carter recognized the fundamentally illiberal nature of U.S. Cold War policy toward the developing world, particularly Latin America. By mandating that the promotion of human rights be "a major objective of U.S. for-eign policy," and by appointing supporters of the initiative in key administration positions, in 1977 and 1978 Carter shifted the locus of human rights advocacy from the nongovernmental sector and Capitol Hill to the White House and Foggy Bottom. That Carter failed to fully institutionalize human rights should not ob-scure just how far the president advanced the debate over U.S. foreign policy as a whole; in light of the previous three decades of U.S. support for right-wing military regimes, the remarkable shift the human rights initiative embodied was clear, even when shorn of rhetorical flourishes and lofty idealism, such as Cyrus Vance's 1977 address at the University of Georgia Law School. "We seek these goals because they are right—and because we, too, will benefit," Vance asserted. "Our own well-being, and even our security, are enhanced in a world that shares common freedoms and in which prosperity and economic justice create the con-ditions for peace. And let us remember that we always risk paying a serious price when we become identified with repression."[50]

Both the power and pitfalls of Carter's human rights policy were starkly evident in U.S. relations with Argentina. In its effort to end state-sanctioned violence, the administration sharply curtailed U.S. grant and commercial transfers of military equipment and training, and consistently opposed or abstained on international financial institution loans to Argentina. With unprecedented intelligence on the extent of political repression in Argentina thanks largely to the efforts of F.A. "Tex" Harris at the U.S. Embassy in Buenos Aires, the Carter administration also made hundreds of consular representations on behalf of human rights.

As a result, human rights entered into the lexicon of U.S. diplomacy toward Argentina, forcing the Argentine military junta to consider international opprobrium as the necessary price for its campaign of extralegal violence. More significantly, the Carter administration's successful effort to convince the Argentine military junta to invite the Inter-American Human Rights Commission (IAHRC) contributed to a dramatic decline in disappearances, improved prison conditions, and increased popular awareness of the government's human rights abuses. Finally, Carter's human rights policy provided an unprecedented mantle of U.S. government legitimacy to Argentine human rights groups, thus providing a modicum of protection against extralegal violence, as well as a much-needed sense of solidarity. Harris played a particularly influential role in establishing the U.S. Embassy as a center for human rights advocacy. As Aída Sarti, a member of the Madres de Plaza de Mayo later recalled, Harris "would receive us, protect us, he kept us away from the military camps." The young foreign service officer, Sarti concluded, "had a disposition for human rights that one could not believe coming from the United States."[51]

By the same token, the declining visibility of human rights in the latter half of the Carter administration dramatically constrained the effort to curtail state-sanctioned violence in Argentina. In the face of deepening economic stagflation, Carter proved unwilling to face down the concerted efforts of the U.S. business community, resulting in an immense influx of private credit and sales to the Argentine military junta. Similarly, the Carter administration's adoption of a more traditional Cold War approach in the face of deepening U.S.-Soviet tension and revolutionary upheaval in the developing world cast the limits of the president's dedication to human rights in sharp relief—a trend particularly evident in the shift toward rapprochement with Argentina following the Soviet invasion of Afghanistan.

In the final analysis, the mixed legacy of the Carter administration's human rights policy toward Argentina most clearly illustrates the abiding significance of the nongovernmental human rights community and its supporters in the U.S. Congress. Not only were Carter's human rights initiatives rooted in the legal foundation established by congressional legislation, but the constant pressure leveled on the administration by the human rights community played a key role in facilitating Carter's own achievements in the human rights arena. The administration's success in eliciting the IAHRC invitation in 1978, for example, was inextricably linked to the impending congressionally mandated U.S. arms cutoff to Argentina; arguably the most significant U.S. human rights initiative toward the military junta, the amendment had passed the previous year over determined White House opposition.

The centrality of the human rights community was a theme that Patricia Derian, the consummate Washington outsider, fully recognized. Describing the future prospects of the U.S. human rights policy, Derian told a gathering of advocates on the thirtieth anniversary of the Universal Declaration of Human Rights that "people have to care enough about it to watch, to complain, to push, to press, to say that this is what we want, that this doesn't match our standard, or that we are not satisfied with it and we must do better. If that doesn't continue, then 15 or 20 years down the pike this will just be something else that happened or still has a little office percolating somewhere. It really depends on the people who are gathered here today." In sum, Derian concluded, "You are the human rights establishment. You are the authors of human rights in American foreign policy."[52]

At the end of the Cold War less than a dozen years later, the human rights movement's effort to remake U.S. foreign policy remained unfulfilled. The formative struggles of the late 1960s and 1970s would serve as a blueprint, however, in the ongoing effort to shape U.S. actions in the international arena in the post–Cold War world. As successive presidential administrations sought to expand the reach of global capitalism and protect U.S. national security from threats ranging from drug trafficking to international terrorism, the human rights movement would remain a powerful influence in the formulation and implementation of U.S. foreign policy. As George Lister enthused to a colleague shortly after the fall of the Soviet Union, "Human rights has become the authentic world revolution, democratic, peaceful and very powerful—so long as we keep it honest."[53]

Abbreviations Used in the Notes

ADP	Argentina Declassification Project (1975–1984)
BA	Buenos Aires
CF	Central Files
CFPF	Central Foreign Policy Files
Christopher Papers	Records of Warren Christopher, 1977–1980
DDRS	Declassified Documents Reference System
DoD	Department of Defense
DoS	Department of State
Derian Papers	Personal Papers of Patricia Derian, Chapel Hill, NC
FAOC	Foreign Affairs Oral History Collection of the Association for Diplomatic Studies and Training
Fraser Papers	Donald M. Fraser Papers, 1951–1995, Minnesota Historical Society, Saint Paul, MN
FRUS	*Foreign Relations of the United States*
GRDS	General Records of the Department of State
GRFL	Gerald R. Ford Library, Ann Arbor, MI
Hill Papers I	Robert C. Hill Papers, Rauner Special Collections Library, Dartmouth College
Hill Papers II	Robert Charles Hill Papers, 1942–1978, Hoover Institution Archives, Stanford University
ILHRR	International League for Human Rights Records, Rare Books and Manuscripts Division, New York Public Library
JCL	Jimmy Carter Library, Atlanta, GA
JFKL	John F. Kennedy Library, Boston, MA
Lake Papers	Policy and Planning Staff, Office of the Director, Records of Anthony Lake, 1977–1981, GRDS, RG 59, NARA
LBJL	Lyndon Baines Johnson Library, Austin, Texas
Lister Papers	George Lister Papers, Benson Latin American Collection, University of Texas Libraries, University of Texas at Austin
NARA	National Archives and Records Administration, College Park, MD

NAUK	British National Archives, Kew, United Kingdom
NSA	National Security Archive
NSF	National Security Files
NYT	*New York Times*
OPLMC	Office of Public Liaison, Margaret (Midge) Costanza
PBS	Public Broadcasting Service
RG 59	Record Group 59
Robinson Papers	Records of Deputy Secretary of State Charles W. Robinson, 1976–1977, GRDS, RG 59, NARA
RRL	Ronald Reagan Library, Simi Valley, CA.
WH	White House
WP	*Washington Post*
WSJ	*Wall Street Journal*
ZBC	Zbigniew Brzezinski Collection
ZBCF	Zbigniew Brzezinski's Country Files, 1977–1981

Notes

INTRODUCTION

1. For lack of a better alternative, "Americans" refers to people from the United States; "Latin Americans" to those living south of the U.S.-Mexico border.

2. The terms "global South" and "Third World" are used interchangeably to indicate political and economic underdevelopment rather than nonalignment.

3. Jimmy Carter, inaugural address, January 20, 1977, Jimmy Carter Library, http://www.jimmycarterlibrary.gov/documents/speeches/inaugadd.phtml.

4. Jimmy Carter, *Keeping Faith: Memoirs of a President* (New York: Bantam Books, 1982), 143.

5. Luis Alberto Romero, *A History of Argentina in the Twentieth Century* (University Park: Pennsylvania State University Press, 2002), 144.

6. Similarly, Amnesty International placed the number of disappeared at twenty thousand in March 1977. DoS memo of conversation, November 21, 1977, subject: "Human Rights Situation in Argentina," ADP.

7. Antonius C.G.M. Robben, *Political Violence and Trauma in Argentina* (Philadelphia: University of Pennsylvania Press, 2005), 134.

8. Jacobo Timerman, *Prisoner without a Name, Cell without a Number* (New York: Alfred A. Knopf, 1981), 31.

9. "Nixon Urges U.S. to Alter Latin Policy," *WP*, May 16, 1967, A12.

10. DoS memo of conversation, October 7, 1976, subject: "Secretary's Meeting with Argentine Foreign Minister Guzzetti," NSA, Electronic Briefing Book 104, Carlos Osorio, ed., posted December 4, 2003 at http://www.gwu.edu/~nsarchiv/NSAEBB/NSAEBB104/index.htm

11. DoS memo, John Bushnell to Patricia Derian, June 13, 1978, subject: "Commentary on Cutler-Hammer Letter," box 13, folder: Human Rights—Argentina III, Christopher Papers.

12. For a useful historiographical overview, see Kenneth Cmiel, "The Recent History of Human Rights," *American Historical Review* 1, no. 1 (2004): 117–135. For more recent historical scholarship on human rights, see, for example, Roland Burke, *Decolonization and the Evolution of International Human Rights*, 1st ed. (Philadelphia: University of Pennsylvania Press, 2010); Rosemary Foote, "The Cold War and Human Rights," in *The Cambridge History of the Cold War*, vol. 3, *Endings*, ed. Melvyn Leffler and Odd Arne Westad (New York: Cambridge University Press, 2010), 445–465; Stefan-Ludwig Hoffmann, ed., *Human Rights in the Twentieth Century* (New York: Cambridge University Press, 2010); Akira Iriye, Petra Goedde, and William I. Hitchcock, eds., *The Human Rights Revolution: An International History* (New York: Oxford University Press, 2012); Michael Cotey Morgan, "The Seventies and the Rebirth of Human Rights," in *The Shock of the Global: The 1970s in Perspective* (Cambridge, MA: Belknap Press of Harvard University Press, 2010): 237–250; Samuel Moyn, *The Last Utopia: Human Rights in History* (Cambridge, MA: Belknap Press of Harvard University Press, 2010). For recent scholarship on human rights in U.S. foreign policy, see, for example, Elizabeth Borgwardt, *A New Deal for the World: America's Vision for Human Rights* (Cambridge, MA: Harvard University Press,

2005); Kenneth Cmiel, "The Emergence of Human Rights Politics in the United States," *Journal of American History* 86, no. 3 (1999): 1231–1250; Barbara Keys, "Congress, Kissinger, and the Origins of Human Rights Diplomacy," *Diplomatic History* 34, no. 5 (2010): 823–851; Kathryn Sikkink, *Mixed Signals: U.S. Human Rights Policy and Latin America* (Ithaca, NY: Cornell University Press, 2004). On transnational human rights advocacy, see, for example, Margaret Keck and Kathryn Sikkink, *Activists beyond Borders: Advocacy Networks in International Politics* (Ithaca, NY: Cornell University Press, 1998); Naomi Roht-Arriaza, *The Pinochet Effect: Transnational Justice in the Age of Human Rights* (Philadelphia: University of Pennsylvania Press, 2006); Sarah B. Snyder, *Human Rights Activism and the End of the Cold War: A Transnational History of the Helsinki Network,* 1st ed. (New York: Cambridge University Press, 2011).

13. On the 1970s, see, for example, Thomas Borstelmann, *The 1970s: A New Global History from Civil Rights to Economic Inequality* (Princeton, NJ: Princeton University Press, 2011); Peter N. Carroll, *It Seemed Like Nothing Happened: America in the 1970s* (New Brunswick, NJ: Rutgers University Press, 2000); Niall Ferguson et al., *The Shock of the Global: The 1970s in Perspective* (Cambridge, MA: Belknap Press of Harvard University Press, 2010); Bruce J. Schulman, *The Seventies: The Great Shift in American Culture, Society, and Politics* (New York: Da Capo Press, 2002). On the concept of the "intermestic," see Campbell Craig and Fredrik Logevall, *America's Cold War: The Politics of Insecurity* (Cambridge, MA: Harvard University Press, 2009), 10.

14. Cmiel, "Recent History of Human Rights," 125–126.

15. For recent positive appraisals of Carter's foreign policy, see, for example, Douglas Brinkley, "Bernath Lecture: The Rising Stock of Jimmy Carter: The 'Hands On' Legacy of Our Thirty-Ninth President," *Diplomatic History* 20, no. 4 (1996): 505–530; John Dumbrell, *The Carter Presidency: A Re-Evaluation* (Manchester, UK: Manchester University Press, 1993); Nancy Mitchell, "The Cold War and Jimmy Carter," in Leffler and Westad, *Cambridge History of the Cold War,* 3:66–87; David F. Schmitz and Vanessa Walker, "Jimmy Carter and the Foreign Policy of Human Rights: The Development of a Post-Cold War Foreign Policy," *Diplomatic History* 28, no. 1 (2004): 113–144; Tony Smith, *America's Mission: The United States and the Worldwide Struggle for Democracy in the Twentieth Century* (Princeton, NJ: Princeton University Press, 1995); Robert A. Strong, *Working in the World: Jimmy Carter and the Making of American Foreign Policy* (Baton Rouge: Louisiana State University Press, 2000).

16. For critical analyses, see, for example, Kenton Clymer, "Jimmy Carter, Human Rights, and Cambodia," *Diplomatic History* 27, no. 2 (2003): 245–278; George C. Herring, *From Colony to Superpower: U.S. Foreign Relations since 1776* (New York: Oxford University Press, 2008); Donna R. Jackson, *Jimmy Carter and the Horn of Africa: Cold War Policy in Ethiopia and Somalia* (Jefferson, NC: McFarland, 2007); Burton I. Kaufman and Scott Kaufman, *The Presidency of James Earl Carter, Jr.,* rev. ed. (Lawrence: University Press of Kansas, 2006); Melvyn P. Leffler, *For the Soul of Mankind: The United States, the Soviet Union, and the Cold War* (New York: Hill and Wang, 2007); A. Glenn Mower, *Human Rights and American Foreign Policy: The Carter and Reagan Experiences* (New York: Greenwood Press, 1987); David Skidmore, *Reversing Course: Carter's Foreign Policy, Domestic Politics, and the Failure of Reform* (Nashville: Vanderbilt University Press, 1996); Donald S. Spencer, *The Carter Implosion: Jimmy Carter and the Amateur Style of Diplomacy* (Westport, CT: Praeger, 1988); Richard C. Thornton, *The Carter Years: Toward a New Global Order* (New York: Paragon House, 1991).

17. Gilbert M. Joseph, "What We Know Now and Should Know: Bringing Latin America More Meaningfully into Cold War Studies," in *In From the Cold: Latin America's New Encounter with the Cold War* (Durham: Duke University Press, 2008), 8. Relatively little has been written on U.S.-Argentine relations during the Cold War. See, for example, Ariel

C. Armony, *Argentina, the United States, and the Anti-Communist Crusade in Central America, 1977–1984* (Athens: Ohio University Center for International Studies, 1997); David Sheinin, *Argentina and the United States: An Alliance Contained* (Athens: University of Georgia Press, 2006); Joseph S. Tulchin, *Argentina and the United States: A Conflicted Relationship* (Boston: Twayne, 1990).

18. On the period of Argentine military dictatorship, see, for example, Martin Edwin Andersen, *Dossier Secreto: Argentina's Desaparecidos and the Myth of the "Dirty War"* (Boulder: Westview Press, 1993); Marguerite Feitlowitz, *A Lexicon of Terror: Argentina and the Legacies of Torture* (New York: Oxford University Press, 1998); Daniel Frontalini and Maria Cristina Caiati, *El mito de la "guerra sucia"* (Buenos Aires: Centro de Estudios Legales y Sociales, 1984); Frank Graziano, *Divine Violence: Spectacle, Psychosexuality, and Radical Christianity in the Argentine "Dirty War"* (Boulder: Westview Press, 1992); Iain Guest, *Behind the Disappearances: Argentina's Dirty War against Human Rights and the United Nations* (Philadelphia: University of Pennsylvania Press, 1990); Donald Clark Hodges, *Argentina's "Dirty War": An Intellectual Biography* (Austin: University of Texas Press, 1991); Paul H. Lewis, *Guerrillas and Generals: The "Dirty War" in Argentina* (Westport, CT: Praeger, 2002); Marcos Novaro and Vicente Palermo, *La dictadura militar (1976–1983): Del golpe de estado a la restauración democrática* (Buenos Aires: Paidós, 2003); Mark Osiel, *Mass Atrocity, Ordinary Evil, and Hannah Arendt: Criminal Consciousness in Argentina's Dirty War* (New Haven, CT: Yale University Press, 2001); María Seoane and Vicente Muleiro, *El dictador: La historia secreta y pública de Jorge Rafael Videla* (Buenos Aires: Sudamericana, 2000).

19. DoS report, November 11, 1978, subject: "Evolution of U.S. Human Rights Policy in Argentina," ADP.

1. FROM COUNTERINSURGENCY TO STATE-SANCTIONED TERROR

1. "During Quiet Coup, TV Offers WWII," *WP*, March 24, 1976, A8.

2. Juan de Onís, "Argentina Is at the Crisis Point," *NYT*, March 20, 1976, 3.

3. DoS cable, BA 6087, U.S. Embassy (Hill) to secretary of state (Kissinger), September 10, 1975, subject: "Analysis of Political Situation Wake of Military Crisis," ADP.

4. DoS cable, BA 2061, U.S. Embassy (Hill) to secretary of state (Kissinger), March 29, 1976, subject: "Videla's Moderate Line Prevails," ADP.

5. DoS cable, Washington (Kissinger) to All American Republic Diplomatic Posts, February 25, 1976, subject: "INR Analysis of Development in Argentina," ADP.

6. "Argentine Junta under Army Chief Assumes Control," *NYT*, March 25, 1976, 73; "Coup in Argentina," *WP*, March 30, 1976, A14.

7. Robert C. Hill, "What New Hampshire Means to Me in This Bicentennial Year," box 1, folder 24, Hill Papers I.

8. Willard F. Barber and C. Neale Ronning, *Internal Security and Military Power: Counterinsurgency and Civic Action in Latin America* (Columbus: Ohio State University Press, 1966), 124. DoS report, "Latin American Internal Security Programs: Under Mutual Security Act 1960, Foreign Assistance Acts, 1961–1965," box 2413, folder: POL 23 Latin America 9/11/65, CFPF, 1964–1966, GRDS, RG 59, NARA. Of the $500 million, roughly 73% went to Brazil, in part to equip a ground force of 25,000 men and an air squadron for deployment to Italy. Mexico, the second-largest recipient, received $40 million, including equipment for an air squadron later sent to the Philippines. DoD report, February 25, 1965, subject: "U.S. Policies toward Latin American Military Forces," box 2, folder 5: Latin America, Volume III, 1/65–6/65, NSF, CF, LBJL.

9. Quote from Greg Grandin, *The Last Colonial Massacre: Latin America in the Cold War* (Chicago: University of Chicago Press, 2004), 5.

10. Mary Ann Glendon, *A World Made New: Eleanor Roosevelt and the Universal Declaration of Human Rights* (New York: Random House, 2002), 15.

11. Paul Gordon Lauren, *The Evolution of International Human Rights: Visions Seen*, 2nd ed. (Philadelphia: University of Pennsylvania Press, 2003), 232.

12. Glendon, *World Made New*, 214.

13. Bricker, quoted in Elizabeth Borgwardt, "'Constitutionalizing' Human Rights: The Rise and Rise of the Nuremberg Principles," in *The Human Rights Revolution: An International History*, ed. Akira Iriye, Petra Goedde, and William I. Hitchcock (New York: Oxford University Press), 78.

14. On the Bricker Amendment controversy, see also Natalie Hevener Kaufman and David Whiteman, "Opposition to Human Rights Treaties in the United States Senate: The Legacy of the Bricker Amendment," *Human Rights Quarterly* 10 (1988): 309–337; and Duane A. Tananbaum, "The Bricker Amendment Controversy: Its Origins and Eisenhower's Role," *Diplomatic History* 9, no. 1 (1985): 73–93.

15. Harry S. Truman, Address of the President to Congress, Recommending Assistance to Greece and Turkey, March 12, 1947, http://www.trumanlibrary.org/whistlestop/study_collections/doctrine/large/index.php.

16. Quoted in Melvyn P. Leffler, *A Preponderance of Power: National Security, the Truman Administration, and the Cold War* (Stanford: Stanford University Press, 1992), 172.

17. Lars Schoultz, *National Security and United States Policy toward Latin America* (Princeton, NJ: Princeton University Press, 1987), 179; Steven G. Rabe, *The Most Dangerous Area in the World: John F. Kennedy Confronts Communist Revolution in Latin America* (Chapel Hill: University of North Carolina Press, 1999), 126. The U.S. effort to establish military predominance in Latin American had continued in the early postwar era, providing $156 million in surplus military equipment to the region between 1945 and 1949. The equipment was provided under the Surplus Property Acts of 1920 and 1944. DoD report, February 25, 1965, subject: "U.S. Policies Toward Latin American Military Forces," box 2, folder 5: Latin America, Volume III, 1/65–6/65, NSF, CF, Latin America, LBJL.

18. Walter LaFeber, *Inevitable Revolutions: The United States in Central America* (New York: W. W. Norton, 1993), 112; Jack Child, *Unequal Alliance: The Inter-American Military System, 1938–1978* (Boulder: Westview Press, 1980), 126; Martin Sicker, *The Geopolitics of Security in the Americas: Hemispheric Denial from Monroe to Clinton* (Westport, CT: Praeger, 2002), 109–113; Leslie Gill, *The School of the Americas: Military Training and Political Violence in the Americas* (Durham, NC: Duke University Press, 2004), 72; J. Patrice McSherry, *Predatory States: Operation Condor and Covert War in Latin America* (New York: Rowman & Littlefield, 2005), 48.

19. Leslie Bethell and Ian Roxborough, "Latin America between the Second World War and the Cold War: Some Reflections on the 1945–8 Conjuncture," *Journal of Latin American Studies*, 20, no. 1 (1988), 183. See also Grandin, *Last Colonial Massacre*, 8–10.

20. Hill, "What New Hampshire Means to Me."

21. David Sentner, "Dulles' Trouble Shooter," *Boston Globe*[?], June 1959[?], box 1, folder 30, Hill Papers I; U.S. Senate Committee on Armed Services, *Nomination of Callaway and Hill: Hearing before the Committee on Armed Services*, 93rd Cong., 1st sess., May 8, 1973 (Washington, DC: Government Printing Office, 1973).

22. Robert C. Hill to Robert Kennedy, Esq., confidential report, rough draft, December 14, 1960, box 5, folder 43, Hill Papers I.

23. According to Hill, Dulles was unconvinced, firmly telling the young executive that he "was the only person who thought so." Robert C. Hill, interview with John T. Mason Jr., Oral History Research Office, Columbia University, October 19, 1972, box 7, folder 16, Hill Papers I; U.S. Senate Committee on Armed Services, *Nomination of Callaway and Hill: Hearing before the Committee on Armed Services*.

24. U.S. Senate Committee on Armed Services, *Nomination of Callaway and Hill.*

25. Personal correspondence, United Fruit president Kenneth H. Redmond to secretary of state Henry Holland, June 28, 1954, Hill Papers I; personal correspondence, José Figueres to Robert C. Hill, April 6, 1955, Hill Papers I.

26. At a Senate hearing on July 27, 1961, Whiting Willauer, who served as U.S. ambassador to Honduras during the implementation of Operation PBSUCCESS, indicated that the "team" working to overthrow Arbenz including Peurifoy, Hill, and Ambassador Tom Whelan in Nicaragua. David Wise and Thomas B. Ross, *The Invisible Government* (New York: Random House, 1964), 167–168.

27. Richard M. Nixon, *RN: The Memoirs of Richard Nixon* (New York: Simon and Schuster, 1990), 192.

28. Personal correspondence, Robert C. Hill to Alvaro Sanchez Jr., July 6, 1962, box 118, folder 10, Hill Papers II.

29. Paul P. Kennedy, "Caribbean Policy Fiercely Debated," *NYT*, April 13, 1959, 11.

30. "Pro-Castro Speech Prompts Queries by Washington—Hill Sees Minister," *NYT*, July 9, 1960, 3; "U.S. Asks, Fails to Get Mexico Stand on Castro," *WP*, July 9, 1960, A4; "5,000 Mexican Students March to Protest U.S. Stand on Cuba," *NYT*, July 13, 1960, 3.

31. Robert C. Hill to Robert Kennedy, Esq., confidential report.

32. W. W. Rostow, "Guerrilla Warfare in Underdeveloped Areas," quoted in Brian Loveman and Thomas M. Davies Jr., *The Politics of Antipolitics: The Military in Latin America* (Lincoln: University of Nebraska Press, 1989), 133.

33. DoS Policy Research Study, Bureau of Intelligence and Research, November 20, 1961, Subject: "Internal Warfare and the Security of the Underdeveloped World," box 98, folder: Counter-Insurgency, President's Office Files, Subjects, JFKL.

34. Roger Hilsman, "Internal War: The New Communist Tactic," *Military Review* 42, no. 4 (1962): 22.

35. DoS Policy Research Study, Bureau of Intelligence and Research, November 20, 1961, subject: "Internal Warfare and the Security of the Underdeveloped World," box 98, folder: Counter-Insurgency, President's Office Files, Subjects, JFKL.

36. Ibid.

37. Andrew J. Birtle, *U.S. Army Counterinsurgency and Contingency Operations Doctrine, 1942–1976* (Washington, DC: Center of Military History, United States Army, 2006), 261–262; Michael I. McClintock, *Instruments of Statecraft: U.S. Guerrilla Warfare, Counterinsurgency, and Counter-Terrorism, 1940–1990* (New York: Pantheon, 1992), 166.

38. Barber and Ronning, *Internal Security and Military Power*, 142; Robert D. Dean, "Masculinity as Ideology: John F. Kennedy and the Domestic Politics of Foreign Policy," *Diplomatic History* 22, no. 1 (1998): 50.

39. Arthur M. Schlesinger Jr., summary guidelines paper, July 3, 1961, subject: "Policy toward Latin America," *FRUS, 1961–1963*, vol. 12 (all *FRUS* documents accessed online unless a page number is indicated).

40. John F. Kennedy, quoted in "John F. Kennedy: Announcing the Alliance for Progress, 1961," reproduced in McPherson, *Intimate Ties, Bitter Struggles: The United States and Latin America* (Washington, D.C.: Potomac Books, 2006), 151–152.

41. DoS guidelines paper, May 1962, subject: "Latin America: Guidelines of United States Policy and Operations," *FRUS, 1961–1963*, vol. 12.

42. Rabe, *Most Dangerous Area*, 2.

43. Letter, Secretary of State Rusk to the chairman of the Subcommittee on American Republic Affairs of the Senate Foreign Relations Committee (Wayne Morse), September 15, 1962, *FRUS, 1961–1963*, vol. 12.

44. Rostow, "Guerrilla Warfare in Underdeveloped Areas," quoted in Loveman and Davies, *Politics of Antipolitics*, 135.

45. DoS circular cable, Chester Bowles to Certain Diplomatic Posts in the American Republics, May 10, 1961, *FRUS, 1961–1963*, vol. 12.

46. Harry F. Walterhouse, "Civic Action: A Counter and Cure for Insurgency," *Military Review* 42, no. 8 (1962): 52.

47. Summary guidelines paper, July 3, 1961, subject: "Policy toward Latin America," *FRUS, 1961–1963*, vol. 12.

48. DoS report, "Latin American Internal Security Programs: Under Mutual Security Act 1960, Foreign Assistance Acts, 1961–1965," box 2413, folder: POL 23 Latin America 9/11/65, CFPF, 1964–1966, GRDS, RG 59, NARA.

49. National Security memo no. 206, December 4, 1962, subject: "Military Assistance for Internal Security in Latin America," *FRUS, 1961–1963*, vol. 12; DoS report, "Latin American Internal Security Programs: Under Mutual Security Act 1960, Foreign Assistance Acts, 1961–1965," box 2413, folder: POL 23 Latin America 9/11/65, CFPF, 1964–1966, GRDS, RG 59, NARA.

50. In the same period, Latin American armies received roughly 70% of MAP funding for civic action projects, air forces received 20%, and 10% went to the navies. DoD report, February 25, 1965, subject: "U.S. Policies toward Latin American Military Forces," box 2, folder 5: Latin America, Volume III, 1/65–6/65, NSF, CF, Latin America, LBJL.

51. The country team consisted of the ambassador and the heads of the MAAG, United States Economic Mission, and United States Information Service. See Samuel T. Williams, "The Practical Demands of the MAAG," *Military Review* 41, no. 7 (1961): 4.

52. At least forty nations were receiving U.S. military aid in 1961, with about five thousand U.S. Army personnel engaged in providing the assistance.

53. National Security memo no. 177, August 7, 1962, subject: "Police Assistance Programs," http://www.jfklibrary.org/Historical+Resources/Archives/Reference+Desk/NSAMs.htm.

54. Martha K. Huggins, *Political Policing: The United States and Latin America* (Durham, NC: Duke University Press, 1998), 109. By 1956, the Eisenhower administration was operating a $25 million police-training program in twenty countries. Two years later the program had expanded to twenty-four countries, with a budget of $35 million (ibid., 86). See also McClintock, *Instruments of Statecraft*, 191.

55. DoD, draft paper, May 19, 1961, subject: "U.S. Policy for the Security of Latin America in the Sixties," *FRUS, 1961–1963*, vol. 12.

56. National Security action memo no. 88, September 5, 1961, subject: "Training for Latin American Armed Forces," *FRUS, 1961–1963*, vol. 12.

57. Barber and Ronning, *Internal Security and Military Power*, 146–147. In addition to providing instruction at U.S. facilities, during the 1960s the United States sent more than one hundred mobile training teams on missions to Latin America.

58. Ibid., 171.

59. Memo, Taylor to Kennedy, October 7, 1961, *FRUS, 1961–1963*, vol. 12.

60. Memo, executive secretary of the DoS (Battle) to the president's special assistant for National Security Affairs (Bundy), February 5,1962, subject: "National Security Action Memo No. 118—Participation of U.S. and Latin American Armed Forces in the Attainment of Common Objectives in Latin America," *FRUS, 1961–1963*, vol. 12.

61. Juan de Onís, "Military Asserts Larger Role in Latin-American Politics," *NYT*, July 29, 1962, 112.

62. Mann acted simultaneously as assistant secretary of state for inter-American affairs, special assistant to the president, and head of the Agency for International Development (AID), which ran the Alliance for Progress. Walter LaFeber, "Thomas C. Mann and the Devolution of Latin American Policy: From the Good Neighbor to Military Intervention,"

in *Behind the Throne: Servants of Power to Imperial Presidents, 1898–1968* (Madison: University of Wisconsin Press, 1993), 197–198.

63. Central Intelligence Agency Intelligence memo, December 9, 1966, subject: "Instability in the Western Hemisphere," box 2, folder 3: Latin America-a, 9/66–12/66, NSF, CF, Latin America, LBJL.

64. Specifically, in section 511(b) of the Foreign Assistance Act of 1965 Congress wrote, "To the maximum extent feasible, military assistance shall be furnished to American Republics in accordance with joint plans (including joint plans relating to internal security problems) approved by the Organization of American States." DoS report, "Latin American Internal Security Programs: Under Mutual Security Act 1960, Foreign Assistance Acts, 1961–1965," box 2413, folder POL 23 Latin America 9/11/65, CFPF, 1964–1966, GRDS, RG 59, NARA.

65. Report on National Security Action memo no. 297, October 1964 [?], box 4, folder: NSAM 297—Latin American Military Aid, NSF, National Security Action Memorandums, LBJL.

66. Joint Study of the Defense Department Representation Abroad, "Report for Latin America," May 1964, box 2, folder 3: Latin America, Volume II, 9/64–12/64, NSF, CF, Latin America, LBJL.

67. DoS memo, secret, subject: "U.S. Regional Policy toward Latin American Security Forces," July 10, 1967, DDRS, document no. CK3100043115.

68. Robert L. Burke, "Military Civic Action," *Military Review* 44, no. 10, (1964): 69.

69. DoD report, February 25, 1965, subject: "U.S. Policies toward Latin American Military Forces," box 2, folder 5: Latin America, Volume III, 1/65–6/65, NSF, CF, Latin America, LBJL.

70. Benjamin Welles, "The Latin Military: A Dilemma for Washington," *NYT*, December 22, 1968, E5; Robert W. Porter, "Look South to Latin America," *Military Review* 48, no. 6 (1968): 89.

71. "U.S. Army School of the Americas," *Military Review* 50, no. 4 (1970): 90; Subcommittee on National Security Policy and Scientific Developments, House of Representatives Committee on Foreign Affairs, "Reports of the Special Study Mission to Latin America on Military Assistance Training and Developmental Television," 91st Congress, May 7, 1970 (Washington: Government Printing Office, 1970).

72. "The Inter-American Defense College," *Military Review* 50, no. 4 (1970): 26.

73. Ibid.

74. "Johnson Welcomes Latin-Bloc Officers," *NYT*, August 4, 1964, 11.

75. DoS Policy Research Study, Bureau of Intelligence and Research, November 20, 1961, subject: "Internal Warfare and the Security of the Underdeveloped World," box 98, folder: Counter-Insurgency, President's Office Files, Subjects, JFKL.

76. Rabe, *Most Dangerous Area*, 133.

77. Memo, Taylor to Kennedy, October 7, 1961, *FRUS, 1961–1963*, vol. 12.

78. Memo of conversation, Washington, April 11, 1962, 5:40 p.m., subject: Inter-American Defense College, *FRUS, 1961–1963*, vol. 12.

79. Ibid.

80. Quoted in Arthur M. Schlesinger, *A Thousand Days: John F. Kennedy in the White House* (Boston: Houghton Mifflin, 1965), 769.

81. Clara Nieto, *Masters of War: Latin America and U.S. Aggression, from the Cuban Revolution through the Clinton Years* (New York: Seven Stories Press, 2003), 92–93; Alain Rouquié, *The Military and the State in Latin America* (Berkeley: University of California Press, 1989), 418. Kennedy also authorized a massive U.S. covert action to overthrow Cheddi Jagan in British Guiana. See Steven G. Rabe, *U.S. Intervention in British Guiana: A Cold War Story* (Chapel Hill: University of North Carolina Press, 2005).

82. Mann's reference to the Latin American military quoted in LaFeber, "Thomas C. Mann and the Devolution of Latin American Policy." "Tempest" quoted from Thomas C. Mann, interview by Richard D. McKinzie, Austin, TX, June 12, 1974, transcript, Mann Papers, Baylor University.

83. Rabe, *Most Dangerous Area*, 141–142.

84. DoS cable, Santiago 702, U.S. Embassy to secretary of state, February 28, 1964, box 1, folder 8: Latin America, Volume 1, 11/63–6/64; DoS cable, Bogota 739, U.S. Embassy to secretary of state, February 28, 1964, box 6, folder 7: Argentina Volume III, 3/67–12/68; DoS cable, Quito 539, U.S. Embassy to secretary of state, February 28, 1964, box 1, folder: 8: Latin America, Volume 1, 11/63–6/64; DoS cable, Guatemala 480, U.S. Embassy to secretary of state, February 26, 1964, box 1, folder 8: Latin America, Volume 1, 11/63–6/64; DoS cable, Lima 1000, U.S. Embassy to secretary of state, February 28, 1964, box 1, folder 8: Latin America, Volume 1, 11/63–6/64; all documents in NSF, CF, Latin America, LBJL.

85. Bert Quint, "Coup Progress Hinders Alliance," *WP*, November 18, 1963, A17.

86. DoS cable, Tegucigalpa 445, U.S. Embassy to secretary of state, February 28, 1964, box 6, folder 7: Argentina Volume III, 3/67–12/68, NSF, CF, Latin America, LBJL.

87. Published in the *Herald Tribune*, October 6, 1963; reprinted as "U.S. Policy regarding Military Governments in Latin America," in *Latin America and the United States in the 1970s*, ed. Richard B. Gray (Ithaca, NY: F. E. Peacock, 1971), 224.

88. DoD report, February 25, 1965, subject: "U.S. Policies toward Latin American Military Forces," box 2, folder: 5: Latin America, Volume III, 1/65–6/65, NSF, CF, Latin America, LBJL.

89. Ibid.

90. DoS report, Harry W. Shlaudeman to secretary of state, September 3, 1976, subject: "ARA Monthly Report (July): The 'Third World War' and South America," ADP. See also Alicia S. García, *La doctrina de la seguridad nacional, 1958–1983* (Buenos Aires: Centro Editor de América Latina, S.A., 1991), 17–20.

91. David Pion-Berlin, "The National Security Doctrine, Military Threat Perception, and the 'Dirty War' in Argentina," *Comparative Political Studies* 21, no. 3 (1988): 385.

92. Jeffrey Stein, "Grad School for Juntas," *Nation*, May 21, 1977, 623–624.

93. Grandin, *Last Colonial Massacre*, 74.

94. Reprinted in Lisa Haugaard, "Recently Declassified Army and CIA Manuals Used in Latin America: An Analysis of Their Content," Latin America Working Group, February 18, 1997, http://www.lawg.org/misc/Publications-manuals.htm.

95. "KUBARK Counterintelligence Interrogation," July 1963, NSA, http://www.gwu.edu/~nsarchiv/NSAEBB/NSAEBB27/01-10.htm.

96. "U.S. Army School of the Americas," *Military Review* 50, no. 4 (1970): 92–93.

97. Quoted in Eduardo L. Duhalde, *El estado terrorista Argentino* (Buenos Aires: Editorial Argos Vergara, S. A, 1983), 42.

2. THE "THIRD WORLD WAR"

1. Andersen, *Dossier Secreto*, 133; Hodges, *Argentina's "Dirty War,"* 134–135; Lewis, *Guerrillas and Generals*, 138–139; Jean Lartéguy, *Les centurions* (Paris: Presses de la Cite, 1960); Roger Trinquier, *Modern Warfare: A French View of Counterinsurgency* (Westport, CT: Praeger Security International, 2006).

2. DoS memo, secret, subject: "Report of Assessment Team on Internal Security Situation in South America," January 10, 1962, DDRS, document no. CK3100112651.

3. DoS cable, BA 2518, U.S. Embassy (McClintock) to secretary of state, June 8, 1962, box 6A, folder: Argentina, General 5/62–6/62, NSF, JFKL.

4. Joseph A. Page, *Perón: A Biography* (New York: Random House, 1983), 69–71.

5. David Rock, *Argentina, 1516–1987: From Spanish Colonization to the Falklands War* (Berkeley: University of California Press, 1985), 259–260.

6. Page, *Perón*, 35–37.

7. Dean Acheson, *Present at the Creation: My Years in the State Department* (New York: W. W. Norton, 1969), 187.

8. Glenn J. Dorn, *Peronistas and New Dealers: U.S.-Argentine Rivalry and the Western Hemisphere (1946–1950)* (New Orleans: University Press of the South, 2005); Gary Frank, *Juan Perón vs. Spruille Braden: The Story behind the Blue Book* (Lanham, MD: University Press of America, 1980); Sheinin, *Argentina and the United States*, 84–88; Tulchin, *Argentina and the United States*, 92–96.

9. Colin M. MacLachlan, *Argentina: What Went Wrong* (Westport: Praeger, 2006), 110.

10. Daniel James, *Resistance and Integration: Peronism and the Argentine Working Class* (Cambridge: Cambridge University Press, 1988), 16.

11. Romero, *History of Argentina*, 104–105.

12. Rock, *Argentina, 1516–1987*, 320–326; Romero, *History of Argentina*, 153–157.

13. Rabe, *Most Dangerous Area,*, 56–58.

14. DoS cable, DoS to U.S. Embassy in Argentina, May 24, 1961, *FRUS, 1961–1963*, vol. 12.

15. Tulchin, *Argentina and the United States*, 121.

16. Rock, *Argentina, 1516–1987*, 338–342. Argentina was one of six nations to abstain on the resolution, along with Brazil, Bolivia, Chile, Ecuador, and Mexico. The resolution passed by a bare two-thirds majority. Frank Manitzas, "Argentina Recalls Envoy in Cuba after Pressure from Military," *WP*, February 3, 1962, A11.

17. "Buenos Aires," *NYT*, December 31, 1961, E3; "Argentina Gets Alliance Loan of $150 Million," *WP*, February 2, 1962, B3.

18. DoS cable, State to U.S. Embassy Argentina, September 27, 1961, *FRUS, 1961–1963*, vol. 12; Tulchin, *Argentina and the United States*, 121.

19. DoS cable, DoS to U.S. Embassy Argentina, February 10, 1962, *FRUS, 1961–1963*, vol. 12.

20. DoS memo, "Report of Assessment Team on Internal Security Situation in South America."

21. DoS cable, BA 1699, U.S. Embassy (McClintock) to secretary of state, March 21, 1962, box 6, folder "Argentina, 3/16/62–3/31/62," NSF, CF, JFKL.

22. Having served under all four geographic bureaus in the Department of State and with United Nations Affairs, McClintock had an unusually wide range of experience including postings in three Latin American embassies as well as eight posts in Asia, the Middle East, and Europe. Fluent in Spanish, French, Italian, Portuguese, and Swedish, McClintock had recently been awarded the State Department's Superior Service Award. "A spruce, wiry man with carefully combed gray hair, Mr. McClintock stands erect and walks briskly," one journalist wrote after McClintock's appointment as U.S. Envoy to Argentina. "Aides say he can be as informal as an old shoe, or formal and determined, as the situation may require." Quote from "R. M. McClintock, Career Man, Next Ambassador to Argentina," *NYT*, December 29, 1961, 6. See also, "McClintock Is Chosen as Envoy," *WP*, January 16, 1962, A5; "Biographic Sketch of Ambassador Robert McClintock," box 6A, folder: "Argentina, General 5/62–6/62," NSF, CF, JFKL.

23. Since his arrival on February 6, the ambassador had repeatedly emphasized to the Argentine president that U.S. military personnel were playing no role in Argentina's political drama. On February 23, McClintock described Frondizi's assertions of U.S. support for the Argentine military's political aspirations as a "morbid fear." Frondizi's vision of "sinister U.S. forces both in and out of our government exercising undue pressures,"

McClintock continued, "borders on fantasy, but it is, nevertheless, a political fact in the president's brain." DoS cable, State 1738, Ball to U.S. Embassy BA, March 23, 1962, box 6, folder: "Argentina, 3/16/62–3/31/62," NSF, CF, JFKL.

24. DoS Cable, BA 1656, U.S. Embassy (McClintock) to secretary of state, March 18, 1962, Box 6, Folder: "Argentina, 3/16/62–3/31/62," NSF, CF, JFKL.

25. DoS cable, State 1666, Ball to U.S. Embassy BA (McClintock), March 19, 1962, box 6, folder: Argentina, 3/16/62–3/31/62, NSF, CF, JFKL.

26. DoS cable, State 1738, Ball to U.S. Embassy BA, March 23, 1962, box 6, folder "Argentina, 3/16/62–3/31/62," NSF, CF, JFKL. McClintock received the department's apparent reversal on March 23 around midnight. The following morning he responded irritably: "I have been working constantly to keep Frondizi in; but Department's first telegram on this subject, instructing me to keep aloof, would not have given impression conveyed belatedly [by State 1738]." DoS cable, BA 1769, U.S. Embassy (McClintock) to secretary of state, March 24, 1962, box 6, folder: "Argentina, 3/16/62–3/31/62," NSF, CF, JFKL; DoS cable, State 1767, Ball to U.S. Embassy BA, March 26, 1962, box 6, folder: "Argentina, 3/16/62–3/31/62," NSF, CF, JFKL.

27. DoS cable, BA 1977, U.S. Embassy (McClintock) to secretary of state, April 6, 1962, box 6A, folder: Argentina, General 4/62, NSF, CF, JFKL.

28. DoS cable, BA 2063, U.S. Embassy (McClintock) to secretary of state, April 13, 1962, box 6A, folder: Argentina, General 4/62, NSF, CF, JFKL.

29. Letter from the ambassador to Argentina (McClintock) to the assistant secretary of state for Inter-American Affairs (Martin) BA, May 31, 1962, in *FRUS, 1961–1963*, vol. 12, 387–388.

30. Tad Szulc, "U.S. Renewing Financial Aid to Argentina," *NYT*, June 7, 1962, 18.

31. Jerome Levinson and Juan de Onís, *The Alliance That Lost Its Way: A Critical Report on the Alliance for Progress* (Chicago: Quadrangle Books, 1970), 80–83.

32. DoS cable, BA 557, U.S. Embassy (McClintock) to secretary of state, August 22, 1962, box 7, folder: Argentina, General 8/62, NSF, CF, JFKL.

33. DoS cable, BA 1304, U.S. Embassy (McClintock) to secretary of state, November 20, 1962, box 7, folder: Argentina, General 11/62–12/62, NSF, CF, JFKL.

34. DoS background paper, Argentine visit of Foreign Minister Muñiz, January 21–24, 1963, subject: "U.S. Military Relations with Argentina," January 18, 1963, box 7, folder: U.S. Policy Statements and Objectives, Bureau of Inter-American Affairs Office of East Coast Affairs, Records Relating to Argentina, 1956–1964, GRDS, RG 59, NARA.

35. DoD bibliographic data, May 1965, box 6, folder 5: Argentina Volume II, Memos, 9/64–2/67, NSF, CF, Latin America, LBJL.

36. DoS memo, Benjamin H. Read to McGeorge Bundy, August 3, 1963, subject: "Military Assistance Program for Argentina," box 3712, folder: Def Defense Affairs ARG 2/1/63, CFPF, 1963, GRDS, RG 59, NARA.

37. Ibid.

38. Enrique Martínez Codó, "The Military Problems in Latin America," *Military Review* 44, no. 8 (1964), 13.

39. See Guillermo O'Donnell, "Modernization and Military Coups: Theory, Comparisons, and the Argentine Case," in *Armies and Politics in Latin America*, ed. Abraham F. Lowenthal and John Samuel Fitch (New York: Holmes and Meir, 1986), 103.

40. DoD cable, no. 11192, U.S. Army Chief of Staff Wheeler to U.S. Embassy BA (McClintock), March 11, 1963, box 7, folder: Argentina, General 2/63–3/63, NSF, CF, JFKL.

41. Henry Raymont, "U.S. Arms Aid Due for Argentines," *NYT*, August 28, 1965, 5.

42. DoS cable, BA 1674, U.S. Embassy (Mein) to secretary of state, March 8, 1963, box 7, folder: Argentina, General 2/63–3/63, NSF, CF, JFKL.

43. Piero Gleijeses, *Shattered Hope: The Guatemalan Revolution and the United States, 1944–1954* (Princeton, NJ: Princeton University Press, 1991), 34.

44. DoS cable, BA 654, U.S. Embassy (McClintock) to secretary of state, October 14, 1963, box 7A, folder: Argentina General 8/63–9/63, NSF, CF, JFKL.

45. Liliana De Riz, *La política en suspenso: 1966–1976* (Buenos Aires: Paidós, 2000), 33–34; DoS cable, USCINCSO to RUEKDA, July 30, 1964, box 6, folder 1: Argentina Volume I, Cables, 11/63–8/64, NSF, CF, Latin America, LBJL.

46. Barber and Ronning, *Internal Security and Military Power*, viii.

47. DoS cable, BA A-826, U.S. Embassy (Martin) to secretary of state, April 27, 1966, subject: "Political-Economic Assessment," box 6, folder 1: Argentina Volume I, Cables, 11/63–8/64, NSF, CF, Latin America, LBJL.

48. Central Intelligence Agency Directorate of Intelligence, *Current Intelligence Weekly Special Report*, November 4, 1966, subject: "Outlook for the Onganía Regime in Argentina," box 6, folder 5: Argentina Volume II, Memos, 9/64–2/67, NSF, CF, Latin America, LBJL.

49. María José Moyano, *Argentina's Lost Patrol* (New Haven, CT: Yale University Press, 1995), 13.

50. DoS cable, BA 35, U.S. Embassy to secretary of state, July 3, 1966, box 1896, folder: POL-Political Aff. and Rel, ARG-U.S., 1/1/64, CFPF, 1964–1966, GRDS, RG 59, NARA.

51. DoS cable, BA A-263, U.S. Embassy (Martin) to DoS, October 1, 1966, subject: "Situation Report," box 6, folder 5: Argentina Volume II, Memos, 9/64–2/67, NSF, CF, Latin America, LBJL; Moyano, *Argentina's Lost Patrol*, 19; Andres Cisneros and Carlos Escudé, *Historia general de las relaciones exteriores de la República Argentina* (Buenos Aires: Centro de Estudios de Politica Exterior, 2003), 40–41.

52. Central Intelligence Agency National Intelligence Estimate, no. 91–67, December 7, 1967, subject: "Argentina," box 9, folder: "91: Argentina," NSF, National Intelligence Estimates, LBJL.

53. "Press in Argentina Leads a Risky Life," *NYT*, May 31, 1970, 121.

54. Speech reprinted in *Geopolitica* 7, no. 25, 61–66. See also Robert Potash, *The Army and Politics in Argentina, 1962–1973: From Frondizi's Fall to the Peronist Restoration* (Stanford: Stanford University Press, 1996), 132–133.

55. Juan de Onis, "Ebb of U.S. Influence," *NYT*, June 29, 1966, 14; Graziano, *Divine Violence*, 19.

56. Potash, *Army and Politics in Argentina*, 148–149; Romero, *History of Argentina*, 152.

57. H. J. Maidenberg, "Argentine Junta Weighs U.S. Stand," *NYT*, July 14, 1966, 11. The United States withheld diplomatic recognition from June 28 until July 15, 1966.

58. Central Intelligence Agency Directorate of Intelligence, *Current Intelligence Weekly Special Report*, November 4, 1966, subject: "Outlook for the Onganía Regime in Argentina," box 6, folder 5: Argentina Volume II, Memos, 9/64–2/67, NSF, CF, Latin America, LBJL.

59. Central Intelligence Agency National Intelligence Estimate, no. 91–61, December 7, 1967, subject: "Argentina," box 9, folder 91: Argentina, NSF, National Intelligence Estimates, LBJL.

60. Dan Kurtzman, "U.S. Resumes Aid to Argentina," *WP*, August 15, 1966, C11.

61. See Laura Kalmanowiecki, "Origins and Applications of Political Policing in Argentina," *Latin American Perspectives* 27, no. 1 (2000): 36–56.

62. Wolfgang S. Heinz and Hugo Frühling, *Determinants of Gross Human Rights Violations by State and State-Sponsored Actors in Brazil, Uruguay, Chile, and Argentina, 1960–1990* (The Hague: Martinus Nijhoff, 1999), 690–691.

63. Ibid., 694, 699–700. See also Center for International Policy, *Human Rights and the U.S. Foreign Assistance Program: Fiscal Year 1978*, part 1, Latin America, in box 74, folder: Human Rights and U.S. Government 12/76–6/77, OPLMC, JCL.

64. Originally printed in *La Razón*, January 4, 1981, quoted in *Nunca Más: The Report of the Argentine National Commission on the Disappeared* (New York: Farrar, Straus, Giroux, 1986), 442.

65. As David Pion-Berlin writes, the Argentine military accepted elements of the U.S. doctrine and rejected others. "The armed forces practiced selective vision, magnifying those components of the doctrine they liked and losing sight of the rest." Pion-Berlin, "National Security Doctrine," 383–384.

66. O'Donnell, "Modernization and Military Coups," 108.

67. DoS cable, BA A-606, U.S. Embassy to DoS, March 2, 1968, subject: "Country Analysis and Strategy Paper (CASP)—Argentina," box 1849, folder: POL—Political AFF and REL, ARG-U.S., 1/1/67, CFPF, 1964–1966, GRDS, RG 59, NARA.

68. Quoted in James Mann, Rise of the Vulcans: The History of Bush's War Cabinet (New York: Viking, 2001), 16.

69. Quoted in Seymour M. Hersh, The Price of Power: Kissinger in the Nixon White House (New York: Summit Books, 1983), 263. In the final volume of his memoirs, Kissinger acknowledged a limited engagement with Latin America. "On being named National Security Adviser in 1968, I had had little direct involvement with Latin America," Kissinger wrote. "The focus of my academic interests had been on the Cold War and its battlefronts, which were located primarily in Europe and Asia. Like many of my contemporaries, I suffered from a distorted geographic perspective: London, Paris, Rome, and Bonn seemed close; Mexico City seemed far away, Rio de Janeiro or Buenos Aires beyond reach. I would think nothing of traveling to Europe for a weekend conference. A visit to Mexico City presented itself as a complex enterprise." Henry Kissinger, Years of Renewal (New York: Simon and Schuster, 1999), 706. That said, in subsequent decades Kissinger demonstrated little willingness to accept criticism for his policy initiatives in the region. In 2004, for example, Kissinger was allegedly involved in the forced resignation of the historian Kenneth Maxwell from an editorial position at the influential journal Foreign Affairs, after Maxwell wrote a favorable review of Peter Kornbluh's The Pinochet File. See Kenneth Maxwell, The Case of the Missing Letter in Foreign Affairs: Kissinger, Pinochet and Operation Condor, Working Papers on Latin America (Cambridge, MA: The David Rockefeller Center for Latin American Studies, Harvard University, 2004).

70. "Nixon Urges U.S. to Alter Latin Policy," WP, May 16, 1967, A12.

71. "Nixon, on Latin Tour, Hails Argentine Military Regime," NYT, May 12, 1967, 19.

72. Nelson A. Rockefeller, The Rockefeller Report on the Americas: The Official Report of a United States Presidential Mission for the Western Hemisphere (Chicago: Quadrangle Books, 1969), 143, 33.

73. DoS memo, BA 4960, U.S. Embassy to secretary of state, December 16, 1970, subject: "Review of U.S. Military Presence in Latin America," box 248, folder: PER Buenos Aires, SNF, 1970–1973, Administration, GRDS, RG 59, NARA.

74. On Argentina's decision to buy European arms, see Eduardo J. Uriburu, El Plan Europa: Un intento de liberación nacional (Buenos Aires: Cruz y Fierro Editores, 1970). Quoted material in DoS cable, BA A-653, U.S. Embassy to secretary of state, December 8, 1971, subject: "Argentine Foreign Policy since 1966," box 2085, folder: POL 1 ARG, SNF, 1970–1973, Political and Defense, GRDS, RG 59, NARA; DoS Country Analysis and Strategy Paper (CASP), FY 1974–1975, May 2, 1973, subject: "Country Analysis and Strategy Paper," box 2092, folder: POL 1 ARG-US 2-5-71, SNF, 1970–1973, Political and Defense, GRDS, RG 59, NARA.

75. DoS Country Analysis and Strategy Paper (CASP), FY 1974–1975, May 2, 1973, subject: "Country Analysis and Strategy Paper."

76. DoS cable, BA A-263, U.S. Embassy (Martin) to DoS, October 1, 1966, subject: "Situation Report," box 6, folder: 5: Argentina Volume II, Memos, 9/64–2/67, NSF, CF, Latin America, LBJL; Malcolm W. Browne, "Argentines Cool to Regime in Poll," NYT, June 28, 1968, 9.

77. Central Intelligence Agency National Intelligence Estimate, no. 91–67, December 7, 1967, subject: "Argentina," box 9, folder: "91: Argentina," NSF, National Intelligence Estimates, LBJL.

78. David Rock, *Authoritarian Argentina: The Nationalist Movement, Its History, and Its Impact* (Berkeley: University of California Press, 1993), 209.

79. Personal correspondence, Robert C. Hill to Alvaro Sanchez Jr., July 6, 1962, box 118, folder 10, Hill Papers II.

80. Robert C. Hill, "The State of Latin America," *Washington World*, August 1966, 4.

81. John M. Goshko, "Latins Anxious about Nixon," *WP*, December 8, 1968, A29.

82. "Ambassador Hill Arrives," undated, box 1, folder 30, Hill Papers I.

83. *Firing Line*, hosted by William F. Buckley Jr., with guests Robert C. Hill and Eduardo Roca, PBS, taped in Buenos Aires on January 31, 1977, subject: "Should the U.S. Pressure Argentina?" transcript, box 3, folder 34, Hill Papers I.

84. See "An Uphill Task for Mr. Hill?" *Buenos Aires Herald*, editorial, February 9, 1974, box 1, folder 30, Hill Papers I.

85. *Firing Line*, PBS, January 31, 1977.

86. Lewis, *Guerrillas and Generals*, 46–47.

87. Richard Gillespie, *Soldiers of Perón: Argentina's Montoneros* (Oxford: Clarendon Press, 1982), 144–153.

88. As the British Embassy in Buenos Aires rather snidely put it, "The only assets she [Isabel Perón] brought to the job . . . were physical attractiveness and personal ambition." Foreign Office report, no. 219/76, April 1, 1976, subject: "Argentina's Flight from Freedom," file: FC07/3927, NAUK.

89. DoS airgram, BA A-143, U.S. Embassy (Montllor) to secretary of state (Kissinger), June 16, 1975, subject: "Political Violence in Argentina," ADP.

90. DoS report, Harry W. Shlaudeman to secretary of state (Kissinger), August 3, 1976, subject: "ARA Monthly Report (July) The 'Third World War' and South America," ADP.

91. DoS airgram, BA A-143; DoS cable, BA 2039, U.S. Embassy (Hill) to secretary of state (Kissinger), March 24, 1975, subject: "25 Political Murders in 48 Hours," ADP.

92. "A No-Nonsense General Throws Isabel Out," *U.S. News and World Report*, April 5, 1976, 38.

93. DoS report, April 16, 1975, subject: "Argentina: Renewed Terrorist Violence," ADP.

94. Milton R. Benjamin, "Exit Isabel, Enter the Army," *Newsweek*, April 5, 1976, 29.

95. *Firing Line*, PBS, January 31, 1977.

96. DoS cable, State 79141, secretary of state (Kissinger) to U.S. Embassy (Hill), April 8, 1975, subject: "Terrorism—Argentina," ADP.

97. DoS cable, BA 698, U.S. Embassy (Hill) to secretary of state (Kissinger), January 30, 1973, subject: "Over View of Terrorist Situation in Argentina," ADP; DoS cable, BA 1415, U.S. Embassy (Hill) to secretary of state (Kissinger), March 1, 1975, subject: "Killing of U.S. Consular Agent," ADP.

98. *Argentina: A Special Report for Those Interested in Argentina, Today and Its Future*, pamphlet, April 1977, published by the Argentine Embassy, Washington, DC, in box 1, folder 29, Hill Papers I.

99. Robert Cox, "Mission Accomplished," *Buenos Aires Herald*, May 4, 1977, box 1, folder 30, Hill Papers I.

100. "Argentina: Safety First," *Newsweek*, February 9, 1976, 39.

101. DoS cable, BA 1042, U.S. Embassy (Hill) to secretary of state (Kissinger), February 16, 1976, subject: "Military Take Cognizance of Human Rights Issue," ADP; DoS cable, BA 1751, U.S. Embassy (Hill) to secretary of state (Kissinger), March 16, 1978, subject:

"Ambassador's Conversation with Admiral Massera," ADP. Similarly, a few weeks after Medus's conversation, Admiral Emilio Massera, the commander in chief of the navy, indicated to Ambassador Hill the military's intention to take political power in the immediate future. The armed forces, Massera informed the ambassador, "were terribly concerned about their public relations in the U.S. should they have to intervene." Admitting the military's inexperience in promoting a favorable image abroad, Massera asked Hill if the latter could recommend reputable public relations firms in the United States to handle "the problem" for a future military government. Hill readily agreed, forwarding a list of firms compiled from the embassy's commercial library. DoS cable, BA 1751, U.S. Embassy (Hill) to secretary of state (Kissinger), March 16, 1976, subject: "Ambassador's Conversation with Admiral Massera," ADP.

102. DoS cable, BA 6087, U.S. Embassy (Hill) to secretary of state (Kissinger), September 10, 1975, subject: "Analysis of Political Situation Wake of Military Crisis," ADP.

103. Letter, Robert C. Hill to George D. Aiken, October 14, 1975, box 1, folder 31, Hill Papers I.

104. On this point, see, for example, Graziano, *Divine Violence*, 27.

105. Camps, originally in *La Prensa*, January 4, 1981, quoted in Frontalini and Caiati, *El mito de la "guerra sucia,"* 31–32.

106. See John Dinges, *The Condor Years: How Pinochet and His Allies Brought Terrorism to Three Continents* (New York: New Press, 2005); McSherry, *Predatory States;* Stella Calloni, *Los años del lobo: Operación Cóndor* (Buenos Aires: Peña Lillo Ediciones Continente, 1999).

107. See Andersen, *Dossier Secreto*, 124–141.

108. See Carlos H. Acuña and Catalina Smulovitz, "Militares en la transición argentina: Del gobierno a la subordinación constitucional," in *Juicio, castigos y memorias: Derechos humanos,* ed. Carlos H. Acuña (Buenos Aires: Nueva Vision, 1995), 28–29.

109. Quoted in Nieto, *Masters of War*, 251.

110. DoS cable, BA 3142, U.S. Embassy (Hill) to secretary of state (Kissinger), May 11, 1975, subject: "Junta's Moderate Line in Doubt," ADP.

111. Dorothy McCardle, "'So Thrilled over Going to Spain,'" *WP*, April 20, 1969, 131.

112. Hill, interview with Mason.

113. Robert C. Hill, "Driving Up from Salvador," *NYT*, April 17, 1955, 21.

114. "Lively U.S. Envoy Is a Hit in Mexico," *NYT*, January 3, 1958, 7. During his tenure in Mexico, Hill also established a reputation for athletic prowess. On one occasion, he made the opening kick at a U.S.-Mexican university football game. "It was by far the best kick of the game and the crowd kept yelling, 'Bring the Ambassador back,'" a *New York Times* stringer reported. Similarly, at an exhibition baseball game, Hill responded to the urging of fans by agreeing to pitch against the Pittsburgh Pirates until they scored. In his shirtsleeves and vest, Hill managed to hold the pitcher's mound for six innings. Ibid.; Holmes Alexander, "Sympathy, Understanding Hill's Trademarks," *Manchester Union Leader,* June [?] 1977, box 1, folder 30, Hill Papers I.

115. McCardle, "'So Thrilled over Going to Spain.'"

116. Statement, October 4, 1976, http://www.gwu.edu/~nsarchiv/NSAEBB/NSAEBB104/index.htm.

117. Latin American Working Group, *LAWG Letter,* vol. 5, no. 2/3, February/March 1978, binder: "Solidarität, Ausland, Argentinien," Forschungs- und Dokumentationszentrum Chile-Lateinamerika, Berlin, Germany.

118. DoS, U.S. Embassy consular section, January 7, 1977, subject: "Record of Human Rights Representations," ADP.

119. DoS cable, BA 5976, September 14, 1976, subject: "W/W: Arrest of Patricia Ann Erb," ADP; DoS cable, BA 6013, September 15, 1976, subject: "W/W: Arrest of Patricia Ann Erb," ADP; DoS cable, BA 6058, September 16, 1976, subject: "W/W: Arrest of Patricia Ann

Erb," ADP; DoS cable, BA 6097, September 17, 1976, subject: "W/W: Arrest of Patricia Ann Erb," ADP.

120. DoS cable, BA 6177, September 21, 1976, subject: "My Call on President Videla," ADP.

121. DoS cable, BA 3376, May 20, 1976, subject: "Welfare/Whereabouts AMCIT," ADP.

122. DoS cable, BA 3576, May 28, 1976, subject: "Demarche to Foreign Minister on Human Rights," ADP.

123. DoS memo of conversation, March 1977 [?], Patricia Derian and Robert C. Hill, U.S. Embassy BA, Derian Papers. To preserve the secrecy of her meeting with Ambassador Hill, Derian subsequently tore off the heading of this remarkable document. In a recent interview, Derian confirmed the date and substance of the meeting. In a separate interview, Fred Rondon confirmed that he drafted the document.

124. Italics mine. DoS memo of conversation, October 7, 1976, subject: "Secretary's Meeting with Argentine Foreign Minister Guzzetti," NSA, Electronic Briefing Book 104, Carlos Osorio, ed., http://www.gwu.edu/~nsarchiv/NSAEBB/NSAEBB104/index.htm.

125. Accordingly to Hill, in a meeting with Kissinger in August, the secretary of state personally related to Hill his June 1976 conversation with Guzzetti—particularly his decision to turn a blind eye to Argentine antisubversion activities. DoS memo of conversation, March 1977 [?], Patricia Derian and Robert C. Hill.

126. DoS cable, BA 6871, October 19, 1976, subject: "Foreign Minister Guzzetti Euphoric over Visit to United States," ADP. The following May, Guzzetti was bludgeoned and shot in the head by left-wing terrorists. The Argentine foreign minister miraculously survived thanks to brain surgery at Bethesda Naval Hospital. Along with two other Argentine military personnel maimed by terrorist attacks, Guzzetti recuperated in the United States.

127. Ibid.

128. Personal interview with Patricia Derian, March 3, 2008, Chapel Hill, NC.

129. For an alternative analysis that emphasizes Kissinger's unique foreign policy approach to the Third World, see Jeremy Suri, *Henry Kissinger and the American Century* (Cambridge, MA: Belknap Press, 2007).

130. "Kissinger's 10-Yr Gap," *Buenos Aires Herald,* July 1978, box 3, folder 30, Hill Papers I. More than two decades later, Kissinger reiterated his limited interest and involvement in Argentina in his memoirs. "Though I met the foreign ministers frequently," he wrote, "it was not until I left government and Argentina had emerged from the Perón/military era that I became personally acquainted with Argentina and grew to love that exciting and sophisticated nation." Kissinger, *Years of Renewal,* 748.

131. Hill died of a heart attack on November 28, 1978. He was sixty-one years old. See "Robert C. Hill, Ex-Envoy, Dies at 61," *NYT,* November 29, 1978, B12.

132. Robert C. Hill, remarks, Pan-America Society of New York, June 28, 1977.

133. Robert C. Hill, "Argentina Today," keynote address, directors and guests of the Argentine-American Chamber of Commerce luncheon given in Hill's honor, June 28, 1977, Metropolitan Club, New York City.

134. DoS memo of conversation, March 1977 [?], Patricia Derian and Robert C. Hill.

135. *Firing Line,* PBS, January 31, 1977.

3. "HUMAN RIGHTS IS SUDDENLY CHIC"

1. Olga Talamante, official affidavit, state of California, October 12, 1976, ADP; Alan Eladio Gómez, "Feminism, Torture, and the Politics of Chicana/Third World Solidarity: An Interview with Olga Talamante," *Radical Historical Review* no. 101 (2008): 171–172.

2. Details from the Talamantes' life from Suzie Dodd Thomas, "Dirty Wars: On the Unacceptability of Torture; A Conversation with Olga Talamante," *Social Justice* 33, no. 1 (2006): 108–109.

212 NOTES TO PAGES 57–60

3. Carol Pogash, "Friends Remember Argentine Prisoner," *San Francisco Examiner,* December 5, 1975.

4. Ibid.

5. Talamante, official affidavit.

6. Congressional correspondence, Michael J. Harrington to Henry Kissinger, March 12, 1976, ADP.

7. Personal letter, Olga Talamante to her parents and brothers, November 27, 1974, box 10, folder 7, Lister Papers.

8. Thomas, "Dirty Wars," 118

9. Ibid., 117. On NACLA's role in the Talamante case, see, for example, "Free Olga Talamante," *NACLA Report on the Americas* 9, no. 6 (September 1, 1975).

10. Official correspondence, Norman Y. Mineta to Robert C. Felder, March 12, 1975, box 10, folder 7, Lister Papers.

11. Since the late 1960s, the term "human rights" has been applied to diverse local, regional, and national movements advocating a wide-range of political, economic, and/ or social and cultural issues. The elasticity of "human rights" was—and remains—both a strength and a weakness for human rights advocates. On the one hand, calls to promote human rights generated widespread support from a broad-based constituency and could be applied to a variety of local contexts. On the other hand, by the end of the 1970s, the use of "human rights" to describe struggles ranging from gay activism in California to opposition to Cuba's command economy denied the human rights movement a clearly defined agenda and prevented a tight organizational structure. "Human rights," in other words, meant different things to different groups at different times. For the sake of clarity, in this book the "human rights movement" refers to the effort to (a) elevate moral and ethical considerations in the formulation and implementation of U.S. foreign policy; and (b) promote the protection of human rights overseas. The term "human rights" defies a single definition in the historical context of the late 1960s and 1970s given the diverse political leanings of human rights advocates, but is broadly construed as (a) freedom from government violation of the integrity of the person; (b) economic and social rights, such as food, shelter, and education; and (c) civil and political rights.

12. Geoffrey Roberts, *Crimes against Humanity: The Struggle for Global Justice* (New York: New Press, 2006), 48–49. On the role of human rights in U.S. foreign policy in the early post–World War II period, see Borgwardt, *New Deal for the World;* Foote, "Cold War and Human Rights," 445–465; Glendon, *World Made New;* Lauren, *Evolution of International Human Rights;* Burke, *Decolonization and the Evolution of International Human Rights.*

13. United States Senate, Committee on Foreign Relations, Subcommittee on Western Hemisphere Affairs, "United States Military Policies and Programs in Latin America," 91st Cong., 1st sess., June 24 and July 8, 1969, Committee Print (Washington, DC: Government Printing Office, 1969), 6.

14. Ibid., 39.

15. DoS memo, deputy coordinator for foreign assistance (Bell) to Secretary of State Rusk, June 26, 1961, subject: "Proposed Presidential Determination under Section 105(b) (4) and 451(a) of the MSA of 1954, as amended, permitting the use of funds to furnish military assistance to Panama, Costa Rica, Nicaragua, El Salvador, Honduras, Guatemala and Haiti," *FRUS, 1961–1963,* vol. 12.

16. Telecon, George W. Ball to Edwin Martin, March 29, 1962, 3:15 p.m., box 149, folder 2, Ball Papers.

17. Letter from Secretary of State Rusk to the chairman of the Subcommittee on American Republic Affairs of the Senate Foreign Relations Committee (Morse), Washington, September 15, 1962, *FRUS, 1961–1963,* vol. 12.

18. Telephone conversation between Lyndon B. Johnson and Thomas C. Mann, March 19, 1964, *FRUS, 1964–1968*, vol. 31, 28–29.

19. "Javits Asks Curb on Alliance Aid," *NYT,* July 18, 1966, 9.

20. WH memo, W.G. Bowdler to W.W. Rostow, October 14, 1966, box 1, folder: "5: Bowdler Memos," NSF, Name File, LBJL.

21. Benjamin Welles, "The Latin Military: A Dilemma for Washington," *NYT,* December 22, 1968, E5; James Sundquist, *The Decline and Resurgence of Congress* (Washington, DC: Brookings Institution Press, 1981), 245.

22. United States Senate, Committee on Foreign Relations, Subcommittee on Western Hemisphere Affairs, "United States Military Policies and Programs in Latin America," 91st Cong., 1st sess., June 24 and July 8, 1969, Committee Print (Washington, DC: Government Printing Office, 1969), 6; A. D. Horne, "Military Aid to Latin America Is Backed by Administration," *WP,* July 9, 1969, B7.

23. United States Senate, Committee on Foreign Relations, Subcommittee on Western Hemisphere Affairs, "United States Military Policies and Programs in Latin America," 91st Cong., 1st sess., June 24 and July 8, 1969, Committee Print (Washington, DC: Government Printing Office, 1969), 73.

24. Frank Church, "Toward a New Policy for Latin America," address to the U.S. Senate, April 10, 1970, box 29, folder 8, Lister Papers.

25. Robert David Johnson, *Congress and the Cold War* (Cambridge: Cambridge University Press, 2006), 179.

26. The amendment was section 510 of the Foreign Assistance Act of 1970 (the Mutual Education and Cultural Exchange Act). "From MAP to FMS: Security on a Cash Basis," *NACLA's Latin America and Empire Report* 10, no. 1 (January 1976), 8.

27. The MAP figure included the transfer of excess defense articles. Child, *Unequal Alliance,* 211; "From MAP to FMS: Security on a Cash Basis," *NACLA's Latin America and Empire Report* 10, no. 1 (January 1976), 8.

28. "From MAP to FMS," 9.

29. Arthur M. Schlesinger Jr., *The Imperial Presidency* (Boston: Houghton Mifflin, 1973).

30. Robert F. Drinan, *Congressional Record,* February 4, 1971, 454.

31. "Tribute to Robert F. Drinan," *Congressional Record,* June 11, 1980, H4813. Rev. Gabriel Richard, also a Catholic priest, served in Congress from 1823–1825, but only as a nonvoting delegate from the Michigan Territory. Four years after Father Drinan's retirement, the Reverend Robert John Cornell (D-WI) served two terms in the House of Representatives. See "Robert Drinan Dies at 86: Pioneer as Lawmaker Priest," *NYT,* January 30, 2007, http://www.nytimes.com/2007/01/30/obituaries/30drinan.html.

32. Robert F. Drinan, *Congressional Record,* April 17, 1972, 3175; Drinan, "Drinan versus Nixon," *Congressional Record,* May 8, 1973, E3016.

33. Cynthia J. Arnson, *Crossroads: Congress, the President, and Central America, 1976–1993* (University Park: Pennsylvania State University Press, 1993), 9.

34. Kenneth B. Dalecki, "Cong. Drinan: Great Guy; 'Devil in Priest's Clothing,'" *Fitchburg Sentinel,* August 13, 1973, 15.

35. Jo Marie Griesgraber, "Implementation by the Carter Administration of Human Rights Legislation Affecting Latin America" (PhD diss., Georgetown University, 1983), 37–38. Fearing an investigation of all OPS activities, the Ford administration shuttered the organization in 1974. See Huggins, *Political Policing,* 195.

36. Fraser's subcommittee was later renamed the Subcommittee on Human Rights and International Organizations.

37. George Lister, interview with *Radio Pacifica,* September 11, 1975, transcript, box 18, folder 22, Lister Papers.

38. U.S. Congress, *Human Rights in the World Community: A Call for U.S. Leadership,* a Report of the Subcommittee on International Organizations and Movements of the Committee on Foreign Affairs, House of Representatives, 93rd Cong., 1st sess. (Washington, DC: Government Printing Office, 1974).

39. Personal interview with John Salzberg, May 6, 2008, Washington, DC.

40. Personal interview with Rev. Joe Eldridge, May 4, 2008, Washington, DC.

41. Personal interview with Roberta Cohen, May 1, 2008, Washington, DC.

42. Quoted in Stephen B. Cohen, "Conditioning U.S. Security Assistance on Human Rights Practices," *Journal of International Law* 76 (1982): 251.

43. In the November 1974 congressional elections, seventy-five new Democrats joined the Ninety-Fourth Congress, the largest freshman class since 1948. Intent on enacting major legislative reform and expanding the power of Congress, the "Watergate Babies" embraced the nascent human rights legislation while working to cut Department of Defense expenditures. Accordingly, Congress increasingly attached country-specific legislation to military assistance authorization bills—an approach initiated the previous year—including limits on U.S. military aid to Turkey, Angola, South Korea, Vietnam, Cambodia, Chile, and Indonesia. See Arnson, *Crossroads,* 9–10; Johnson, *Congress and the Cold War,* 205; Cohen, "Conditioning U.S. Security Assistance on Human Rights Practices," 254.

44. Kissinger, *Years of Renewal,* 755.

45. Roberta Cohen, "Integrating Human Rights in U.S. Foreign Policy: The History, the Challenges, and the Criteria for an Effective Policy," statement at the Foreign Service Institute, 2008, http://www.brookings.edu/speeches/2008/04_human_rights_cohen.aspx.

46. James M. Wilson, "Diplomatic Theology: An Early Chronicle of Human Rights at State," undated, James M. Wilson Papers, box 1, folder: Human Rights and Humanitarian Affairs—Wilson Memoir, GRFL.

47. Donald M. Fraser, address at the Human Rights Day Commemorative Conference, Chicago, December 9, 1976, box 149.C12.4F, folder: Don Fraser, Fraser Papers; congressional correspondence, Donald M. Fraser to Stephen Pflange, October 26, 1976, box 149.G.9.8F, folder: Human Rights 1976 [1], Fraser Papers.

48. In June Fraser apprised Kissinger of the recommendations in *Human Rights in the World Community,* and three months later he pointedly informed the State Department that he was "disturbed of our lack of responsiveness when governments commit gross violations of human rights." The following year, Fraser requested information from Kissinger on human rights cases in more than a dozen countries. Congressional correspondence, Donald M. Fraser to Henry A. Kissinger, June 27, 1974, box 149.G.13.7B, folder: Human Rights; and Fraser to William D. Rogers, September 13, 1974, box 149.G.13.8F, folder: Foreign Affairs Committee Subcommittee on International Org. and Movements 1974, Fraser Papers. For Fraser's correspondence on specific countries, see Fraser to Kissinger, box 149.G.13.7B, folder: Human Rights; and Fraser to Kissinger, box 149.G.9.7B, folder: Human Rights, 1975 [1], Fraser Papers.

49. DoS memo of conversation, December 17, 1974, subject: "Human Rights," box 7, folder: Human Rights (D/HA), Robinson Papers.

50. Ibid.

51. Personal interview with Rev. Joe Eldridge, May 4, 2008, Washington, DC.

52. Patrick Breslin, "Human Rights: Rhetoric or Action?" *WP,* February 27, 1977, 33.

53. John P. Salzberg, "A View from the Hill: U.S. Legislation and Human Rights," in *The Diplomacy of Human Rights,* ed. David D. Newsom (Lanham, MD: University Press of America, 1986), 17.

54. Cohen, "Conditioning U.S. Security Assistance on Human Rights Practices," 252–253.

55. Clair Apodaca, *Understanding U.S. Human Rights Policy: A Paradoxical Legacy* (New York: Routledge, 2006), 40; "House Votes to Ban Foreign Aid for Human Rights Violations," *NYT,* September 11, 1975, 18.

56. DoS memo, J.M. Wilson to Henry Kissinger, October 1, 1976, subject: "D/HA Monthly Report," box 7, folder: Human Rights (D/HA), Robinson Papers.

57. DoS cable, State A-1285, secretary of state (Kissinger) to all ARA diplomatic posts, February 26, 1975, subject: "Human Rights and Protection of U.S. Nationals in Latin America," box 63, folder 25, Lister Papers.

58. Ibid.

59. DoS cable, BA 6870, U.S. Embassy BA (Hill) to secretary of state, October 15, 1975, ADP.

60. DoS cable, BA 4645, U.S. Embassy BA (Hill) to secretary of state, July 14, 1975, ADP.

61. DoS cable, State 239839, assistant secretary of state (Shlaudeman) to U.S. Embassy BA (Hill), October 8, 1975, ADP.

62. DoS cable, BA 6870.

63. Congressional correspondence, Robert J. McCloskey to Edward M. Kennedy, November 13, 1975, ADP.

64. "The Armed Forces' Decision to Assume the Direction of the State, 1976," reprinted in *The Politics of Antipolitics: The Military in Latin America,* 2nd ed., ed. Brian Loveman and Thomas M. Davies Jr. (Lincoln: University of Nebraska Press, 1989), 158–160.

65. Thomas, "Dirty Wars," 117.

66. Ibid., 118. See also Joanne Omang, "Argentines Release Jailed American," *WP,* March 29, 1976, A17; "Freed American Tells of Torture in Argentine Jail," *NYT,* March 29, 1976, 9.

67. Thomas, "Dirty Wars," 118.

68. Ibid., 108.

69. Ibid.

70. Pogash, "Friends Remember Argentine Prisoner."

71. Gómez, "Feminism, Torture, and the Politics of Chicana/Third World Solidarity," 165.

72. Ibid., 164.

73. Ibid., 166.

74. Talamante, official affidavit.

75. Ibid.

76. Ibid.

77. Olga Talamante, "Surviving to Tell the Tale of Torture," *Los Angeles Times,* March 25, 2006, B17.

78. Olga Talamante, excerpt of personal correspondence reprinted in "Free Olga Talamante," *NACLA's Latin America and Empire Report* 9, no. 6 (September 1975), 30.

79. Ibid.

80. Apodaca, *Understanding U.S. Human Rights Policy,* 39.

81. DoS memo, Don Tice to Charles W. Robinson, July 16, 1976, subject: "Fraser Human Rights Hearings," box 7, folder: Human Rights (D/HA), Robinson Papers.

82. U.S. Congress, House of Representatives, Committee on International Relations, Subcommittee on International Organizations, *Human Rights in Argentina,* 94th Cong., 2nd sess., September 28–29, 1976, Committee Print (Washington, DC: Government Printing Office, 1976), 41.

83. Laurie S. Wiseberg and Harry M. Scoble, "Monitoring Human Rights Violations: The Role of Nongovernmental Organizations," in *Human Rights and American Foreign Policy,* ed. Donald P. Kommers and Gilbert D. Loescher (Notre Dame: University of Notre Dame Press, 1979), 183–185.

84. Jeri Laber, *The Courage of Strangers: Coming of Age with the Human Rights Movement* (New York: PublicAffairs, 2002), 73–74.

85. *U.S. Policy on Human Rights in Latin America (Southern Cone): A Congressional Conference on Capitol Hill* (New York: Fund for New Priorities in America, 1978), 81.

86. Memo, Roberta Cohen, undated, personal papers of Roberta Cohen, Washington, DC.

87. The Lawyers Committee was later renamed Human Rights First.

88. Kathleen Teltsch, "Human Rights Groups Are Riding a Wave of Popularity," *NYT*, February 28, 1977, 2.

89. Robert F. Drinan, *Cry of the Oppressed: The History and Hope of the Human Rights Revolution* (San Francisco: Harper & Row, 1987), 153.

90. David B. Ottaway, "The Growing Lobby for Human Rights: Time for Action," *WP*, December 12, 1976, 31. On Amnesty's early history, see Tom Buchanan, "'The Truth Will Set You Free': The Making of Amnesty International," *Journal of Contemporary History* 37, no. 4 (2002): 575–597; William Korey, *NGOs and the Universal Declaration of Human Rights: "A Curious Grapevine"* (New York: Palgrave Macmillan, 2001), 159–169; Moyn, *Last Utopia*, 129–133.

91. Cmiel, "Emergence of Human Rights Politics in the United States," 1235.

92. Ottaway, "Growing Lobby for Human Rights," 31.

93. Amnesty International, *Report on Torture* (London: Amnesty International Publications, 1973); Darius Rejali, *Torture and Democracy* (Princeton, NJ: Princeton University Press, 2007), 43.

94. DoS general correspondence, Harry W. Shlaudeman to all [?] U.S. embassies in Latin America, October 28, 1976, ADP.

95. Robert Cox, "Argentina: Despite New Rule, Nightmare of Violence Continues," *WP*, May 11, 1976, A8.

96. Robert Cox, "Argentines Spend Hours in Line to Learn the Fate of Arrested Kin," *WP*, May 31, 1976, A19.

97. Juan de Onís, "Argentina Fighting Both Leftist Subversion and Counterterrorism by Right," *NYT*, June 28, 1976, 12.

98. See, for example, Amnesty International, "List of Refugees Detained or Missing in Argentina," press release, June 17, 1976, ADP; AI, "List of Politically Motivated Deaths in Argentina between 3 January and 3 June 1976," press release, July 2, 1976, ADP; AI, "Attack on Academic Freedom in Argentina," report, September 6, 1976, ADP.

99. Robert F. Drinan, "Death Squads in Argentina Go Unchecked," *Congressional Record*, July 2, 1976, E 3780; Drinan, "Political Assassinations and Illegal Detentions Increase in Argentina," *Congressional Record*, August 25, 1976, H 9064.

100. Robert F. Drinan, "Religious and Political Repression in Argentina," *Commonweal*, February 18, 1977, 103.

101. DoS memo of conversation, December 5, 1976, ADP. In fact, at least three other individuals who had met with the AI group in Córdoba also disappeared shortly thereafter, a fact the U.S. Embassy apparently decided not to share with Representative Drinan. Exemplifying the decentralized nature of the Argentine antisubversive campaign, the victims were most likely kidnapped by security services operating independently of the Córdoba central military command. According to the Argentine Human Rights Working Group, an organ of the military government, Martinez was freed on December 10, 1976, a statement belied by Drinan's continued efforts on her behalf through early 1977. DoS cable, BA 7722, U.S. Embassy to secretary of state, November 26, 1976, ADP; DoS cable, BA 8039, U.S. Embassy to secretary of state, December 10, 1976, subject: "Josefa Martinez Freed; Letelier Sotomayor," ADP.

102. *Report of an Amnesty International Mission to Argentina, 6–15 November 1976* (London: Amnesty International Publications, 1977).

103. "Statement of Congressman Robert F. Drinan upon Release of the Report of an Amnesty International Mission to Argentina," March 23, 1977, box 392, folder: Subject HR, ARG, Robert F. Drinan Papers, John J. Burns Library, Boston College, Boston, MA.

104. Lars Schoultz, *Human Rights and United States Policy toward Latin America* (Princeton, NJ: Princeton University Press, 1981), 84.

105. Telephone interview with Olga Talamante, March 28, 2008.

106. Argentine Commission for Human Rights, press release, November 10, 1977, box 73, folder: Human Rights 12/76–11/77, OPLMC, JCL.

107. Telephone interview with Talamante.

108. Jimmy Carter, inaugural address, January 20, 1977, http://www.jimmycarterlibrary.gov/documents/speeches/inaugadd.phtml.

109. Jerome J. Shestack to Jimmy Carter, March 2, 1977, box: 4, folder: Foreign Policy and Human Rights, 1/77–3/77, OPLMC, JCL.

110. "I appreciate your organization's contribution to an area in which I have a deep, personal concern," Carter wrote Shestack. WH correspondence, Jimmy Carter to Jerome J. Shestack, March 9, 1977, box: 4, folder: Foreign Policy and Human Rights, 1/77–3/77, OPLMC, JCL. Shestack turned down the UN position in 1977 due to commitments in the nongovernmental sector. Offered the position again two years later, Shestack accepted and served as the U.S. delegate to the 1980 commission. See Guest, *Behind the Disappearances,* 190–191.

111. "Thanks in large measure to the initiatives of the President of the United States," the review asserted, "there is a new focus on the human rights of the world's peoples. The League rejoices in this development. For 35 years, we have worked in the barren soil with all too few champions to help." International League for Human Rights, *Annual Review, 1976–1977.* Underscoring the shift from the Nixon-Ford years, in its previous report the ILHR had dourly reported, "One surveys the human rights scene with a certain despair." International League for the Rights of Man, *Annual Review, 1974–1975.*

112. DoS memo, Warren Christopher to Cyrus Vance, April 14, 1977, subject: "U.S. Foreign Policy on Human Rights: A Status Report," box 2, folder: TL 4/1–4/15, Lake Papers.

113. Congressional official correspondence, Tom Harkin to Cyrus Vance, November 11, 1977, box 13, folder: Human Rights—Argentina I, Christopher Papers. Donald Fraser concurred with Harkin's assessment. Similarly, despite noting "a certain amount of ad hocery," "preachiness," and inconsistency in its application of the human rights policy, Fraser praised Carter's support for human rights in April 1977, and later described Carter's human rights policy as "the singular achievement of this administration." Congressional correspondence, Donald M. Fraser to Virgil C. Sullivan, April 1, 1977, box 151.H.3.6F, folder: Human Rights 1977 [4], Fraser Papers; Donald M. Fraser, testimony before the Subcommittee on International Organizations of the House Committee on Foreign Affairs, August 2, 1979, box 152.K12.9B, folder: Human Rights, Fraser Papers.

114. Argentine Commission for Human Rights, "Statement Prepared for the International Symposium on Human Rights and American Foreign Policy, April 27–30, 1977, University of Notre Dame," box: 74, folder: Human Rights: Argentina and Chile 1/76–11/77, OPLMC, JCL.

115. Griesgraber, "Implementation by the Carter Administration of Human Rights Legislation Affecting Latin America," 71.

116. Patricia Erb, "A mis compañeros y compañeras les regalé mi voz," in *Testimonios de la solidaridad internacional* (Buenos Aires: Ministerio de Relaciones Exteriores, Comercio Internacional y Culto, 2007), 143.

117. Olga Talamante and Horacio D. Lofredo to Jimmy Carter, June 3, 1977, box 74, folder: Human Rights: Argentina and Chile 1/76–11/77, OPLMC, JCL.

118. Schoultz, *Human Rights and United States Policy toward Latin America*, 84.

119. Burton I. Kaufman and Scott Kaufman, *The Presidency of James Earl Carter, Jr.* (Lawrence: University Press of Kansas, 2006), 52.

120. DoS memo, John Bushnell to Patricia Derian, June 13, 1978, subject: "Commentary on Cutler-Hammer Letter," box 13, folder: Human Rights—Argentina III, Christopher Papers; Sandy Vogelgesang, *American Dream, Global Nightmare: The Dilemma of U.S. Human Rights Policy* (New York: W.W. Norton, 1980), 220.

121. On this point, see, for example, DoS cable, BA 5172, U.S. Embassy (Castro) to secretary of state (Vance), June 26, 1979, subject: "Ambassador Discusses Human Rights with General Viola," ADP.

122. Quoted in Gómez, "Feminism, Torture, and the Politics of Chicana/Third World Solidarity," 119.

4. "TOTAL IMMERSION IN ALL THE HORRORS OF THE WORLD"

1. Patricia Derian, interview on "The Current," radio broadcast, March 24, 2006, Canadian Broadcasting Company, http://www.cbc.ca/thecurrent/2006/200603/20060324.html.

2. DoS memo of conversation, March 1977 [?], Patricia Derian and Robert C. Hill.

3. Personal interview with Patricia Derian, March 3, 2008, Chapel Hill, NC.

4. Ibid.; Karen De Witt, "Carter Aide in Argentina to Gauge Rights Impact," *WP*, March 31, 1977, 17.

5. DoS general correspondence, Fernando E. Rondon to Robert C. Hill, April 7, 1977, ADP.

6. Ibid.

7. Ibid.

8. Derian subsequently divorced, remarrying in 1978 the Mississippi journalist and fellow civil rights activist Hodding Carter III. Carter served as Jimmy Carter's (no relation) assistant secretary of state for public affairs and spokesman for the Department of State.

9. Karen De Witt, "On-the-Job Human Rightist," *WP*, August 11, 1977, B1.

10. Patricia Derian, résumé, box 16, folder: Human Rights—Early Efforts, Christopher Papers.

11. Ibid.

12. Patricia Derian, interview by Charles Stuart Kennedy, March 12, 1996, transcript, FAOC, copy provided to the author by Patricia Derian.

13. Jere Nash and Andy Taggart, *Mississippi Politics: The Struggle for Power, 1976–2006* (Jackson: University Press of Mississippi, 2006), 27.

14. Derian, interview by Kennedy.

15. In the 1968 election, Wallace's American Independent Party ticket won just under 10 million votes and carried five southern states. Other than his native Alabama, Wallace received more votes from Mississippi than any other state. Richard Pearson, "Former Ala. Gov. George C. Wallace Dies," *WP*, September 14, 1998, A1; Nash and Taggart, *Mississippi Politics*, 30–31.

16. Barbara Gamarekian, "Human Rights Spokeswoman," *NYT*, June 23, 1977, 43.

17. Patricia Derian, résumé.

18. Gamarekian, "Human Rights Spokeswoman."

19. Derian, interview by Kennedy.

20. Gamarekian, "Human Rights Spokeswoman."

21. Arthur M. Schlesinger, "Human Rights and the American Tradition," *Foreign Affairs* 57, no. 3 (1978): 513.

22. The second presidential debate, Palace of Fine Arts Theater, San Francisco, October 6, 1976, transcript printed in Sidney Kraus, *The Great Debates: Carter vs. Ford, 1976* (Bloomington: Indiana University Press, 1979), 486.

23. Italics original. Laber, *Courage of Strangers,* 80.

24. Jimmy Carter, *Why Not the Best? The First Fifty Years* (Nashville: Broadman Press, 1975), 35.

25. Jimmy Carter, remarks and a question-and-answer session at a public meeting in Yazoo City, MS, July 21, 1977, *Public Papers of the Presidents of the United States, Jimmy Carter: 1977* (Washington, DC: Government Printing Office, 1978), 2:1328–1329.

26. Kaufman and Kaufman, *Presidency of James Earl Carter, Jr.,* 16.

27. Zbigniew Brzezinski, *Power and Principle: Memoirs of a National Security Adviser, 1977–1981* (New York: Farrar, Straus, Giroux, 1983), 48.

28. Carter, *Keeping Faith,* 142–143.

29. See Brinkley, "Bernath Lecture," 522.

30. Carter, *Keeping Faith,* 143.

31. Quote from the San Francisco debate; see Kraus, ed., *Great Debates.*

32. Bill Adler, *The Wit and Wisdom of Jimmy Carter* (Secaucus, NJ: Citadel Press, 1977), 113.

33. Carter, *Keeping Faith,* 142–143.

34. "Secretary Vance's News Conference of March 4," March 4, 1977, reprinted in *Department of State Bulletin,* vol. 76 (1977), 277; Zbigniew Brzezinski, remarks at the White House commemoration of the thirtieth anniversary of the Universal Declaration of Human Rights, December 6, 1978, box 48, folder: Human Rights Day, 12/6/78, Staff Offices, Assistant for Communications—Press Events, Rafshoon, JCL.

35. Elizabeth Drew, "A Reporter at Large: Human Rights," *New Yorker,* July 18, 1977, 36–62.

36. Cmiel, "Emergence of Human Rights Politics in the United States," 1235.

37. Wiseberg and Scoble, "Monitoring Human Rights Violations," 183–185.

38. On Jackson and détente, see, for example, Robert Gordon Kaufman, *Henry M. Jackson: A Life in Politics* (Seattle: University of Washington Press, 2000), 242–260; Anna Kasten Nelson, "Senator Henry Jackson and the Demise of Détente," in *The Real Policy Makers: Shaping American Foreign Policy from 1947 to the Present* (Lanham, MD: Rowman and Littlefield, 2008), 83–106.

39. Stephen S. Rosenfeld, "Secretary of State Scoop Jackson?" *WP,* June 18, 1976, A27.

40. Schlesinger, "Human Rights and the American Tradition," 515.

41. Kaufman and Kaufman, *Presidency of James Earl Carter, Jr.,* 19.

42. Carter, *Keeping Faith,* 145.

43. Brzezinski, *Power and Principle,* 125. Bernard Gwertzman, "Human Rights: It's Harder to Admonish Allies," *NYT,* February 6, 1977, E1; "The Right Tack on Rights," *WP,* February 27, 1977, 38.

44. Breslin, "Human Rights."

45. Jimmy Carter, news conference, March 9, 1977, *Public Papers of the Presidents of the United States, Jimmy Carter* (Washington, DC: Government Printing Office, 1978), 1:341.

46. Quoted in Drew, "Reporter at Large," 42.Similarly, the UN ambassador Andrew Young maintained that "the human rights emphasis by this administration was never really set down, thought out and planned." David S. Broder, "Pushing Human Rights: To What Consequence?" *WP,* June 15, 1977, A17.

47. DoS action memo, Anthony Lake to Cyrus Vance, February 4, 1977, subject: "Human Rights," box 2, folder: TL 2/1–15/77, Lake Papers.

48. Ibid.

49. Brzezinski, *Power and Principle,* 126.

50. "The Push for Human Rights," *U.S. News and World Report,* June 20, 1977, 46.

51. DoS memo, Cyrus Vance to all assistant secretaries, February 1977, subject: "Human Rights," box 2, folder: TL 2/1–15/77, Lake Papers; De Young, "Carter Aide in Argentina to Gauge Rights Impact."

52. Hedrick Smith, "Aid Cut to Rights-Violating Nations Is Break with U.S. Pragmatism," *NYT*, February 25, 1977, 3.

53. "Moral Policeman to the World? Six Senators Six Up Carter's Stand," *U.S. News and World Report*, March 14, 1977, 21.

54. Robert Keatley, "Human Rights and Diplomatic Pitfalls, *WSJ*, March 22, 1977, 22; see also Vogelgesang, *American Dream, Global Nightmare*, 139.

55. Drew, "Reporter at Large," 43–44.

56. "Human Rights at Different Weights," *NYT*, February 27, 1977, 133.

57. Breslin, "Human Rights."

58. Center for International Policy, "Human Rights and the U.S. Foreign Assistance Program: Fiscal Year 1978, Part 1—Latin America," box 74, folder: Human Rights and U.S. Government 12/76–6/77, OPLMC, JCL. Moreover, the U.S. FMS reduction did not apply to items previously purchased by Argentina but not delivered, or to unspent credits "in the pipeline." As a result, despite the reduction, in FY 1977 Argentina purchased $14.4 million in U.S. equipment (not including commercial sales). See Coalition for a New Foreign and Military Policy, "International Human Rights and the Administration's Security Assistance Program for Fiscal Year 1979: A Critique," March 1978, box 13, folder: Human Rights—Country Evaluation Papers, Christopher Papers.

59. Estimate by the Permanent Assembly for Human Rights member Emilio Mignone. DoS memo of conversation, January 1, 1977, subject: "Military Rule, Human Rights, and U.S. Policy," ADP.

60. DoS cable, BA 696, U.S. Embassy (Hill) to secretary of state (Vance), January 28, 1977, ADP.

61. DoS miscellaneous, June 3, 1977, subject: "United States—Argentine Relations," ADP.

62. Quote from "DoS miscellaneous," R.W. Zimmerman, December 9, 1976, subject: "U.S.-Argentina Relations," ADP. See also Juan de Onís, "Argentina and Uruguay Reject U.S. Assistance Linked to Human Rights," *NYT*, March 2, 1977, 10.

63. Derian, interview by Kennedy.

64. Arriving at her office on her first day, Derian found it still occupied by Jim Wilson, the acting human rights coordinator under Henry Kissinger. When Derian learned that Wilson would probably have to "walk the hall" until receiving another assignment—a rather notorious element of the State Department's personnel system—she refused to humiliate Wilson by asking him to leave. Although Derian was able to temporarily occupy an office in Warren Christopher's suite, her difficulties continued: on her first day, "someone walked in with a stack of paper about 14 inches high and said, 'The Secretary wants you to read this,'" Derian later recalled. After dutifully reading the massive document, entitled "Law of the Sea," Derian walked into Christopher's office and told the surprised deputy secretary, "I don't think this belongs to me. I think it belongs to you." Derian's sympathy for Wilson eventually waned; weeks after her appointment, she was surprised to learn that the former human rights coordinator had conveniently "forgotten" to hand over the parking permit reserved in her name at the department. Confronting Wilson in his office, Derian was blunt: "You pack up and put it on the desk," she told him. "I don't like games like this." Ibid.

65. Breslin, "Human Rights."

66. The functional bureaus perform administrative tasks or analysis in areas such as economics, politico-military, consular, and human rights. Prior to the New State's completion during the Kennedy administration, the operations of the State Department had been dispersed among nearly three dozen buildings distributed throughout the capital. See Anthony Lake, *Somoza Falling* (Boston: Houghton Mifflin, 1989), 1–2.

67. See Caleb Rossiter, "Human Rights: The Carter Record, the Reagan Reaction," *International Policy Report* (September 1984): 5.

68. Derian, interview by Kennedy.

69. Ibid.

70. DoS cable, BA 2053, U.S. Embassy (Hill) to secretary of state (Vance), March 17, 1977, subject: "Argentine Reactions to Human Rights Issue," ADP.

71. Foreign Office memo, British Embassy BA, March 31, 1977, FC07/3276, NAUK.

72. DoS cable, BA 2053, U.S. Embassy (Hill) to secretary of state (Vance), March 17, 1977, subject: "Argentine Reactions to Human Rights Issue," ADP; Juan de Onís, "Argentina Says Carter Interferes," *NYT,* March 1, 1977, 6.

73. *Report of an Amnesty International Mission to Argentina, 6–15 November 1976.*

74. Robert F. Drinan, "Amnesty International Report Details Human Rights Violations in Argentina," *Congressional Record*, March 23, 1977, H2537–2538. Similarly, when asked why the Carter administration supported human rights in mid-June, Derian responded, "Because it's the right thing to do." "Push for Human Rights," *U.S. News and World Report.*

75. Graham Hovey, "Liberals Resisting Naming of a Black to Key Latin Post," *NYT,* January 13, 1977, 9.

76. Lake, *Somoza Falling,* 26.

77. Fernando E. Rondon, interview by Charles Stuart Kennedy, June 4, 1997, transcript, FAOC, http://hdl.loc.gov/loc.mss/mfdip.2004ron01.

78. Terence A. Todman, interview by Michael Krenn, transcript, June 13, 1995, FAOC, http://hdl.loc.gov/loc.mss/mfdip.2004tod01.

79. On this point, see Schoultz, *Human Rights and United States Policy toward Latin America,* 187.

80. Derian, interview by Kennedy.

81. DoS chronology, May 17, 1978, subject: "Argentine Human Rights Chronology," ADP.

82. Gaddis Smith, *Morality, Reason, and Power: American Diplomacy in the Carter Years* (New York: Hill and Wang, 1986), 110.

83. Jimmy Carter, "Pan American Day and Pan American Week, 1977," proclamation 4491, March 21, 1977, *Public Papers of the Presidents of the United States, Jimmy Carter,*, http://www.presidency.ucsb.edu/ws/index.php?pid=7203&st=&st1=.

84. Robert A. Pastor, *Exiting the Whirlpool: U.S. Foreign Policy toward Latin America and the Caribbean* (Boulder: Westview Press, 2001), 42.

85. NSC memo, Robert A. Pastor to Zbigniew Brzezinski, March 14, 1977, subject: "PRC Meeting on Latin America," box 24, folder: Meetings—PRC 8:3/24/77, ZBC, Subject File, JCL.

86. Underscoring the importance Carter assigned to Latin America, less than a week after his inauguration the president expanded the Policy Review Memorandum (PRM) on Panama into a general review of U.S. policy toward Latin America and the Caribbean. NSC, Presidential Review Memorandum/NSC-17, January 26, 1977, subject: "Review of U.S. Policy toward Latin America," box 105, folder: "Presidential Review Memorandum 11–35," Presidential Review Memoranda 10 through Presidential Memoranda 36–47, JCL.

87. NSC memo, "Policy Review Committee Meeting," March 24, 1977, box 24, folder: Meetings—PRC 8: 3/24/77, ZBC, Subject File, JCL.

88. NSC memo, Robert Pastor to Zbigniew Brzezinski, subject: "NSC Contributions to the Carter Administration's Policy to Latin America," ZBC, box 34 NSC Accomplishments—Latin America: 1/81 File, JCL.

89. WH memo, Zbigniew Brzezinski to Jimmy Carter, March 31, 1977, subject: "PRC Meeting on Latin America."

90. Robert Pastor, "The Carter Administration and Latin America: An Assessment," October 28, 1980, box 27, folder: Latin America, 1/12/80, National Security Affairs, Staff Material—North/South, Pastor—Country Files, JCL.

91. "Text of Carter's Address to OAS Council Outlining Policy toward Latin America," *NYT,* April 15, 1977, 10.

92. On this point, see Richard E. Feinberg, "U.S. Human Rights Policy: Latin America" *International Policy Report* 6, no. 1 (1980): 1; Schoultz, *Human Rights and United States Policy toward Latin America,* 372.

93. As Robert Pastor later asserted, "The amount and the quality of attention which you and your Administration gave to Latin America in 1977 probably exceeded that of any other Administration's first year, including that of Kennedy and the Alliance for Progress." Pastor, "Carter Administration and Latin America."

94. Quoted in Graham Hovey, "Carter's Latin Policy: No Big Pledges but 'Honest Concern,'" *NYT,* September 28, 1977, 12.

95. Jimmy Carter, address before the United Nations General Assembly, March 17, 1977, *Public Papers of the Presidents of the United States, Jimmy Carter,* 1:449.

96. DoS cable, State 54798, secretary of state to all diplomatic and consular posts, March 23, 1977, subject: "USG Emphasis on Human Rights," box 13, folder: Human Rights—Early Efforts, Christopher Papers.

97. Underlined text in original. DoS memo, Warren Christopher to Cyrus Vance, April 14, 1977, subject: "U.S. Foreign Policy on Human Rights: A Status Report," box 2, folder: TL 4/1–4/15, Lake Papers.

98. Drew, "Reporter at Large," 44.

99. Underlined text in original. DoS memo, Warren Christopher to Cyrus Vance, April 14, 1977, subject: "U.S. Foreign Policy on Human Rights: A Status Report," box 2, folder: TL 4/1–4/15, Lake Papers.

100. Albert R. Hunt, "House Coalition's Plan on Human Rights Likely to Prove Embarrassing for Carter," *WSJ,* April 6, 1977, 10; William Goodfellow and James Morrell, "U.S. Aid and Comfort for World Torturers: Legislation to Withhold Loans from Repressive Regimes Is in Trouble," *Los Angeles Times,* May 19, 1977.

101. DoS question and answer guide, box 17, folder: Human Rights—Interagency Group I, Christopher Papers.

102. Emphasis original. DoS memo, Warren Christopher to Cyrus Vance, April 14, 1977, subject: "U.S. Foreign Policy on Human Rights: A Status Report."

103. Hunt, "House Coalition's Plan on Human Rights."

104. Ibid.; Mary Russell, "Hill Bars Softening on Rights," *WP,* April 7, 1977, A1.

105. "Stunning Human Rights Victory Scored in House," *Coalition for a New Foreign and Military Policy,* newsletter, undated, box 74, folder: Human Rights and Foreign Policy, 2/77–6/77, OPLMC, JCL.

106. See Arnson, *Crossroads,* 9–15; Johnson, *Congress and the Cold War,* 205–206; Kaufman and Kaufman, *Presidency of James Earl Carter, Jr.,* 23–34.

107. WH memo, Zbigniew Brzezinski to Jimmy Carter, April 13, 1977, subject: "Proposed Position on Human Rights Amendments to International Financial Institution Legislation," box 19, folder: Human Rights (Re International Finance Institutions Legislation), 4–8/77, Records of the White House Office of the Counsel to the President, 1977–1981, Robert J. Lipshutz's Files, 1977–1979, JCL.

108. The human rights advocates were Bishop Donal Lamont (Rhodesia), Paul Cardinal Arns (Brazil), and Stephen Cardinal Kim (South Korea).

109. Jimmy Carter, address at commencement exercises at the University of Notre Dame, May 22, 1977, *Public Papers of the Presidents of the United States, Jimmy Carter,* 1:956.

110. Ibid., 958.

111. Bernard Gwertzman, "Carter Enunciated a New, but Somewhat Used, Foreign Policy," *NYT,* May 29, 1977, 109.

112. DoS cable, State 124544, secretary of state to all diplomatic posts, May 28, 1977, box 13, folder: Action Plans, Christopher Papers.

113. Trained as a lawyer, Vance was appointed general counsel for the Department of Defense in 1960, and subsequently served a brief stint as secretary of the army before being appointed deputy secretary of defense in 1963 by Lyndon B. Johnson. An early proponent of U.S. intervention in Vietnam, by the end of the decade, the West Virginia native had become disillusioned with the conflict, returning to private legal practice in 1968.

114. Cyrus R. Vance, *Hard Choices: Critical Years in America's Foreign Policy* (New York: Simon and Schuster, 1983), 46.

115. Cyrus Vance, "Human Rights and Foreign Policy," address at Law Day ceremonies at the University of Georgia School of Law in Athens, GA, April 30, 1977, reproduced in *Department of State Bulletin,* May 23, 1977, 505.

116. Ibid., 508. Vance's emphasis on the potential for promoting the first category of human rights opened the administration to accusations of de-emphasizing the second and third categories of human rights; see, for example, Lars Schoultz, "U.S. Diplomacy and Human Rights in Latin America," in *Latin America, the United States, and the Inter-American System* (Boulder: Westview Press, 1980), 180.

117. Vance, "Human Rights and Foreign Policy," 506.

118. "Mr. Vance on Human Rights," *WP,* May 4, 1977, A16.

119. DoS memo, Anthony Lake to Warren Christopher, June 30, 1977, subject: "PRM 28 on Human Rights," box 2, folder: TL 6/16–10/77, Lake Papers.

120. Ibid.

121. DoS memo, Sandy Vogelgesang to Warren Christopher, July 1, 1977, subject: "Human Rights PRM," box 2, folder: TL 7/1–15/77, Lake Papers.

122. Presidential directive/NSC-30, February 17, 1978, subject: "Human Rights," box: 18, folder: Human Rights, 12/77, Records of the White House Office of the Counsel to the President, 1977–1981, Robert J. Lipshutz's Files, 1977–1979, JCL.

123. WH memo, Zbigniew Brzezinski to Jimmy Carter, February 10, 1978, subject: "Human Rights Foundation (HRF)," box 224, folder: Human Rights, 3/7–16/77, Office of Congressional Liaison, Bob Beckel's Subject Files, 1977–1980, JCL.

124. Rossiter, "Human Rights," 6.

125. Library of Congress Congressional Research Service, Foreign Affairs and National Defense Division, *Human Rights and U.S. Foreign Assistance: Experiences and Issues in Policy Implementation (1977–1978),* prepared for the U.S. Senate Committee on Foreign Relations, 96th Cong., 1st sess., November 1979, Committee Print (Washington, DC: Government Printing Office, 1979).

126. Susana McBee, "Fears That Carter Is Easing on Rights Expressed on Hill," *WP,* October 25, 1977, A3.

127. Laurent E. Morin, interview by Charles Stuart Kennedy, March 24, 1992, transcript, FAOC, http://hdl.loc.gov/loc.mss/mfdip.2004mor09.

128. Kenneth N. Rogers, interview by Charles Stuart Kennedy, October 21, 1997, transcript, FAOC, http://hdl.loc.gov/loc.mss/mfdip.2004rog01.

129. Griesgraber, "Implementation by the Carter Administration of Human Rights Legislation Affecting Latin America," 109–110.

130. John A. Bushnell, interview by John Harter, December 19, 1997, transcript, FAOC, http://hdl.loc.gov/loc.mss/mfdip.2007bus01.

131. Paul M. Cleveland, interview by Charles Stuart Kennedy, October 20,1996, transcript, FAOC, http://hdl.loc.gov/loc.mss/mfdip.2004cle02.

132. Georgie Ann Geyer, "Latin America: Carterites' Whipping Boy," *Los Angeles Times,* March 27, 1978, C27.

133. Bushnell, interview by Harter.

134. Tulchin, *Argentina and the United States,* 141.

135. Personal interview with Roberta Cohen.

136. *U.S. Policy on Human Rights in Latin America (Southern Cone),* 53–55

137. Rossiter, "Human Rights," 6.

138. WH memo, Zbigniew Brzezinski to Cyrus Vance and secretary of treasury, April 1, 1977, subject: "Decision-Making on Human Rights Issues as They Related to Foreign Assistance," box 13, folder: Human Rights, Christopher Papers.

139. DoS memo, Cyrus Vance to Zbigniew Brzezinski, April 6, 1977, box 13, folder: Human Rights, Christopher Papers.

140. DoS memo, Warren Christopher to Denis [?], April 6 [?], 1977, box 13, folder: Human Rights, Christopher Papers.

141. Rossiter, "Human Rights," 6.

142. Personal interview with John Bushnell, May 5, 2008, Leesburg, VA.

143. Rossiter, "Human Rights," 9–10.

144. Center for International Policy, "Human Rights and the U.S. Foreign Assistance Program: Fiscal Year 1978, Part 1—Latin America," accessed in box 74, folder: Human Rights and U.S. Government 12/76–6/77, OPLMC, JCL.

145. Rossiter, "Human Rights," 10.

146. The MDBs included three subsidiaries of the World Bank: the International Bank for Reconstruction and Development (IBRD), the International Development Association (IDA), and the International Finance Corporation (IFC), as well as the Asian Development Bank (ADB), the African Development Bank (AFDB), and the Inter-American Development Bank (IDB).

147. Vance, *Hard Choices,* 41.

148. Donnie Radcliffe, "Warren Christopher and the Deputy's Dilemma," *WP,* March 16, 1980, H1.

149. Rossiter, "Human Rights," 6.

150. Radcliffe, "Warren Christopher and the Deputy's Dilemma."

151. Personal interview with Patricia Derian, March 3, 2008, Chapel Hill, NC. See also Library of Congress Congressional Research Service, Foreign Affairs and National Defense Division, *Human Rights and U.S. Foreign Assistance,* 2.

152. DoS memo, March 5, 1978, subject: "The Interagency Group on Human Rights and Foreign Assistance," box 13, folder: Human Rights—Congressional Relations, Christopher Papers; Rossiter, "Human Rights," 20.

153. DoS briefing memo, Patricia M. Derian to Cyrus Vance, November 10, 1977, subject: "Status Report on U.S. Policy on Human Rights," box 19, folder: Human Rights—Status Reports, Christopher Papers.

154. Gamarekian, "Human Rights Spokeswoman."

155. Jimmy Carter, remarks at the swearing in of the United States attorney for the Southern District of Indiana, the chairman of the Equal Employment Opportunity Commission, and the State Department coordinator for human rights and humanitarian affairs, June 17, 1977, *Public Papers of the Presidents of the United States, Jimmy Carter,* 1:1132.

156. On Carter's human rights policy toward the Soviet Union, see, for example, Dumbrell, *Carter Presidency,* 121–130; Raymond Garthoff, *Détente and Confrontation: American-Soviet Relations from Nixon to Reagan* (Washington, DC: The Brookings Institution, 1994); Scott Kaufman, *Plans Unraveled: The Foreign Policy of the Carter Administration* (Dekalb: Northern Illinois University Press, 2008), 37–46; Leffler, *For the Soul of Mankind,* 265–271; Snyder, *Human Rights Activism and the End of the Cold War,* 81–114.

157. John P. Salzberg, "The Carter Administration and Human Rights," in *The Diplomacy of Human Rights*, ed. David D. Newsom (Lanham, MD: University Press of America, 1986), 62.

158. Robert Pastor, "Accomplishments in the First Six Months: U.S. Policy to Latin America," July 15, 1977, box 27, folder: Goals/Initiative: 6/77–12/78, National Security Affairs, Brzezinski Material, Subject File, JCL.

159. Mark L. Schneider, testimony before the U.S. Congress House of Representatives, Committee on International Relations, Subcommittee on International Organizations, October 25, 1977, accessed in box 74, folder: Human Rights Reports 3/77–11/77, OPLMC, JCL.

160. Ibid.

161. Cohen, "Conditioning U.S. Security Assistance on Human Rights Practices," 262.

162. DoS memo, Steven Oxman to Warren Christopher, June 8, 1978, subject: "Meeting with Patricia Derian," box 16, folder: Human Rights—HA, Christopher Papers.

163. Rossiter, "Human Rights," 5.

164. DoS memo, Oxman to Christopher, June 8, 1978, subject: "Meeting with Patricia Derian."

165. Personal interview with Patricia Derian, March 3, 2008, Chapel Hill, NC.

166. Vance, *Hard Choices*, 29.

167. Quoted in Dumbrell, *Carter Presidency*, 118.

168. David Hawk, "Human Rights at Half-Time," *New Republic*, April 7, 1979.

169. Mark L. Schneider, testimony before the U.S. Congress House of Representatives, Committee on International Relations, Subcommittee on International Organizations, October 25, 1977.

170. DoS memo, Steven A. Oxman to Warren Christopher, October 28, 1977, box 13, folder: Human Rights, Records of Warren Christopher, 1977–1980, GRDS, RG 59, Office of the Deputy Secretary, NARA.

171. Graham Hovey, "Brzezinski, U.S. Diplomats' Guest, Is Told White House Ignores Them," *NYT*, December 12, 1977, 14.

172. Susana McBee, "Fears That Carter Is Easing on Rights Expressed on Hill," *WP*, October 25, 1977, A3.

173. Rondon, interview by Kennedy. For the memorandum of Derian's conversation with Harguindeguy, see DoS cable, State 193418, State (Christopher) to U.S. Embassy, August 15, 1977, subject: "Derian Meeting with Minister of Interior," ADP.

174. DoS cable, BA 5889, U.S. Embassy (Chaplin) to secretary of state (Vance), August 11, 1977, subject: "Derian Call on President Videla," ADP; DoS cable, BA 5493, U.S. Embassy (Chaplin) to secretary of state (Vance), August 12, 1977, subject: "Derian Visit with Economy Minister Martinez de Hoz," ADP.

175. Capturing the position advanced by the majority of U.S. diplomats, Bushnell concluded, "I don't think such confrontations helped human rights or our policy." Bushnell, interview by Harter.

176. Personal interview with Patricia Derian, March 3, 2008, Chapel Hill, NC. For the memorandum of Derian's conversation with Massera, see DoS cable, State 192822, State (Christopher) to U.S. Embassy, August 15, 1977, subject: "Derian Visit with Admiral Massera," ADP. An estimated five thousand people were tortured and killed in the Naval Mechanics School, which was turned into a memorial museum in 2007. See Daniel Schweimler, "Argentina Hands on Dirty War Site," *BBC News*, October 3, 2007, http://news.bbc.co.uk/2/hi/americas/7026833.stm. See also Horacio Verbitsky, *El vuelo: "Una forma cristiana de muerte"; Confesiones de un oficial de la Armada* (Buenos Aires: Editorial Sudamericana, 2004).

177. Foreign office cable, British Embassy BA to foreign office, September 5, 1977, subject: "U.S./Argentine Relations: Visits of Mrs Derian, Mr Todman, Senators and Congressmen," file: FCO82/743, NAUK.

178. For the memorandums of Todman's conversations with Argentine officials, see DoS cable, BA 6045, U.S. Embassy (Chaplin) to secretary of state (Vance), August 16, 1977, subject: "Ambassador Todman's Meeting with Minister of Economy Martínez de Hoz—Draft Message," ADP; DoS cable, BA 6218, U.S. Embassy (Chaplin) to secretary of state (Vance), August 24, 1977, subject: "Asst Sec Todman's Meeting with President Videla," ADP; DoS cable, BA 6606, U.S. Embassy (Higgins) to secretary of state (Vance), September 9, 1977, subject: "Todman Meeting with Argentine Politicians," ADP. On Todman's support for Videla, see also the heavily excised—but nonetheless illuminating—DoS memo, ARA (Todman) to secretary of state (Vance), September 27, 1977, subject: "A Time to Support Argentina's Videla," ADP.

179. Lt. Gen. (Ret.) Vernon Walters, address to Inter-American Defense Board, Council of Delegates, session 688, March 10, 1977, box 62, folder 30, Lister Papers. Underscoring his long-standing support for right-wing regimes in Latin America, following Juan Perón's election in 1973, then-Deputy Director of the CIA Walters made a secret visit to Buenos Aires to convey U.S. apprehension regarding a possible political shift to the left. Andersen, *Dossier Secreto,* 108.

180. DoS cable, BA 2595, U.S. Embassy to secretary of state, April 11, 1977, subject: "Visit to Argentina of LTG Gordon Sumner, Chairman, Inter-American Defense Board (IADB)," ADP.

5. ON THE OFFENSIVE

1. DoS officer evaluation report, F. Allen Harris, period covered: July 31, 1977–April 15, 1978, Derian Papers.

2. *Nunca Más,* 2.

3. Ibid., 25.

4. Guest, *Behind the Disappearances,* 26.

5. Matilde Herrera, statement, November 1, 1977 [?], ADP.

6. DoS cable, BA 3627, U.S. Embassy to secretary of state, May 16, 1977, subject: "Admiral Massera Sees Terrorism as Part of World War," ADP.

7. The Argentine military junta was made up of the chiefs of the three Argentine military service branches, Jorge Rafael Videla (army), Eduardo Emilio Massera (navy), and Orlando Ramón Agostí (air force).

8. DoS cable, BA 4443, U.S. Embassy (Chaplin) to secretary of state (Vance), June 14, 1977, subject: "Argentine Human Rights Situation; A General Review," ADP.

9. DoS cable, BA 9843, U.S. Embassy (Castro) to secretary of state (Vance), December 23, 1977, subject: "Human Rights Roundup," ADP.

10. DoS cable, BA 4443, U.S. Embassy (Chaplin) to secretary of state (Vance), June 14, 1977. The military junta initially divided Argentina into four military zones corresponding with the jurisdiction of each army corps. A fifth zone was later added. Heinz and Frühling, *Determinants of Gross Human Rights Violations,* 681.

11. DoS officer evaluation report, F. Allen Harris.

12. Personal interview with F. A. Harris, October 9, 2007, Washington, DC; Guest, *Behind the Disappearances,* 168.

13. Ulises Gorini, *La rebelión de las Madres* (Buenos Aires: Grupo Editorial Norma, 2006), 109.

14. Jo Fisher, *Mothers of the Disappeared* (London: Zed, 1989), 60.

15. Personal interview with F. A. Harris, October 9, 2007.

16. F. A. Harris, transcribed discussion in Cynthia J. Arnson, *Argentina-United States Bilateral Relations: An Historical Perspective and Future Challenges* (Washington, DC: Woodrow Wilson International Center for Scholars, 2003), 50.

17. DoS transcript of one-way recorded telephone message, F. A. Harris to Michele [Bova], Patt [Derian], and Mark [Schneider], March [?] 1978, ADP.

18. DoS officer evaluation report, F. Allen Harris.

19. Personal interview with F. A. Harris, October 9, 2007.

20. Personal interview with Fred Rondon, May 8, 2008, Falls Church, VA.

21. DoS officer evaluation report, F. Allen Harris.

22. Ibid.

23. DoS general correspondence, Fred Rondon to F. A. Harris, January 31, 1978, ADP.

24. DoS miscellaneous, May 4, 1977, subject: "Multilateral Assistance to Argentina in IDB and IBRD," ADP.

25. DoS miscellaneous, May 23, 1977, subject: "Argentina—Human Rights," ADP.

26. DoS memo, Steven Oxman to Warren Christopher, May 18, 1977, subject: "Results of Today's Meeting re Upcoming IFI Loans," box 16, folder: Human Rights—Foreign Assistance, Christopher Papers.

27. DoS miscellaneous, May 23, 1977, subject: "Argentina—Human Rights," ADP.

28. DoS cable, BA 4368, U.S. Embassy (Chaplin) to secretary of state (Vance), June 22, 1977, subject: "GOA Notes Human Rights Improvements," ADP.

29. Daniel Southerland, "State Department Rights Proponents Flex Muscles," *Christian Science Monitor*, June 27, 1977.

30. DoS memo, M. E. Gonzales to files, June 20, 1977, subject: "Board Discussion of the $100 Million Industrial Credit to Argentina, June 16, 1977," box 17, folder: Human Rights—Interagency Group IV, Christopher Papers.

31. Ibid.

32. Quoted in Schoultz, *Human Rights and United States Policy toward Latin America*, 252–253.

33. Cohen, "Conditioning U.S. Security Assistance on Human Rights Practices," 261–262.

34. DoS memo, William P. Stedman Jr., Patricia Derian, and Leslie M. Gelb through Lucy Wilson Benson to Cyrus Vance, August 19, 1977, box 13, folder: Human Rights—Argentina I, Christopher Papers.

35. On evidence of the Argentine military government's use of helicopters, see DoS cable, BA 4072, U.S. Embassy (Chaplin) to secretary of state (Vance), June 2, 1977, subject: "Possible Use of U.S. Helicopters in GOA Anti-Subversion Activities," ADP. On HA's recommendation regarding the Bell-Textron sale, see DoS memo, William P. Stedman Jr., Patricia Derian, and Leslie M. Gelb through Lucy Wilson Benson to Cyrus Vance, August 19, 1977.

36. DoS memo, Lucy Benson to Cyrus Vance, August 19, 1977, box 13, folder: Human Rights—Argentina I, Christopher Papers.

37. DoS memo, Douglas J. Bennet Jr. to Terence Todman and Lucy Wilson Benson, September 29, 1977, subject: "Bell Helicopter Sale to Argentina," box 13, folder: Human Rights—Argentina I, Christopher Papers; Senate correspondence, Lloyd Bentsen to Cyrus Vance, October 5, 1977, box 13, folder: Human Rights—Argentina I, Christopher Papers.

38. DoS cable, State 211744, Warren Christopher to U.S. Embassy BA, September 3, 1977, box 13, folder: Human Rights—Argentina I, Christopher Papers.

39. DoS memo, Douglas J. Bennet Jr. to Terence Todman and Lucy Wilson Benson, September 29, 1977, subject: "Bell Helicopter Sale to Argentina," box 13, folder: Human Rights—Argentina I, Christopher Papers.

40. Senate correspondence, Lloyd Bentsen to Cyrus Vance, October 5, 1977, box 13, folder: Human Rights—Argentina I, Christopher Papers.

41. DoS memo, Stephen Oxman to Warren Christopher, August 20, 1977, box 13, folder: Human Rights—Argentina I, Christopher Papers.

42. DoS Memo, Lucy Wilson Benson through Warren Christopher to Cyrus Vance, September 20, 1977, subject: "Argentine Arms Transfers," box 13, folder: Human Rights—Argentina II, Christopher Papers.

43. Congressional correspondence, Silvio O. Conte and Thomas P. O'Neil Jr. to Cyrus Vance, October 5, 1977, box 13, folder: Human Rights—Argentina I, Christopher Papers.

44. Senate correspondence, Edward W. Brooke to Lucy Wilson Benson, October 7, 1977, box 13, folder: Human Rights—Argentina I, Christopher Papers.

45. DoS memo, Fred Rondon to Mr. Arellano, October 13, 1977, subject: "Arms Transfers to Argentina: Congressional Interest," box 13, folder: Human Rights—Argentina I, Christopher Papers.

46. Pennsylvania Congressional Delegation Steering Committee to Cyrus Vance, April 27, 1978, box 13, folder: Human Rights—Argentina III, Christopher Papers.

47. Karen DeYoung and Charles A. Krause, "Our Mixed Signals on Human Rights in Argentina," *WP*, October 29, 1978, A1.

48. DoS memo, Warren Christopher to Cyrus Vance, October 26, 1977, box 13, folder: Human Rights—Argentina IV, Christopher Papers.

49. DeYoung and Krause, "Our Mixed Signals on Human Rights in Argentina."

50. As the Washington Office on Latin America director Rev. Joe Eldridge asserted in a congressional conference the following year, "The administration has also demonstrated of late a certain insensitivity to the power of symbolic action. The most disturbing setback was the series of tête-à-tête meetings between Latin America's most notorious violators of human rights and President Carter, following the signing of the Panama Canal treaties." *U.S. Policy on Human Rights in the Latin America (Southern Cone)*, 5.

51. DoS cable, State AL-160, secretary of state (Vance) to U.S. Embassy BA, September 26, 1977, subject: "List of Political Detainees," ADP; DoS miscellaneous, October 12, 1977, subject: "Aide Memoire," ADP.

52. On the factions within the Argentine military, see Rock, *Argentina, 1516–1987*, 370–371.

53. Cyrus Vance, handwritten notes, September 12, 1977, box 10, folder 27, Cyrus R. and Grace Sloane Vance Papers, Sterling Memorial Library, Yale University, New Haven, CT.

54. DoS cable, State 262832, secretary of state (Vance) to U.S. Embassy BA, subject: "Letter to President Videla from President Carter," November 3, 1977, ADP.

55. Jimmy Carter meeting with Jorge Rafael Videla, September 9, 1977, remarks to reporters following the meeting, in *Public Papers of the Presidents of the United States, Jimmy Carter*, 2:1555.

56. WH memo, Zbigniew Brzezinski to Jimmy Carter, September 29, 1977, subject: "Information Items," box 3, folder: 9/16/77–9/30/77, National Security Affairs, Brzezinski Material, Daily Report File, JCL.

57. WH correspondence, Jimmy Carter to Jorge R. Videla, December 1, 1977, box CO-10, folder: CO-8, 1/20/77–1/20/81, WH Central File, Subject File, Countries, JCL. For a rather humorous discussion of Carter's passion for classical music, see Brzezinski, *Power and Principle*, 23.

58. "Vance Arrives in Argentina," *WP*, November 21, 1977, A16.

59. DoS memo of conversation, November 21, 1977, subject: "Courtesy Call on Admiral Massera," box: "FOIA, Mick 1949–1973," folder: "1977," Martin Edwin Andersen Collection, NSA.

60. Lewis H. Diuguid, "Vance to Take Rights Roster to Argentina," *WP*, November 13, 1977; George Gedda, "Vance Departs Today on 3-Nation Latin Tour," *WP*, November 20, 1977, 21.

61. DoS cable, State 282605, secretary of state (Vance) to U.S. Embassy BA, November 25, 1977, subject: "List of 7500 Detainees and Disappeared," ADP.

62. DoS memo of conversation, November 21, 1977, subject: "Human Rights Situation in Argentina," ADP.

63. DoS memo of conversation, January 16, 1977, subject: "Information concerning the Disappearance of Two French Catholic Nuns," ADP; DoS transcript of one-way recorded telephone message, F. A. Harris to Michele [Bova], Patt [Derian], and Mark [Schneider].

64. Osiel, *Mass Atrocity, Ordinary Evil, and Hannah Arendt*, 36.

65. Fisher, *Mothers of the Disappeared*, 68.

66. DoS cable, BA 9420, U.S. Embassy (Castro) to secretary of state (Vance), December 12, 1977, subject: "Disappearances Reported of Mothers of Plaza de Mayo and Their Supporters," ADP. See also Gorini, *Rebelión de las Madres*, 157–165; John Simpson and Jana Bennett, *The Disappeared: Voices from a Secret War* (London: Robson Books, 1985), 161–163.

67. DoS cable, BA 9420.

68. DoS memo, John A. Bushnell to deputy secretary, January 26, 1978, subject: "Diplomatic Efforts on Behalf of the Thirteen Argentines and Two French Nuns Who Disappeared in December," ADP.

69. DoS cable, BA 0482, U.S. Embassy (Castro) to secretary of state (Vance), January 20, 1978, subject: "Disappearance of French Nuns and Mothers' Group Supporters," ADP.

70. DoS cable, BA 0766, February 1, 1978, subject: "AMB Discusses Human Rights, Right of Option and Beagle Channel with DEP FONMIN Allara," ADP.

71. DoS cable, State 37632, secretary of state to U.S. Embassy BA, February 13, 1978, subject: "Ambassador's Goals and Objectives," box 17, folder: TL Sensitive 1/1–3/31/78, Lake Papers.

72. An estimated five thousand individuals were killed by naval personnel operating at the ESMA. See "Generals Object to Torture Museum," *BBC News*, March 25, 2004, http://news.bbc.co.uk/2/hi/americas/3568795.stm.

73. DoS cable, BA 1919, U.S. Embassy (Castro) to secretary of state (Vance), March 15, 1978, subject: "Rumors of Bodies Disposed at Sea," ADP. Corroborating Mignone's report, nearly two decades later the retired navy officer Francisco Scilingo revealed to the investigative journalist Horacio Verbitsky that between fifteen and twenty victims had been thrown from navy airplanes into the Atlantic on a weekly basis for two years. Horacio Verbitsky, *The Flight: Confessions of an Argentine Dirty Warrior* (New York: New Press, 1996), 51.

74. Exhumed in 1984, the bodies of Villaflor, Esther Ballestrino de Careaga and María Ponce de Bianco were positively identified in 2005. See Nora Cortiñas, "Que los Culpables Vayan a Cárceles Communes," *Pagina 12*, accessed online (May 7, 2006) at http://www.clarin.com/diario/2005/12/12/conexiones/azucena.htm.

75. DoS cable, BA 02346, U.S. Embassy (Castro) to secretary of state (Vance), March 30, 1978, subject: "Report of Nuns Death," ADP.

76. Regarding the Christmas promise, Videla told the press, "For our part, we hope for peace this Christmas; but if the other part, the subversives, do not want to coexist in peace, they will get the rightful response." DoS cable, BA 9843, U.S. Embassy (Castro) to secretary of state (Vance), December 23, 1977, subject: "Human Rights Roundup," ADP. On advancing the moderate agenda, see DoS transcript of one-way recorded telephone message, F. A. Harris to Michele [Bova], Patt [Derian], and Mark [Schneider]; DoS report, Bureau of Intelligence and Research, April 5, 1978, subject: "INR Weekly Highlights of Developments in Human Rights," no. 51, ADP.

77. DoS cable, State 027853, secretary of state (Vance) to U.S. Embassy BA, April 7, 1978, subject: "Report of Nuns' Death," ADP.

78. DoS cable, BA 2663, U.S. Embassy (Castro) to secretary of state (Vance), April 10, 1978, subject: "Conversation with President Videla on Nuns' Death," ADP. Gen. Dennis P. McAuliffe was the son of the late general Anthony McAuliffe, who had rejected German surrender demands at Bastogne with the memorable response "nuts." On the younger McAuliffe's actions on behalf of human rights during the Carter administration, see Jack Anderson, "Human Rights in Latin America," *WP*, February 23, 1978, A15.

79. DoS briefing memo, Richard Feinberg to Cyrus Vance, November 19, 1977, subject: "President Videla: An Alternative View," box 3, folder: TL 11/16–30/77, Lake Papers.

80. Massera participated in secret operations under the alias "Black" or "Zero." See *Nunca Más*, 122–123.

81. Seoane and Muleiro, *Dictador*, 240.

82. Riveros, testifying at the Inter-American Defense Junta on January 24, 1980, quoted in *Nunca Más*, 2. Similarly, the military junta's "Statute" issued on April 28, 1983, asserted that "all anti-subversive and anti-terrorist operations under-taken by the armed forces and by the Security, Police, and Penitentiary Services under operational control and in fulfillment of Decrees 2770, 2771 and 2772/75 were carried out in accordance with plans approved and supervised by the official high commands of the armed forces and by the military junta from the time it was constituted." Quoted in Amnesty International, *Argentina: The Military Juntas and Human Rights, Report of the Trial of Former Junta Members* (London: Amnesty International, 1987), 39.

83. Romero, *History of Argentina in the Twentieth Century*, 216. On this point, see also Seoane and Muleiro, *Dictador*, 231.

84. Amnesty International, *Argentina*, 76–77; Lewis, *Guerrillas and Generals*, 220.

85. DoS memo, Steven Oxman to Warren Christopher, April 12, 1978.

86. DoS report, "Argentine Human Rights Strategy Paper," March [?] 1978, box 13, folder: Human Rights—Argentina II, Christopher Papers.

87. DoS memo, Steven Oxman to Warren Christopher, April 12, 1978, subject: "Argentine Arms Transfer Cases," box 13, folder: Human Rights—Argentina III, Christopher Papers.

88. DoS memo, Terence Todman to Cyrus Vance, March 3, 1978, subject: "Results of the ARA Chiefs of Mission Conference," box 17, folder: Human Rights—Latin America, Christopher Papers.

89. See the heavily redacted, DoS memo, ARA (Todman) to secretary of state (Vance), September 27, 1977, subject: "A Time to Support Argentina's Videla," ADP.

90. DoS memo, Terence A. Todman to Warren Christopher, undated, subject: "IDB Loan for Argentina," box 13, folder: Human Rights—Argentina I, Christopher Papers.

91. Personal interview with Lawrence Birns, May 2, 2008, Washington, DC.

92. Terence A. Todman, "The Carter Administration's Latin American Policy: Purposes and Prospects," address at the Center for Inter-American Relations, New York, February 14, 1978, box 17, folder: Human Rights—Latin America, Christopher Papers; DoS cable, BA 1406, U.S. Embassy (Chaplin) to secretary of state (Vance), February 24, 1978, subject: "Argentine Reaction to Todman Human Rights Speech," ADP.

93. Council on Hemispheric Affairs, press release, February 23, 1978, subject: "Conflict in Administration's Latin-American Human Rights Policy," box 17, folder: Human Rights—Latin America, Christopher Papers.

94. DoS memo, Patricia Derian to Warren Christopher, April 1978, subject: "Human Rights Policy in Latin America," box 17, folder: Human Rights—Latin America, Christopher Papers. See also Rossiter, "Human Rights," 20–21.

95. John M. Goshko, "Todman Asks Out of State Post," *WP*, April 8, 1978, A12. With a reputation for opposing Carter's human rights policy, Todman received a tepid welcome in post-Franco Spain. "A lot of people are upset," a Spanish diplomat told the *Washington*

Post's Stanley Meisler. "Here we are trying to create a system that will lean over backwards in favor of human rights, and you are sending us someone who lost his job for failing to support the program on human rights." Stanley Meisler, "Spanish in Flap over Prospect of Todman as U.S. Envoy," *WP*, May 4, 1978, A20.

96. DoS cable, secretary of state to U.S. Embassy BA, May 11, 1978, subject: "Argentine Human Rights," box 13, folder: Human Rights—Argentina III, Christopher Papers.

97. Newsom had previously served as head of Arabian Peninsula affairs at the Department of State, director of North African affairs, and assistant secretary of state for African affairs, as well as holding ambassadorships to Libya and Indonesia. Foreign Office cable, British Embassy in Washington 1621002, March 16, 1978, subject: "Appointment of Under Secretary of State For Political Affairs, State Department," file FC082/876, NAUK.

98. DoS memo, Richard Feinberg to all S/P members, June 15, 1978, subject: "Paper on U.S. Policy Goals and Achievements in Latin America," box 1, folder Misc.: re Issues and Priorities '78 etc., Lake Papers. See also Salzberg, "Carter Administration and Human Rights," 62.

99. DoS memo, Steven Oxman to Warren Christopher, May 23, 1978, box 13, folder: Human Rights—Argentina III, Christopher Papers.

100. Telephone interview with Robert Cox, April 14, 2008.

101. DoS officer evaluation report, F. Allen Harris.

102. Quoted in Gorini, *Rebelión de las Madres*, 248.

103. DoS officer evaluation report, F. Allen Harris.

104. Official correspondence, Bruce Allan Kiernan to Warren Christopher, July 30, 1979, box 2, folder 5, Lister Papers. For the AAAS report, see Lawyers Committee for International Human Rights, *Human Rights in Argentina: Case Histories of Arrested, Abducted and Disappeared Doctors and Scientists* (New York: Lawyers Committee for International Human Rights, September 1978).

105. See Andersen, *Dossier Secreto*, 252.

106. DoS general correspondence, Patricia Derian to Raúl H. Castro, June 5, 1979, ADP.

107. Personal interview with F. A. Harris, October 9, 2007.

108. Anthony Freeman, interview with Don Kienzle, February 7 and 13, 1995, FAOC, Georgetown University Library, Washington, DC.

109. Bonnie Henry, "Castro, Ever a Fighter, Battled to the Top," *Arizona Daily Star*, January 11, 2009, http://www.azstarnet.com/sn/bonnie/275236.

110. Castro, quoted ibid.

111. Ibid.

112. DoS memo, Cyrus Vance to Jimmy Carter, August 18, 1977, subject: "Nomination of Raul H. Castro as Ambassador to Argentina," box F0-5, folder: F0 2/CO 8/A, 1/20/77-1/20/81, WH Central File, Subject File, Foreign Affairs, JCL.

113. Freeman, interview with Don Kienzle.

114. DoS general correspondence, Raúl Castro to Claus Ruser, February 28, 1978, ADP.

115. DoS cable, BA 6123, U.S. Embassy (Castro) to secretary of state (Vance), August 8, 1978, subject: "U.S. Interest Human Rights Cases—Embassy Presents 500th Case," ADP.

116. Personal interview with F. A. Harris; Guest, *Behind the Disappearances*, 169.

117. Tex Harris, quoted in Arnson, *Argentina-United States Bilateral Relations*, 51–52.

118. "The Foreign Service views its primary role or essence as the maintenance of smooth and cordial relations with other governments," Stephen Cohen wrote in an early assessment of the Carter administration's human rights policy. Cohen, who served in the State Department Human Rights Bureau, continued: "It believes that military aid and arms sales are an indispensable means to achieving this goal. When provided, the other government is grateful and more inclined to get along with the United States. When refused, a cordial relationship may be harder to maintain, especially if the other government

suspects that the reason for refusal is a judgment that it has mistreated its own citizens." Cohen, "Conditioning U.S. Security Assistance on Human Rights Practices," 257.

119. See Seoane and Muleiro, *Dictador*, 268.

120. DoS cable, State 027853, secretary of state (Vance) to U.S. Embassy BA, April 7, 1978, subject: "Report of Nuns' Death," ADP.

121. DoS transcript of one-way recorded telephone message, F. A. Harris to Michele [Bova], Patt [Derian], and Mark [Schneider], March [?].

122. DoS officer evaluation report for F. A. Harris, August 15, 1977, Derian Papers.

123. Personal interview with Jeanie Harris, June 21, 2009, McLean, VA.

124. DoS officer evaluation report for F. A. Harris. In an interview with the author, Maxwell Chaplin declined to comment on Harris's tenure at the embassy or the 1978 evaluation report. Telephone interview with Maxwell Chaplin, September 29, 2008.

125. DoS cable, BA 3767, U.S. Embassy (Castro) to secretary of state, May 15 [?], 1978, subject: "Export Import Bank Loans to Argentina," box 13, folder: Human Rights—Argentina III, Christopher Papers.

126. DoS general correspondence, F. A. Harris to Michele [Bova] and Jim [Bumpus], April 26, 1978, ADP.

127. For memorandums of Newsom's meetings, see DoS memo of conversation, March 24, 1978, subject: "Detainees, disappearances and other Human Rights Concerns," ADP; DoS memo of conversation, March 24, 1978, ADP; DoS memo of conversation, March 24, 1978, subject: "Human Rights and United States Relations with Argentina," ADP.

128. DoS cable, BA 4040, U.S. Embassy (Castro) to secretary of state (Vance), May 25, 1978, ADP.

129. DoS cable, State 134918, secretary of state (Vance) to U.S. Embassy BA, May 26, 1978, subject: "Argentina Human Rights," ADP.

130. DoS cable, BA 4086, U.S. Embassy (Castro) to secretary of state (Vance), May 29, 1978, subject: "Argentine Human Rights," ADP.

131. DoS cable, BA 4741, U.S. Embassy (Castro) to secretary of state (Vance), June 21, 1978, subject: "Argentina Invites OAS Human Rights Commission Visit," ADP.

132. Export-Import Bank official correspondence, John L. Moore Jr. to David C. Scott, July 17, 1978, subject: "Argentina—Entidad Binacional Yacyreta," box 13, folder: Human Rights—Argentina III, Christopher Papers.

133. Harris in Arnson, *Argentina-United States Bilateral Relations*, 45.

134. E-mail, F. A. "Tex" Harris to the author, August 31, 2009.

135. Harris in Arnson, *Argentina-United States Bilateral Relations*, 46–47.

136. Ibid.; personal interview with F. A. Harris.

137. E-mail, F. A. Harris to the author, December 3, 2008.

138. Harris in Arnson, *Argentina-United States Bilateral Relations*, 46–47.

139. DoS cable, State 161503, secretary of state (Vance) to U.S. Embassy BA, June 24, 1978, subject: "Under Secretary Newsom's Meeting with Deputy Foreign Minister Allara," ADP.

140. DoS cable, State 162533, secretary of state to U.S. Embassy BA, June 26, 1978, subject: "Human Rights and U.S. Programs in Argentina," box 13, folder: Human Rights—Argentina III, Christopher Papers.

141. DoS cable, BA 5748, U.S. Embassy (Castro) to secretary of state (Vance), July 25, 1978, subject: "Continuing Argentine Reaction to Exim Bank Letter to Allis Chalmers," ADP.

142. DoS cable, BA 6834, U.S. Embassy to secretary of state, August 4, 1978, subject: "Human Rights; Note of Protest from FONMIN," box 13, folder: Human Rights—Argentina III, Christopher Papers.

143. DoS cable, State 151569, secretary of state to U.S. Embassy BA, June 14, 1978, subject: "Presidential Correspondence to President Videla," box 13, folder: Human Rights—Argentina III, Christopher Papers; DoS memo, Cyrus Vance to Jimmy Carter, June 28, 1978, box 13, folder: Human Rights—Argentina III, Christopher Papers.

144. WH memo, Zbigniew Brzezinski to Jimmy Carter, confidential, subject: "Your Question about the Human Rights Situation in Argentina," July 13, 1978, DDRS, document no. CK3100117377; president's evening reading, July 28, 1978, box 13, folder: Human Rights—Argentina IV, Christopher Papers.

145. WH memo Zbigniew Brzezinski to Jimmy Carter, undated, subject: "Argentina Alert Item," box: 4, folder: Argentina, 1/77–12/78, Office of the National Security Adviser, ZBCF, JCL.

146. Derian testimony, reprinted in "Testimony of Assistant Secretary Derian before the Subcommittee on Inter-American Affairs of the Committee on Internal Relations," House of Representatives, August 9, 1978, subject: "Arms Trade in the Western Hemisphere," ADP.

147. "The human rights organizations here are ecstatic over the EXIM decision and Patt's statement," Tex Harris wrote the State Department Human Rights Bureau. "They have all streamed into my office to express their pleasure and profound thanks." DoS official-informal, F. A. Harris to Roberta Cohen, September 13, 1978, ADP.

148. DoS cable, BA 6232, U.S. Embassy (Castro) to secretary of state (Vance), August 10, 1978, subject: "Derian Testimony to House Foreign Affairs Committee," ADP.

149. DoS memo of conversation, September 15, 1978, subject: "Videla-Mondalc, Military Unity, Political Activity," ADP; DoS memo, secret, Warren Christopher to Jimmy Carter, September 13, 1978, DDRS, document no. CK3100503818.

150. DoS cable, BA 8473, U.S. Embassy (Castro) to secretary of state (Vance) October 25, 1978, subject: "Ambassador's Meeting with General Viola," ADP.

151. Seoane and Muleiro, *Dictador*, 233.

152. DoS report, November 11, 1978, subject: "Evolution of U.S. Human Rights Policy in Argentina," ADP.

153. DoS cable, BA 5172, U.S. Embassy (Castro) to secretary of state (Vance), June 26, 1979, subject: "Ambassador Discusses Human Rights with General Viola," ADP.

154. DoS cable, BA 7875, U.S. Embassy (Castro) to secretary of state (Vance), September 21, 1979, subject: "The IAHRC Visit: Not Much Changed," ADP. In a more recent estimate, Marcos Novaro and Vicente Palermo place the number of individuals that were disappeared at 137 in 1979, and 58 in 1980. Novaro and Palermo, *Dictadura militar (1976–1983)*, 119.

155. DoS memo of conversation, March 2, 1979, subject: "Current Argentine Developments," ADP.

156. Seoane and Muleiro, *Dictador*, 228–229.

157. Novaro and Palermo, *Dictadura Militar (1976–1983)*, 119.

158. DoS handwritten notes by Patricia Derian, March 16, 1979, ADP.

159. Rita Arditti, *Searching for Life: The Grandmothers of the Plaza de Mayo and the Disappeared Children of Argentina* (Berkeley: University of California Press, 1999), 38.

160. Quoted in Gorini, *Rebelión de las Madres*, 334.

161. DoS cable, BA 7875, U.S. Embassy (Castro) to secretary of state (Vance), September 21, 1979, subject: "The IAHRC Visit: Not Much Changed," ADP.

162. Organization of American States, Inter-American Commission on Human Rights, *Report on the Situation of Human Rights in Argentina* (Washington, DC: OAS, April 6, 1980), 6. See also Guest, *Behind the Disappearances*, 177.

163. Patrick J. Flood, "U.S. Human Rights Initiatives concerning Argentina," in *The Diplomacy of Human Rights* (Lanham, MD: University Press of America, 1986), 133.

164. Ann Crittenden, "Human Rights and Mrs. Derian," NYT, May 31, 1980, 16.

6. "TILTING AGAINST GRAY-FLANNEL WINDMILLS"

1. Crittenden, "Human Rights and Mrs. Derian."
2. Ibid.
3. Carter, *Keeping Faith*, 74.
4. Jimmy Carter, press conference 20, December 15, 1977, Washington DC, box 2, folder: Human Rights 1977[1], Hendrik Hertzber's Speech Files, JCL.
5. Kaufman, *Plans Unraveled*, 100–103.
6. See Erwin C. Hargrove, *Jimmy Carter as President: Leadership and the Politics of the Public Good* (Baton Rouge: Louisiana State University Press, 1988), 22; Kaufman and Kaufman, *Presidency of James Earl Carter, Jr.*, 65; Sean Wilentz, *The Age of Reagan: A History, 1974–2008* (New York: HarperCollins, 2009), 78–85.
7. Carter, *Keeping Faith*, 78.
8. Quoted in Vogelgesang, *American Dream, Global Nightmare*, 228.
9. Personal interview with Larry Birns, May 2, 2008, Washington, DC.
10. The Exim Bank is a credit and insurance agency that aims to stimulate U.S. exports by assuming commercial and political risks that would otherwise deter exporters or private financial institutions. Similarly, OPIC "insures equity investments of U.S. corporations in the Third World against three kinds of political risks—expropriation, currency inconvertibility, and war, revolution or insurrection." Center for International Policy, "Human Rights and the U.S. Foreign Assistance Program: Fiscal Year 1978, Part 1—Latin America," box 74, folder: Human Rights and U.S. Government 12/76–6/77, OPLMC, JCL. For a useful overview of congressional human rights legislation, see David D. Newsom, *The Diplomacy of Human Rights* (Lanham, MD: University Press of America, 1986), 223–235.
11. "Human Rights Export Policy Called Failure," *Aviation Week and Space Technology*, October 15, 1979, 23.
12. "A No-Nonsense General Throws Isabel Out," *U.S. News and World Report*, April 5, 1976, 38.
13. Paul H. Lewis, *The Crisis of Argentine Capitalism* (Chapel Hill: University of North Carolina Press, 1990), 460–462.
14. In addition to the United States, Burson-Marsteller worked to generate positive publicity for the Argentine military junta in Belgium, Britain, Canada, Colombia, Holland, Japan, and Mexico. See Guest, *Behind the Disappearances*, 69.
15. Andrea Fishman and Richard Alan White, "The Selling of Argentina: Madison Ave. Packages Repression," *Los Angeles Times*, June 11, 1978, 12.
16. In a 1978 *Washington Post* op-ed, Jack Anderson denounced Burson-Marsteller's contract with the Argentine military junta. "Madison Avenue hucksters are trying to improve the image of the military dictatorship of Argentina with the same flair they use to sell deodorants and cigarettes," he wrote. Anderson, "Projecting New Image for Dictator," *WP*, May 30, 1978, B11. In 1996, the sociologist Marguerite Feitlowitz interviewed Victor Emmanuel, who had spearheaded the Burson-Marsteller report for Argentina. When asked whether he condoned the military junta's use of abductions and clandestine detention centers, Emmanuel responded, "It was arguably almost necessary. The situation required full military force." Emmanuel concluded that "given the opportunity he would do the job again." Feitlowitz, *A Lexicon of Terror*, 42.
17. R. Scott Greathead, "Truth in Argentina," *NYT*, May 11, 1995, A29; Schoultz, *Human Rights and United States Policy toward Latin America*, 52–53.
18. "U.S.-Argentine Relations," editorial, *Argentina Outreach: Bulletin of the Argentine Information Service Center*, vol. 3, October–November 1978, box 84, folder: Argentina, 1978, ILHR.
19. Schoultz, *Human Rights and United States Policy toward Latin America*, 66–72.
20. Ibid., 51. "U.S.-Argentine Relations," editorial, *Argentina Outreach*.

21. "Military's Radical Cure for Argentina," *U.S. News and World Report*, October 15, 1979, 84.

22. "A Show of Confidence in Economic Recovery," *BusinessWeek*, May 30, 1977, 40.

23. "Despite Kidnappings and Murder, Americans Are Returning to Argentina," *U.S. News and World Report*, November 21, 1977, 26.

24. "Argentina: Budget Reforms Lure Foreign Investment," *BusinessWeek*, April 24, 1978, 47.

25. Postdictatorship testimony indicated that some international firms actively helped the Argentine military carry out dirty war violence, including Ford and Mercedes-Benz. See, for example, Larry Rohter, "Ford Motor Is Linked to Argentina's 'Dirty War,'" *NYT*, November 27, 2002, http://www.nytimes.com/2002/11/27/international/27ARGE.html; "Argentina Checks Ford's 'Military Ties,'" *BBC News*, http://news.bbc.co.uk/2/hi/americas/2410551.stm; Kenneth Ofgang, "Court Rejects Suit over Argentine Rights Violations," *Metropolitan News-Enterprise*, August 31, 2009, http://www.metnews.com/articles/2009/baum083109.htm.

26. DoS report, "Argentine Human Rights Strategy Paper," March [?] 1978, box 13, folder: Human Rights—Argentina II, Christopher Papers.

27. E. B. Fitzgerald to Clement J. Zablocki, December 12, 1977, box 13, folder: Human Rights—Argentina II, Christopher Papers.

28. Jimmy Carter, Presidential Directive/NSC-30, February 17, 1978, http://www.jimmycarterlibrary.gov/documents/pddirectives/pd30.pdf.

29. DoS action memo, Anthony Lake to Cyrus Vance, January 20, 1978, subject: "The Human Rights Policy: An Interim Assessment," box 19, folder: Human Rights—Policy Implementation, Christopher Papers.

30. Library of Congress Congressional Research Service, Foreign Affairs and National Defense Division, *Human Rights and U.S. Foreign Assistance*, 47. Ironically, McDonald was later killed when the Soviet military destroyed Korean Air Lines flight 007 in midflight on September 1, 1983.

31. Earl C. Ravenal, "Carter's Year of Human Rights," *Inquiry*, January 23, 1978. A professor at the Georgetown University School of Foreign Service, Ravenal later joined the Cato Institute, where he became a distinguished senior fellow.

32. Karen DeYoung, "Argentina Woos and Wins Its Visiting Americans," *WP*, August 30, 1977, A17.

33. NSC memo, Jessica Tuchman Mathews to Zbigniew Brzezinski, September 25, 1978, subject: "Thoughts on the Attached," box 4, folder: Argentina, 1/77–12/78, ZBCF, JCL.

34. E. B. Fitzgerald to Clement J. Zablocki, December 12, 1977.

35. Alton K. Marsh, "Rights Policy Confusion Halts Air Ambulance Sale," *Aviation Week and Space Technology*, July 31, 1978, 18.

36. DoS draft memo, Julius L. Katz to Cyrus Vance, July 15 [?], 1977, box 13, folder: Human Rights—Arms Transfers, Christopher Papers.

37. Robert Hotz, "Carter's Export Muddle," editorial, *Aviation Week and Space Technology*, August 7, 1978. On Hotz, see "Robert B. Hotz, 91: Arms-Control Expert Ran Aerospace Publication," *Los Angeles Times*, February 12, 2006, http://articles.latimes.com/2006/feb/12/local/me-hotz12; Jeremy Pearce, "Robert B. Hotz, 91, a Critic of NASA's Disaster Response, Dies," *NYT*, February 15, 2006, http://www.nytimes.com/2006/02/15/national/15hotz.html?fta=y.

38. DoS memo, William C. Harrop to Warren Christopher, August 11, 1978, subject: "The Allis-Chalmers Argentine Project," box 8, folder: Memoranda from WC to Bureaus—1978, Christopher Papers.

39. Emphasis original. DoS memo, Paul H. Kreisberg to Patt Derian, Jules Katz, and Steve Oxman, September 20, 1978, subject: "Human Rights Advisory Group," box 4, folder: TL 9/16–30/78, Lake Papers.

40. Rowland Evans and Robert Novak, "'Undiplomatic' Incident," *WP*, September 6, 1978, A15.

41. Rowland Evans and Robert Novak, "Human-Rights Zeal That Costs U.S. Jobs," *WP*, September 18, 1978, A23.

42. "Report of the Interagency Group on Human Rights and Foreign Assistance concerning the Effectiveness of U.S. Human Rights Actions in the International Financial Institutions,' April 30, 1978, box 18, folder: PD-30—Response (Final), Christopher Papers.

43. Vogelgesang, *American Dream, Global Nightmare*, 222.

44. In addition to Argentina, the United States denied Exim Bank transactions based on human rights considerations to Chile, Brazil, and Uruguay. Library of Congress Congressional Research Service, Foreign Affairs and National Defense Division, *Human Rights and U.S. Foreign Assistance*.

45. DoS cable, BA 3767, U.S. Embassy (Castro) to secretary of state, May 15 [?] 1978, subject: "Export Import Bank Loans to Argentina," box 13, folder: Human Rights—Argentina III, Christopher Papers.

46. DoS action memo, Patricia Derian and Anthony Lake to Cyrus Vance, March 31, 1978, subject: "Human Rights Considerations in Department Contacts with the Private Sector," box 3, folder: TL 3/16–31/78, Lake Papers.

47. It was a pattern that was repeated throughout the hemisphere. "When the Carter Administration has withheld foreign aid," wrote the journalist Michael Massing in early 1979, "Latin America's dictators usually have responded with a virulent verbal outburst and then simply turned to prominent members of the U.S. banking and business community for assistance." Indeed, by June 1978 U.S. banks had lent $34.6 billion to Latin American regimes, with roughly $12 billion earmarked for governments or public sector enterprises. Massing, "Are U.S. Banks Funding Latin American Repression?" *Los Angeles Times*, April 22, 1979, F2.

48. Roberta Cohen, "The Carter Administration and the Southern Cone," *Human Rights Quarterly* 4 (1982): 239.

49. Italics added. DoS memo, Steven Oxman to Warren Christopher, November 15, 1978, box 13, folder: Human Rights—Argentina IV, Christopher Papers.

50. DoS memo, John Bushnell to Patricia Derian, June 13, 1978, subject: "Commentary on Cutler-Hammer Letter," box 13, folder: Human Rights—Argentina III, Christopher Papers; Vogelgesang, *American Dream, Global Nightmare*, 220.

51. DoS memo, Richard N. Cooper to Warren Christopher, July 25, 1978, subject: "Four-Bureau Memo on EXIM Bank Transactions Involving Argentina, Dated July 22," box 13, folder: Human Rights—Argentina III, Christopher Papers.

52. John T. Norman, "Plan for National Export Policy Is Sent to President by Administration Officials," *WSJ*, July 26, 1978, 14.

53. DoS draft memo, Julius L. Katz to Cyrus Vance, July 15 [?], 1977, box 13, folder: Human Rights—Arms Transfers, Christopher Papers.

54. DoS memo, William C. Harrop to Warren Christopher, August 11, 1978, subject: "The Allis-Chalmers Argentine Project," box 8, folder: Memoranda from WC to Bureaus—1978, Christopher Papers.

55. DoS memo, Warren Christopher to Steven Oxman, 1978, box 13, folder: Human Rights—Argentina II, Christopher Papers.

56. President's evening reading, July 28, 1978, box 13, folder: Human Rights—Argentina IV, Christopher Papers.

57. DoS memo, Anthony Lake to Warren Christopher, August 10, 1978, subject: "Human Rights 'Sanctions,'" box 4, folder: TL 8/1–8/15/78, Lake Papers.

58. DoS cable, New York 3249, American ambassador to the United Nations to secretary of state, August 8, 1978, subject: "Eximbank Loan to Argentina: Human Rights, Development, and Export Policy," box 13, folder: Human Rights—Argentina IV, Christopher Papers.

59. "I had long been convinced that the idea of basic human rights had a powerful appeal in the emerging world of emancipated but usually nondemocratic nation-states and that the previous Administration's lack of attention to this issue had undermined international support for the United States," Brzezinski wrote in his memoirs. "I was concerned that America was becoming 'lonely' in the world. I felt strongly that a major emphasis on human rights as a component of U.S. foreign policy would advance America's global interests by demonstrating to the emerging nations of the Third World the reality of our democratic system, in sharp contrast to the political system and practices of our adversaries. The best way to answer the Soviets' ideological challenge would be to commit the United States to a concept which most reflected America's very essence." Indeed, Brzezinski claimed authorship of Carter's inaugural assertion that the U.S. commitment to human rights would be "absolute." Brzezinski, *Power and Principle*, 124–125.

60. Ibid., 128.

61. Robert Pastor, interview December 12, 2006, Washington, DC, conducted by the Red de Archivos Orales de la Argentina Contemporánea, Programa de Historia Política del Instituto de Investigaciones Gino Germani, Programa de Historia Política—IIGG –UBA, Buenos Aires, Argentina.

62. DoS cable, New York 3249, American ambassador to the United Nations to secretary of state, August 22, 1978, subject: "Eximbank Loan to Argentina: Human Rights, Development, and Export Policy," box 13, folder: Human Rights—Argentina IV, Christopher Papers.

63. WH memo Zbigniew Brzezinski to Cyrus Vance, September 5 [?], 1978, box 4, folder: Argentina, 1/77–12/78, ZBCF, JCL.

64. Schoultz, *Human Rights and United States Policy toward Latin America*, 311.

65. Flood, "U.S. Human Rights Initiatives concerning Argentina," 133.

66. Karen DeYoung and Charles A. Krause, "Our Mixed Signals on Human Rights in Argentina," *WP*, October 29, 1978, A1. A total of $35,787,000 in U.S. transfers contracted prior to the cutoff remained undelivered. DoS miscellaneous, November 27, 1979, subject: "Argentina Human Rights," ADP.

67. NSC memo, Robert A. Pastor to Zbigniew Brzezinski, August 14, 1978, subject: "Your Question about Patt Derian's Testimony on the Argentine Human Rights Situation," box 1, folder: Argentina, 1–8/78, National Security Affairs, Staff Material—North/South, Pastor—Country File, JCL.

68. NSC memo, Robert A. Pastor to Zbigniew Brzezinski, August 31, 1978, subject: "U.S. Policy to Argentina," box 4, folder: Argentina, 1/77–12/78, ZBCF, JCL.

69. Ibid.

70. NSC memo, Robert A. Pastor to David Aaron and Zbigniew Brzezinski, September 25, 1978, subject: "U.S. Policy to Argentina," box 1, folder: Argentina, 9–12/78, National Security Affairs, Staff Material—North/South, Pastor—Country File, JCL.

71. Cohen, "Carter Administration and the Southern Cone," 239.

72. Juan Pablo Bohoslavsky and Veerle Opgenhaffen, "The Past and Present of Bank Responsibility: Financing the Argentinean Dictatorship," paper presented at New York University School of Law, April 14, 2009.

73. Charles A. Krause, "Argentine Rights: One Issue Settled, Many Remain," *WP*, September 27, 1979, A27.

74. DoS cable, BA 6150, U.S. Embassy (Castro) to secretary of state (Vance), July 27, 1979, subject: "Periodic Human Rights Trends Reporting," ADP.

75. Marguerite Guzmán Bouvard, *Revolutionizing Motherhood: The Mothers of the Plaza de Mayo* (Lanham, MD: Rowman and Littlefield, 1994), 139.

76. DoS cable, BA 10212, U.S. Embassy (Chaplin) to secretary of state (Vance), December 14, 1979, subject: "President Videla's Press Conference," ADP.

77. DoS memo, Patrick J. Flood to Patricia Derian, April 18, 1979, subject: "The Human Rights Situation in Argentina," ADP.

78. The Permanent Assembly for Human Rights, for example, estimated in 1979 that the government was holding 5,200 clandestine prisoners, while other human rights organizations set the figure far higher. See Joanne Omang, "Rights Criticism Solidifies Argentine Rule a Year after Coup," *WP*, March 24, 1977, A14.

79. DoS cable, BA 6150, U.S. Embassy (Castro) to secretary of state (Vance), July 27, 1979, subject: "Periodic Human Rights Trends Reporting," ADP.

80. Ariel C. Armony, "Transnationalizing the Dirty War: Argentina in Central America," in *In from the Cold: Latin America's New Encounter with the Cold War* (Durham, NC: Duke University Press, 2008), 146–159.

81. DoS memo, Patricia Derian to Warren Christopher and Cyrus Vance, January 26, 1979, subject: "Next Steps in Argentina," box 13, folder: Human Rights—Argentina IV, Christopher Papers.

82. Roger Smith, "Rockefeller Hits Tying of Human Rights to Trade," *Los Angeles Times*, February 23, 1979, E17.

83. DoS memo, Roberta Cohen to Mark Schneider, May 11, 1979, subject: "The Non-Governmental Community's Recommendations for Strengthening US Human Rights Policy," Cohen Papers.

84. Odd Arne Westad, *The Global Cold War: Third World Interventions and the Making of Our Times* (Cambridge: Cambridge University Press, 2005), 276–277. See also Jackson, *Jimmy Carter and the Horn of Africa*, 120–128.

85. Quoted in Leffler, *For the Soul of Mankind*, 301.

86. Central Intelligence Agency, Secret, January 20, 1978, subject: "Assassination of Pedro Chamorro, the Somoza Regime's Most Prominent Domestic Critic, Discussed," DDRS, document no. CK3100250749.

87. On the Carter administration's participation in the Nicaraguan mediation talks, see William Michael Schmidli, "'The Most Sophisticated Intervention We Have Seen': The Carter Administration and the Nicaraguan Crisis, 1978–1979," *Diplomacy & Statecraft* 23, no. 1 (2012): 66–86.

88. Dumbrell, *Carter Presidency*, 201.

89. Jimmy Carter, North Carolina address at Wake Forest University, Winston-Salem, March 17, 1978, http://www.presidency.ucsb.edu/ws/index.php?pid=30516. See also Kaufman, *Plans Unraveled*, 117; Thornton, *Carter Years*, 185.

90. Leffler, *For the Soul of Mankind*, 288.

91. Skidmore, *Reversing Course*, 48.

92. Alan Riding, "Nicaragua Must Rebuild, But Who Will Lead—And Where?" *NYT*, July 22, 1979; Pastor, *Exiting the Whirlpool*, 52.

93. Leffler, *For the Soul of Mankind*, 285.

94. Quoted in Jackson, *Jimmy Carter and the Horn of Africa*, 136.

95. Skidmore, *Reversing Course*, 49; Kaufman, *Plans Unraveled*, 141–145.

96. Patrick Vaughan, "Zbigniew Brzezinski and Afghanistan," in *The Policy Makers: Shaping American Foreign Policy from 1947 to the Present*, ed. Anna Kasten Nelson (Lanham, MD: Rowman and Littlefield, 2009), 124.

97. Brzezinski, *Power and Principle*, 49.

98. Smith, *Morality, Reason, and Power*, 37.

99. Brzezinski, *Power and Principle*, 128.

100. Kaufman, *Plans Unraveled*, 117–118.

101. In a September 1977 poll, for example, 59% of respondents approved of Carter's "public criticism of nations that deny human rights to their citizens," while only 19% disapproved. Asked the same question in March 1979, support for the human rights policy remained high, with 53% of respondents approving, and 24% disapproving. Roper Organization, "Roper Report, 77–9," September 1977; "Roper Report 79–4," March 1979, Roper Center for Public Opinion Research, University of Connecticut.

102. Griesgraber, "Implementation by the Carter Administration of Human Rights Legislation Affecting Latin America," 305; Eric Pianin, "Fraser Returns to Minneapolis to Run for Mayor," *WP*, May 15, 1979, A2.

103. "Is Carter Abandoning His Policy on Human Rights?" *U.S. News and World Report*, December 4, 1978, 34.

104. Emphasis original. DoS memo, Patricia Derian to Cyrus Vance, October 22, 1979, subject: "Goals and Objectives for the Next 18 Months," box 18, folder: Next Seventeen Mos.—Mtgs w A/S, Lake Papers.

105. Ibid.

106. Memo, Patricia Derian to Hamilton Jordan, undated [spring 1980], subject: "Holding onto the Human Rights Issue," Derian Papers.

107. DoS memo, Roberta Cohen to Mark Schneider, May 11, 1979, subject: "The Non-Governmental Community's Recommendations for Strengthening US Human Rights Policy," Cohen Papers.

108. DoS memo, Paul Kreisberg to Warren Christopher, October 23, 1979, subject: "Human Rights Goals and Objectives," box 18, folder: Next Seventeen Mos.—Mtgs w A/S, Lake Papers.

109. "In Argentina, the families of the thousands of disappeared victims of official abduction live a daily agony of uncertainty and anxiety about the fate of their missing relatives," Derian told the gathered assembly. "The Government steadfastly refuses to give them any information about their relatives and even denies having information. . . . What we say to the Argentine authorities is this: for Humanitarian reasons, tell the families of the living where they are, tell the families of the dead what they need and deserve to know." Patricia Derian, "Human Rights in Latin America," address at Florida International University, Miami, Florida, May 18, 1979, reprinted in *Current Policy*, no. 68, United States Department of State Bureau of Public Affairs, June 1979, box 31, folder 3, Lister Papers.

110. NSC memo, Thomas Thornton to Zbigniew Brzezinski, June 15, 1979, subject: "Argentinian Human Rights," box 1, folder: Argentina, 1–7/79, National Security Affairs, Staff Material—North/South, Pastor—Country File, JCL.

111. Juan de Onís, "Argentine Policies Please U.S. Business," *NYT*, December 7, 1979, A8.

112. John L. Moore, *Congressional Quarterly: President Carter, 1979* (Washington, DC: Congressional Quarterly, 1980), 41.

113. Jimmy Carter, state of the union address, January 23, 1980, http://www.jimmy-carterlibrary.gov/documents/speeches/su80jec.phtml.

114. Daniel W. Drezner, *The Sanctions Paradox: Economic Statecraft and International Relations* (New York: Cambridge, 1999), 74–75.

115. Brzezinski, *Power and Principle*, 433.

116. Charles A. Krause, "U.S. General Asks Argentine Aid on Embargo," *WP*, January 25, 1980, A16; "Soviets Seek to Buy Argentine Grain," *NYT*, January 31, 1980, A3.

117. DoS memo, John A. Bushnell to secretary of state, January 20, 1980, subject: "Your Meeting with General Andrew J. Goodpaster, U.S. January 22, 1980, at 3:00 p.m.," ADP.

118. DoS memo, Nelson Ledsky to Newsom, February 21, 1980, subject: "Your Meeting with Argentine Ambassador Aja Espil," ADP.

119. Juan de Onís, "4 Years after Coup, Argentina Is Regaining Favor," *NYT*, March 26, 1980, A2.

120. DoS memo of conversation, February 1, 1980, subject: "Videla Talks to Newspaper Editors about Goodpaster Visit," ADP.

121. DoS cable, BA 2469, U.S. Embassy (Castro) to secretary of state (Vance), March 21, 1980, subject: "U.S.-Argentine Relations: A Rocky Road," ADP.

122. DoS briefing book, "Bureau Priorities," May 22, 1080, box 20, Lake Papers; DoS briefing memo, William G. Bowdler and Anthony Lake to acting secretary [Christopher], May 14, 1980, subject: "PRC Meeting on Argentina," box 6, folder: TL 5/1–15/80, Lake Papers.

123. DoS memo, Edmund S. Muskie to Jimmy Carter, October 18, 1980, subject: "U.S. Policy toward Argentina," box 24, folder: Meetings—Muskie/Brown/Brzezinski: 10/80–1/81, ZBC, Subject File, JCL.

124. DoD memo, W. Graham Claytor Jr. to Jimmy Carter, October 27, 1980, subject: "U.S. Policy toward Argentina," box 24, folder: Meetings—Muskie/Brown/Brzezinski: 10/80–1/81, ZBC, Subject File, JCL.

125. John Kelly Damico, "From Civil Rights to Human Rights: The Career of Patricia M. Derian" (PhD diss., Mississippi State University, 1999), 266.

126. John Goshko, "U.S., Concerned about Soviets, Seeks New Argentine Rapport," *WP*, May 29, 1980, A6.

127. Ray Bonner, "Bolivia Becomes a Battleground," *Los Angeles Times*, August 31, 1980, F3.

128. Armony, "Transnationalizing the Dirty War," 137; K.D. Lehman, *Bolivia and the United States: A Limited Partnership* (Athens: University of Georgia Press, 1999), 176–177.

129. Carter appointed Muskie on April 29 following Vance's resignation in the aftermath of the administration's failed attempt to rescue U.S. Embassy personnel held hostage in Iran. Quote from DoS memo, Edmund S. Muskie to Jimmy Carter, October 18, 1980, subject: "U.S. Policy toward Argentina," box 24, folder: Meetings—Muskie/Brown/Brzezinski: 10/80–1/81, ZBC, Subject File, JCL.

130. NSC memo, Thomas Thornton to Zbigniew Brzezinski, November 18, 1980, subject: "M-B-B Lunch—Argentina and Chile," box 24, folder: Meetings—Muskie/Brown/Brzezinski: 10/80–1/81, ZBC, Subject File, JCL.

131. Carla Hall, "A Farewell to Derian," *WP*, January 15, 1981, D3.

132. Ibid.

CONCLUSION

1. Committee of Santa Fe, *A New Inter-American Policy for the Eighties* (Washington, DC: Council for Inter-American Security, 1980), 53. See also James M. Scott, *Deciding to Intervene: The Reagan Doctrine and American Foreign Policy* (Durham, NC: Duke University Press, 1996), 14–39.

2. Quoted in Robert A. Pastor, *Not Condemned to Repetition: The United States and Nicaragua* (Boulder: Westview Press, 1987), 190.

3. Jeane Kirkpatrick, "Dictatorships and Double Standards," *Commentary*, November 1979, 34.

4. David P. Forsythe, *Human Rights and U.S. Foreign Policy: Congress Reconsidered* (Gainesville: University Press of Florida, 1989), 181.

5. Quoted in Richard Cohen, "Principles," *WP*, May 25, 1982, C1.

6. Roger Fontaine, transcript of presentation for Presidential Candidates Forum Series: U.S. Policy toward Latin America, organized by the Center for Inter-American Relations, June 25, 1980, box 110, folder: Latin America: 1980, ILHRR.

7. Bill Roeder, "Reagan's Man in Argentina," *Newsweek*, June 30, 1980, 15.

8. DoS memo, Townsend B. Friedman, August 21, 1980, subject: "Human Rights," ADP.

9. Guest, *Behind the Disappearances*, 276; Rossiter, "Human Rights," 23.

10. *Nunca Más*, 445.

11. Quoted in Guest, *Behind the Disappearances*, 277.

12. See Armony, *Argentina, the United States, and the Anti-Communist Crusade in Central America, 1977–1984*.

13. William M. LeoGrande, *Our Own Backyard: The United States in Central America, 1977–1992* (Chapel Hill: University of North Carolina Press, 1998), 116.

14. Quoted ibid., 292.

15. DoS, memo of conversation, March 31, 1977, ADP.

16. Timerman, *Prisoner without a Name, Cell without a Number*, 22, 33.

17. Following Timerman's abduction, Congressman Drinan declared, "It is evident that the Argentine Government is cracking down viciously on the few remaining independent journalists. All those who respect the freedom of the press and the fundamental human rights of the individual must protest the arrest of Mr. Timerman and other journalists. By their recent actions, Argentina's military leaders have demonstrated once again that they merit condemnation by all civilized men and nations." Robert F. Drinan, "Argentina's Military Junta Arrests Leading Independent Journalist," *Congressional Record*, April 19, 1977, E2266. See also Drinan, *Congressional Record*, June 21, 1979, H4934; and Drinan, "The Release of Yacobo Timerman [sic]," *Congressional Record*, September 26, 1979, E4771.

18. State Department cable, BA 6137, U.S. Embassy (Chaplin) to secretary of state (Vance), August 19, 1977, subject: "Interior Minister Sees Jacobo Timerman; Congressman Gilman also to be Permitted Interview with Timerman," ADP.

19. WH official correspondence, Jimmy Carter to Jacobo Timerman, November 5, 1979, box: 4, folder: Argentina, 1/79–1/80, ZBCF, JCL.

20. John M. Goshko, "Argentinian Visits Lefever Hearing, Criticizes 'Quiet Diplomacy' Policy," *WP*, May 20, 1981, A3. See also Richard Cohen, "Shhh! And Pretend You Can't Hear the Screams," *WP*, May 21, 1981, C1.

21. Aryeh Neier, *Taking Liberties: Four Decades in the Struggle for Rights* (New York: Public Affairs, 2003), 179.

22. George Lardner Jr., "Human Rights Spokesman Reported Chosen," *WP*, October 30, 1981, A12; Neier, *Taking Liberties*, 185.

23. Quoted in A. Glenn Mower Jr., *Human Rights and American Foreign Policy: The Carter and Reagan Experiences* (New York: Greenwood Press, 1987), 26.

24. Greg Grandin, *Empire's Workshop: Latin America and the Roots of U.S. Imperialism* (New York: Metropolitan Books, 2005), 71; Walter LaFeber, *Inevitable Revolutions: The United States in Central America* (New York: W.W. Norton, 1983), 362–363.

25. Grandin, *Last Colonial Massacre*, 188.

26. Quoted in LeoGrande, *Our Own Backyard*, 63.

27. Peter Kornbluh, "The U.S. Role in the Counterrevolution," in *Revolution and Counterrevolution in Nicaragua* (Boulder: Westview Press, 1991), 333. On the Reagan administration's human rights policy, see also David Carleton and Michael Stohl, "The Foreign Policy of Human Rights: Rhetoric and Reality from Jimmy Carter to Ronald Reagan," *Human Rights Quarterly* 7, no. 2 (1985): 205–229; Hauke Hartmann, "U.S. Human Rights Policy under Carter and Reagan, 1977–1981," *Human Rights Quarterly* 23, no. 2 (2001):

402–430; Tamar Jacoby, "The Reagan Turnaround on Human Rights," *Foreign Affairs* 64, no. 5 (1986): 1066–1086.

28. Apodaca, *Understanding U.S. Human Rights Policy,* 107.

29. Ibid., 106–110.

30. George Lister, "Human Rights: Our World's Best Chance," address at George Washington University, February 5, 1998, box 18, folder 8, Lister Papers.

31. MacLachlan, *Argentina,* 154.

32. Romero, *History of Argentina in the Twentieth Century,* 242–247; Tulchin, *Argentina and the United States,* 154–156.

33. Alison Brysk, *The Politics of Human Rights in Argentina: Protest, Change, and Democratization* (Stanford: Stanford University Press, 1994), 58–62; Rock, *Argentina, 1516–1987,* 385–387.

34. Ronald Dworkin, introduction to *Nunca Más,* 2. See also David Pion-Berlin, *Through Corridors of Power: Institutions and Civil-Military Relations in Argentina* (University Park: Pennsylvania State University Press, 1997), 77–106.

35. Ronald Dworkin, introduction to *Nunca Más.*

36. Ibid., 5.

37. Ibid., 3.

38. Brysk, *Politics of Human Rights in Argentina,* 71.

39. Amnesty International, *Argentina,* 76–81; Carlos Santiago Nino, *Radical Evil on Trial* (New Haven, CT: Yale University Press, 1996), 89.

40. Brysk, *Politics of Human Rights in Argentina,* 79.

41. Thomas C. Wright, *State Terrorism in Latin America: Chile, Argentina, and International Human Rights* (Lanham, MD: Rowman and Littlefield, 2007), 145.

42. *Nunca Más,* 442–445.

43. Neier, *Taking Liberties,* 175; Sikkink, *Mixed Signals,* 154.

44. Lydia Chavez, "Testimony on Argentine Junta," *NYT,* June 14, 1985, A10; William Montalbano, "Argentine Witnesses Tell of Terrorism by Military," *Los Angeles Times,* July 9, 1985, 6.

45. Jackson Diehl Washington, "Reagan-Alfonsín Chat Marks Upswing in U.S.-Argentine Ties since Falklands," *Washington Post,* April 10, 1984, A15.

46. Theodore E. Gildred, interview by Hank Zivetz, April 26, 1990, transcript, FAOC, http://hdl.loc.gov/loc.mss/mfdip.2004gil03.

47. DoS memo, Elliott Abrams, H. Allen Holmes, and Rozanne Ridgway to secretary of state, July 7, 1987, subject: "Consolidating Democracy in Argentina: U.S. Strategy for Strengthening Military Support," Latin American Affairs Records, box 92356, folder: PRG Meeting: Argentina/United Kingdom/ United States Relations, RRL.

48. Thomas Carothers, *In the Name of Democracy: U.S. Policy toward Latin America in the Reagan Years* (Berkeley: University of California Press, 1991), 132–135.

49. Mann, *Rise of the Vulcans,* 133–134, 136.

50. Cyrus Vance, "Human Rights and Foreign Policy," statement made at the University of Georgia School of Law at Athens, GA, April 30, 1977; reprinted in the *Department of State Bulletin,* vol. 76, May 23, 1977.

51. "Este Mr. Harris nos recibía, nos protegía, nos sacaba de la comisaría." Aída Sarti in Madres de Plaza de Mayo Línea Fundadora, *Memoria, verdad y justicia a los 30 años X los treinta mil* (Buenos Aires: Ediciones Baobab, 2006), 89.

52. Patricia Derian, remarks at the White House commemoration of the thirtieth anniversary of the Universal Declaration of Human Rights, December 6, 1978, box 48, folder: Human Rights Day, 12/6/78, Staff Offices, Assistant for Communications—Press Events, Rafshoon, JCL.

53. Official correspondence, George Lister to Oliver T. Covey, November 5, 1992, box 11, folder 3, Lister Papers. Lister retired in 1981, but continued to work on human rights in the State Department without compensation until 2001. In 1992, Lister was recognized by the government of Chile for his participation in the restoration of Chilean democracy. Six years later Lister was also recognized by the South Korean president Kim Dae Jung for his assistance during Kim's exile and house arrest. Although in the second half of his career Lister faced repeated attempts to oust him from the State Department, in 1997 he was nominated for the Warren Christopher Award, for "sustained outstanding achievement on behalf of democracy and human rights."

Primary Sources

MANUSCRIPT COLLECTIONS

Ball, George W., Papers. Seeley G. Mudd Manuscript Library, Princeton University.
Cohen, Roberta, Personal Papers. Washington, DC.
Derian, Patricia, Personal Papers. Chapel Hill, NC.
Drinan, Robert F., Papers. John J. Burns Library, Boston College.
Fraser, Donald M., Papers, 1951–1995. Minnesota Historical Society.
Hill, Robert C., Papers. Rauner Special Collections Library, Dartmouth College.
Hill, Robert Charles, Papers, 1942–1978. Hoover Institution Archives, Stanford University.
International League for Human Rights Records. Rare Books and Manuscript Division, New York Public Library.
Lister, George, Papers. Benson Latin American Collection, University of Texas Libraries, University of Texas at Austin.
Mann, Thomas Clifton, Papers. Texas Collection, Baylor University.
Vance, Cyrus R., and Grace Sloane, Papers. Sterling Memorial Library, Yale University.

ORAL HISTORIES AND ROUNDTABLES

Jimmy Carter, interview. Carter Presidency Project, Miller Center of Public Affairs, University of Virginia, Charlottesville, VA.
Falklands Roundtable. Ronald Reagan Oral History Project, Miller Center of Public Affairs, University of Virginia, Charlottesville, VA.
Foreign Affairs Oral History Collection. Georgetown University Library.
Foreign Affairs Oral History Collection of the Association for Diplomatic Studies and Training. Library of Congress, Manuscript Division, Washington, DC.
Personal interviews: Cynthia Arnson; Mechtild Baum; Osvaldo Bayer; Lawrence Birns; Michelle Bova; John Bushnell; Maxwell Chaplin; Roberta Cohen; Robert Cox; Patricia Derian; F. A. "Tex" Harris; Michael Posner; Fernando E. Rondon; John Salzberg; Olga Talamante.
Red de Archivos Orales de la Argentina Contemporánea, Programa de Historia Política del Instituto de Investigaciones Gino Germani, Buenos Aires, Argentina.

NATIONAL ARCHIVES AND RECORDS ADMINISTRATION, COLLEGE PARK, MD

Record Group 56 General Records of the Department of State

Office of the Under Secretary for Monetary Affairs, Records of Assistant Secretary for International Affairs C. Fred Bergsten, 1977–1979
Office of Assistant Secretary for International Affairs; Office of the Deputy Assistant Secretary for Developing Nations; Office of International Development

Record Group 59 General Records of the Department of State

Bureau of Inter-American Affairs, Office of East Coast Affairs, Records Relating to Argentina, 1956–1964
Central Foreign Policy Files, 1963
Central Foreign Policy Files, 1964–1966

Subject Numeric Files, 1970–1973: Administration; Political and Defense
Office of the Deputy Secretary, Records of Warren Christopher, 1977–1980
Policy and Planning Staff, Office of the Director, Records of Anthony Lake, 1977–1981

PRESIDENTIAL LIBRARIES

Jimmy Carter Library, Atlanta, GA.
Gerald R. Ford Library, Ann Arbor, MI.
John F. Kennedy Library, Boston, MA.
Lyndon Baines Johnson Library, Austin, TX.
Ronald Reagan Library, Simi Valley, CA.

DOCUMENT COLLECTIONS

Declassified Documents Reference System. Farmington Hills, MI: Gale Group, 2007,
    http://infotrac.galegroup.com.
Department of State. Argentina Declassification Project (1975–1984). Freedom of
    Information Act (FOIA) Electronic Reading Room, http://foia.state.gov/Search-
    Colls/CollsSearch.asp.
——. Foreign Relations of the United States, 1961–1963, vol. 12.
——. Foreign Relations of the United States, 1964–1968, vol. 31.
National Security Archive, George Washington University, Washington, DC.: Elec-
    tronic Briefing Book no. 27; Electronic Briefing Book no. 104; Martin Edwin
    Andersen Collection.

INTERNATIONAL ARCHIVES

Asamblea Permanente por los Derechos Humanos, Buenos Aires, Argentina.
Centro de Estudios Legales y Sociales, Buenos Aires, Argentina.
Bibliothèque de Documentation Internationale Contemporaine, Paris, France.
British National Archives, Kew, United Kingdom.
Forschungs- und Dokumentationszentrum Chile-Lateinamerika, Berlin, Germany.
Memoria Abierta, Buenos Aires, Argentina.

Index

Abrams, Elliott, 186
Acheson, Dean, 31
Afghanistan, Soviet invasion of, 5, 157, 175,
   176, 178, 180, 192
Alfonsín, Raúl, 188, 189, 190
Alianza Anticomunista Argentina (AAA), 47
Allara, Gualter, 150
Allende, Salvador, 43, 100
Alliance for Progress: Argentina as model for,
   30, 33; congressional objections to, 60–61;
   Johnson and, 21; Kennedy and, 16–18,
   24, 30, 60; shift away from, 36
Allis-Chalmers decision, 148–50, 151; backlash
   against, 155, 156–57, 165–66, 168, 169–70,
   181; as high-water mark in Carter's human
   rights policy, 171
American Association for the Advancement of
   Science, fact-finding visit to Argentina, 142
American Civil Liberties Union (ACLU), 75
American Friends Service Committee, 71, 82
Amnesty International, 3, 75–78, 91, 96
anticommunism: Ambassador Hill's, 14–15,
   45, 49, 50, 54; Argentine military's, 37, 40,
   41; vs. democracy in Latin America, 42–43;
   of Latin American military regimes, 23. See
   also Cold War
anti-Vietnam War movement: and human
   rights movement, 1, 59, 74; impact on U.S.
   Congress, 61, 62–63
Apodaca, Clair, 186
Arbenz, Jacobo, 14
Argentina: under Frondizi, 2, 30, 32–35;
   invasion of Malvinas/Falkland Islands,
   187–88; military coup of 1955, 32;
   military coup of 1962, 35, 60; military
   coup of 1966, 2, 39–40, 41; military coup
   of 1976, 8–9, 48, 69; under Onganía,
   30, 37–41; under Perón (Isabel), 47,
   57–58, 69, 72, 159; under Perón (Juan),
   31–32, 45, 46; restoration of democracy
   in, 188–90; revolutionary terrorism in,
   46, 47–48; Western European military
   assistance to, 29–30, 37, 41–42, 44. See
   also Argentina, U.S. policy toward; dirty
   war; military; military junta

Argentina, U.S. policy toward: Bolivian
   coup of 1980 and, 180; under Carter,
   4–5, 79–82, 127–34, 155–72, 177–78,
   191–92; Cold War considerations and, 2,
   9, 33–36, 94–95, 155–57, 178, 190, 192;
   economic interests vs. human rights in,
   129–32, 148–50, 155–57, 158–72; human
   rights considerations and, 4, 79–82; IFI
   loan conditionality and, 126–29; under
   Johnson, 41; under Kennedy, 30–31, 33–38;
   limited leverage in, 34, 118–19; nuclear
   nonproliferation vs. human rights in,
   129–30; under Reagan, 183–84, 190–91;
   Santa Cruz kidnapping and, 134–37. See
   also military assistance to Argentina
Argentine Human Rights Commission.
   See Comisión Argentina por Derechos
   Humanos (CADHU)
Armony, Ariel, 173
Astiz, Alfredo, 134–35
Avebury, Lord Eric, 77

Badillo, Herman, 94, 102, 103
Baird, Peter, 58
Baldwin, Roger, 75
Batista, Fulgencio, 14
Bell-Textron sale, 129–30, 131
Benenson, Peter, 75
Benson, Lucy, 111, 129–30, 131
Bentsen, Lloyd, Jr., 130
Bergsten, G. Fred, 111
Bethell, Leslie, 13
Birns, Lawrence, 140, 158, 181
Boeing Vertol sale, 131–32, 164
Bolivia, 49, 180
Bonner, Ray, 180
Bowdler, William G., 61
Bowdoin, Cecilia, 13
Bowles, Chester, 18
Braden, Spruille, 31, 109
Brazil: Argentine military and, 38, 41, 49;
   bureaucratic-authoritarian rule in, 26, 41;
   human rights activists in, 78, 103; military
   coup of 1964, 41; U.S. policies toward, 22,
   26, 41, 68, 133, 158, 170

CPSIA information can be obtained
at www.ICGtesting.com
Printed in the USA
LVOW09*0621170317

527469LV00006BA/153/P

9 780801 451966